THE EVOLUTION OF HUMAN
CONSCIOUSNESS

C000183614

THE EVOLUTION OF HUMAN CONSCIOUSNESS

JOHN HURRELL CROOK

CLARENDON PRESS · OXFORD

Oxford University Press, Walton Street, Oxford OX2 6DP

Oxford New York Toronto
Delhi Bombay Calcutta Madras Karachi
Kuala Lumpur Singapore Hong Kong Tokyo
Nairobi Dar es Salaam Cape Town
Melbourne Auckland

and associated companies in
Beirut Berlin Ibadan Mexico City Nicosia

Oxford is a trade mark of Oxford University Press

© Oxford University Press 1980

First published 1980
Reprinted 1985

Published in the USA by Oxford University Press, Inc, New York

*All rights reserved. No part of this publication may be reproduced,
stored in a retrieval system, or transmitted, in any form or by any means,
electronic, mechanical, photocopying, recording, or otherwise, without
the prior permission of Oxford University Press*

British Library Cataloguing in Publication Data

Crook, John Hurrell
  The evolution of human consciousness.
  1. Genetic psychology
  I. Title
  128'.2   BF701   79-41389

  ISBN 0 19 857174 7
       0 19 857187 9 p. back

Printed in Great Britain by
Richard Clay (The Chaucer Press) Ltd,
Bungay, Suffolk

To Stamati and Tanya

The mind moves uneasily between two poles:

Human consciousness in identification

In most British universities, scholars in the arts often give themselves airs of gentility that among scientists are rare. The stance of the scientific psychologist may thus have about it something of the air of a self-made man: a compound of self-confidence and rigidity that overlays a more subterranean sense of not belonging. . . . And although, like the businessman, he sometimes aspires to liberal pursuits, to the study for instance of creativity, he only does so on his own reductive, assimilative terms. On this view the softer tend to react to their harder neighbours as waning gentlefolk react to those who persist in building bungalows on good arable land: with ineffectual disdain.

Liam Hudson 1972

Human consciousness in disidentification

At one with the food we eat we identify with the Universe.
At one with the Universe we taste the food.
The Universe and the food we eat
Partake of the same nature.

Zen mealtime ceremonial; from the *Vimalakirti Sutra*

To the better comprehension of this polarity this work is dedicated.

Preface

Evolution and enlightenment: is there a connection? What are the biological roots of the higher forms of human consciousness and cognitive ability? Are we for ever faced with a dichotomy between biology and a metaphysics of awareness, as one might call the tentative psychological approaches to such problems. In the great advances in Darwinian theory of the last ten years can we trace any increased ability to wrestle, not so much with the sources of human *behaviour* but with the origins of the elaborate intersubjective and introspective capacities of the human self?

In this book I set out to explore possible ways of coming to grips with questions such as these. My early academic life was devoted to field studies of the social systems of birds and primates and to developing the groundwork of evolutionary theory utilized in contemporary discussions. More recently I learnt how to facilitate encounter groups of several types, to practice Gestalt psychotherapy, as well as continuing in academic ethology as best I could. This book attempts to link the two sides of my interest, or as some might say, the two sides of my mind. I believe such a linkage is not only possible but essential if we are to develop an ethological understanding of the human mind. Ethologists nowadays are often psychologists with evolutionary obsessions. We use animals to speculate about motivational mechanisms for behaviour, their development in individuals, and their sources in evolution. We also try to erect theories that explain the historical extrapolations we infer. To me it is apparent that ethologists have devoted themselves so exclusively to behaviour observation that they have omitted, as also did the behaviourists, any adequate study of the origins of the uniquely distinctive human mind. Yet, if Darwin was right, this too must have an evolutionary history. It is time we began to unravel it. I agree with Don Griffin that the question of animal awareness forms a prelude to the exploration of the human mind. But we need to grasp the uniqueness of this mind as well as the possible sources of its development in more lowly forms. The merely comparative method is not enough. It is essential also to use evidence usually considered only by psychologists and anthropologists to build up a picture for ethological reflection.

A further point. We should not flinch in a wide survey of this preliminary nature to broach topics that concern some of the strangest aspects of mental life. Sometimes very ancient theories of cultures other than our own present a deeper analysis than contemporary thought has done. The Buddhists in particular, by virtue of a 'subjective empiricism', have systematically explored states of consciousness to a depth not reached in the modern West. Parallels between these old reflective analyses and modern research are striking and give us much material that needs evolutionary consideration. Even though some of these theories became as fossilized as the cultures that gave birth to them the validity of their original insights is often striking.

In the concluding part of the book we shall attempt tentatively to adopt a position on the meaning of our exploration at the present time. The contemporary mind at its most creative is open not closed, exploratory not overcontrolled by a cybernetics of needs, hopeful and active rather than passive and moderately optimistic for human development in the future. The gene machine is mindless but it has produced mind that creates meaning. If the end is paradox may not that paradox also be made meaningful? If to create meaning is to organize information in culturally specific ways then the future is by no means closed.

November 1978   J.H.C.
The Maenllwyd
Pant-y-dwr

Acknowledgements

In a work of this breadth I clearly owe much to many diverse friends and thinkers. The attempt at a two-way linkage, on the one hand between evolutionary ethology and the psychology of self and, on the other, between Western and Eastern psychological models indicates an association over several years with at least three lineages of thought.

My interest in interdisciplinary studies was fostered during my research years at Cambridge (1955–62) through participation in a behaviour discussion group that used to meet in Bill Thorpe's rooms in Jesus College. Those meetings were an attempt by psychologists and ethologists to find common ground. The sophisticated debates that took place were profoundly instructive to a young subaltern fresh from National Service and seeking to orient himself to academic life. It was also perhaps Oliver Zangwill's stimulating lectures to student psychologists comparing the work of Pavlov and Sherrington and approaching ethology from the viewpoint of psychology that alerted me particularly to the profound scholasticisms that prevailed and still prevail in much psychological thinking. How different from zoology, where Darwin and comparative physiology reigned supreme creating a field of almost monolithic comprehensibility.

My interest in Zen Buddhism began during my National Service in the Army in Hong Kong in 1953. I shall always remember Shi Liang Yen and his kindness in allowing me to participate in his Ch'an group even though this meant giving me a running commentary throughout in translation from the Cantonese. In India I had the immense good fortune to join a small discussion group with Krishnamurti which ran for several months in Poona in 1959. This acquaintance created in me not only an endeavour to comprehend his philosophy but also to realize within myself something of the insights he so clearly knew. Along this path brief contacts with several Japanese Masters of Zen, the Roshi Jiyu Kennett, Dr. Irmgard Schloegl, Chögyam Trungpa Rimpoche, Geshe Damchös Yonten, and Douglas Harding have all been of inestimable benefit.

My practical involvement with psychotherapy began in California in 1969 while working as a Fellow at the Centre for Advanced Study in the Behavioural Sciences at Stanford. I subsequently developed this interest and together with Ken Waldie founded the Bristol Encounter Centre in my home city. I am especially indebted to Jeff Love for training in the facilitation of groups using the Zen communication exercise of Charles Berner and for his personal guidance through several such events in which I was a participant.

Fundamentally this book arises from my fascination with evolutionary theory, especially in its application to social life. I wish to record an especial indebtedness to the major theoretical contributions of William Hamilton, Robert Trivers, and Richard Alexander who have done so much to advance evolutionary ethology. To Robert Trivers especially I am grateful for his outstanding paper on reciprocal altruism which plays a major role in the argument of this text. Several of the themes of this book received an early airing during my participation in the Summer symposium on Animal Behavior of the College of Science, Utah State University in 1974 and in my 'keynote' address to the Animal Behavior Society during the annual meeting in Boulder in 1976. I remain most grateful for those opportunities to explore broad themes. I am also grateful to Robert Hinde for his warm encouragement on reading an early attempt to put together some ideas in eastern and western psychology.

At a more proximate level this book would never have been written without the kindness of my old friend Klaus Immelmann, now Professor of Ethology at the University of Bielefeld, who invited me there to participate as visiting professor in a 6-month marathon of a conference on developmental psychology and ethology in 1977. At the Zentrum für Interdisziplinäre Forschung (ZIF) I found exactly the right blend of privacy and scholarly company that brought these thoughts to fruition. I benefited greatly from the friendship and conversational companionship of the scholars in residence of whom Jack Block, Marten de Vries, Klaus and Karen Grossmann, Hanus Papouçek, Mary Main, Arnold Sameroff, and Michael Studdent-Kennedy particularly influenced the development of my ideas. I am especially grateful to Mary Main for her thoughtful and insightful criticisms of an early draft of Chapters 9 and 10. Sverre Schölander arranged for my comfort and regulated all administrative problems for me at the ZIF with a skill made doubly impressive by his ability to write lengthy letters of substance in advanced English slang.

I am grateful to my colleagues at Bristol for their willingness to allow my lengthy absences. To my younger ethological friends I acknowledge gratefully a constant reminder to focus on my primatological career when 'higher things' loomed too attractively. My earlier evolutionary thinking which is reflected in this book owes much to lively interaction with Pelham Aldrich-Blake, John Archer, Penny Butterfield, John Deag, Robin and Patsy Dunbar, John Goss-Custard, Steve Gartlan, Jim Ellis, Jenny Ingram, Ken Simmons, Nick Thompson, and Richard Wrangham and at an earlier stage with Ronald Hall who originally established me at Bristol.

I thank Jerome Barkow, Napoleon Chagnon, Marten de Vries, Mildred Dickeman, Robin Dunbar, Mary Main, Klaus and Karen Grossman, Olwyn Rasa, Ian Vine, Michael West, and Richard

Wrangham for allowing me to quote material still in press or preparation at the time of writing. I am indebted also to Robin Dunbar, Hazel Russell, and Henri Tajfel for readings of certain sections of the text.

In a work of this scope I have certainly made many errors of judgement in the selection and presentation of material as I attempted to build bridges to disciplines not my own. As to these I can only plead guilty and anticipate constructive criticism from my readers.

Lastly and not at all least I owe much to the patience and skill of Cornelia Fulland at the ZIF and Jean Britten and Pam Aldren in Bristol who laboured hard at converting my shocking MSS. into readable typescript.

Hazel Russell, by her interest in my long preoccupation with this book and her enthusiasm in discussion of its central themes, supported my endeavours more than either of us have probably realized.

I am grateful to the following for permissions to reproduce material: to Associated Book Publishers for Table 2 from *Ecological adaptations for breeding in birds* by D. Lack and published by Chapman & Hall Ltd; to Richard D. Alexander and The Academy of Natural Sciences for Figures 2 and 5 from 'Natural selection and the analysis of human sociality' in *The changing scenes in natural sciences, 1776 to 1976*, Academy of Natural Sciences publication 12 (1977); to Victor Gollancz Ltd. and Harper & Row, Inc. for the quotations from *Krishnamurti's notebook* by J. Krishnamurti which conclude Chapter 14; to Prentice-Hall, Inc. for Figures 2.2, 4.2, and 4.3 from *Tribesmen* by Marshall D. Dahlins © 1968; to Adriaan Kortlandt for Fig. 4.2; to Jossey-Bass, Inc. for Figure 1 from *Beyond boredom and anxiety: the experience of play in work and games* by M. Csikszentmihalyi; to John Wiley & Sons, Inc. for Fig. 9.6 which was originally published in *Interpersonal diagnosis of personality: a functional theory and methodology for personality evaluation* by Timothy Leary © 1957; and to Thames & Hudson Ltd. for Figure 4 from *Tantra* by P. Rawson.

Contents

Preamble to an ethology of cognition

> Darwin . . . showed that a natural history of mind
> might be written and that this method of study
> offered a wide and rich field for investigation. Of
> course those who regarded the study of mind only as
> a branch of metaphysics smiled at the ineptitude of
> the mere man of science. But the investigation, on
> natural history lines, has been prosecuted with a
> large measure of success. Much indeed remains to
> be done; for special training is required, and the
> workers are still few.
>
> C. Lloyd Morgan 1909

'That's not it at all.'

In one of the novels of Albert Camus an unfortunate man is walking at night on the banks of the Seine when a suicide, having cast himself upon the waters, cries for help. Unable to summon the courage to enter the cold dark of the river the man, a lawyer by profession, finds himself at odd moments thereafter, and even in the courtroom, increasingly assailed by a laugh at the back of his mind, a laugh that mocks his whole posture in the world, a laugh that progressively exposes in him what he chooses to see as a guilty pretence.

I suspect that a number of ethologists of my generation occasionally feel the same way about ethological generalizations to human beings. Certainly ten years ago, in the flood-tide of my research interest in wild primates, I began wondering more critically than before about the applications of ethological theories to man, the species. Increasingly as I examined the implications of primate studies for ourselves and tried to see some convincing link between baboons and men a voice began muttering in the back of my head 'Hey—that's not it at all.'

Falteringly, I sought to express these misgivings in my conclusions to a number of papers, conclusions that certainly brought no joy to my more optimistic colleagues in an emerging human ethology rooted firmly in the objective analysis of behaviour sequences and components. So, in a paper written to commemorate the life and work of Danny Lehrman, whose critical interest in ethology and psychiatry had been considerable, I argued pessimistically (Crook 1977a) that an understanding of the primate behaviour I had been reviewing 'provides no more than a kind of educational backcloth—a reference literature for university courses on human evolution and that it cannot begin to touch upon the *existential* issues that are the central focus of living human relations'.

Grabbing the nettle I went on:

Ethologists have not yet begun to grasp at the crucial characteristic of human beings that tends to invalidate all but the most cautious inferences from other animals to Man. Surprisingly too, many psychologists have also . . . failed to recognize the point I am about to make. As a species Man possesses the characteristic of self-reference. This means that not only do we describe ourselves to ourselves and create identity constructs but we can also face the issue of whether we want to alter those constructs and become another kind of person. I feel there can be only one conclusion. If ethologists are truly interested in an ethology of human relating we have to drop the pretence that, given present knowledge, evolutionary arguments are any more than a game for the psychologically literate. Instead we should look directly in the place where the answer lies . . . the proper study of Mankind.

Of course, since I first penned these stirring lines E. O. Wilson has brought forth his spectacular synthesis of ethology and population genetics and opened anew the vigorous debate concerning the roles of the biological and the socially acquired in the determination of human behaviour. This is all very much to the good but my inner voice keeps muttering 'That's not it at all'—because studies of this kind never attempt to cross the boundary-line between behaviour and inner experience, and thus tend to side-track the issue I am raising here. The ghost of J. B. Watson, who cast 'consciousness' out of psychology because it was too difficult to handle, still walks and ethologists and psychologists alike often fail to see that such a borderline exists. The continuing separation between those who are interested in what people say about their experiences (psychoanalysts, psychotherapists, counsellors, phenomenologists, novelists) and those who pay attention only to what they do (behaviourist psychologists, human ethologists) is based upon important choices in research orientation related to conceptions of the social role and implications of the studies themselves.

The study of what people say is ultimately to do with cognition. At present an ethology of cognition is almost a contradiction in terms.

In this book I hope to show that behaviour scientists interested in what people say can talk to those observers who prefer the voyeurism of much contemporary human study. The growth of ethology can continue only if we find a way of talking about human experience that opens the whole range of the activities of men and women to inspection.

The uniqueness of man

Most inferences from animals to the human species are based in anatomical, behavioural, or sociological comparisons. They deal with patterns of observable structure and employ well-established methods of comparative analysis, often based upon the principles of taxonomy established by earlier generations of zoologists faced with the enormous diversity of the animal kingdom. There is a plausible consistency about a well-developed derivational argument (for examples see pp. 96–9) that cannot be gainsaid except by a more inclusive one, for most such theses are not open to a direct test.

The evolutionary theory fundamental to understanding the human emergence has recently acquired a firmer basis than ever before (see Chapter 3). The line of thought initiated by William Hamilton in his interpretation of the evolution of altruism (see p. 42) and developed by Robert Trivers's theory of reciprocation (see p. 43) provides a tight biological model for social change that is to a considerable degree applicable to man. Although there is actually little that is novel in 'sociobiology', for the key elements have been in the air since the writings of Sir Ronald Fisher and J. B. S. Haldane, the extensive if not exhaustive application of population genetics to social evolution means that the relevance of evolutionary biology in the social sciences can no longer be ignored.

The enthusiasm generated by this approach can, however, blind; the simplicism, the 'nothing butism' as Julian Huxley would have said, of reducing all functional explanations of complex behaviour to calculations concerning the relative fitnesses (see p. 42) of gene-bearers tends to miss the major significance of human beings to other human beings. Jerome Barkov begins a recent paper (1978a):

Are you reading this article in order to maximize your inclusive fitness? Is human behaviour reducible to 'nothing but' an endless struggle to maximize one's genetic representation in the next generation? Are we really nice to others only to the extent that they carry the genes we do, or to the extent that our 'niceness' will definitely be reciprocated.

Extreme reductionism is usually a sign of restricted outlook and it seems safe to say that sociobiology will not remain long in so puritanical a stage.

In his definitive review 'Functional ethology and the human sciences' Niko Tinbergen (1972) showed that functional analysis of single behaviours in animals offered analogies for human studies in spite of the added complexities at this level. Yet, it is the unique features of *Homo sapiens* that become crucial in any comparison of animals with men. The unique feature of human adaptability, emphasized by Tinbergen, is the cultural transmission of information between generations. It is this that has allowed the astonishingly rapid conquest of the terrestrial environment and the anthropogenic changes in habitat resulting from accelerating rates of population increase and extension of urban environments. Tinbergen argues further that human adaptations to older agricultural and pre-agricultural ways of life may be failing to cope with the societal artefacts of cultural success, and he gives evidence from several areas of mental health and education.

Certainly, after the extremely rapid evolution of brain and skull structure in the early hunting phase of human social development, the prime cause of behavioural change switched to rapid cultural evolution with strong feedback effects whereby one cultural shift produced another like a series of cascades; agricultural surpluses needing markets, cities being formed, kings and statesmen gaining dominance, states and statecraft managing economies, and so on. The mechanism of change, the cultural 'instruction' as Cloak (1975) calls it, has much the same function in the historical process as genes have had in biological evolution, but the 'instruction' in cultural change is usually an acquired behavioural injunction existing in a world of meanings: the cognitive, although not always conscious, appreciation of their social environment by a human community.

It is particularly when we turn from comparisons with animals to the more characteristically human manifestations of our species that we hit the problem. There is little understanding about how animal behaviour evolved through time to produce the human 'mind'. Human beings relate to one another not as complex reflex machines but as persons for whom the focal point in behaviour is the mutual transaction between one individual's psychosocial experience and that of another. Ethology has always been profoundly concerned with evolutionary development, with phylogeny. Yet, curiously, there is almost no evolutionary ethology of the human 'person'.

The word person or 'persona' refers to the face each one of us puts on the world. For it is to this that another reacts and it is to the face of another that I speak. The term implies that there is a something that lies behind the face. Indeed the face may be a mask covering a very different existential reality from that which it portrays (de Levita 1965).

The idea of an 'internal world' is not however new in ethology; it was indeed a prime preoccupation of one of its key founding fathers, Jacob von Uexküll, who through studies of the perceptual apparatus of a variety of species deduced the nature of the experiential worlds to which they gave rise. This experiential world he called an *Umwelt*. So cogent and imaginative were his descriptions and inferences that his name remains well known today even though almost nothing in the same vein has followed from his work. It was the questions he implied rather than their apparently subjectivist formulation that ensured his place in current history.

To von Uexküll (1909), the *Umwelt* of an animal comprised two parts, the world as sensed and the world of actions. The latter was accessible to an observer but the nature of the former could only be inferred. This dualism tended to reinforce a form of psychophysical parallelism in ethology. The subjective inner world of animals was not denied and an evolutionary development of sensed-worlds was assumed because of the complexity indicated by the increasing sophistication of perceptual and communicational mechanisms, but only the behaviour could be charted and recorded in the actual passage of time.

This two-sidedness in ethology harks back in fact to the seventeenth-century dualism of Descartes, the mind–body dichotomy into different 'things' (see Chapter 2). So long as philosophers and psychologists of the nineteenth century had to wrestle with an implicit mind–body problem, it was virtually impossible for evolutionists to tackle the evolution of higher mental processes of a distinctively human kind. For the most part they contented themselves with the material evidence available in the form of bones and artefacts, yet even when they began to observe living animals good behavioural description did not expose the factors that transformed the infrahuman primate society into a human one.

The idea of the *Umwelt* has re-emerged in ethology in Griffin's book *The question of animal awareness* (1976), in which he argues that recent research in animal orientation, navigation, and social communication implies cognitive processes of a high order and even mental experiences of them. Griffin, whose own contribution to the experimental investigation of bird navigation and bat orientation is immense, argues that the objectifying abstractions of both behaviourist learning theory and much contemporary ethology simply ignore these issues. Griffin, however, writes with a glance over his shoulder. He asserts cautiously that there is a 'possibility that both genetic and environmental influences, and interactions between them, may be important in the causation of mental processes, including awareness' and goes on to say that awareness probably has survival value because it enables animals to respond to the complexities of the world in which they behave. William Mason (1976) comments

The interesting question is not whether such functions exist, for they are clearly implied in the phenomena we call behaviour. The interesting questions relate to how they are expressed in different species. What has been their probable evolutionary course? How do they develop in the individual? How do they work? Finally one might hope that some useful distinctions could be drawn between 'having a mental experience' and 'being aware of having such an experience' which seems much closer to our usual view of consciousness and must certainly be an emergent property in evolution.

Indeed, it is precisely from this 'being aware of having experience' and being able both to communicate its features to another and to distinguish between oneself as experiencing agent and another's reported experiences that the prime features of humanity arise.

Behaviourist learning theory, which so dominated psychology from around 1914 until the revival of cognitive studies in the 1950s, was particularly concerned with the 'laws' relating stimulus and response. The intervening processes were not directly examined. Most studies of animal cognition focused on the gaining of an experimental control of learning processes in order to examine their nature. Stimulus–response theory leaves both 'consciousness' and the 'organism' out of account and is purely operational in its establishment of the laws under which animals learn. Even when, as in Hull's learning theory, the organism is introduced, its place is taken by a formal set of mediating processes in which neither mental life nor biological processes as such are revealed.

Yet, as Mary Ainsworth (1969) points out in relation to the concept of attachment between mother and child (monkeys included), a mental or physiological condition can be said to be present even when it is not visible in behaviour. She argues that the attachment between individuals—the relationship—resides in an inner structure which has both cognitive and affective aspects and affects behaviour. The existence of such an inner structure can, however, be inferred only from behaviour:

Studies of responses to both separation from the attachment object and subsequent reunion with it, yield unequivocal support to the proposition that attachments can and often do survive periods of absence, undiminished in strength, despite the fact that attachment *behaviour* may diminish in strength during the period of absence.

If this quotation were referring to attachments between adult human subjects, most such persons would probably say that they were aware of their state of attachment, even though in their daily lives this would not necessarily be detectable in their behaviour. They may or may not choose to express their awareness of themselves to another person. This capacity for choice, implicit rather than active in so many people, can in fact be taken as one criterion for human maturity. And such behaviour must of course be the expression of a psychobiological apparatus that needs description.

Few human ethologists have been interested in the existential issues of human subjectivity implied by the recognition of inner structure. Much of our work focuses on externals, using the methods of an observational animal ethology well versed in the quantitative analysis of frequencies of tail flicks in relation to their context and the construction of elegant models of the systemic relations between them. For the most part this paradigm allows only a study of non-verbal social behaviour. Some authors indeed have argued that topics such as self-image, leadership, and attitudes, all belong to 'social psychology' and are not appropriate problems for ethologists to examine. Yet the evolutionary and developmental origins of behaviours that are contingent on esteem, attitudes, leadership, and similar factors are of vital importance in any study of humanity. Social psychologists, apart from those educated in ethology, have no evolutionary theory. To gain one, syntheses of method and approach are essential.

In the early 1950s the anthropologist A. Irvin Hallowell reconsidered the whole issue in the light of what it meant to be a human person. He was clearly influenced by a reading of Freudian psychoanalytic writings in attempts at historical reconstructions of cultural stages in anthropology. He pointed out that the structural basis of human behaviour must be rooted in the gregarious nature of primates and the potentialities thereby offered for the socialization of individual experience. The study of personality structure, he argued, the genesis of which lies in social interaction, offers the beginning of a conceptual resolution of the old mind–body dichotomy while at the same time relating the individual to his social setting. Since personality arises out of social interaction its structure is not reducible to organic structure even though it remains dependent upon the whole psychoendocrine and neural system of a human being. Both the 'social matrix of conduct and the expansion of the cortex are among the necessary conditions for the emergence of a human mind. Just as bodily evolution and mental evolution cannot be separated, neither can psychological structuralization and the social evolution of mankind.'

Hallowell (1950, 1956) went on to argue that the emergence of culture was due to a novel psychological structure rooted in the social behaviour of the gregarious primate that gave rise to Man. Organic evolution, behavioural evolution, and the old problem of mental evolution come to a common focus in a study of this structure. Hallowell was in effect establishing the whole field of inquiry with which this book is concerned. His argument, although rarely quoted, is basic to an attempt at understanding the evolution of the complex psychodynamics that characterize our species (Barkov 1978b). As I put the question again in 1974, 'Why is Man so restless and so divided an animal? What is the root of his ever-present seeking for something other than he has—happiness, nirvana or what you will? An answer to this depends on a correct definition of human uniqueness rather than looking at those features Man shares with animals.'

Hallowell argued for a species-specific type of psychic structure in the human being that clearly differentiates the 'person' from the psychological make-up of primates and other animals. 'This structure is the foundation of Man's specialized form of adaptation as a species as well as the basis of his personal adjustment as an individual.'

Self-consciousness in humans is a conceptually structured awareness of self-processes that are unique to man. Relatively simple observation of the activities going on within one's head would produce such a phenomenological definition. Whereas we may postulate 'awareness' as a basic property of any behaviour, the ongoing 'here-and-now' relating together of incoming sensations to provide a consciousness of 'oneself as an object' requires a sustained act of attention utilizing a coded representation of reality in which the self as agent is included.

Although this psychobiological structure is unique, it makes use of functional processes that are well established in other higher animals. It follows, then, that an evolutionary argument must attempt to establish exactly what the continuity may have been that led from the level of the higher animals to that of Man.

Behaviour and the environment of evolutionary adaptedness

In considering the evolution of the mental capacities of the human being we need to remind ourselves that evolution occurs through the differential selection of traits with survival value in the habitat adopted by the animals. The word 'habitat' implies more than simply the physical environment of an animal. It includes the presence of other animals that may be predators or competitors for food, animals of other species that may communicate with it in finding food or raising an alarm, and individuals of its own species that interact with it in many ways, competitively, nepotistically, and in co-operation. The structure of the animal's behaviour will be adapted to all these features in ways that in past generations have been most successful in transmitting the gene complexes of individuals into the future. The 'design for living' shown by a species is the outcome of this selective process and is related not at all to any eventuality that may arise but to the set of conditions, the 'niche', to which the evolutionary process has confined the species. Robins live mostly on the floors of woods while titmice explore the twigs. This restriction to particular 'niches' in the environment is the result of a partitioning out of competing species over a limited range of resources; each comes to live in the portion of a habitat it can exploit best for reproductive purposes. Every living organism is thus constrained as a result of selection to live in what John Bowlby terms its 'environment of evolutionary adaptedness', using stable strategies of exploitation which are the best available to it.

Tinbergen argued that rapid cultural change may have pushed human systems into an environment which is no longer that to which the species has adapted through evolution. If this is the case, it implies that some at least of the feedback systems maintaining human well-being may be in difficulties simply because they are being called upon to function near the limits of their capacity. We can expect such systems to show varying degrees of ability to acclimatize. The environmental conditions with which the system is in equilibrium may shift, and only so long as the equilibrium can be set at new and workable positions can the species survive. There are likely to be limits to the extent to which such acclimatization is possible.

To what then is the human psychobiological system adapted and what are the limits to which it can adjust without an excessive strain leading ultimately to reduced reproductive ability? We simply do not know the answer to this question but brief mention of the complexity of a human individual's environment may suffice at this point to indicate how elaborate the considerations will have to be.

If we were asking this question of an amphibian or reptile, which lays its eggs and goes away to live solitarily except when the mating season comes around again, we would answer it purely in terms of the physical ecology of the species. Human ecology includes a vast complexity of social elements, themselves functioning in relation to modes of economic exploitation in varying regional ecologies. In a tribal village, in Africa say, a boy is born to a particular woman who, obeying the customs of her people, proceeds to rear him either under conditions of high sociability or relative isolation and according to a particular regime of toilet training and weaning. The child then becomes relatively independent of his mother and enters a sequence of periods in which his identity is established by the role that custom decrees for his age-group. Family structures, age stages, and the sharpness of the transition between stages, accompanied perhaps by initiation rites that may be both physically and psychologically painful, all vary between peoples, often in extreme ways. Each of these stages is an element in a complex societal structure and cultural context. The overarching cultural structure includes a system of rights and obligations, the family organization and the child-rearing practices, yet each of these levels is distinct in that, to a degree, it can shift independently of the others. Culture or social structure may change and child-rearing may remain the same. Conventions of weaning may alter while family structure does not. Change from one state of a system to another may occur at different rates at contrasting levels. Economic pressures producing changes in family structure may, for example, influence the higher-order structure of society only a generation or two later.

The original environment of human evolutionary adaptedness cannot be clearly defined because our evolution has been such an extraordinary progression of expansive diversifications in adapting to an immense range of environments. Even so, the extreme length of the hunter–gatherer phase (Chapter 8) suggests that our main behavioural attributes were formed in that period. These attributes clearly included immense potential for societal and cultural modification in relation to economic exploitation of the environment. It is also possible that cultural adaptations during this phase may have selected genetic bases for behaviour in ways that ensured the development of social strategies designed to ensure that individuals fitted well into the existing social structure.

Extrapolation theory as a background to understanding human action

In the past some psychologists have written as if there were a kind of biological, genetically determined 'bang' at the beginning of human life and that cultural learning took over immediately afterwards. This form of body–mind dualism merits rejection. Biological factors operate throughout an individual's life with differing degrees of importance at different stages. Studies of the natural constraints on learning suggest that what is learnt, and when, is probably under a genetic surveillance so that learning does not normally occur outside the context of an evolutionary stable strategy. This does not, however, mean that a biological reductionism is an appropriate mode of explanation for all types of human behaviour.

As we shall see inter-group behaviour in modern times is explicable primarily in terms of the social identities people adopt in relation to cultural and economic stresses, and the place for a biological factor in the discussion is here a very small one (p. 390). Nonetheless an evolution-ary approach to human social life permits a broad perspective in which the emergence of the social psychological domain from the biological can be traced. The understanding of human action requires a temporal perspective which only a sufficiently broad evolutionary approach can supply.

This book is much concerned with what I shall call 'extrapolation theory'; that is to say the drawing of inferences regarding the sequence of changes whereby one psychobiological state has shifted to another—from chimp-like language, say, to human speech. Here no single-factor theory of language will do, for brain size and anatomy, symbolic coding linguistics, social system, and dietary distribution are all plausibly involved and operate in interaction during the evolution of language systems. Clearly we must think in terms of changes in state of complex systems, of transitions involving various types of 'catastrophe' (in the sense of René Thom).

An adequate extrapolation theory must have at least the following features:

(1) A concern with change within systems.
(2) A capacity to explain temporal shifts, i.e. a sequence of stages and the duration of different stages.

(3) An explanation of the increasing complexity of systems with time.
(4) A treatment that allows for a basic continuity underlying the emergence of novelty. The appearance of later stages is usually a development from earlier ones using the same components, and not a radical replacement.
(5) An account of how later stages often serve similar or identical biological strategies as lower stages but employing more complex mechanisms (e.g. compare hunting in wolves and man).
(6) An account of where in the development of individuals evolved changes productive of shifts in adult behaviour are expressing themselves.

The sources of extrapolation theory, like those of evolutionary theory generally, are numerous. They include current selection theory describing the mechanisms of biological change, accounts of animal studies that provide evidence concerning the psychobiological 'platform' from which human life ascended, inferences from infrahuman primates and other animals to man, and finally a treatment of the evolution of the component faculties that go to make up the human mind.

Evolutionary theory is by nature synthetic. Most evolutionary propositions, especially those referring to historical derivations, are not directly testable, however precisely one may attempt to erect alternative hypotheses for testing. This means that derivational arguments stand or fall by their plausibility according to the effective use of evidence; advance in theory is achieved primarily through the incorporation of new material. Some of this evidence may be factual: the occurrence of certain fossils in certain strata, for example. Some may consist of correlational studies of behaviour in relation to social systems and ecology, perhaps combined with observational or experimental tests of the causality of the correlations found. Some evidence may consist of tightly controlled laboratory experiments on motivational systems or genetics.

Evolutionary theory, especially when applied to so complex a creature as man, has often advanced by what E. O. Wilson in his book *Sociobiology: the new synthesis* has slightingly termed the 'advocacy' method. An author has a 'hunch' and infers an evolutionary scenario informed by the proposition he has created. Robin Fox (1971, 1972) and Lional Tiger (1969) in influential books have perhaps pushed this approach to an extreme, but they have thereby generated an important renewal of interest in biology among anthropologists. A good hunch is heuristic, productive of preliminary explanatory propositions and capable of analysis into *a priori* axioms that can be reformulated into hypotheses, some of which may be practically testable. It is quite pointless for critics of evolutionary thinking to waste time and space on a denigration of the hunches of earlier phases of an evolutionary inquiry when neither contemporary sources of information nor current developments in selection theory had arisen. The context of hypothesis creation quite normally remains the realm of imaginative speculation. Without an advocacy stage few general theories in biology would ever have arisen. The sterility of Wilson's final chapter with its severely reductionistic interpretation of human nature reveals the effects of a puritanical fundamentalism.

The advocacy of a plausible explanation in science is open-ended and self-correcting. Evidence bearing upon it will be finely sifted. Some propositions can be subjected to experimental test and the results used in the creation of an extended thesis or alternatively an antithesis. Other propositions may not be testable even in principle but may remain for the time as a necessary component of an overall paradigm. A good theorist should be aware of the weaknesses in his theory, and his prime advocacy will be for more imagination in examining the issues involved and better experimentation wherever possible.

The chapters that follow do not present a tight theory. They do, however, survey a wide range of material relating to cognitive evolution. The result is a set of viewpoints on contemporary man down the long corridor of his evolutionary past. To see ourselves in this way is to gain a perspective rather than to advocate a policy, yet the relation of these two activities will inevitably remain in the background of our work.

Summary
(1) Ethologists concerned with the evolution of human behaviour have stopped short of attempting to explain the further reaches of the human mind; consciousness, self-reference, the construction of identity, and intersubjective relating. Instead of defining clearly the uniqueness of man their efforts have focused on aspects of human life comparable to those of animals.
(2) Man has a biologically unique history defined by an extreme development of complexity in his cognitive functions, perceiving, remembering, analysing, states of awareness, and communicating. These areas are the stock in trade of psychologists who busy themselves with mechanisms and models but never fully with origins or evolutionary history. This indeed is a task for the ethological evolutionist concerned to understand humanity.
(3) Recent developments of Darwinian theory provide us with a new and deeper understanding of the processes of natural selection. There is little doubt that higher cognitive functions are associated with complex social life and elaborate means of communication. The modern

sociobiological approach to evolution contains much of major importance for this inquiry.

(4) In this book I develop the question of animal awareness into a
quest for the evolutionary roots of self-consciousness and identity.
There are many considerations. One is that we must admit verbal
reports of inner experiences of human beings as valid evidence for
studies of consciousness. Contemporary psychology has come a long
way from the time when J. B. Watson, the first behaviourist, forbade
the consideration of non-observable entities. Struggle as it might,
psychology has not been able to remain behaviourist.

(5) One of the consequences of advanced cognitive ability has been the
emergence of cultural life. Mind and culture go together in evolution,
for culture depends on the emergence of capacities for learning and the
retention of novel practices of environmental exploitation and social
organization. Culture in man depends on the development of
psychological traits not found in other primates. The capacity to form a
concept of one's own identity and a process of comparison allowing an
estimation of one's esteem among one's fellows that affects one's view of
oneself are central features of humanity.

(6) This book is to a large extent an exercise in extrapolation. I attempt
to clarify the roots of human cognition in their primordial states. An
ethology of man that accepts human uniqueness can thus begin.
Observation of behaviour is no longer enough, for the cognitive processes of transactions between people and within a person are also
essential topics for an ethologist's exploration.

2 On the biological function of mind

> Mental processes are the accompaniments or con-
> comitants of the functional activity of specially
> differentiated parts of the organism. They are in
> some way dependent on physiological and physical
> conditions. But though they are not physical in their
> nature, and though it is difficult or impossible to
> conceive that they are physical in their origin, they
> are, for Darwin and his followers, factors in the
> evolutionary process in its physical or organic
> aspect. By the physiologist within his special and
> well defined universe of discourse they may be pro-
> perly regarded as epiphenomena; but by the
> naturalist in his more catholic survey of nature they
> cannot be so regarded.
>
> C. Lloyd Morgan 1909

The concept of mind

We begin with an exploded concept, for 'mind' no longer signifies the
entity it once did. Even so, the tradition of several centuries does not die
easily and for many people mind remains opposed to matter, remains
the opposite of the body. The origin of this very basic and particularly
European way of thought lies in the experience that I appear to exist as
a conscious entity within my body, and yet remain distinguishable from
my body.

Within the European intellectual tradition, conscious awareness, the
soul, became the seat of all that is angelic in Man, the part having the
possibility of eternal life through resurrection after death. The body,
bound to the soil to which it is destined to return, remained the source
of those evil behaviours that, judged by God, lead to hell. In some
Christian doctrine the flesh is the source of evil and the soul or mind is
elevated as the moral agent with behavioural choice. In the Hindu folk
tradition, rebirth of the spiritual entity in a hell or a heaven is likewise
dependent upon its moral behaviour while in the bodily container.

In secular philosophy this doctrine, in the form given to it by
Descartes, has remained until very recently a basic element in European thought and science. The relation between mind and body in this
set of ideas is such that the two retain distinct properties and function as
discrete entities. Every human being has both a body and a mind.
Bodies are substantial, exist in space, obey mechanical laws. In that
bodies are observable, they can be inspected by others. The behaviour

of bodies can be evaluated according to criteria, as beautiful or ugly, sane or mad.

Bodily life is a public matter. With mind all is opposite; minds are not substantial, do not apparently obey physical laws, cannot be directly observed or inspected, unless it is my own mind that is in question. Mind life is private.

Clearly there is a relation between the body and the mind that inhabits it. Indeed the positing of such a relationship lies at the root of moral judgement. Even though it is the body that offends, it is none the less the mind that is found accountable. Descartes himself, using the little mechanical and physiological knowledge available to him, went to great lengths in trying to account for this relationship. He did it by suggesting the nervous system as an intermediary.

You have a mind and I have a mind. We can both observe our bodies but I can never observe your mind nor you mine. In this respect, you and I remain unknowable to one another. Yet since you 'have' your body and I 'have' mine we can infer the general features of each other's minds by observing each other's bodily behaviour. Behaviour carries the expression of the mind. Yet, at best, this is unreliable, as when I am thinking of your beautiful wife while discussing with you the state of the nation.

The idea that minds exist as separate entities within bodies has been termed by Gilbert Ryle 'the dogma of the Ghost in the Machine'. In his important book *The concept of mind* (1949) Ryle exploded the dogma by successfully demonstrating that, as used in the Cartesian 'myth', the term represents the facts of mental life as if it belonged to one logical type or category, when it actually belongs to another. Ryle uses a set of powerful illustrations to demonstrate his point.

A foreign visitor to Oxford is shown the colleges, libraries, playing fields, laboratories, and administrative offices. He then asks 'But where is the University?' A child watches the march-past of an army division. He has seen the battalions, squadrons, tanks, infantry, and so on. He then asks 'When is the Division going to appear?'.

In both these cases the confusion arises because a term is considered to belong to the same category as the ones that are being demonstrated. In the case of Oxford University all the parts of the university comprise the University. There is no extra entity, for the term 'university' assembles collectively all those visible objects that are known by the term.

Similarly, when a psychologist has observed numerous activities of the body, he may be inclined to ask 'Ah—but now where is the mind?'. Ryle's point is that, since the terms 'mind' and 'body' are not of the same category, it is illegitimate to relate them logically in this way. But

. . . the argument will not show that either of the illegitimately conjoined propositions is absurd in itself. I am not, for example, denying that there occur mental processes. Doing long division is a mental process and so is making a joke. But I am saying that the phrase 'there occur mental processes' does not mean the same sort of thing as 'there occur physical processes', and, therefore, that it makes no sense to conjoin or disjoin the two.

Ryle wishes not to dissipate the contrast between mind and matter by absorbing one by the other but by showing that the contrasting of the two is as illegitimate as contrasting 'She came home in a flood of tears' and 'She came home in a sedan-chair'. Thus, to argue that minds exist and that bodies exist is correct, so long as the 'logical tones of voice' are maintained as distinct. Here there are two different senses of 'exist', in the same way as 'the tide is rising' and 'the cost of living is rising' differ in the sense in which 'rising' is used. One might argue from this that 'mind' simply refers to the subjective aspect of a complex bodily process of cognition.

Ryle's examination of the relation between mind and body should not be confused with the behaviourist tenet that all 'unobservables', such as consciousness, should be eliminated from the programme of psychology. J. B. Watson in 1914 and other behaviourist thinkers (Hull, Skinner) believed that an acquired behaviour element, the conditioned reflex for example, could be made to account for all behaviour, because such an element could be treated as a 'building block' in theory much in the same way that nineteenth-century physicists used 'atoms' to build up a theory of matter. This extreme reductionism has failed simply because elements such as Pavlov's 'conditioned reflexes' cannot account for all aspects of behaviour. By establishing a paradigm for psychological investigation that lasted for some forty years, behaviourists seriously delayed the understanding of human cognition. Such is probably always the result of an excessive zeal in the application of Occam's Razor.

Ryle points out that the psychologist's dream of creating a behavioural science on a Newtonian basis must be abandoned. Psychology is no more the name of an unique body of theory or inquiry and in physics Newton has given place to Einstein. While, on the one hand, my stammering only in the presence of persons in particular roles, or talking excessively after giving a lecture, pose genuine psychological problems that find expression in certain types of theorizing, so too, on the other hand, do questions about the effects of adrenalin on sitters in an examination room, or family genetics on the choice of career. Likewise, the neurology of the cerebral hemispheres is significant for the localization of cognitive attributes and the evolution of the nervous system is one way of describing the evolution of mental life. Indeed, so interlinked have become questions of psychology with those of biology that the two words are gradually eliding. So we have psychobiology, sociobiology, biosocial anthropology, and so on, to indicate the common roots of the two sciences in the structuring of life.

Evolution of mind

When I reflect upon the nature of my experiential life, my 'inner' life if you will, I become aware of the presence of structure. Some of this structure I hold in common with the structural elements of other people. Their behaviour in resembling mine often allows me to make correct interpretations of their experience. At least they may tell me so. But some of my structure is unique to me, my history for example, and no one else can know much of this unless I choose to relate it to them. I am aware too that, in spite of other similarities, no amount of relating will allow me to converse in more than a most elementary way with a chimpanzee. Generalizing from these reflections that began in my own subjectivity I may ask 'objective' questions about the origin of my self-awareness, of my structure, and that of others. I am led very rapidly into the field of evolution as applied to my behaviour, my experiencing, and that of others.

As early as 1901 L. T. Hobhouse wrote a book entitled *Mind in evolution*—a work singularly ignored by most modern scholars. Hobhouse concerned himself directly with the evolution of mind at a time when the behaviourist dogma had not yet arrived to inhibit such a discussion. He began by arguing that adaptive radiation in the animal kingdom produces diversity and specialization, but that such a process may as commonly entail a structural atrophy, as in the case of parasites or cave fish, as it does some directional increase in complexity. Furthermore, stability rather than change is commonly a result of evolution. Thus many primitive animals retain an ancient form and subsist to the present day. Evolution multiplies and defines but 'does not necessarily elevate'.

In posing the question as to whether there is some consistent direction from lower to higher states of biological organization, Hobhouse concluded that the one consistent change of this type lies in the growth of mind. He largely avoided the Cartesian dilemma by saying

We shall not endeavour to trace the origin of Mind out of something that is not mind. So far as its origin is concerned, we shall take it as a factor in organic evolution, and shall content ourselves with pointing out certain more primitive features of which it is the natural development. In regards to its nature, we shall be principally occupied, not with what Mind is felt to be by its possessor, but rather with its operations as apparent to an onlooker.

Hobhouse went on to state:

Mind . . . is known by its functions. The function which modern philosophy seized upon as expressing the vital essence of Mind was that of bringing things together so that they have a bearing upon one another. Where there is Mind there is order and system, correlation and proportion, a harmonising of forces and an interconnection of parts. The organisation which is gifted with intellig- ence shows it by arranging its actions on a certain plan. . . . Its scheme of action may include the good of its young or its mate . . . along with its own. In proportion as its acts tend to promote the same end, its conduct may be termed organised and its several actions correlated.

Hobhouse goes on to point out that although instinct is a

basis for the adjustment and co-ordination of action unsurpassed in its own way . . . evolution consists in the gradual replacement of instinct by reason and, it is the final goal of reason . . . to bring all the experience of the race to bear in organising the whole life of the race.

He then went on, chapter by chapter, to provide an evolutionary ethology of behaviour as known in his time, treating reflexes, instincts, intelligence (with learning experiments), social behaviour, and finally conceptual thought and purposive self-conscious development.

Like the Victorian evolutionists before him, Hobhouse saw no error in seeking an element of progressive change in evolution. Yet evolution- ists of the next generation paid little attention to his views and others like them. Early writers had not analysed clearly enough the elements that by changing constituted a directional advance. Subjective an- thropomorphism, undoubtedly present in these theories, led to the criticism that an evolutionary direction was purely relative to human evaluations. This reaction attributed evolution to pure chance and held the opinion that complex animals could not be considered better adapted to their environments than more lowly forms: all represented degrees of specialization. However, in 1942, Julian Huxley rein- troduced both the notion of directional change and that of levels of adaptation. The objective criteria for a hierarchy of types of adaptive organization have been variously discussed (see also Simpson 1944; Rensch 1950) but Huxley greatly advanced the analysis by suggesting two types of shift in levels: first, an increasing control by the organism over its environment; secondly, an increasing physiological and behavioural independence of the organism from its environment.

This idea may be expressed in terms of population dynamics. An evolutionarily successful species is likely to populate its habitat fully and individuals are likely to be forced into peripheral regions where they face a greater environmental variance. For many individuals, tolerance of the increased environmental stresses will be inadequate, reproduction will not be successful, and a high mortality may occur. However, for those individuals which natural variation has endowed with greater tolerance, survival and reproduction will be possible. The progeny of such individuals, when compared with the parental populations, will have probably shown advance in both features listed by Huxley. From this point on a number of contingencies are possible. One is that descendants of the marginal stock enter into competition with the parental stock in a third area of colonization. The individuals adapted through increased capacities to control environmental changes and to exist independently of them will then be the more successful.

Near the end of his book, Hobhouse introduced an interesting argument. He stated that his purpose had been 'to ascertain the character and function of Mind as the organising principle in Evolution. In the absence of intelligence and in its lowest stages, Life is, as we expressed it, unorganised.' He pointed out that the occurrence of conflict rather than co-operation and the fact that evolution 'rests on a struggle for existence' shows 'a want of that organic unity in which the good of one part is necessarily the good of the rest'. Evolution by natural selection is 'the direct negation of organic growth. It is in no way parallel to the regular unfolding of a germ. It is more like a slow process of sifting, in which, by a long series of stages, and with many pauses, grains of one kind tend to come together in a heap'. Evolution thus does not proceed in a particular direction but types emerge which deal most effectively with their particular environments. Mind is that capacity of individuals to correlate past experience with ongoing reactions. In this way a knowledge of the patterning of events makes possible 'a mutual understanding of individuals and the impulses of aid to mate or young are thereby transformed into sympathetic actions'. The extension of such knowledge produce a corpus of thought in which actions are adapted to 'broad views of the purpose of life'. And from this stems the origin of ethical systems governing behaviour. Hobhouse saw the end-point of this direction in 'a co-ordination of thought and conduct . . . in which the whole experience of the species would be used in furtherance of one end that can embrace all human action, the development of the human species towards whatever perfection it may be within its power to attain'.

Hobhouse, in these paragraphs, was using the word 'mind' to refer particularly to a knowing capacity that functions in the construction of effective policies of behaviour with respect to individual and group survival and reproduction. The shift from the 'blind' control of individual strategies by innate behaviour repertoires through the various stages of capacity in acquiring new behaviour through learning and intelligence is a marked feature of evolutionary direction seen clearly, for example, in the development of complex societies from simpler beginnings (Chapter 8).

Models of mind

In modern parlance, Hobhouse placed his emphasis on cognition and was discussing the evolution of cognitive capacity. But cognition cannot exist independently of its data base and for data to be evaluated it must first be perceived. The relation between percept and concept, between processes of perception and those of cognition, thus becomes a key focus of our attention. Clearly it is no mere anthropomorphism to point out that the functional relation between these two and their capacity in man to render the species largely independent from and a controller of his natural environment has become a prime factor in the advance of man over other primate species.

If we are to comprehend how this has come about, we need to start with some simple modelling of the relations between mental functions. Much as the University of Oxford is understood by reference to a model of its operational system so may we approach the operations of 'mind' from this point of view.

Through their effort in extreme simplification the early behaviourists treated the organism as a 'black box' with inputs (stimuli) and outputs (responses). This black box model represented so:

$$S \rightarrow \boxed{} \rightarrow R$$

allows the study of animal behaviour through an analysis of the lawful relations between stimulus conditions and responses. Surprisingly perhaps, the results were highly productive and the basic laws of learning under certain strictly controlled laboratory conditions were achieved through the monumental labours of B. F. Skinner and his colleagues using such amenable subjects as the white rat and the domesticated pigeon. Another prodigious worker, Clark Hull, endeavoured to infer the processes within the black box that intervened between the stimulus and response. Without actually opening it, which would have been to examine the beast physiologically, Hull inferred numerous relationships between levels of motivation (drive) and the extent of learning (habit strength) that rendered a response more or less probable. Interestingly enough, as many writers have pointed out, this process led to the positing of numerous agencies with high-sounding names purporting to do exactly what the older and rejected vocabulary of pre-behaviourist mentalism had attempted to do. These erudite analyses and subtle experiments thus led back to precisely the point at which they had started. Clearly, if not the ghost, then the organism in the black box could not be ignored. The model sketched below was inevitable:

$$S \rightarrow \boxed{O} \rightarrow R$$

The great physiologist Sir Charles Sherrington had approached the problem of the emergence of cognitive control in behaviour along a very different route. Throughout a life spent in experimental anatomy he worked primarily with the spinal mammal and its reflexes. He summarized his findings in his book *The integrative action of the nervous system* (1906). Animals came in two kinds, radially and bilaterally symmetrical. As the term indicates, radially symmetrical animals have a globular or circular plan such as do *Volvox*, sea anemones, starfishes, or jellyfishes. The nervous systems of these creatures are loosely organized with many more-or-less interdependent parts. An extensive nerve network receives stimulation on the surfaces, and when stimulation exceeds a threshold, responses are generated by activation of an equally diffuse system of motor neurons. Many such creatures contain nervous organelles that operate independently of the other systems. Such are the nematocysts of sea anemones: cells containing a coiled spring filament with a harpoon on the end. When stimulated by contact the dart shoots out to impale a passing animalcule as prey.

Within the effector (motor) nervous system are neuronal circuits that cause periodic movements, so that the animal's basic needs are met. Sea worms, living in tubes, aerate their burrows periodically by washing water through them and thereby both receive oxygen from the fresh flow of water and keep their tubes clean. Some jellyfish beat the edges of the bell rhythmically and thereby rise in the water to remain near the surface. At night they slowly sink. This maintains them within the layer of plant plankton upon which they feed. Such 'wired-in' behavioural programmes controlled by neuronal pacemakers are innate response repertoires activated endogenously or in relation to shifts in local conditions. Similarly, reception of certain stimuli, usually by specialized neuronal receptors, sets off appropriate responses to the appearance of food, a predator, or a potential mate. Such organisms have evolved their complex response repertoires as the means whereby they can relate to stimuli impinging from outside, either through direct tactile contact or at a short distance, by vibration or chemosensory means. Behaviour here is a genetically programmed capacity for an adaptive response to environment. These responses ensure the maintenance and survival of an individual and its reproduction. These simple response systems, often only very loosely integrated, comprise elementary programmes with strategic designs.

Bilateral animals move in a constant direction in such a way that one end is the front and the other the back. Many such creatures increase in size by segmentation, each segment containing a batch of similar organs, legs, excretory devices, and reproductive organs, so that each is partially independent of the remainder. Even so the activity of the whole animal is co-ordinated by superordinate controls in the central nervous system. The earthworm (*Lumbricus*) is an example. Evolution in bilateral animals has usually consisted in a tendency towards more effective integration of segments. In some cases, as in certain molluscs such as snails or octopods, the segments have become closely coalesced so that the original plan is largely hidden. In vertebrates, the division of the spinal cord recalls the original segmentation, and the organization of the nervous system is still largely based on a segmental arrangement of both receptor and effector nerves.

The consequence of having a front end is that stimuli tend to make their impact there first. It is thus that the 'head' as bearer of an impressive array of receptor organs (sight, sound, odour) has evolved. And to integrate this bombardment of sense stimulations and to organize responses to them, the ganglion of this segment (often plus several additional ones) becomes greatly enlarged to form the brain. In vertebrates the brain is the much expanded front end of the spinal cord.

Sir Charles Sherrington (1906) paid close attention to the evolutionary importance of the development of the 'head'. In each vertebrate segment the 'reflex arc' is based upon two neurons: the afferent sensory root and the efferent motor root. 'And . . . on the junction between these two are superposed and functionally set, mediately or immediately, all the other neural arcs, even, those of the cortex of the cerebrum itself'. In the head the segmental receptors are especially developed and differentiated into sense organs responding to environmental stimuli emanating often at a distance from the animal. The main modalities of touch and smell, hearing and sight are all specializations to different modes of 'distance reception'. Sherrington underlines the statement that 'the brain is always the part of the nervous system which is constructed upon and evolved upon the "distance receptor" organs'. Now distance receptors provide information about a possible event in the immediate future such that, through neural connections to innate movement controllers, an animal may make 'precurrent' reactions enabling it to adjust to the new information, for example, by approaching prey, or by preparatory behaviour for escape in relation to possible alarming stimuli. These 'anticipatory' reactions are thus 'precurrent' to final or 'consummatory' reactions such as swallowing or escape. A strong 'affective tone' accompanies these consummatory reactions so that once stimulated an animal may show a motivated persistence in completing the behavioural event that finalizes the sequence. In a simple instance, such as hunger, the stimulus is particularly noticeable to a hungry animal, which then works hard to obtain the food. Furthermore 'the relative haste with which an animal when hungry approaches food offered to the visual field, suggests that conation attaches to the visual reaction by association through memory with affective tone'. Here then

Sherrington perceives that learning and memory may intervene between stimulus and response and guide the animal with respect to the satisfaction of its metabolical or productive needs. Along a different line of thought, Sherrington had thus reached similar conclusions to those of Pavlov in his famous conditioning experiments. The 'conditioned reflex' is an element in the learning process.

To achieve this effect the complex sets of alternative motor patterns available to meet the contingencies presented by the distance receptors need to be managed. This involves a substantial intercalation of neurons to form an association area between the sensory and motor parts of the elementary brain. The consequence of course, is a major enlargement of the whole structure. In addition, the neuronal representation and control of complex innate behavioural repertoires of strategic importance is based here. Lorenz (1950, 1970) and Tinbergen (1951) have constructed influential models describing possible relations between such innate motor systems and the environment. These ideas, together with their Sherringtonian anticipations, form the historical roots of much contemporary ethological theory and debate.

Animals rarely live in completely stable environments. The successful colonization of the land from the original marine environment not only necessitated the production of entirely new means of acquiring oxygen and supporting the weight of the body, but also exposed animals to habitats of much greater variability in temperature, humidity, and other conditions. Innate behaviour repertoires only change through natural selection over successive generations and, although their range of tolerance, their capacities, can be extended, their capability in responding to rapid day to day environmental shifts is clearly limited. Increased ability to learn directly from the environment evolved to allow organisms to acquire new information and thus to build up simple programmes of response to such exigencies. Expansion of neuronal material provided areas devoted to 'association' so that the necessary correlations between stimulus patterns and their effects in terms of comfort or discomfort (see below, p. 26) could be made. Association areas were initially closely linked to innate programmes and extended their capacity. As learning ability developed, however, whole response repertoires of acquired behaviour became possible and functioned largely independently of the innate bases.

In considering the maintenance and reproductive functions of an advanced organism, we find that there is an especially pronounced development of the capacity to correlate classes of information originating from the environment, not only with one another, but also with information arising from monitoring the interior metabolic condition. This enhancement leads on to new stages in cognitive complexity:

(1) An increased capacity to store past events in memory, together with the responses given to them and their results. In fact whole past programmes and their effects are stored.

(2) The capacity to recircuit neurophysiologically the ongoing experiencing of the senses in such a way that the subject becomes 'aware' of its situation through introspection of this analogue. This process seems to occur in much the same way as a plan position indicator in a radar system monitors the movement of targets recorded on the radar sets by reference to the stable map of the background locality. This recycling of the present is the root of consciousness and of the perception of time.

(3) The capacity to re-represent in conscious awareness what was once a 'presentational continuum' of past events. In this way elements of past experience can be 'recalled' from memory for comparison with the ongoing situation. This is the basis for discriminatory planning and foresight. It is the essential condition for higher forms of intellectual functioning.

We may now represent the mental capacities of the cerebral hemispheres of an advanced organism in a simple model that gets us far closer to the condition of our own species (Fig. 2.1). There are four interacting systems within the organism's black box that enable it to function effectively. First in the diagram is the *perceptual system* which monitors the environment by means of distance receptors: eyes, ears, nose, and tactile organs. The internal state of the organism is monitored by means of receptors, mostly situated in the brain stem. These record the ambient blood temperature, the levels of oxygen and CO_2 in the blood, sugar and various nutrient levels, and the levels and presence of numerous endocrine substances related to symptoms of stress or reproductive physiology. This input is fed to certain parts of the brain stem and filtered. The filtering operation is crucial, because the total amount of environmental information could swamp virtually any receiver not adapted to selective perception. In brief, filtering consists of a monitoring for novelty by a match–mismatch comparison with expected values based on physiological norms and established knowledge (see further in Chapter 9). The selected novel information is then fed to the *cognitive system*.

In higher organisms one prime function of this system is the maintenance of consciousness as a kind of screen upon which both novel information and the background presentational continuum can be projected. Past scenarios may also be called up and reprojected in relation to the ongoing situation, so that the probable outcome of a current dilemma may be assessed. Much of this assessment occurs in a kind of calculating room that is perhaps rather rarely available to conscious inspection and where information concerning bodily condi-

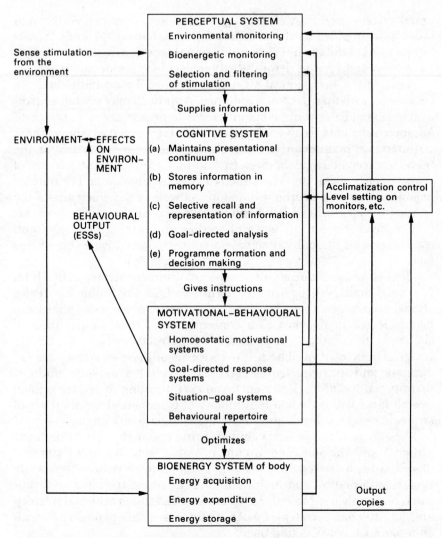

FIG. 2.1. Interdependent systems in the operations of mind.

tions, unconsciously held programmes highly prejudicial to the outcome, and the current motivational bias are consulted. The outcome eventuates in a decision and instructions are passed to the *motivational–behavioural system.*

The motivational system of a higher organism is complex, comprising several distinct types of mechanism expressed through differing behavioural means. Gone are the days when Hull among behaviourists or Lorenz among the classical ethologists could assume that all motivational mechanisms were of the similar type. The activation of a motivational system (say, fear, escape, aggression, sex) is expressed through behaviour provided by the neuromuscular systems of the body. Social interactions entail the use of complex signal repertoires, many of which have been analysed in detail by ethologists (see Hinde 1960).

Many of the behavioural strategies initiated by an individual are concerned with approach or avoidance. Approach may lead to aggression or sexual behaviour; avoidance leads to preservation. But basic to all such schemata is the supplying of energy reserves above those required for maintenance metabolism. The *bio-energy system* of the body is exceedingly elaborate. In addition to maintaining levels of crude energy from sugars, it includes the maintenance of complex chemicals basic to neuronal functions as well as the efficiency of the endocrine system. Basic behaviour must maintain the efficiency of this system, and the current wave of studies on foraging strategies and exploitation of the habitat signals a contemporary awareness of this fact.

The behavioural output affects the environment strategically. John Maynard Smith (1976) used the term Evolutionary Stable Strategies (ESSs) to describe those regular performances of a species that have been selected in the past as a consequence of their contribution to success in differential reproduction and the structure of which is largely under genetic control. The prime concerns of these strategies are (1) foraging and nutrient acquisition, (2) predator avoidance, and (3) mating, pair bonding (if present), and care of young (if present). Each overall label will include a multiplicity of behavioural mechanisms of strategic design subordinate to the main functional system.

The effects of behavioural activity bring about changes in both the physical and the social environment and a shift in the information provided to the perceptual system. The organism is thus constantly cycling information and maintaining an alertness to change. Organisms commonly need to rest this apparatus and this is achieved by sleep and its attendant strategies, such as finding a safe place or, as with chimpanzees, constructing one.

One of the most crucial features of the model we are describing is the occurrence of feedback. Information from the bio-energy and motivational–behavioural systems is returned in the form of an 'output copy' to the perceptual system. On this basis the detection of discrepancy or 'dissonance' is possible. Likewise, within the cognitive system the interplay between memory and ongoing circumstances involves repeated cycles of selective recall established according to highly complex sets of individualized criteria forming elaborate hierarchical systems.

Mind as information processing

The recognition that all parts of the psychobiological system governing the lives of individuals are interrelated is surprisingly recent. The current emphasis on systems analysis tends to hide this fact, yet in both Konrad Lorenz's famous hydraulic model and Niko Tinbergen's attempt to relate this to the functioning nervous system no feedback loops at all were incorporated. This omission, which now seems curious, was based upon the conventional notion of the organism as respondent. Programmed by the genes or by the acquisition of conditioned operant behaviour, the organism emitted responses acquired through natural selection or learnt through reinforcement by rewards. The insight, particularly in psycholinguistics, that the linear sequence was contrived through a hierarchical logic necessitating feedback, came as a revolution. The consequence is a realization that it is precisely the hierarchical and cybernetic attributes of living organisms that enabled evolution to acquire the direction emphasized by Hobhouse at the start of the century.

Julian Huxley's directional component in evolution is made possible only by an increasing subtlety of internal integration of the body and a corresponding increase in the inter-individual integration in societal processes involved in reproduction. Both of these depend on the capacity of organisms to integrate previously separated functions through the imposition of a superordinate system relating its subordinate parts; and this requires the open transfer of information between those parts. Once a hierarchical order of open systems had come into being, natural selection, operating on the elaboration of new hierarchies and new cybernetics, became capable of generating states of greater heterogeneity with integrative systemic control. Systems originally independent, become interdependent components of higher-order systems. While retaining a measure of separate functioning, these systems may again become components of yet more highly complex ones. Cells become elaborated into tissues, tissues into organs, colonies become individuals; organisms relate in societies that in many respects replicate the functions of individual organisms.

The cybernetic approach to biological systems is especially useful in an examination of the place of mind in bodily organization (Lazlo 1969). The cognitive apparatus with its subjective aspect is above all concerned with the manipulation of information governing the conduct of the organism in relation to the environment through the flexible expression of evolved strategies. Information processing is the prime function of 'mind'; its organismic role. As Sayre (1976) points out, a cybernetic approach also has philosophical advantages. It allows a degree of reductionism without deserting a monism of mind for dualism. The cybernetic approach is tailored to make sense of statements regarding body–mind interaction and to increase our understanding of both terms.

The interpretation of 'mind' as information processing with a self-monitoring facility called consciousness goes a long way towards resolving the problem of body–mind interaction which Popper and Eccles (1978) have recently revived. It seems that these authors see mind as an entity distinct from the processes that support it. While their criticism of reductionism is just and their emphasis on 'downward' causation (mind influencing matter) timely, it seems to me that the problem of 'interactionism' largely disappears when the systemic position of information processing in the life of a subjectively aware organism is understood.

There is no doubt that information is held and manipulated in cytochemically encoded structures. Information is physically represented. The mind is thus *materially* present in the world. The problem of dualism seems to arise from the way in which we experience ourselves. Dualistic experiencing is a property of the way in which information is processed by action in the brain. Consciousness, we may argue, comes into being when information is re-presented to a monitoring faculty under deliberative attention. Attention is a holding in consciousness of an object that may be a thing, person, state of mind, a self-experience, another's opinion, or a mathematical abstraction. Only as attending proceeds, however, does it become possible to describe the immediately antecedent experience of a conscious episode. In fact mental experience can be consulted only retrospectively and such experience, as evidence for the existence of mind, can appear only as an introspective report of past events. Inferences about mind are thus made from descriptions.

By contrast, if one seeks in the present continuum for 'that which attends', nothing is to be found. Only observation itself exists; the 'attender' escapes observation (see also Sherrington 1940, p. 334). It is because the attender is unobservable and can only be inferred from retrospective description that mental experiencing includes a strong tendency to dichotomize the 'I' (attender) from the 'me' (self-description); a dichotomy that parallels that between 'I' and my body.

Interactionism derives then from these two modes of experiencing (the monist present continuum and dualist self-description) which, on analysis, simply appear as inherent properties of the human cognitive process. The philosophical splitting-off of mind from brain arises mistakenly from the necessity of retrospective insight in the affirmation of the mind's existence.

This is not to deny in any way that informational processing leads to decisions that have 'downward' psychosomatic effects. Of course it does. It is the function of the cognitive analyser to perform in exactly

this way and thereby to relate the organism more closely to environmental and social change. There is no case beyond this for some
mysterium, an agent of non-material origins, unless information processing itself is given that status.

Pursuing, perhaps riskily, a computer analogy we can argue that
while the body resembles the hardware of a computer the mind comprises the software, the programmes that analyse and organize information to produce responses to inputs. There is thus a valid distinction
between body and mind. Mind is synonymous with information in two
categories; that governing instructions for operations and the raw
information operated upon prior to decision-making. Yet, in reality, we
have much greater complexity. The 'biogrammar' of evolutionary
stable strategies and the acquired 'sociogrammar' of social rules and
roles are not so distinctly separated; they interlace functionally and
epigenetically in ways that are not yet understood.

Consciousness

Many of the operations of mind, for example high-speed addition,
skilled typing, or playing a musical instrument are not readily
examined through introspection. The roots of these activities remain
unconscious to the performer whose attention illuminates the product
more than the underlying process. The selectivity and control of conscious attention remains poorly understood; very clearly it is not at all
coextensive with information processing for much of this is never
observed and cannot be summoned up for examination.

What then is consciousness? It is as if the information processed by
the senses becomes integrated to form an analogue of the energy
patterns impinging upon them. This interior analogue of the exterior
world is actively 'seen'; and this we may presume is no accidental
metaphor, for the dominance of visual perception in human life extends
into the inner world of experiencing as a dominant mode providing a
basic 'map' of an ongoing continuum. Auditory consciousness with its
markedly linear character dependent upon the sequencing of events in
time is a powerful vehicle for emotion, perhaps especially because the
human voice is experienced in this mode, but it lacks the map-like
quality of the inner visual panorama. The tactile consciousness too,
powerful as it may be in intimate contact, cannot represent our wide
apprehension of the world to so marked a degree. Vision, distance
perception, maps our world and its analogue within is the experience of
'seeing'.

Within consciousness one can experience a focal and a peripheral
area. It is as if within the wider panorama particular topics become a
focus of especial attention. And, curiously, this focus may utilize a

different mode from the more global picture. Thus, while driving to work, an awareness of the road, other vehicles and the surrounding environment may become quite peripheral while the attention focuses upon a conversation, a recent argument at home, or a coming confrontation with a boss or client. More curiously, since the complexities of threading one's vehicle through the traffic is successful, this peripheralization of awareness does not result in a reduction in efficiency. The focusing of consciousness often appears to be concerned with the attempted resolution of unfinished business. It is intentional. In the moment of performing a task this recall of the past is precluded but when the ongoing continuum can be switched to 'automatic' the lines are cleared and old problems are worked over again. In sleep, when the outer world is no longer dominant, the themes of such problems, often transposed into the curious symbolism of fantasy, again intrude associating with eye movements that emphasize their visual patterning.

The priorities that produce the recall of particular themes doubtless relate to the histories of the persons concerned. Yet a consciousness can occur in which the focal attentiveness on a theme is absent; in a deeply relaxed mood one simply gazes upon the world. Consciousness is both the stage and the action upon it. Consciousness is not always a patterning in words. While the inner metaphors of sensory experience are, as Jaynes (1976) affirms, verbal, consciousness is clearly not confined to linguistic themes. The inner analogue is not just an interpretation of experience, it is a re-presentation of experience itself. Indeed, subjectively, an individual is his experience, is his consciousness. Consciousness is 'being'. Verbal thinking, by creating the object, is 'having' (Fromm 1978). About these polarities hang the varying states of consciousness that can and do arise (see Chapter 11).

Consciousness is intimately related to attending. Attention is the focusing of conscious awareness. This may involve a narrowing of consciousness, a division of awareness into a more- and a less-focal area, a widening of consciousness until it has no especial object, or a flickering of consciousness when steady attending is for some reason precluded. Attention creates the foreground of consciousness, letting the rest slip into peripheral awareness. Gaining control of attending is to control the mind and the states of experiencing. It is one of the main disciplines of spiritual training (Chapters 12 and 13).

In learning a task, how to ride a bicycle, for example, one attends at first to every muscular movement. As one gains in skill the performance of the task of riding is released to the periphery of awareness. It becomes 'automatic' and an attempt to introspect the components of skilled movement often breaks up the quality of the performance. Meanwhile conscious awareness is freed to survey the landscape, to plan a route, to talk with fellow cyclists, or to dream on what might have been or what once was. Consciousness is the forefront of the mind particularly concerned with the intentionality of the moment.

The consciousness we experience is most usually a structure derived from complex processing of information from the senses and elaborately categorized to make a consistent 'picture' against which fresh information can be sorted and 'understood'. Interaction with the environment is a complex transaction between biological structure and the energy flows of the world 'out there' mediated by the categories we impose upon raw experiencing. In social life we build personal 'constructs' (Kelly 1955) and use them to create consistent patterns of relating with others.

Some of the key properties of consciousness are spatialization, excerption, narratization, and conciliation (Jaynes 1976). Spatialization is the invention of a spatial world as the map upon which we plot experience. Inside the solid lumps of our brain lives the experience which appears to the subject as an ordered world, the room in which I write for example. Yet not all is seen at once, we excerpt from possible scenarios those bits most relevant to the moment. For example, in 'conceiving' of my car I literally create it in awareness by putting together an interior abstraction. To remember an event, I first create an excerpt from the drama of the past and build from there. Narratization is story telling. The creation of linear sequences from the excerpts of our lives. And a highly biasing and prejudicial process it can be. Conciliation is the working through of ideas to produce an internally consistent view of the material. For example, we create the space within which the action occurs and the social scenario of a given personal drama. The 'I' and the 'me' (p. 247) are likewise structures excerpted and narratized from experience. These are not the immutable basis of our world but rather the constructs we create to produce a stable world of subject and object within which to act.

Inevitably this means that not only are individual consciousnesses unique but that the consciousnesses of one epoch may differ as greatly from those of another as do the construed worlds of a polar Eskimo and a city dweller in New York. It also implies that the history of human consciousnesses is the history of human social life. There is every reason to suppose that the conscious life of the Homeric heroes, for example, was most unlike that of modern man. So unlike indeed that Jaynes (1976) does not refer to it as consciousness at all. The Homeric heroes, the personalities of the early old Testament, individuals of the old empires of Babylon and Egypt have all come down to us as individuals driven by interior forces. Gods speak to them from inside, hallucinating voices perhaps originally those of actual ancestors, later projected into statues but still 'heard' within. It seems likely that as these authoritarian empires arose the simple egalitarianism of hunter–gathering peoples gave place to the stress of hierarchy. Early human consciousness would have been a world of certainties based upon simple social conventions and the fact of being born irrevocably into a clear cut role in life. These empires, run by the internalized voices of deified ancestors, demanded a firm control of classes and sections of society.

Jaynes argues that at this stage in human history conscious examination of self was absent. For this to arise an increase in social complexity with a need for analytical flexibility in contact with diverse persons of other cultures was necessary. And this came about through a sequence of catastrophes, movements of people, and trade. Jaynes in fact argues that the shift to self-critical awareness involved a major alteration in the use of the brain with a new emphasis on the analytical functions of the right hemisphere and the subordination of the more holistic left (see Chapter 11). Whatever the paths that may have been taken, the relatively late arrival on the human stage of the self-preoccupied consciousness of Indian, Chinese, late Greek, Roman, and European civilizations seems certain. The form of consciousness is a product of the myth generating socio-economic forces of its time. To this we shall later return.

The symbol and the world

In *The biology of ultimate concern* Dobzhansky (1967) argued that the emergence of life from non-living matter, the development of air-breathing land-dwelling animals, and the appearance of other major shifts in structural organization that preceded great adaptive radiations are examples of 'evolutionary transcendence'. By 'transcendence' he simply meant surpassing or going beyond the limits of previous organization. The emergence of the information-processing capacity of the human brain is clearly a major transcendence in this sense.

The model of mental functioning we have been elaborating here shows clearly that the evolutionary direction in higher organisms has been particularly focused in the development of cognition. Jean Piaget, in his profound yet often obscure work *Biologie et connaissance* (1967), remarks that 'cognitive mechanisms constitute the actual organs of regulation during exchanges with the environment' and infers that some isomorphism between theories of biological and cognitive integration is inevitable.

Glancing at the animal kingdom as a whole it is apparent that biologically simple organisms regulate their transactions with the environment primarily through a genetic endowment of relatively inflexible action patterns. The addition of learning skills and the intelligent construction of knowledge through exploration gradually becomes a predominant feature of the transactional style. This is particularly so in homoiotherms, whose constant body temperature ensures a steady level of functioning in the central nervous system and hence the possibility of extensive exploration in varied environments.

Cognitive mechanisms managing intelligence are extensions of self-regulating processes in living organization. They necessarily become the specialized regulators of behavioural interactions with the environment. We have seen that a prime cognitive function in higher animals is the re-presentation of organized information for cognitive, sometimes conscious, evaluation in relation to the current experiential continuum.

In Piaget's system the behavioural components are functional forms of organic structure. These 'schemata', as he calls them, comprise the strategic elements of the organism's elementary transactions with the world. With increased capacity for learning and intellectual functioning the *concept* replaces the *percept* as the controller of schematic behaviour. These interiorized schemata are constantly shuffled together, remodelled, discarded, or replaced as the subject shows cognitive adaptation to the objects of its knowledge as an extension of the overall adaptation of the organism to its environment. Piaget does not believe that concepts take their origin from linguistic structures. Rather they derive from associated events in experience that antedate linguistic structure both phylogenetically and, in man, in individual development. Thus, for Piaget, concepts derive from operational schemata: 'logico-mathematical structures are extracted from the general conditions of actions long before they make use of language, either natural or artificial'—for example, a mother's non-verbal interactions with her baby (see Chapters 9 and 10).

Thought forms, at first perhaps pictorial and in modern man very largely linguistic, set up a re-presentational environment possessing a dynamic stability that is distinct but not separable from the biological organization that maintains it. These thought-systems contain behavioural norms, expectations, ethics, and ideals as well as simpler components probably present in all higher mammals at a non-verbal level. The extraordinary benefit that this environment of thought confers upon its inhabitant is the possibility of advanced cognitive anticipation. The capacity of the mature human individual to run through whole sets of possible scenarios as imagined responses to a problem situation or as a means to achieve a goal so far existent only in thought, is the secret of human ascendancy. Even so this attribute of mind has a biological basis, and intercalates with thought forms of a very different nature. These belong to a paralogical world of symbol and fantasy deeply rooted in non-verbal experiences. Head, heart, and body remain indivisibly organic and he who would divide them does so at his peril.

In their treatment of this theme both Cassirer and Hallowell point out that the crucial link between the inner world of representation and the outer 'reality' lies in the human capacity to symbolize percepts; symbolization of events in the perceptual continuum provides the units for a pictorial logic from which the abstraction of grammar eventually emerged as a concomitant of sound production in the development of verbal communication. Symbolization is involved not only in the psychic functions of reason but also in all forms of selective attention and perception, dreams and fantasy, and in imagination.

'Representative processes,' says Hallowell, 'are at the root of Man's capacity to deal with the abstract qualities of objects and events, his ability to deal with the possible or conceivable, the ideal as well as the actual, the intangible along with the tangible, the absent as well as the present object or event, with fantasy and with reality. Every culture as well as the personal adjustment of each individual gives evidence of this, both at the level of the unconscious as well as conscious processes.'

An animal capable of symbolization can carry away from a situation an inner trace that stands in for the response it may make when it next encounters the situation. A central process comes to function as a substitute for actual sensory cues. The operations of this central process cannot be conveyed to another without employing some convention which allows a communicational interchange, whether it be by gesture, facial expression, or language. Extrinsic signals representing the inner symbols are what make it possible for groups of humans to share a meaningful world. Externalized graphic, plastic, dramatic, or electronic representations make up the 'media' and provide that cultural environment that is so inextricably intercalated with the biology of the performers and the physicality of the environment.

This view of the mind as the prime organ of the body in its transactions with the environment is a profound one. It totally replaces the archaic dualism of the Cartesian myth, and has the form of a modified holism based on the cybernetic analysis of living systems. Mental activity becomes, not the movement of a disembodied sprite anxiously wandering the corridors of the brain, but rather a mode of relating by which the organism contacts, interprets, and acts on its world. Experience is necessarily an act of relating in a relationship that can never be free of paradox. For that of which we relate is our interpretation, our presentational continuum coloured not so much by the world as by our own senses. Real, yet not real, the world we see remains in itself mysterious, ineffable, sometimes a world of suffering, sometimes of joy and wonder.

But to leave this chapter with such a peroration would close prematurely the development of the very argument we need to pursue if a clarification of 'biological mind' is to follow. The transactions of our perceptual, cognitive, and motivational systems occur primarily between ourselves and another. The context of mental functioning is social. The imagery of thought, the sequencing of behaviour, and our foci of attention are primarily concerned with the world of other people. The mind 'runs on' social information, for our environment is a society. The paradox is thus a social one and to clear the ground for an attempt at its resolution we must take an extensive detour of several chapters. In these we shall attempt to say what it means to be social, for in that attempt lies a further definition of 'mind'.

Summary
(1) The word 'mind' connotes all those most complex features of human cognition. It has been a focal point in philosophies attempting to relate subjective experience to the objectivity of the body.
(2) The idea that mind and body were separate yet in some sense connected has dominated European thought. Gilbert Ryle in 1947 showed, however, that this dualism was based in a mistake in the categorization of ideas relating to the two terms. To contrast 'mind' and 'body' strictly as opposites is logically illegitimate. Interest lies in the investigation of the activities called 'mental' which occur concurrently with the activities of an entity we term 'the body'.
(3) Introspection of my inner life and behaviour reveals structure. In 1901 Hobhouse made an early attempt at accounting for the evolution of mental structure. He concluded that a consistent direction of evolutionary change has been an elaboration of processes of perception and knowing towards an emergence of what we call the mind. Sir Charles Sherrington argued that the evolution of neuronal integration of reflexes concerned with movement gave rise to large ganglia situated at the front end of mobile animals, for that is where the sense organs develop. The head bears not only the senses but also the machinery for integrating information and organizing appropriate responses.
(4) A model of the physiological processes concerned with cognition requires at least a four-part system with feedback loops between them. The four parts are the perceptual apparatus, the input analysers, the motivational and behavioural controllers, and the energy regulator. Cognitive activities are essentially involved in relating perception, analysis, and action. A prime activity is the recognition of novelty, for it alerts the animal to the presence of danger, a food object, or a mate. Consciousness of the world comprises a form of re-presentation of the current perceptual input on a mental screen so that a constant awareness of a monitoring process arises.
(5) Awareness occurs in the context of stable strategies of behaviour

evolved in relation to the satisfaction of the key needs of an organism for food, for avoidance of predation, and for reproduction.

(6) The idea that all parts of the psychobiological system are closely interwoven is relatively recent. It is precisely the integration of cybernetic mechanisms in a hierarchical order that enables animals to develop the more complex cognitive functions. Sir Julian Huxley argued that the directional component in cognitive evolution was made possible by an increasing stability of internal integration in the body together with increases in social integration that allow for stable social systems in which individuals can learn while young. Successive levels of integration, each more fully developed and dependent on more complex mechanisms, have succeeded one another throughout the evolution of the animal kingdom. Man is the latest creation of this process.

(7) Many cognitive processes are carried through without conscious awareness. Consciousness is the experiencing of an integrated analogue of the information received by the senses. It is however highly selected by mechanisms of attention. Within consciousness there are often focal and peripheral concerns—again the result of differential attention. Conscious awareness is the forefront of the mind and is particularly concerned with the intentionality of the moment. Consciousness is structured and there are reasons for supposing that this structure differs with the socio-economic situation of the experiencing subject.

(8) Jean Piaget, in arguing that cognitive mechanisms constitute the actual organs of regulation during exchanges with the environment, emphasizes that the development of complexity arises through the assimilation of new functions on to older structures. He points to an inevitable parallel here between biological evolution and cognitive development in the life of an individual.

(9) The mind is the cognitive organ of the body—the perceiver, the knower, and the actor in its relations with the environment. This notion entirely replaces the old body–mind dichotomy that once dominated Western thought. Yet a paradox remains, for what we relate to in actual experience remains our interpretation of a presentational continuum coloured as much by our own senses as by the realities they perceive.

3 The social environment and its evolution

No man is an island   John Donne

Evolution, social selection, and altruism

It is impossible to understand the activities of the human person without considering what it means to be social. Man, furthermore, shares sociality with a wide array of other living organisms and to treat the specifically human kind without a look at other species would be to assume too narrow a perspective. Indeed, it is precisely on the difficulties posed by making inferences from social animals to social man that a great contemporary debate concerning the mechanisms of social evolution has had its focus.

The theory of natural selection first propounded by Charles Darwin (1858) is a cornerstone of biological thought and its appreciation is essential to anyone asking evolutionary questions in relation to human social behaviour. There is an enormous body of data in support of the theory and it is as close to being a factual representation of the nature of evolutionary change as any theory can be. None the less there remain a number of common misapprehensions that need constant clarification. As we are about to see, Darwin's use of Herbert Spencer's resounding phrase 'survival of the fittest', does not actually represent the nature of the process adequately and over-emphasizes part of it.

Animals live in populations that are dispersed in characteristic ways in the environment, ways that can usually be interpreted as a function of the behaviour of individual members operating as strategies for survival and reproduction. Some groups of animals found in nature are simple 'associations' assembled either through overwhelming influences of nature, such as tide-washed plankton on a sandy shore, or through responses to temperature or light held in common by all participants. Most assemblies are, however, 'consociations' resulting from behaviours in which animals respond to each other's presence in ways that establish their spacing in relation to one another and their occurrence in groups of certain age and sex composition. Dispersion patterns in a population are thus usually a consequence of social responses producing a societal organization.

As examples of societal organization consider the herds of wildebeest on the Serengeti plains of East Africa, kittiwake gulls in cliff colonies, weaver birds in their dense colonies of thousands of nests in trees or marshes in Africa, elephant seals in vast assemblies on the Californian island of Anna Nuevo, or the troops of baboons wandering in the

African savannah. Examples of equal interest, of course, are the ant or bee colonies. But not all social responses result in sociable congregation. A response that maintains wide spacing, as in territorial animals or solitary nomads, may be equally social in that it is an interaction between two or more individuals. Its effect may produce dispersal rather than crowding according to the characteristic response repertoire of the species. Solitariness is thus a result of social behaviour and may produce particular societal structures involving wide dispersion.

Within populations animals differ in their success in leaving offspring; they show differential reproductive ability. This comes about in two ways. Spencer's colourful phrase refers to differences between organisms in death-rates (i.e. differential mortality). Obviously, individuals that either fail to find enough food for themselves or unwisely and fatally expose themselves to predators tend to die young and to leave few offspring. Differential reproductive success also occurs in other ways, however. The main process is competition. Whenever one individual leaves more offspring than another and this capacity is inherited, in time its genes will come to dominate the population gene pool. Eventually the rarer genes will disappear and the genetic types leaving fewer offspring will become extinct. An exception arises only where there are concomitant changes that confer an advantage on the rarer types.

Evolution by selection is a balancing process. Animals that are too aggressive, too daring, or too timid for their own good in terms of reproduction are gradually eliminated so that in a stable environment the median values tend to become the population norms. In general, intermediates have more offspring in repeated generations than do extremes and, for this reason selection favouring intermediates is called 'stabilizing'. In biology, one says that where an intermediate type is leaving on average more progeny than others then it is the more 'fit'. In this sense fitness is measurable by the number of offspring surviving in succeeding generations.

In a changing environment things are different. The average individuals may now not be the most fit. Rather those, perhaps at first rare, types best equipped to deal with the changed conditions may have this characteristic. In time then, as their potential representation is realized through actual selection, these types increase their proportional occurrence in the population as a whole. If the environment then stabilizes it will be these types that will probably emerge as the intermediates.

The habitat of an animal population offers only finite resources for its use. As individuals reproduce these resources are necessarily depleted and the relation between the speed of their renewal and the rate of population growth governs the numbers of individuals that can live there. The geese feeding on grassy maritime flats at Slimbridge in England or at Caelaverock in Scotland arrive in large numbers in autumn. The grass is quickly cropped. Unless it grows fast enough to sustain recropping the birds must move elsewhere. In a population confined to a particular habitat competition for limited resources is an inevitable feature of life so long as reproduction occurs. This indeed has been the case ever since self-replicating molecular assemblages evolved to exploit finite resources. Competition and selection are logically inevitable features of ecology, and this must be true on any planet on which life-forms reproduce and depend on supplies that can run out.

Efficiency in competition is thus a prime source of selection and occurs in many aspects of social life. It is indirect in the case of two flocks of geese quartering the same ground; direct in the case of two titmice fighting over a piece of fat on a bird table. Both these processes in the long term are effective agents of selection, especially when applied to differential capacities to obtain mates and to care for and rear young.

These fundamental ideas in population dynamics emphasize the individual as the subject of selection. In biological writing it has often been said that a character is advantageous or detrimental to a *species*. Sir Ronald Fisher in the 1958 edition of his great book *The genetical theory of natural selection* (first published in 1930) cautioned against this fallacy and suggested that arguments about the benefit of a given trait to a species were misleading. The term 'species' simply denotes a population of interbreeding organisms which have a 'pool' of genes in common. The pool is not, however, selected as such; rather its genetic constituents are constantly reshuffled into individual organisms which contain subsets of gene-pool elements. These individuals are then subjected to differential survival through the operation of a range of mortality factors that eliminate them either before or after reproduction.

There has been much debate about this question of the unit of natural selection. Some earlier writers have considered that the characteristic groups that make up populations could be selected as such. While this is theoretically conceivable, every writer who has recently examined the problem has considered that in nature it must be a very rare event and certainly not a common factor in the evolution of animal traits. Characteristics of groups, like the characteristics of species, are thus considered by most theorists today to be the result of the selection of genes as they manifest themselves in the individuals comprising populations (G. C. Williams 1966; Lewontin 1970; E. O. Wilson 1975).

Dawkins (1976, 1978) has argued strongly that considering the individual animal as the unit of selection is a form of shorthand for what is actually selected down the generations is the gene, or over short time spans, groups of associated genes. Logically and philosophically Dawkins's argument is important. Ultimately it is indeed the individual genes that are selected. However genes do not act independently; often blocks of genes operate together in determining traits and sets of traits in individual organisms. This inevitably means that in each generation the loss of individuals from the population through mortality prior to breeding or through failure to breed, eliminates not isolated genes but sets of associated genes from the pool of genes that represents the total population of that species. Over short time spans then genes are not the separate units of selection Dawkins supposes. And again, over a longer time span.genes will have changed by mutation or altered their effects by chromosomal recombination so that the effect they exert on traits can never be considered in isolation. It looks as if the concept of the isolated gene as a unit of selection is an idealized abstraction from reality. Alexander and Borgia (1978) have re-examined the problem of the unit of selection at different levels of biological organization. After considering a variety of cases their main conclusion is that, operationally, the genome (the genes of an individual animal) is a common unit of selection and that to refer to individuals as units of selection is not necessarily in error. Individual organism and genic selection are two among several processes of selection that produce species populations. A total reductionism to genic selection is a distortion of the complexities involved.

A classic case of the evolution of social features within a species is the process described by Charles Darwin (1871) as 'sexual selection'.

Sexual selection depends on the success of certain individuals over others of the same sex in relation to the propagation of the species; whilst natural selection depends on the success of both sexes, at all ages, in relation to the general conditions of life. The sexual struggle is of two kinds; in the one it is between individuals of the same sex, generally the male sex, in order to drive away or kill their rivals, the females remain passive; whilst in the other the struggle is likewise between the individuals of the same sex, in order to excite or charm those of the opposite sex, generally the females, which no longer remain passive, but select more agreeable partners.

Darwin used several criteria for distinguishing sexual characteristics selected in this way: (1) the features acquired by sexual selection are confined to one sex; (2) the features develop fully only at sexual maturity; (3) the features often appear only during the reproductive season; and (4) males are in most species the most active in courtship. In the context of reproduction, males make use of weapons (teeth, horns, etc.) in competitive encounters with male rivals and also make use of their courtship display characteristics in the presence of females in order to attract them.

An example of sexual selection emphasizing male-to-male exclusion (intrasexual selection) is provided by the antlers of deer. These enormous structures vary with age and are closely related to the dominance of their owners in the hierarchy. While fights may occur in the context of displays of rivalry, the exhibition of the character in question is often sufficient. Sexual selection emphasizing attraction of the opposite sex is commonly recorded in relation to the elaborate displays of polygamous birds. The extraordinary plumages of the male suffice to attract several females, who then rear their young alone (see Selander 1972).

Darwin's argument emphasized that sexual selection depends on the 'success of certain individuals over others of the same sex in relation to the propagation of the species'. The word 'propagation' in most of the literature since then has been understood to mean fertilization leading to the birth of new individuals in the population. Indeed, in most examples, the emphasis has been on social systems in which males sporting the elaborate character are polygamous and have little to do with other aspects of reproduction. In 1972 I suggested a fresh categorization of the processes involved to take into account an additional meaning of 'propagate'; namely to rear to sexual maturity.

Social selection results from (a) effects of competition between the subject and others of either sex with respect to commodities essential to survival in the situation that will allow attempt at reproduction, (b) competition for access to preferred members of the opposite sex for mating and (c) effects of competition between subjects for access to commodities in the environment essential for rearing of their young or those of relatives to reproductive age. Of these (b) is the process most commonly referred to as sexual selection. Social selection is undoubtedly one of the main evolutionary processes responsible for the emergence of . . . behavioural characteristics.

We can see easily enough that in a competitive world social selection for a selfish maximization of an individual's capacity to reproduce will result in the predominance of certain traits in a population. The presence of these traits in an individual often means a very 'fit' animal. However, when that same individual is observed spending some of its vital time and energy budget assisting others to survive or rear their young the logic of Darwin's theory would suppose it to be engaged in activities that would tend to lower its biological fitness. For a long time the only way in which a truly selfless behaviour could arise seemed to be through a differential advantage accruing to groups of individuals that showed sacrifice in relation to their companions to a degree greater than in other groups. We have already seen, however, that on present evidence, and on the basis of extensive efforts at modelling, such a process of group selection seems unlikely to be important in evolution.

None the less, observers of animal behaviour know that altruistic acts with differing degrees of self-sacrifice are of common occurrence, ranging from parental care to group defence and rescue behaviour to complex forms of co-operation. How such behaviours have evolved in the face of selection favouring the maximization of individual reproduction has been a great and tantalizing mystery to evolutionary theorists.

This puzzle was at last unravelled in a series of brilliant papers of a rather technical and mathematical nature by the English geneticist and entomologist William Hamilton (1964, 1971a, b, 1972). The essence of his argument is simple enough. An individual's genes are not unique to itself; they occur also in animals to which it is genetically related through genealogical descent. The proportion of genes which an individual shares with a relation depends on how close the relationship is. For example, I share a greater proportion of my genes with my sister than I do with my cousin. The number of genes I share with my relations by marriage is again smaller, and those I share with people from other countries is yet smaller still. Given sufficient information on the 'family trees' of individuals it is possible to calculate their relatedness. Similar calculations, in the absence of information from pedigrees, can be made from studies on the similarities of blood types and other traits.

The sharing of genes means that it is possible to sacrifice myself for my sister in such a way that, even if I die in the process, a proportion of my genes will survive in the next generation. My behaviour is thus far from unfit. In fact since my sister is likely to share half my genes my behaviour is probably only one-half less fit than if I had behaved totally selfishly. My cousin probably shares with me only one-sixteenth of my genes, so that to sacrifice myself for her would be an activity of less fitness than sacrificing for my sister. There are exceptional circumstances, such as my total castration or my taking vows as a monk, where my only residual fitness is that which accrues to me through my assistances to relatives.

If, at times in an ordinary reproductive life, I am moved not only to look after my own progeny but those of my sister as well, then I clearly increase my fitness above that due solely to selfish interests. Hamilton had the brilliance to see the simple point that had not been elaborated before; namely that overall fitness is the sum of fitness owing to selfish behaviour plus fitness owing to altruistic behaviour to relatives. This overall value he named 'inclusive fitness'. Now, it is intuitively clear that an individual has the evolutionary option of operating strategies that either maximize individual fitness or provide varying degrees of assistance to relatives. To what extent its reproductive strategies emphasize such altruism depends on the pay-off of such strategies in terms of inclusive fitness. Different pay-offs are related to contrasting social systems of reproduction, which are in turn correlated with features of the environment, as we shall see.

Hamilton's theory indicates that since altruism is only of survival value if it enhances fitness, it can evolve only where the recipients are relatives. It will diminish rapidly with the distance in relatedness between individuals. Some have therefore concluded that behaviour in this category cannot be termed altruism at all. Alexander (1974) expresses the nature of the process most succinctly in the term 'nepotism'. Nepotism is selfish behaviour having the appearance of altruism since it benefits relatives as well as ones own concerns. Strategies that maximize the individual fitness component may be termed selfish. Those that increase inclusive fitness through behaviour facilitating reproduction by relatives are nepotistic. The process by which such behaviour arises is often called kin selection. Social selection has thus yielded two main strategic components in the behaviour responsible for societal organization. Upon the balance between them depends the enormous variety of societies seen in the animal kingdom. Both, however, exist to maximize the inclusive fitness of breeding in their exponents. A biological case for 'true' altruism does not exist.

An extension of Hamilton's theory has been provided by Trivers's (1971) analysis of the evolution of reciprocal altruism. Altruism is reciprocal when the assistance rendered to an individual by another is returned in an appropriate interaction, usually at a later date. In reciprocal altruism individuals are not required to have any particular genetic relatedness with one another. Indeed, reciprocation may develop in behaviour occurring between different species. The phenomenon depends upon an exchange of benefits and not upon the fact that, as in Hamilton's theory, the gene in question benefits its duplicate in another organism. The behaviour will spread in a population where the net benefits accruing to reciprocators exceeds that to non-altruists. Trivers argues that the chances of selection favouring altruistic behaviour in which individuals dispense a benefit to another greater than the cost of the act will be improved when many potentially altruistic situations arise in the population, when there are repetitive interactions of the same kind within a small group of individuals, and where symmetrical situations favouring the return of benefits are common. Generally, then, one would expect to find reciprocation in populations of highly social animals living in small intensely interactive groups. Trivers's theory has in fact received a convincing demonstration in Packer's observations on the baboon *Papio anubis* living at Gombe in Tanzania (see p. 76) as well as in numerous less-quantified examples cited in Trivers's paper. Finally, in man, reciprocal altruism is supported by an elaborate psychological system based in friendship, sympathy, and moral rules (see further p. 176).

A possible response to receiving a benefit is to cheat; to fail to return the favour. Selection is likely to penalize a cheater if cheating has subsequent adverse effects on his life that are greater than the benefits of not reciprocating. For example, altruists may learn to withdraw benefits from cheaters and their offspring. In man discrimination against known cheaters is intense, going so far as imprisonment and other forms of punishment. Short-term gains by cheating are likely to be offset by long-term losses that may affect one's offspring and those of relatives. We shall see later (p. 244) that the monitoring of trustworthiness in companions probably played a major role in the evolution of self-awareness in higher primates.

Ecology and social organization

One of the main thrusts in the social ethology of the 1960s was the clarification of the adaptiveness of social organizations. Why did some birds of the same taxonomic family move in flocks while others were solitary? Why do some antelopes mate in lekking grounds much as ruffs do while others attempt to round up small harems in a moving herd? Why do gelada and hamadryas baboons form bonded harems based on long-term relations between the sexes while olive baboons have short consortships in a patterned promiscuity? Why do human beings form sexual bonds and show a tendency to monogamy? These and other questions emerged from a classical ethology primarily concerned with the evolution, motivation, and function of social signals but which began to focus on ecology as the adaptiveness of social structure to habitat gradually became apparent (see Crook 1970b; Crook and Goss-Custard 1972).

Gross correlations between social organization and ecology sometimes yield valuable clues which lead to the formulation of hypotheses for testing in later studies. One of the most productive themes has been the association between two major types of selection pressure (see below) and differing reproductive strategies of species under ecological constraint. A mountain of research has shown that the population of a species is commonly limited by shortages of resources in a density-dependent manner; the larger the population the greater the shortage and the more marked the effects of starvation. The research of the great ecologist David Lack (1954) showed for example that in many bird species of temperate zones, individuals were reproducing as fast as they were able and that the subsequent population was cut back every year by winter mortality. The state of control depended on the relationship between the success of breeding in the preceding summer and the carrying capacity of a location under varying conditions of weather and vegetative production.

The pattern of food production varies in different ecologies. In the tundra there is a massive growth of ground vegetation and insect life in a very short spring and summer. Much the same situation, although both a more productive and prolonged one, obtains in temperate woodland, where a great table of riches is spread every summer, declining to a low level of diminishing resources in the autumn. By contrast equatorial forests lack extreme seasonal variation; where productivity varies little during the year the resource fluctuations are never so great as in savannah or temperate regions. These contrasted conditions pose different problems for individuals of a reproducing population.

In the first condition individuals that breed soonest produce young at the peak of a rich and often superabundant period of food production. Competition and selection may be expected to yield traits that maximize rapid and early reproduction and the production of the largest possible brood or litter. By contrast, where food resources are relatively constant the population will be close to the carrying capacity of the environment and successful reproduction will only balance mortality. Beyond this the young and frail newcomers will starve. Under these circumstances bood sizes would be expected to be low and behavioural traits to emphasize careful and effective rearing and foraging under difficult circumstances.

Technically these two conditions are said to yield so-called r and K selective circumstances respectively: r being the 'intrinsic rate of natural increase' and K the 'carrying capacity of an environment'. Where seasonal conditions favour a high r, selection favours maximal reproduction in terms of both brood size and speed. Where a steady K is maintained animals aim at optimizing their success with more limited numbers of carefully reared young. r and K selection tend to produce widely contrasting strategies for individual success in reproduction, which are in turn given expression in the types of social organization in which individuals live and breed. Their contrasted influences have been found again and again in widely differing animal groups. r and K symbolize contrasted extremes of course; many conditions lie in intermediate positions so that the terms are used in a purely comparative sense to indicate the extent to which a set of r or K habitat conditions is reached for comparable situations.

My original concern with these problems was expressed in a series of papers on African and Asian weaver birds culminating in a monograph in 1964. Over six years some 50 out of 105 species of weavers (Ploceinae) were observed in field studies in West and East Africa, the Seychelles Islands, and the Indian subcontinent. The birds inhabit tropical forests, savannah, and arid semi-desert conditions. Some specialize in grassland living. In arid country (r conditions) the weaver birds, small passerines related to sparrows, tend to be seasonally and sexually dimorphic, to breed polygynously (one male mated with several females), and to have short or capricious breeding seasons. In humid forest (K conditions) by contrast, plumage colour does not change seasonally, monogamy is the rule, and colonies are occupied for long breeding seasons with individual pairs breeding in successive relays. Why was this so?

I found that weaver species could be sorted into six different types of population dispersion, varying from the solitary to very sociable. All forest weavers were relatively unsociable as well as being monogamous and eating insects. Grain- and seed-eaters of grassland and savannah were gregarious and tended to breed in colonies. The crowding of nests varied with the vegetation, being generally most dense in the more protected sites in tall grass, over water, or in trees infested with fierce ants.

Weavers also showed six types of pair formation. In the forest insectivores with non-sociable behaviour, the male pursues the female, courts her, and leads her to the nest he has built. In savannah trees, the male advertises the nest and pursues a female that approaches him, bringing her back to the nest after a chase. In the most colonial species this chase is omitted and all courtship occurs at the nest. The female is attracted there by a colourful advertisement display given on the nest itself.

These correlations suggested four grades of social organization in weaver birds in which features of population dispersion and pair formation correlated functionally with ecology (see Table 3.1).

My interpretation of the functional significance of these grades began by following Lack's (1954) view that the primary adaptations of birds, so far as their dispersion was concerned, were to ensure an adequate food supply. The solitary feeding of insectivores in forests was therefore attributed to a foraging strategy involving the pursuit of cryptic and easily disturbed prey by singletons. This would naturally associate with relatively solitary living in separate territories. In the forest home of these birds the obscured vision in dense foliage necessitates a courtship strategy in which females are pursued and shown to their nest sites. Monogamy is interpreted as a bonding strategy enhancing the co-operation of paired parents in rearing young. The relatively unchanging conditions of forest life (i.e. K conditions) suggest that the adult population is near the food limit at all times and that adults have difficulty in rearing young; they therefore need to collaborate in pairs. The unvarying conditions also promote long breeding seasons with breeding in relays.

In open savannah, gregarious species forage in flocks from colonies or roosts from which the daily dispersal occurs. In open country, birds are easy targets for predators, and many authors have argued that

TABLE 3.1
Relations between types of breeding, degree of sociability, and clutch size and food and habitat types forming the environments of weaver birds in Afro-Asia

Main food	Main habitat	Dispersion of nests				Pair-bond			Mean clutch on tropical mainland (no. of species)
		Solitary (or 2–4 pairs together)	Grouped territories	Colonial	Solitary or colonial	Mono-gamous	Poly-gynous	Probably both	
		Number of species in each category							
Insects	Forest	15(+2)	0	1	0	17	0	0	2·1 (8)
Insects	Savannah	4	0	2	0	5	0	1	2·4 (5)
Insects and seeds	Forest	2	0	0	1	3	0	0	—
Insects and seeds	Savannah	1	0	4	3	1	4	3	2·2 (7)
Insects and seeds	Grassland	1	0	0	1	1	(1?)	0	2·9 (2)
Seeds	Savannah	0	1	16	0	2	10	1	2·6 (14)
Seeds	Grassland	0	13	2(+1)	0	0	14(+1 Pr.)	0	2·7 (17)

Source: Crook 1964; table after Lack 1968.

flocking increases the likelihood of an individual's survival in the event
of an attack, if only because of the cover provided by its fellows (Vine
1971; Hamilton 1971a). In addition flocking may assist individuals in
finding food through enhancing their searching efficiency: several
advantages may therefore result from such behaviour (Crook and
Goss-Custard 1972; Thompson, Vertinsky and Krebs 1974). The seeds
on which weavers feed do not of course require spaced hunting, and
flocking facilitates the location and congregation of birds on patchily
distributed resources. As J. Fisher (1954) and Ward and Zahavi
(1973) have argued, dispersal systems based on roosts probably provide centres for information exchange whereby birds can detect contrasts in the foraging success of other individuals and follow the more
successful back to good feeding patches. In open country, trees
becomes sites for breeding colonies which may also facilitate synchron-
ization of breeding. The sudden release of many young into the savannah at the same time may perhaps swamp the waiting predators and
thus constitute in itself a survival strategy. Colonies are easily detected
by females at a distance, especially in species where advertisement
displays on the many nests are given in synchrony to produce a vivid
tree-sized orchestration of sound and movement. Polygyny occurs in
these environments because the short food-rich breeding season is a
period of such abundance (r circumstances) that females can rear
young by themselves. Males thus tend to maximize their reproductive
success by attracting and mating with several females and establishing
them in nests in their territories. Weavers are not totally promiscuous.
The number of a male's females is limited and males do assist them in
rearing their broods. In grassland colonies the nests are hidden in the
greenery and the males have developed especially prominent aerial
displays which attract females to the territories. Males then show them
where the nests are. Away from the territories the birds remain gregarious.

The weaver birds in fact reveal a fascinating range of societal variation broadly correlated with points on an r–K continuum stretching
from the arid near-desert conditions of sub-Saharan Sahel landscapes
to the almost non-seasonal equatorial forests of the Congo basin. Under
the most northern conditions the Quelea of Mauritania breeds in
exceptionally short rainy seasons. The males establish the nest as in
other weavers and attract females to it. Living in extremely dense
colonies, often covering several acres of thorn bush, they simply posture
on their nests in display and do not pursue their prospective mates.
Males do not go on to construct further nests as polygynous weavers of
more productive lands do. Instead they assist females in rearing young,
working extremely hard at collecting insect food. Clearly in this arid
region with its brief period of insect food availability for raising young

such assistance is vital if both sexes are to participate in a successful breeding (Crook and Butterfield 1970).

As we have seen, at the other end of the r–K continuum, in the rain forests, monogamy is again the rule. But in this case the explanation lies in the relatively poor food resources due to the stabilized population–resource equilibrium under conditions of very limited seasonality. I was able to study only a few of these birds but Brosset's (1978) research on the *Malimbus* weavers of the Gabon forests has usefully extended the story. While the male of one of these species constructs the nest alone (as in other weavers), in others the female also involves herself in this activity and in two cases receives the active assistance of additional apparently adult birds. In *M. coronatus* the nest is built by a mixed party of males and females (3–6 birds) all working together. In *M. racheliae* and *M. cassini* the nest is built by a female and a multi-male party of two or three individuals. In this case one male drives off the others when the nest is completed. In all these advanced cases only a pair finally incubate, brood, and feed the young.

The social complexity correlates here with the complexity of nest construction and the difficulty of the siting (protectively slung from the ends of vines or tendrils). In these birds with long breeding seasons the protective quality of the nest is important. Collaboration is probably related to relay breeding under these K circumstances. Some degree of collaboration in the *Malimbus* was predictable from comparative studies of other avian families where collaboration in incubation and rearing associate with K conditions. In these weavers the importance and complexity of the nest seems to have focused co-operative behaviour in this area but it will be interesting to see whether further research shows an extension of the behaviour to incubation or rearing in any of them.

The weaver bird study suggested that the motivational systems of individual members of different species were producing contrasting strategies of dispersion and pair formation neatly graded to suit environmental conditions. The social structure arising from the interactions between the birds was thus an expression of individual adaptedness and formed an important societal component of the environment in which individuals were seeking to survive and procreate descendants. Following the weaver bird example, an array of studies appeared analysing the societal organizations of related species through correlating behaviour and ecology. In 1968 Lack published a survey of birds from this viewpoint and the idea took root also among mammalogists. In particular, surveys of African antelopes, carnivores, primates, and certain bats have been most instructive.

One of the most interesting bird examples, and one that reveals rather different principles from the weaver study, is Nelson's (1970,

1978) long series of investigations on the oceanic boobies and gannets. In particular there are close associations between nesting density on islands or islets, foraging habits, breeding ecology, and behaviour. Some of the principles illustrated follow.

Where nest sites on islands are plentiful and there are no special advantages arising from social stimulation the birds (all boobies of oceanic areas) space their nests on the ground or in trees. Here there is little site competition, little aggression, and a development of displays based on locomotion. Some of these species feed far off shore, necessitating very long foraging trips (up to 300 m). In these species the clutch is very small (1–2), eggs are large, growth is slow, and starvation may occur. The breeding cycles are very long. In species that forage inshore, clutches are usually larger but brood reduction may occur under adverse circumstances. Growth is quicker. Many details of behaviour are associated with these contrasts.

Dense nesting arises either because the chosen sites are small or because high levels of social stimulation are advantageous in ensuring breeding synchronicity in short optimal breeding seasons. In the gannet there is strong competition for sites with much aggression, little aerial display, and a great deal of mutual social stimulation. Together with these traits go highly ritualized, short-range threat posturings, intense mutual preening, developed site ownership displays, and a meeting ceremony of mates functioning in reassurance. Nelson's detailed account is well worth close scrutiny for it illustrates many aspects of socio-ecology most cogently.

Turning to the mammals, Jarman's (1974) study of antelopes describes five types of foraging strategy differing in their selectivity of plant species and parts and the utilization of food items dispersed in different ways. Since these ungulates are primarily exploiters of vegetation, it is natural that the range of feeding strategies should be related to different types of browsing and grazing.

The 74 species of African antelope share certain basic features: all are exclusively vegetarian and bear one large and precocious calf each year. Body size, mating systems, nomadism, and dietary composition as well as other minor features all vary and correlate with numerous details of display and behaviour.

Class-A antelopes are small and good at selecting plant parts to comprise a good diet. Such animals remove the most important plant parts so that group foraging does not occur. These selective feeders exploit their territories well throughout the year and correspondingly they defend them vigorously.

By contrast the larger class-D animals, living on grasslands where rainfall varies, are less selective and so long as they do not crop the grass too close many animals can cover the same foraging area in a short time. Herds are favoured (protection from predation) and nomadism develops. The larger size of these nomads allows them to cover ground and move over longer distances than smaller animals.

The class-A animal on his small territory is likely to be monogamous, whereas the nomad males may attempt to round up harems on the move or establish temporary territories for mating purposes.

The mating systems of these animals are often dependent upon the dispersion patterns of the females and these in turn are related to patterns of optimum food exploitation. The Uganda kob females, for example, tend to congregate over good foraging. The males perforce come within such an area to mate and establish small 'leks' thereon. Females are attracted by males' displays and go to them for mating. Males are exhausted fairly soon and replace one another quickly as the prime maters on site (Buechner 1961).

The wildebeest of the Ngorongoro crater in Tanzania show an interesting ecological dependency in their patterning of dispersion and mating (Estes 1966). Near the central lake there is rich grass where females assemble. Males take territories here and attract temporary harems of females on to them. Around the fringe of the crater grass growth is seasonal and the animals move in nomadic herds. Here males attempt to acquire harems on the move rather than on topographically defended areas.

Among the mammalian carnivores there are likewise relationships between social organization and feeding ecology. Carnivores are among the most socially complex mammals, although only a few of them form sociable groups. Their importance is great, for they form the peak of the ecological pyramid and their prey comprises many of the antelopes already described. Carnivores themselves are rarely preyed upon by other animals. There are several distinguishable types of foraging behaviour and food preference, varying from tracking and pursuit of prey animals by running them down through stealth and pouncing methods to omnivory or insect eating. There are four types of social organization: isolated animals with mother–litter families, monogamous pairs, groups or bands of associated litter–mates with their parents, and colonial animals living in burrow systems. Some principles of association that emerge are that solitary hunters feed on prey they can subdue individually which they kill suddenly after a stealthy approach. By contrast, hunters in packs are usually small relative to their prey and collaborate in diverse and very complex ways in hunting, in transport of food to dens, and in feeding and care of the young. Some smaller carnivores such as mongooses are colonial, social, and highly altruistic, using group burrows for protection and as a refuge from which they then forage.

We can usually show that social organization correlates closely with a species ecology yet we are often far from clear about the processes by which this association has come about. Patterns of grouping and spatial dispersion are closely related to food resources and foraging strategy and come to constitute the demographic environment within which social selection determining behaviour responsible for mating and rearing strategies occurs. These strategies are to a degree autonomous from the dispersion patterns within which they arise and may radiate in a number of directions.

Reproductive strategies

There are two distinguishable questions concerning social evolution. The first is: why do groups form anyway? The second concerns why groups have the size and membership composition that they do. We have already seen that the first question has usually been answered by emphasizing either the primary value of the protection the group gives to individuals from predators or the value of gregariousness in relation to finding food. I am inclined to back Alexander's argument that grouping would occur in most predated species if it were not for additional factors dispersing the individuals in relation to their food supply. It seems likely that in most species these two selection pressures interact to produce a compromise weighted according to (a) the particular foraging requirements of a species in a given habitat and (b) alternative means of protection from whatever predators may be present.

The actual composition and size of groups seems to be largely a consequence of the formation of particular types of mating and rearing unit. These types vary according to the investment in time and energy that the male and female place respectively in their mating and rearing roles. Trivers (1972) points out that the sex that invests most time and energy in parental behaviour becomes a 'limiting resource' for the other sex. For example, a male is rarely limited reproductively by his capacity to produce sperm but a female is restricted in her output of eggs. Females are often limited further by the necessity to rear offspring by brooding or lactation. It follows that in paired individuals the male's breeding capacity is limited by that of the female. He can, however, improve his reproductive performance by mating with another female. In general, then, males tend to compete with one another for females. In more abstract terms, the sex that invests less will compete for the sex investing more in the production of young. In effect males usually invest more in mating than in rearing but under certain circumstances must assist in rearing to ensure the survival of their offspring. These circumstances play a major role in determining the variety of rearing systems found in nature.

In North America many marshland bird species show polygyny, a condition in which a male is mated to several females who occupy his territory. Ornithologists, especially Orians and his colleagues, interpret this in terms of the effect of competition between the territorial males for the areas most productive in food for breeding. Females tend to disperse themselves among the males but in cases where a male has an especially good territory a female may opt to breed with him even if he already has a mate, rather than go for one without. Such a male has a territory so much better than that of neighbours that a 'polygyny threshold' is surpassed and he gains a second mate.

Among the weaver birds polygyny occurs in territories within a colony but these do not include a foraging area because the birds forage in flocks away from the breeding location. The nests are intricate structures beautifully woven by the male birds, who then display on them to attract females to the nest. Females inspect several nests before allowing courtship with a chosen male to proceed. The females seem to be choosing between males of contrasting building skills. A male that has a string of prime sites and well-made nests attracts the most females. A male's vigour in display may also indicate to the female a mate with whose genes hers can mix with a high chance of being passed on through future generations. Male vigour in display could also indicate vigour in caring for the young. Male weavers assist females as the young hatch and the extent of their help to successive mates may greatly promote each female's reproductive success.

It is not always clear that polygyny is of such reproductive value to females as the views of Orians and his colleagues suggest. In marmots, large ground-dwelling squirrels, for example, adult males are territorial and aggressive. Each male's territory holds 1–4 breeding females. Naturally the male's reproductive success rises with the number of females on his territory: but this is not the case for the females themselves. The existing system seems to be a compromise between a female strategy that would favour monogamy and a male one favouring polygyny (Downhower and Armitage 1971). However, it has also been suggested that since there is a dominance hierarchy among the females and only the subordinates do badly, it may be that it is only younger females that fare worse in big harems than they would if they were monogamous. Since these females may breed more effectively when older the system is not necessarily disadvantageous to them (Elliot 1975).

Some male birds spend all their time mating and do not provide the female with any benefits other than indications of their vigour. This condition, called polybrachygyny, means that males that show the most effective displays are most persuasive in attracting females. These displays are given at localized courting places called leks. Among many dramatic examples the ruff has perhaps been studied the most thoroughly (Hogan-Warburg 1966).

The male ruff is a long-legged wading bird whose head and neck feathers are specially developed for use in a jumping display on a lek display ground. The leks are placed within areas favoured by reeves (female ruffs) for breeding, probably because of a good food supply. There are two types of ruff plumage and these are associated with two types of courtship behaviour. 'Resident' males display on their leks and are attended by 'satellite' males. In large leks the satellites have little chance of mating as they are driven away by the residents. But in smaller leks the favourite residents are so busy mating that their satellites succeed in attracting waiting females and mate with them. The interesting point about the satellites is that their behaviour includes many submissive components that trick the resident males into allowing them to remain near their sites. Some 30 per cent of ruff matings are owing to satellites, and selection has yielded a stable dimorphism of the two forms of male structure and display.

A contrasting condition is found in a number of Arctic sandpipers studied by Pitelka and his ornithological group (Pitelka, Holmes, and Maclean 1974) based at Berkeley University, California. Sandpipers show varying tendencies to breed polyandrously. A female courts one or more males and then goes round laying eggs in nests prepared by them on the ground. This odd reversal of polygyny has been attributed to a very high rate of ground predation whereby clutches are easily lost. If a female, in a short breeding season, has to re-establish her clutch in relation to a single mate, clutch loss becomes a very serious matter which the male can do little about. If, however, she keeps mating and not only gets several clutches going but is able to re-establish those that get lost, then she maximizes her chance of a successful breeding season. In this case too, by maximizing their caring role, males ensure as far as possible that their young are 'got off' successfully. In these birds male care is the limiting resource and females show the increased size and dominance which in polygynous species accrue to the males (see Jenni 1974).

The incidence of mating systems differs in mammals and birds. Among birds the need to supply a nest and incubate the eggs externally to the body evidently produces conditions under which the female commonly requires male assistance. Bringing up the fledglings necessitates a great deal of work in finding food, and polygyny, as we have seen, is possible only when food is exceptionally abundant under r conditions. Among mammals by contrast, viviparity and lactation mean that the limiting resource is nearly always the female's rearing capacity. Polyandry and monogamy are thus rather rare among mammals and polygyny the most common reproductive strategy (see Table 3.2).

TABLE 3.2

Contrasting partitions of parental investment between the sexes in birds and mammals

	Reproductive strategy			
	Polyandry	Monogamy	Polygyny	Promiscuous competition by males and females
Birds	Unusual	Frequent	Occasional	Unusual
Mammals	Rare	Occasional	Common	Frequent

After Daly and Wilson 1978. See also Crook 1965, 1977a; Crook, Ellis, and Goss-Custard 1976.

Selective circumstance and the evolution of co-operation

Hamilton's theory of the evolution of nepotistic behaviour as a consequence of maximizing the inclusive fitness of individuals through kin selection (p. 42) has opened a passage from a nature red in tooth and claw to a no less rigorous nature in which the appearance of much gentler forms of interaction is comprehensible.

Among birds, the New World jays show a wide range of societies. One line of development parallels the weaver-bird route culminating in the colonial breeding of paired individuals, each defending its own small territory but foraging as a group gregariously. Another route has led to the formation of bands of close relatives in which only a small number of adults breed and these are assisted by helpers that live communally with them in a group territory. These helpers are young of previous broods which defer breeding 'altruistically' to assist in the rearing of close relatives under ecological conditions which make this difficult. In one study a comparison was made between pairs of *Aphelocoma coerulescens* unassisted by helpers and those that were. Among the former the number of fledglings produced per pair on average was $1 \cdot 1$ and the average number of offspring still alive after three months after fledging was $0 \cdot 5$ ($n = 47$). For pairs assisted by helpers the corresponding figures were $2 \cdot 1$ and $1 \cdot 3$ ($n = 59$). Thus the presence of helpers increased the replacement rate of the jay family by a factor of 2–3. This held true through a number of further evaluative studies of the data (Brown 1974).

One of the most remarkable accounts of collaboration in mammals comes from recent research by Olwyn Rasa (1977) on the dwarf mongoose (*Helogale*), which lives in colonies in arid parts of Africa, often burrowing a refuge in the base of a termitarium. The animals live in matriarchal family groups of about a dozen to thirty individuals in which adult offspring remain as group members but do not breed under normal circumstances. Instead they participate vigorously in the reproductive activities of their parents. Dwarf mongooses are diurnal and feed mainly by hunting invertebrates such as insects, spiders, and millepedes. Eggs, lizards, smaller mammals, birds, and snakes are also eaten. The family goes foraging as a group within a large home range and establishes a variety of bases for refuges which seem to be used at different times of the year. In the captive group studied by Rasa the founding pair lived with several generations of offspring. The family is led by the mother (designated 'alpha') with the founding father ranking immediately beneath her. The older offspring tend to be lowest in the rank.

Only the alpha female breeds and it seems that the monogamous reproductive male suppresses sexual interactions between siblings. The young are visited by the alpha female only for suckling. Otherwise the babies are continuously attended by two or three baby-sitters. These evidently clean and warm them and retrieve them if they wander. In other collaborative activities individuals take turns in sitting vigilantly alert while others feed, thereby functioning as watchdogs or guards. There is a regular changeover between individuals in the performance of this activity. When the alarm is given the group assembles and may mob collectively a potential predator. Males are usually most involved in attacking predators and may collaborate to kill snakes as dangerous prey. They are also prominent in investigating potentially dangerous occurrences in the day's routine. The group also collaborate in offering food to the young still in the nest. Apparently, it is group care for the young that leads to the higher rank of younger rather than older non-reproductives in the group.

These features may be interpreted in terms of a high degree of social selection responsible for the care shown by the non-reproductives in the group. Suppression of an individual's own breeding allows a slow rate of reproduction, which is probably of survival value in a harsh environment where over-exploitation of resources can easily develop. Conversely, co-operative feeding and care increases the likelihood of rearing those young that are produced. All individuals are closely related and the behaviour probably maintains a high degree of inclusive fitness for all parties. Research on these animals is continuing.

Among primates, especially close collaboration between parents has developed in a few forest-dwelling animals as diverse as gibbons on the one hand and the tiny marmosets on the other. The marmoset mother produces twins or occasionally, in the laboratory, triplets. It seems that in times past marmosets were bigger but, perhaps in adaptation to an almost bird-like life in the high branches of South America forests, they have shown an evolutionary trend of decreasing size. This has meant that big single babies no longer easily pass through the birth canal. Individuals having two small young have evidently been the more successful and twins have become the rule. But two small marmosets need much attention, and insect hunting with two babies clinging to her fur may not be easy for the mother. Whatever the reason, male marmosets have developed a rearing strategy whereby they greatly assist the mother by carrying, holding, and generally caring for infants while she is away eating elsewhere. Furthermore, when the next young come along, their brothers and sisters of the preceding litters may assist the male in his carrying and caring tasks. It is certain that to rear the twins successfully this kind of collaborative endeavour has become essential. It is perhaps not surprising to find then, that here the female is the larger sex and is dominant over her male (Ingrams, personal communication).

One of the best-documented analyses of altruism and kin selection in group-dwelling mammals is Bertram's (1976) study of the lion pride. These animals show evidence of considerable kin selection in that the females show communal suckling while the two males in the pride not only show no sexual competition for the females but are very tolerant towards all cubs.

From his field-study of the species Bertram has drawn up a list of features that in general characterize the lion pride. These are:

(1) A pride comprises two adult males and seven adult females.
(2) Four females usually give birth and rear cubs together.
(3) The litter size is three cubs.
(4) The two males share the fathering of the cubs.
(5) Three subadult female cubs remain in the pride.
(6) Subadult females replace adult females that have died or left during the period. Pride size thus remains constant.
(7) All male cubs are expelled.
(8) The adult males have grown up together in a similar pride, left before maturity, and stayed together. They have taken over and breed in a pride which is not the one in which they were born.
(9) Adult males retain a pride only long enough to father one batch of young females for the pride.
(10) Prides are stable and are maintained in this way over generations.

Bertram's calculations of average relatedness among the pride's members show that the adult males are on average about as closely related as half siblings while the females are as related as full cousins. Bertram explains the male's tolerance of cubs at kills by the fact that there is a high probability that it is his child or at least the child of the

other male, which is itself closely related to him. They tolerate cubs
more than the females possibly because their reproductive life in the
pride is so short. The absence of competition for the females is also
associated with the very close genetic relationship of the males and
their potential for harming one another should they fight. The relationship between the females likewise favours a sharing in suckling
young.

Closely knit groups of interacting and co-operating animals are
common in some 60 bird species, in wolves, wild dogs, mongooses,
elephants, and in many primates. The fact that small groups tend of
necessity to comprise a membership of close kin favours the occurrence
of kin selection and hence a high probability that cooperative behaviour
will evolve. Group formation may arise as a result of factors favouring
defence or resource acquisition and the sizes and compositions of groups
express the effects of social selection within them.

The day of large inclusive socio-ecological theories is probably over.
So much detail is now accumulating on so wide a range of taxonomic
groups that a mini-theory can be erected for virtually every one of them.
The general postulates of each theory have, however, much in common: the contrasts between them depend on the phylogenetic features
brought to the varying ecological conditions of life in which the animals
live.

Many mini-theories involve the r–K continuum. Co-operative
behaviour is often clearly associated with species which, when compared with their relatives, live under the more K selective circumstances. We must recall, however, that the application of these ideas is
necessarily comparative. It does not follow that species reproducing
under r conditions will always lack co-operative ability. The need for
theoretical analysis of many more cases such as the lion is clearly
apparent and major studies of this kind are already on the way.

Social systems evolve in close relation to ecology. The environment
calls the tune and the strategic behaviour of individuals is a response to
the circumstances affecting their lives. The evolution of mating and
rearing systems with attendant complexities of nepotistic behaviour
occurs within and is part of this process. Social evolution without
ecological reference is ultimately a logical impossibility in a world of
finite resources. This we shall see to be as true of man as of any of his
relatives in the animal kingdom.

Summary
(1) Most animals show societal organizations that are the expression
of the social responses of individuals one to another. An understanding
of human sociality demands a biological theory of animal social life and
evolution.

(2) The individuals of a species differ in reproductive ability. Whenever one individual leaves more offspring than another and this capacity is inherited, its genes will in time come to dominate the gene pool.

(3) Competition for limited resources is an inevitable feature of life so long as reproduction occurs in the context of finite supplies. Selection of successful competitors is the prime mechanism in evolution.

(4) The unit of selection is the individual phenotype: this, however, implies that the ultimate unit of selection is the gene that contributes successful traits. Such genes increase their proportional representation in a gene pool.

(5) Social selection, of which three types are distinguished, is a major process responsible for the evolution of behaviour.

(6) Altruistic behaviour, for long a puzzle to evolutionists, may now be explained largely in terms of kin selection for the inclusive fitness of individuals. Assistance to relatives enhances the fitness of individuals accruing solely from selfish behaviour. We thus have a general sociobiological theory that accounts for both altruistic and selfish social behaviour.

(7) Reciprocal altruism evolves where the net benefits received by individuals that show co-operative reciprocity exceeds that of non-altruists.

(8) Elaborate social organization with co-operation tends to evolve in species attempting to reproduce under conditions where the carrying capacity of the environment is more or less filled. These K circumstances play an important ecological role in influencing the evolution of advanced social behaviour.

(9) Many studies have correlated features of social organizations with ecology and shown that the strategies of their members are adapted to habitat conditions, often in very elaborate ways. Examples are described.

(10) Reproductive strategies involve patterns such as polyandry, monogamy, polygyny, and promiscuity. Sexual selection under environmental constraints from a species habitat accounts for the adaptive radiation apparent in taxonomic groups.

(11) Some cases of elaborate co-operative behaviour are outlined and their evolutionary explanations discussed.

4 Monkeys, apes, and man

> If no organic being excepting man had possessed
> any mental power, or if his powers had been of a
> wholly different nature from those of the lower ani-
> mals then we should never have been able to con-
> vince ourselves that our high faculties had been
> gradually developed.
>
> Charles Darwin

The primate scene

While the primates comprise only one of the several orders into which
the class of mammals is divided, the group is of surpassing significance
because man himself is classified within this order. Of the mammalian
orders, the insectivores, the ungulates, the Cetacea, the carnivores, and
others, each comprises an array of forms of which every one is adapted
to a particular habitat with a mode of life enabling it to live and
reproduce there. In each order an adaptive radiation has proceeded in
the manner of an opening fan, eventually yielding the variety of forms
extant today. The earliest mammals (Eutheria), the insectivores, arose
during the time that reptiles dominated the earth. Together with some
dinosaurs, perhaps, and with birds, which also emerged from a different reptilian stock at this time, they developed the capacity for regulating their own body temperature. Homoiothermy allows the mammalian and avian body to maintain a constant high level of activity that
does not depend upon the temperature of the environment; and it
allows the colonization of environments that would be otherwise too
severe to inhabit.

A great diversification of herbivorous and carnivorous forms
developed from the insectivores. The development of large herbivorous
mammals was accompanied by a radiation of the carnivorous forms
that preyed upon them. The landscapes of the earth were thus 'peopled'
with an interdependent range of forms comprising a natural system,
itself dependent upon the grass and vegetation provided by soil, rain,
and sun. Today most of these assemblages are broken up by human
activity but, for example, on the great plains of Serengeti in East Africa
the relationships between seasonal vegetation, nomadic herbivores,
and dependent beasts of prey can still be discerned and studied in
detail.

Radiation and socio-ecology

The primate radiation took its own particular path. The most primitive representatives are extremely similar to the insectivores. Prosimians, such as the nocturnal mouse lemur of Madagascan forests, feed on invertebrates and are active at night. Socially they live in loose communities comprising a set of juxtaposed home ranges utilized by females and their dependent young. The adult males move in larger home ranges that are superimposed spatially upon those of the females. Each male may meet and perhaps mate with several females in the course of moving through his range. Males compete for females and thereby come to exclude one another from their ranges and, since male ranges are larger than those of females, there tend to be fewer males than females in any local community. The excluded males range over large areas on the outskirts of the little community.

These important studies, made at night with great patience (Charles-Dominique and Martin 1972), show that at the very root of the primate evolution we have an extremely loose kind of relationship between the sexes. Socially, the males are dependent on the whereabouts of the breeding females, themselves located in places well suited for the nourishment and protection of their young. The female, with her heavy investment in producing and raising her babies, is both the spatial and the behavioural focus of the social system while the males compete for ranges that contain mateable females. Only a proportion of them are successful and the rest must struggle as best they can to obtain mates. With increasing age, strength, and experience, most of them probably inherit a vacated range, take one over, or succeed in establishing a new community where younger females are setting up new ranges.

The mouse lemur's pattern of life focuses especially on the female's feeding ecology, upon which the males dispersion is contingent. Indeed, since the female has the prime investment in young, this is exactly what would be expected from Trivers's elaboration of Darwin's account of sexual selection (p. 52). We shall see that explanations of social systems in terms of a male reproductive strategy contingent on a female rearing strategy make good sense in attempts at understanding the evolution of primate societies.

Early work on primate social systems yielded the first model of their social evolution in the mid-1960s. In conjunction with Steve Gartlan, who like myself had conducted field research in Africa, I undertook a survey of existing studies (1966). The outcome was a set of correlations much in the manner of my earlier weaver-bird work. In brief, we argued that the primates could be classified into five grades of socio-ecological adaptation (see also Table 4.1);

TABLE 4.1

Classification of primates according to grades (diet, activity, socio-sexual behaviour) shown in relation to ecology and demography

Species, ecological, and behavioural characteristics	Grade I	Grade II	Grade III	Grade IV	Grade V
Species	*Microcebus* sp. *Chirogaleus* sp. *Phaner* sp. *Daubentonia* sp. *Lepilemur Galago Aotus trivirgatus*	*Hapelemur griseus Indri Propithecus* sp. *Avahi Lemur* sp. *Callicebus moloch Hylobates* sp.	*Lemur macaca Alouatta palliata Saimiri sciureus Cobbus* sp. *Cercopithecus ascanius Gorilla*	*Macaca mulatta*, etc. *Presbytis entellus Cercopithecus aethiops Papio cynocephalus Pan satyrus*	*Erythrocebus patas Papio hamadryas Theropithecus gelada*
Habitat	Forest	Forest	Forest–Forest fringe	Forest fringe, tree savannah	Grassland or arid savannah
Diet	Mostly insects	Fruit or leaves	Fruit or fruit and leaves. Stems, etc.	Vegetarian-omnivore Occasionally carnivorous in *Papio* and *Pan*	Vegetarian-omnivore *P. hamadryas* occasionally also carnivorous
Diurnal activity	Nocturnal	Crepuscular or diurnal	Diurnal	Diurnal	Diurnal
Size of groups	Usually solitary	Very small groups	Small to occasionally large parties	Medium to large groups. *Pan* groups inconstant in size	Medium to large groups, variable size in *T. gelada* and probably *P. hamadryas*
Reproductive units	Pairs where known	Small family parties based on single male	Multi-male groups	Multi-male groups	One-male groups
Male motility between groups	—	Probably slight	Yes—where known	Yes in *M. fuscata* and *C. aethiops*, otherwise not observed	Not observed
Sex dimorphism and social role differentiation	Slight	Slight	Slight—Size and behavioural dimorphism marked in *Gorilla*. Colour contrasts in *Lemur*	Marked dimorphism and role differentiation in *Papio* and *Macaca*	Marked dimorphism. Social role differentiation
Population dispersion	Limited information suggests territories	Territories with display, marking, etc.	Territories known in *Alouatta, Lemur*. Home ranges in *Gorilla* with some group avoidance probable	Territories with display in *C. aethiops*. Home ranges with avoidance or group combat in others.	Home ranges in *E. patas. P. hamadryas* and *T. gelada* show much congregation in feeding and sleeping. *T. gelada* in poor feeding conditions shows group dispersal

Source: Crook and Gartlan 1966; see also text.

(I)   The relatively solitary invertebrate-eating nocturnal forest animals such as the mouse lemur.

(II) Forest fruit-eaters living diurnally in small family parties usually with a single reproductive male.

(III) Diurnal forest vegetarians living in large multi-male parties.

(IV) The terrestrial primates of savannah with a vegetarian omnivore diet living in multi-male troops.

(V)   This grade comprises the terrestrial 'harem' dwellers moving either as small parties in huge ranges or in large troops.

Our main inference was that as insectivorous primates radiated within the forest they took to fruit-eating and became diurnal. The larger troops, plausibly, were developed as protection from diurnal predators. Given sufficient food males were thus distributed with the females in large groups forming a hierarchically ordered collective collaborating in protection.

In a 1972 paper I suggested that during the evolution of terrestrial open-country monkeys, two main selection pressures operated on the individuals whose collective strategies lead to the interactions and relationships that are responsible for the social structure (see also Fig. 4.1). On the one hand, the argument goes, predation pressure tended to select individuals which travelled in groups in which males often performed the role of protectors in collaboration. Within such groups the males' competitiveness for females produced a strongly hierarchical

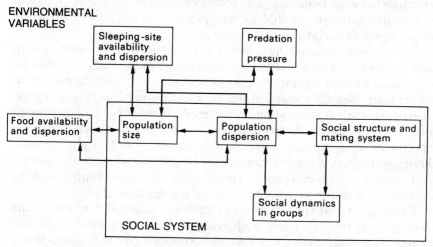

Fig. 4.1. Diagram of relations between environmental factors and aspects of a primate social system. Note how population size and dispersion are functions of interactions between food availability and dispersion, sleeping site distribution and predation pressure. The social structure of population units results from reproductive and rearing strategies that express universal social behaviour patterns of species. (After Crook 1970, see also Crook, Ellis, and Goss Custard 1976.)

sequence of ranks. In environments with seasonally poor supplies the large troop hoovering its way across the countryside would however soon clean up the food and many individuals would not get enough to eat. Under these circumstances, as in the fringe areas of species ranges (Aldrich-Blake, Bunn, Dunbar, and Headley 1971), the troop splits into smaller parties so that when food patches are discovered all can feed adequately. Competition for mates would tend to partition males among such parties and sexual selection would tend to favour males that retained a harem of females and assisted them in rearing young. The relatively large size of males compared to females is probably due to sexual selection also, although the value of the male, unencumbered by a baby, in the protection of a harem against predators may also favour a large body size. Predation risk would also maintain a tendency whereby harems would join others to form herds whenever feeding conditions allowed. Much debate has centred round the relative significance of these interacting factors, and how they may apply to related baboons such as drills which range on the floors of rain forests. Some problems faced by this approach are discussed later in the chapter.

These researches and others like them are based on innumerable hours of field study in remote places. They formed the starting-point for contemporary sociobiological theory and the main data bank of facts. In some respects, however, the theory was running ahead too fast. Recent studies are attempting more quantified analyses of the exact relations between behaviour and ecology in day-to-day living. This will eventually make it possible to manipulate ecology so as to test the dependence of social structure upon it.

Correlations between the broad characteristics of a taxonomic group and species ecologies yield suggestive associations that can then be expressed as evolutionary hypotheses that are in principle open to direct tests. Not all social features of a species need be direct expressions of ecological adaptation, however. As Struhsaker (1969) pointed out, uncertainties and irregularities in attempts to allocate primate species to socio-ecological grades may be attributed to phylogenetic heritage. Indeed, a kind of inertia may be present whereby the genetic constitution of a species prevents it following the same adaptive route in relation to a common ecology as other species may show.

Furthermore, at refined levels of analysis, subtle differences at the species level may correlate with ecological adaptations that are obscured by grosser analyses of a whole taxonomic group. Clutton-Brock (1974), for example, using finer instruments and methods than the earlier work, and applying it to species contrasts, was able to show that differences between two colobus species living in the same forest were functions of their feeding ecology. Both the red colobus and the black and white colobus monkeys eat a mixture of leaves and fruit and have a fully arboreal life. The black and white feeds in a narrow range of tree species and when none is fruiting it eats leaves. It lives in small troops in defended home ranges that supply its needs. The red colobus, however, needs fruit all the year round and takes it from a greater variety of dispersed tree species; it thus requires a larger range which can support a correspondingly larger troop. In these contrasts, the temporal and spatial patterning of food availability are important factors (see also Richard 1977).

As the number of species studied increases the simple classification into adaptive grades begins to break down as the variance within species and between species begins to exceed that between the categories described as grades. None the less in a broad survey of recent studies a number of socio-ecological correlations are still sustained (Clutton-Brock and Harvey 1977).

Apes and man: the argument from descent

Man's place in the primate order is that of an ape derivative. To understand the details of human social evolution the nearest point of interspecific comparison lies among the apes. The apes, however, are all forest-dwelling specialists while man evolved primarily in open country as a savannah animal. There are thus two possible lines of inquiry; the first, the argument from descent, is to look to relationships likely to connect the human species with ape-like ancestors; the second is to compare man with less closely related primates that have followed a similar evolutionary path in invading the savannah lands, an argument therefore by analogy. Taken together these approaches provide a startlingly comprehensive picture for a plausible understanding of the socio-ecological origins of human life.

Beginning then with our closer relatives, we are faced with three rather similar forms, the orang-utan, the gorilla, and the chimpanzee, and a rather more distant set of relatives, the gibbon, and the siamang. Gibbons and siamangs (the hylobatids) are restricted today to south-east Asia, as also is the orang-utan among the true great apes. The chimpanzee lives in thick forest conditions of central Africa and in savannah woodland in western and eastern Africa. It extensively overlaps the gorilla in its forest range but generally shows adaptations to lighter drier woodlands.

Many attempts have been made to compile a genealogical tree showing the relationships of these animals to one another and to man. Authorities are in agreement that the hylobatids represent a branch sprouting early off the stem leading from the Old World monkeys towards the great apes. They became highly specialized arboreal forest-dwellers feeding on fruit, moving by brachiating from tree to tree, and living at high densities in food-rich forests where resources are generally constant and predictable. The resulting competition probably causes the animals to occupy small but adequate territories which are vigorously defended by a monogamous pair. The male assists the female in rearing the young. The gibbon and siamang societies seem to be products of strong K selection.

The orang-utan, gorilla, and chimpanzee are usually depicted as arising from a stock separate from that leading to man. More recently, however, Kortlandt (1972), in an extensive summary of palaeogeographical palaeoecological, and biochemical evidence, has argued that the orang-utan split off early from the stem leading to the root of the African radiation of ancestral apes into gorilla, chimpanzee, and man (Fig. 4.2). It seems plausible that the Asian orang-utan represents an early forest specialization. Dendrograms of this type are notoriously labile as new information appears and opinion changes.

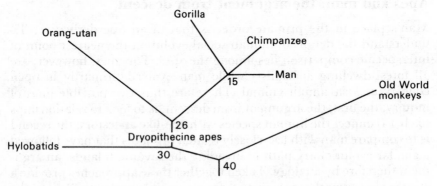

FIG. 4.2. Kortlandt's dendrogram of the genealogy of the great apes. The dates of divergence are shown in millions of years.

The radiation of the African great apes and man represents a set of adaptations by a common stock, the Dryopithecine apes, to differing ecological conditions. Kortlandt argues that the formation of the Great Rift Valley system in East Africa combined with the Nile and Zambezi drainage systems to constitute a geographical barrier to the east of which the Dryopithecine apes adapted to a progressive desiccation of the landscape caused by the rise of the Rift mountain ridges in combination with climatic trends. This form developed bipedalism and other adaptations to the newly opening arid savannah landscape and eventually became the ancestor of man. By contrast, to the West of the Rift the mosaic nature of the relatively dry forest woodlands north of the Niger–Benue river system constituted a cradle for the evolution of the adaptable, partly terrestrial, chimpanzee with its variable fruit food supply and capacity for mobility. To the south of this, the gorilla specialized as an evergreen-forest-dweller feeding on rich evenly dispersed vegetable food resources, mostly at ground level.

The earliest forms resembling man, the hominoids, were in fact widely distributed in Africa and Asia between 15 and 10 million years ago. Pilbeam, in a continuing series of investigations in the sedimentary beds formed by rivers flowing from the Himalayas, themselves dating back only to about 20 million years ago, considers that of these forms *Ramapithecus*, because of its dental structure with large molars and smaller incisors and canines, is the most plausible ancestral form of the late Pliocene. It was a small animal, probably about 1·2 m tall, living in woodland savannah. This savannah covered huge areas as the great forests of 15 million years ago decreased following global changes in climate. *Ramapithecus* was one of several primates, such as the baboons, which came down from the trees to develop terrestrial living. Its dental adaptations to hard savannah fruits and seeds probably preceded the development of bipedalism, which may itself have been originally connected with foraging, reaching upward to browse on bushes for example. *Ramapithecus* lasted for about 7 million years and may have then given rise to the first true hominid, *Australopithecus*, which has a similar dental structure. *Ramapithecus* may not have been carnivorous, and the association between hunting, travel, and bipedalism probably emerged only with the true hominids.

The evolutionary story of early man remains a complexity of fossils and uncertain interpretations (Leakey and Lewin 1977). It now seems clear that evolution in a hominid direction occurred over a widespread area. A mosaic of characteristics developed, generally heading towards bipedalism in grass savannahs, the consequent freeing of the hands for foraging and later for weapon-making and hunting. These changes coincided with the rapid development of the brain in response to the need for additional intelligence in social life and in the chase (Chapter 6). Conceivably, different forms, changing at different rates and showing contrasting combinations of characteristics, were present in different areas. In East Africa a gracile and a robust form of man–ape seem to have coincided and overlapped ecologically for a time—perhaps in a manner comparable to chimpanzees and gorillas in certain areas of their ranges today. Eventually one form became pre-eminent, perhaps through warfare and forced intermating between the divergent stocks.

Recent field studies of the extant great apes by Wrangham, MacKinnon, and Dian Fossey allow us to formulate new models of the relations between social organization and ecology of these species and to present them in terms of the reproductive and social strategies of individuals.

The orang-utan studied by MacKinnon (1974) in Sabah, Borneo, and in Sumatra live in large home ranges in the trees of the rain forest.

They feed on large tough fruits and other vegetable matter, including bark which they can tear apart with their strong hands. The fruit is irregularly spaced throughout the forest and the fruiting of trees is not easily predictable. These large-bodied apes thus require a sizeable home range. Unlike the gibbon, which tends to specialize in figs of a predictable and often continuous availability that allows it to live in small territories and at a large population density, the orang-utan is a great wanderer. Group size is very small, rarely amounting to more than a singleton or a mother with a dependent infant. The scattered nature of the food evidently makes dispersed foraging essential, since the animals are slow-moving and cover a small area each day. Congregation at feeding sites would lead to a rapid exhaustion of local supplies. The orang-utan shows no tendency to join up with others socially except for sex. There is no greeting behaviour and a general lack of interest in other orang-utans, and tension between animals is rare. The males wander over a wider area than females and make contact with those whose ranges they overlap. Short mating consortships last a few days. Females are evidently often afraid of the male's approach, for he may assault and rape her. This seems unlikely to lead to fertilization, however, for the male's short penis makes female cooperation necessary for successful copulation. Males give loud long calls which seem to function in spacing the males, and the dispersion of the females may well be related to this. Long calls may also attract females or enable dispersed individuals to remain in contact with a dominant male. In Sumatra, MacKinnon found that the orang-utans of an area moved into the near-by hills when the largest calling male did so.

MacKinnon believes that a robust medium-sized Dryopithecine ape fossil (*D. sivalensis*), with the highly crenellated teeth that characterize the orang-utan, was the animal's probable ancestor. The dental remains indicate little more than a dependence on a hard-fruit diet, and there may have been several species with this inclination. The orang-utan itself was not present in the well-known Siwalik fossil fauna of northern India and appears therefore to have evolved in Indo-China. The South Chinese fauna suggests an open woodland environment but, by the early Pleistocene, humid forest conditions were established. The orang-utan thus probably reached its definitive form by evolution from a rather more terrestrial animal but at a later date than that suggested by Kortlandt. MacKinnon thinks that the orang-utans may once have been more sociable with a way of life suited to the more open woodland habitat of the suggested ancestor. In addition, a decrease in size seems to have accompanied adaptation to an exclusively arboreal life. But orang-utans were never as terrestrial as chimpanzees, for the species lacks the knuckle-walking adaptations of the African apes and its limb proportions indicate a long arboreal history. MacKinnon's further suggestion that the social life of the orang-utan could resemble that of early arboreal ape ancestors and to antedate the more terrestrial adaptations of the chimpanzee and gorilla seem borne out by the most recent studies.

Wrangham's (1975, 1977) research at the Gombe Stream reserve, a locality originally made famous by the pioneering efforts of Jane Goodall on the chimpanzee, has clarified many mysteries presented by contrasts between the Gombe findings and those of Japanese workers in the Mahali Mountains elsewhere in Tanzania. Wrangham found that by following chimpanzees daily, he could establish the ranging relationships of the animals. While anoestrous females are dispersed in overlapping home ranges, they may also congregate at food trees in areas where their ranges overlap. The dispersion of adult reproductive males resembles that of females when food is poor, but they form large groups utilizing ranges in common at other times. This group range is in effect a male-group territory and is defended as such against groups of other males. Although the females' ranges are smaller than those of individual males they overlap those of several of them and may therefore turn up in more than one male community; females in oestrus range widely, consorting with a male for a few days.

Parties of chimpanzees congregate at fruiting trees irregularly spaced in both location and time and, since the animals eat small soft-bodied fruits in dense clumps, they can feed together and then move on or separate without producing an immediate over-exploitation of resources. The chimpanzee is highly mobile and semi-terrestrial, showing great adaptability to a wide range of woodlands. During periods of relative food shortage males tend to move less; dispersion evidently reduces competition for resources. In good feeding conditions wider ranging groups occurs, evidently for reproductive reasons.

Chimpanzees often feed in groups and come together with loud demonstrations in the feeding trees. Individuals then occupy particular feeding sites in the trees and there is competition for the best ones. These parties are occasions for much social behaviour, including mating. Wrangham's results show that party-size was largest when food was most abundant. This means that information about food obtained by following others was most available to a given individual when it appears to be of least importance. Eating may not then be the main reason for gathering in parties. Such congregations seem more easily explained in terms of opportunities for relating and for sexual behaviour.

The congregation of animals at rich food sources necessarily increases local party size. We have noted that a male community defends a group territory and the outcome of aggressive interactions between different communities is known to be in part dependent upon party size. The giving of 'food calls' by males assembles a large party, ostensibly for feeding purposes. It can, however, have the additional effect of producing large parties that could then effectively win any encounter with males of an opposed community. Furthermore, when such encounters happen the females do not necessarily retreat with the losers; the winners thereby gain more potential mates. Wrangham argues that the formation of large feeding parties (in which individuals actually eat less than in smaller ones) may improve the reproductive success of a male community through increasing its probability of winning territorial encounters and hence females. Indeed, the evolution of the communal behaviour of individual males may be due to strategies whereby co-operative action increases the chances of individuals mating with females. The resulting group territoriality is possible in the chimpanzee since the locomotory costs in maintaining it are sufficiently low.

Ever since the pioneering field-work on chimpanzees of the Reynolds (1965) the species has been known to have a markedly 'loose' society when compared, for instance, with baboon troops. Wrangham's work goes far to provide us with the essential spatial structuring that underlies this flexibility. The chimpanzee social system turns out to be structurally rather primitive, offering temptations at a comparison with the social systems of nocturnal lemurs and even insectivores. The separate spatial patternings of male and female reveal an absence of close intersexual bonding, and this impression is supported by the casual sexual arrangements and rather brief courtships of these animals. These spatial arrangements are interpretable as (i) adaptations of individuals to the fluctuating availability of the dietary items, (ii) the fact that the size and local density of fruits encourage joint exploitation in parties, and (iii) to conditions of food abundance that periodically allow greater social activity, formation of male parties, and group territoriality. It seems that male spatial arrangements are contingent upon those of females, who are themselves dispersed in relation to dietary ecology, and yet in this species it is females rather than males that move between social units.

If chimpanzee social structure is primitive, the actual behaviour whereby chimpanzees relate to one another is on a level far advanced beyond that of prosimians. The animals show a sociable disposition that contrasts markedly with the isolationist features of the orangutans, the 'loner' among apes. It is in the features of this sociable disposition rather than in societal structure that the chimpanzee most resembles man. Let us examine several of these features.

The chimpanzee's mode of life calls for an ability to adjust to rather sharp motivational changes associated with shifts in party size and composition during group gatherings. In the fluctuating combination and recombination of groups, old friends and old antagonists come across one another in shifting social contexts. Reassurance behaviour by touch, caress, mutual clasping, and other tactile means establishes a mutual support between animals known to one another that promotes, on the one hand, confidence in the face of potential antagonists and, on the other, a support that makes aggression unnecessary since simple assertion can maintain an individual's security. Animals of high status commonly provide the reassurance that stabilizes interaction, and relations between close kin clearly underlie most of the contacts that take place. An advanced system of emotional equilibration has thus developed which, on the one hand, resembles that of other sociable animals such as dogs and wolves among carnivores and, on the other, has a clear primate character. A key to this combination is the unique association of emotionality with a social intelligence which has developed along somewhat different lines in man. Emotional equilibration tends to reduce the possibility of social interactions of aggression or avoidance that would lower the maintenance of an individual's potential inclusive fitness. The striking resemblance between this type of mutual support and that occurring in the human species accounts for much of the fascination of the chimpanzee for man. A chimpanzee is an easy recipient for human projections since humans can easily identify with the emotional expressions of chimpanzees.

Chimpanzee males combine to capture prey which is then torn up and shared. The imaginative may not unreasonably see in these actions the source of communal meal-taking in man and its importance to social life and ritual. What do chimpanzees actually do?

Extensive descriptions of predation and meat sharing by chimps are now available (Teleki 1973; Wrangham 1975). Chimpanzees eat many small animals. Juvenile or infant monkeys, baby baboons, and piglets are the main dietary items providing meat, at least in the area of the Gombe Stream Reserve. Adult males do most of the killing although adolescents and females also do so occasionally. Killers are skilled at choosing the right moment, snatching a baby baboon when large baboon males are not looking, chasing monkeys out on to limbs of emergent trees from which there is no escape except a jump—into the hands of other co-operating chimps below. Meat is nutritionally important and chimps are a serious source of predation for their prey.

Once an individual obtains meat he attempts to protect it and eat it privately. This is rarely possible, for chimps join in an excited melée as soon as a killing occurs. Wrangham opines that while attacks on a possessor are rarely successful, such harassment often prevents eating.

Food is shared to reduce risks of damage in fighting and to prevent interference with eating. Meat is not the staple item in a chimp diet but a desirable extra. Individuals vary in the success they have in getting meat from others, and old animals seem to do best. Perhaps they risk less in terms of a damaged reproductive potential if they lose a challenge for possession, and hence persist more in harassment? Conversely the cost of aggression in defence of meat against a female might be a reduced chance of mating. Sharing food with females also seems linked to kinship. Wrangham explains the higher success of older animals in terms of cost per effort decreasing with age. Damage to an animal affects less of his reproductive potential as age increases. In any case older animals may be socially more skilful.

Meat-sharing among chimpanzees should not therefore be ascribed totally to altruism. It is, rather, the outcome of balancing costs and benefits in a competitive situation where clustering occurs around an obtained item of food. Sharing in these circumstances clearly differs greatly from sharing in man, where the items shared go mainly to family members or other close kin. Sharing is rare in primates and the chimpanzee behaviour may indicate the sources of human mealtime ceremonials. The underlying functions and motivational causation are, however, different, for the chimpanzee's behaviour does not occur in the same setting of structured kinship and family relations as happens in man.

Chimpanzee communication is complex and extends into the formation and use of simple forms of language (p. 127). Such language usage is, however, clearly described only from animals especially taught in laboratories. We do not yet know to what extent chimps use their potential in the wild. Menzel (1973) has shown that non-speaking chimpanzees can convey the location of food to one another in a large field enclosure; Wrangham notes that individual awareness of food resources in the natural environment is acute; but how much information transfer occurs in the wild remains unknown.

Chimpanzee society turns out to be a loosely organized system of overlapping male and female strategies. It differs greatly from the family-based structuring of human life with its stress on the long-term bond between mates. In this respect the gorilla resembles man more than the chimpanzee. Gorillas move about in small parties usually containing one large adult 'grey-back' male. These groups move in extensive and exclusive home ranges so that the freely forming parties so common in chimps do not occur. Gorillas, as mentioned above, are terrestrial animals feeding on ample vegetation found at ground level whereas chimps congregate and move between fruiting trees irregularly dispersed through the forest in space and time.

The incorporation of the gorilla male into a more-or-less permanent party is probably associated with certain benefits in relation to the terrestrial feeding niche. The abandonment of trees makes the species, especially the young, prone to ground predation. Against this the presence of the large male and his spectacular charging displays is an ample response. The more even distribution of food is commonly associated with exclusive ranging in mammals and the presence of potentially aggressive males may enhance dispersion. The cost of having a large male feeding together with females and young on the same resources is probably not great given the even distribution of food and its abundance. Such a cost none the less needs setting against the advantages in any ecological study of gorilla social behaviour.

The apes provide us with much information concerning possible roots of sociable behaviour in man. They are much less helpful, however, in a search for the source and significance of our social organization. This is probably because they are all adapted to forest or woodland conditions and none of them has developed the close-knit social formations that are characteristic of open-country animals. Man originated in arid lands, and for an understanding of his societal arrangements we may turn to look at those other terrestrial primates that adapted to a closely similar niche.

The baboon in the mirror: the argument by analogy

In the waters of the monsoon pools of East Africa it is as if man sees a baboon in the mirror, for the development of baboon societies in the very regions in which human social life must have also evolved seems to reflect in extraordinarily detailed ways the emergence of features otherwise unique to human life. Even if the personal relations of baboons lack the human quality shown by chimpanzees, their societal organization is at once recognizably similar to hominid structures. The following features are particularly striking:

(1) These open-country terrestrial primates mostly move in large groups of both sexes which are often elaborately structured.

(2) The membership of groups is socially organized in pronounced hierarchies of dominance, rank, or status.

(3) In some species males and females consort socially in long-term relationships that may last many years. Such relationships comprise uni-male reproductive groups or 'harems'.

(4) In 'harem'-forming societies the non-reproductive male population may form a 'bachelor' section of the social unit which is organized rather differently in species of contrasting ecologies. Young males leave harems to live in these sections of the community until ready for sexual reproduction.

(5) Males compete for sexual access to the females. This results in changes in their status leading to their participation in sexual life.

(6) Extensive collaboration between males is common in defence of a group against predators and in certain social circumstances.

(7) Males are generally the more mobile sex socially; females commonly remain part of the same social unit throughout their lives and their relationships often provide a basic stability to it. Their organization into lineages descended from ancestral females has been demonstrated in some populations. In some baboons, however, females move between social units more than males, for example the hamadryas (Abbeglen 1976).

Among the terrestrial open-country baboons there are two basic kinds of social unit: the multi-male and the uni-male reproductive unit. The former, large troops of 40 or more animals, occur in the more wooded and fertile parts of the savannah with less seasonal aridity than the more arid 'Sahel' regions. The several fully adult males of these groups are ranked in such a way that only top rankers usually mate with females in the mating season. Such hierarchies tend to be stable with a powerful 'alpha' animal at the top. Low rankers sometimes leave the troop. In the case of the socially similar Japanese macaques such individuals may live as solitaries for a long time, growing in size and strength. Eventually they may take over a small group when the large parent troop undergoes fission as increasing size produces social instability. Among African baboons, males transfer between groups and a powerful male begins travelling with a stranger troop, gradually gaining acceptance as a member. He may later fight his way to the very top of the hierarchy in a series of tactically staged combats.

The uni-male harem occurs in at least three kinds of population dispersion pattern. Among patas monkeys each harem moves in a very large and exclusive home range. In the hamadryas baboons the harems cohere in a band in which numerous non-breeding males also occur. Gelada baboons often move in large herds; individual harems move separately and the 'bachelor' males are found in their own discrete and coherent social units. Under conditions of poor food supply gelada harems tend to separate and travel independently. Small parties seem to serve their members better when food patches are found for in larger units only a few of the animals present could then be fed (Dunbar 1977).

The basic function of both multi-male and uni-male groups concerns the provision of a safe social environment for rearing young. These groups are rearing units and not merely mating consociations. The animals within them are often closely related and both co-operative and competitive behaviours occur.

Hierarchies in baboons

The work of Robert Seyfarth (1976) has demonstrated that wild female baboons in a multi-male troop structure maintain a hierarchy just as males do. Female and male hierarchies none the less differ in important ways that seem to be consequences of the contrasting strategies by which the two sexes seek to maximize their inclusive fitness.

Among the females of Seyfarth's study those of highest rank were most preferred as grooming partners. This preference could not of course be satisfied for all members of the troop at once since baboons groom in couples. Competition is thus established and the second-ranker comes effectively to prevent those of lower status from grooming the female above her. Similarly number 3 can prevent number 4 from gaining access to either 1 or 2. Females thus tend to groom those nearest to them and immediately above them in rank. High-ranking females by and large receive more grooming than others. The structure of the female group is thus based upon the relatively simple social dynamic principles of preference for high rank and the consequent competition, which in its turn maintains the hierarchy. Fluctuations in this system occur when, for example, a female has a baby, for the mother–infant pair is a source of immediate attraction. The more dominant females then tend to gain access more easily to the new mother irrespective of her rank.

As we have already mentioned, adult male baboons characteristically compete for sexual access to ovulating females. This seems to be the main process ordering them into ranks. Males will also compete for other resources, food for example, but the status hierarchies for access to different commodities are not necessarily always correlated (Rowell 1972). It seems that the nature of the physiological factors involved in the motivation for competition play an important role in differentiating these rank orders. Competition for a female or other sex object may not produce the same hierarchy as that for food, simply because a sexually aroused animal, say, is not necessarily a hungry one. He will work hard at competition for a female but not so hard for food. The establishment of the alpha male of a group seems, however, to be primarily a consequence of ranking in relation to sexual access to females.

The behaviour of young males and females in Seyfarth's study already foreshadowed the adult outcome. Immature females interacted with adult females primarily when the latter were lactating; immature males did so when they were in oestrus. Furthermore, immature females tended to spend proportionately more of their grooming time with females ranking higher than their mothers. Immature males tended to groom more with adult females ranking lower than their mothers. In addition, immature females already competed for opportunities to groom mothers of higher rank than their own. Among immature males this does not occur, but they are liable to be displaced by adult males if they attempt sexual interactions with high-ranking females.

The behaviour of males appears to be the expression of an underlying strategy that optimizes the probability of sexually effective mating while reducing agonistic competition. Their rankings in relation to one another arise both through learning their relative strengths in play and because the strength of the tendency to compete for sexual partners is differentially distributed among them. The advantages of female access to dominant females is less clear. One of the functions of grooming lies in the causal relation between interactions and mutual support. Thus grooming partners may form a coalition during agonistic encounters. If one is threatened it can call upon the other's aid and give a 'protected threat' to its adversary. The attractiveness of dominant females may derive from the advantage accruing to an individual from having a powerful 'friend'. In addition, high rankers tend to have access to scarce resources so that in competitive encounters the possession of a powerful ally will increase the subject's chance of obtaining some. This will be important where the resources are vital for the well being of a subject's dependent young (see also Cheney 1978; Wrangham 1977).

Mothers and daughters tend to develop a close grooming association which tends to persist so that these close relatives have about the same rank, the daughter's being contingent upon that of the mother. This tendency to a kin-based preference in the distribution of associations naturally biases the distribution of ranks among group members so that close kin tend to acquire similar rank as their genetic elders. The attraction to mothers with neonates often leads to 'aunt' behaviour ('baby-sitting') providing valuable learning opportunities in the handling of infants that will be valuable when the subject's own baby is born.

Reciprocal collaboration in social conflict
The multi-male troops of *Papio anubis* baboons studied by Packer (1977) at Gombe illustrate two important principles governing the lives of these animals. The first striking feature is the mobility of the male baboons. At or soon after puberty they leave the troops in which they were born and work their way into new ones. The breeding males of a particular unit are all animals that have transferred into it from elsewhere. While sexually mature males may remain in their natal troops they have little access to females, unless they are of especially high dominance.

During conflict, baboons may seek assistance from others by soliciting their participation in an attack upon an opponent. The solicited animal is enlisted by the solicitor's repeated turning of the head from a direct look at the solicited animal towards the potential opponent. Every enlisting event thus involves three animals, the enlister, the opponent, and the solicited. A partner may be solicited to enable the enlister to achieve dominance in an altercation which does not necessarily involve any disputed object; such partners were not involved in the incident until they were solicited and thus had a 'choice' as to whether to collaborate or not. One of the most significant occasions is when one male enlists the collaboration of another to separate an opponent from an oestrus female in consort with him. When the solicited animal joins in the harassment, it may end with the enlister going off with the female and leaving the other two to fight it out. The enlister thus creates for himself a very real opportunity for mating, while the collaborator faces a real risk of injury.

Packer believes that nepotism plays no role in the explanation of these events because the males of a troop, having transferred into it from elsewhere, must be only very distant relatives of one another. The criteria for reciprocal altruism seem fulfilled as the interactions seem based upon expectations of reciprocation. Of the 140 occasions observed by Packer, 97 solicitations succeeded in enlisting a partner. On 20 of these occasions, the target was consorting with an oestrus female and, in general, partners were more likely to join in coalition when this was the case. On six occasions the attack resulted in the initiator gaining the female. Packer remarks that the greater willingness to join in collaboration against a consorting male may be related to the greater benefits that the altruism bestows on the recipient in these cases. The most striking finding is that individuals which most frequently gave aid are those which most frequently receive it. Favourite partners of an animal tended in turn to request aid most frequently from that animal. Collaboration is thus a mutual matter between animals well known to one another who have established a reciprocating relationship. Preferences for partners are probably based on the frequency of reciprocation. Indeed, reciprocation is perhaps the operational basis for friendship.

Reciprocation is infrequent when females and young are the enlisters. Here the expectation of effective aid and return will be small since males are so much bigger than non-males and most encounters of males are with other males. Reciprocation seems to depend on the expectation of assistance from the beneficiary at a later time. This must imply that the possibilities of gain are overall greater than the risks of injury. Certainly the number of offspring that a male may sire as a result of reciprocating coalitions will be greater than if he did not participate, while his lifespan is probably only slightly affected by such activity.

Reciprocating coalitions are an important feature of these multi-male groups and particular friends at the top of the hierarchy can effectively 'police' the unit, reducing the frequency of quarrels and maintaining a low level of disturbance of pregnant and lactating females. Indeed it is remarkable that transferring males have the persistence and strength to rise in rank and gain mates for themselves in the face of such opposition. Much of their success lies in their skills in social manipulation whereby their rise is assisted by partners whose status and mating success likewise improves. As existing dominant males age so doubtless can the collaborative attacks of younger animals prove increasingly effective.

On holding a harem

The prime difference between the multi-male and uni-male groups is that in the latter sexually maturing males quickly leave the reproductive unit. This arises not only because fathers tend to reject young sons at puberty but also because young males show a preference for their own kind for company. Young male and female geladas begin to differentiate their preferences in this way well before the male separates to join an all-male group. The motivational system of the developing male makes a positive contribution to separation in these animals.

Young females usually remain within the natal group, although transference to other groups through affiliation with young male reproductives reduces the probability of incest (see below) with the father. The females within a harem form a team in which there is much mutual support for one another. The strength of this support differs between species and effects the role the male plays in the social dynamics of the harem and the types of relationship that maintain the structure.

Among patas monkeys the male behaviour is adapted to the large territory through which the group ranges in open grassland (Hall 1965). The male spends much time perched in trees on the lookout both for other Patas and for potential predators. His alarm call causes the females to slink off undetected while he may produce a diversionary display to confuse a predator or male rivals. He thus does little to 'lead' his group and he does not dominate the females.

The opposite condition is shown by the hamadryas baboon: the male enforces a direction of march through biting the necks of recalcitrant females until they follow him. Male geladas are intermediate. During the formation of harems they are assertive, dominant, directive. As the harem matures, however, the females show a close collaboration that can oppose a male effectively; they determine the direction of movement and the male has little control. His main preoccupation becomes the demonstration of prowess through chasing off other males that attempt to gain access to his females.

The study of interactions and relationships that constitute the social structure of these various rearing units has begun to provide a description of the rules whereby the structure is maintained from generation to generation. These rules express the interactional dispositions of the individuals concerned which constrain their potential for acquiring novel behaviour randomly through learning. Baboons are highly intelligent animals and learn to satisfy their biological needs in many often diverse ways. The routes to satisfaction are patterned by internal or dispositional constraints so that the behaviours concerned tend to lead to an end that is characteristic of a species. The behavioural routes to that end thus show an 'equipotentiality'. However far out an animal may seem to be going there is a tendency to swing back into a pre-ordained behaviour or orbit within which motivational satisfaction may be most probably attained.

Young baboons are reared in social units of complex structure. They are born into a nexus of interactions and relationships that shape the expression of their own needs from the very beginning. At each stage of life relationships are the outcome of relatively temporary associations between individuals in which the needs of the partners are balanced. 'Reinforcement of the behaviours related to such needs cements the associations at least for a time. While it may be strategic for a juvenile male to appease larger ones for a period and while he may learn elaborate social skills in the process, his ultimate strategy is to replace the dominant animal in terms of access to required commodities—especially mates. Relationships are dynamic . . . the status system is a kind of social front, a temporary balance of forces, behind which individuals develop the social skills needed for the . . . resolution of intergenerational competition' (Crook 1975).

The study of the mechanisms responsible for group structure at any one time thus requires a through-time or 'diachronic' perspective if the functional role of these mechanisms in relation to the overall reproductive strategies of individuals is to be perceived. A static model, such as that of Homans in sociology, emphasizing structural maintenance through a form of 'social approval', neglects the inherent dynamism of reproductive strategies that necessitate risk in competition and possibly conflict for their fulfilment. The maximization of inclusive fitness requires a motivational assertion in the performance of strategies that necessarily conflict with the similar strategies of others, for animals (and humans) live in a world of finite supplies.

Young males in harem societies are faced with a problem of acquiring mates against a gradient of mate possession established by a 'gerontocracy' of their fathers. Likewise young females have the problem of choosing mates that will provide them with vigorous young and possibly the assistance they need to rear them. An ageing father is not the best bet, yet very often his behaviour is coercive and restricts his daughter's access to potential suitors. The mode of resolution of these conflicts is the key theme in any study of social dynamics.

The first exploration of this theme was made by Kummer (1968) in research on hamadryas in Ethiopia. The male of the species is an unadulterated chauvinist who will not allow the females of his harem to move more than a few feet from him. If they do so he grabs them by the neck and hauls them back to the fold. These males are also sexually attracted to their daughters so that young suitors are vigorously rejected. However, males from the bachelor section of the band harass owners until they are able to travel with the harem as a second male in what emerges as a two-male team. The young male thereafter protects very young sexually immature females so that they are attracted to him and form a close relationship. There thus emerges a harem of juvenile females in association with the secondary male, but this male is as yet unable to mate with them because they are too young. As they mature he leads them out of the harem to an independent existence. Recent research on the hamadryas shows that the males who join harem owners tend to be their sons. This means that harem females are being passed down from father to son in a patrilineal fashion. Bands of hamadryas evidently comprise several patrilineal lineages of this kind (Abbeglen 1976). It also means that the males and females are not unrelated animals.

Kummer (1975) has also done much to clarify the rules that govern the formation of a gelada harem. His work on this topic is experimental and consists of introducing a series of animals to one another and watching them as they 'convene' a group in a field enclosure. The regularities he observed in this process suggest that the species behaves according to rules that limit the possible variety of behaviours that could occur as they meet one another.

Every time two geladas are introduced to one another they go through a series of steps in which, characteristically, a fight precedes presenting, which precedes a mounting, which in turn precedes mutual grooming. These presentings and mountings, although sexual expressions, are not overt sexual acts but rather reflect the relative dominance and submission of the two. All pairs go through this sequence irrespective of their sex and it ends with a clear dominance—subordination relationship in which grooming indicates compatibility and resolution of tension. The establishment of compatibility is slower and it remains less stable when the two animals are both of high initial dominance; thus two males are less compatible than a male–female dyad. The latter dyads are also more compatible than female–female pairs, although in the latter case there is little fighting in the convening sequence. It seems that the initial agonism derives from a conflict over dominance and the subsequent sexual posturing reduces both aggressive and escape tendencies as the conflict over dominance is resolved. Grooming, says Kummer, is the behaviour typical of a mature and relatively stable couple.

If an established pair is subjected to the presence of a new animal their compatibility may become less and the interaction mode may regress to one of the earlier behavioural stages. The less compatible a pair the greater the probability that their relationship will regress in the presence of another animal. Three animals cannot establish two dyads of high compatibility, for the sight of an interacting pair in a threesome tends to reduce the capacity of the onlooker for developing his relationship with either of the other two. Males, in particular, are quickly inhibited from approaching a female if she is already interacting with a male partner.

As more animals are introduced, males seek to maximize the number of compatible relations with females while the latter seek to make their relation with a particular male exclusive. There is thus a strong tendency for individual males to intervene in every friendly dyadic interaction in which they do not have a part. Intervention occurs when the intruder is dominant to at least one member of the couple approached. When he is subordinate to both of them then a partnership with either animal may be established as an aid to intervention. The outcome of these behaviours in a captive colony is the formation of one-male groups similar to those found in the wild. All females become part of such groups but socially inhibited males may lack mates.

Robin and Patsy Dunbar (1975) have developed my pioneering studies of gelada baboons in Ethiopia (1966) through detailed analyses of interactions within harems in the natural habitat. The number of females with whom the male frequently interacts decreases with the size of the group. This means that in larger groups most of the interactions and mutual grooming go on between members of female pairs while the male only grooms with one or two of them. The male can maintain a fairly equable distribution of grooming up to a harem size of five females. Above this size he is unable to maintain this rate of involvement.

Whereas newly formed harems are small, with an active male who is both the dominant animal and the leader within it, older well-established and larger groups contain not only a strongly bonded group of females but a male who no longer leads and whose dominance can also be challenged by a consortium of females. The male is now primarily involved in breaking up quarrels between females and in repelling approaches by other males either bidding for access to the harem through the formation of a two-male team or, more dangerously, seeking a fight for total replacement.

Large gelada harems develop instability from a variety of causes. First, the male–female bonding is weakened owing to the low frequency of male interactions with most of his female companions. Secondly, the male shows little sexual interest in his sexually mature daughters. Thirdly, since dominant females have most young it follows that the more subordinate females there are in the harem the lower the potential reproductive success of any one of them. The implication is clear. Young, subordinate females will do better if they mate with a new male. Opportunities may be expected to exist for a young male to join the harem.

Members of all-male groups maintain a regular monitoring of harems through a system of challenges I called the 'yelping chase'. By approaching the harems the male owners are stimulated to come out and chase the interlopers. The approach of a body of unmated males to a group of harems is always the signal for a whole series of challenges and chases of this kind often initiated by the harem owners themselves. The presence of a weakening harem owner must be easily detected.

Young males that regularly harass a particular harem owner finally get accepted as a member of the harem. Sexual relations between the newcomer and the old man's daughters are not resented, and after a period of mutual co-existence the young male leads the daughters into a separate existence as a new harem. The process is slowed down by the young females' strong attachments to their mothers some of whom may occasionally defect and move off with the young males too.

Males without harems sometimes opt for a frontal attack. Fighting may go on intermittently for days and the original owner does not tire easily. If the newcomer is persistent, however, some of the females may transfer their attention to him. If this happens it seems the old male is doomed. Soon he is defeated and becomes peripheral to the social unit now dominated by the sexually active newcomer. The Dunbars have observed only a few such fights to completion but the outcome is quite remarkable. In other harem-forming species the takeover by another male or males is commonly followed by either the killing or complete ejection of the old owner and by the slaughter of babies and infants (Hrdy 1974). Such incidents have now been reported sufficiently often in langurs and in lions, for example, to invalidate an early explanation attributing them to a high population density. In terms of selection theory it makes sense for an incoming male to kill the young, for the females then come into oestrus quickly and he can get his genes into the assembly line at the earliest opportunity. Otherwise he would not only have to wait till the young of a non-related male were reared but would probably have to protect them as well in order to prevent other males from supplanting him. The old gelada male, by contrast, is not driven forth, his young are not killed, and he may assist the newcomer in preventing a further takeover of the group.

Robin Dunbar (personal communication) is of the opinion that the reason why this happens in gelada is that the two males strike a bargain, as it were. The newcomer trades his forbearance of the existing young against the collaboration of the old male in retaining the harem. There is a real possibility that the newcomer is not only exhausted but possibly wounded by the time he has won the harem. Other gelada males without harems have been seen to sit watching such a fight. As soon as it is over and both males are exhausted they have a brief opportunity during which they can launch an attack and win the harem from both of them, and this has been seen to happen. The collaboration of the two males tends to prevent this. The old male remains loosely attached to the harem and spends a great deal of time caring for his infants. No longer active sexually, he now invests his time and energy in caring for his last offspring. The newcomer mates as soon as females are in oestrus.

Male geladas may thus obtain a harem in several ways that seem to depend on age. Most seem able to enter a harem by harassment and then acquire the group's daughters. A harem owner may have several sets of daughters creamed off in this way. He is not interested in them sexually, so there is no direct confrontation between him and the newcomer. A simple incest taboo is in operation here. Males that are not successful at this manoeuvre are losing reproductive time; they are older and bigger. On theoretical grounds, they must needs stake a venture to gain a maximum prize; so they risk a battle for the harem. While this gets them both young and older females there is a price to pay, since big harems are the least stable and most easily taken over by other males.

The Dunbars have shown that whereas harems taken over in combat only last an average of three and a half years, those established by way of two-male team formation last eight and a half. Over a lifetime these two strategies yield almost the same number of offspring but an older male clearly needs the quicker success and he takes the greater risk. Who the cunning ones may be who calculatingly steal a harem from exhausted combatants after a battle is a question yet to be answered.

Homosexual behaviours between male gelada baboons
Young male geladas acquire the skills essential for obtaining a harem within the context of life in an 'all-male' group. Whereas the young hamadryas baboon males move in the periphery of the bands of harems the geladas establish groups of consistent membership, close bonding between individuals, and reciprocal collaborations in several aspects of life. When Wrangham joined our Bristol team after his chimpanzee research at the Gombe National Park (p. 69) he concentrated his

rainy season observations on a unit of gelada males. Unfortunately, owing to changes in Ethiopian political life, the studies he began, together with those of the Dunbars, had to be terminated early, thus leaving many questions inconclusively answered. One especially interesting question concerns homosexuality in these animals.

Wrangham (1976) made some striking observations. He describes overt sexual behaviour of two kinds occurring between bachelors. Neither of these behaviours comprised pseudosexual behaviour of the sort aimed at reducing tension and regulating dominance interactions which is quite common in mammals. In such behaviour a submissive individual presents his bottom to a dominant male and is briefly mounted, but without penile erection or ejaculation by either animal. Wrangham writes that in his observations the mounter could be either older or younger than the partner and that approaches were made in situations commonly lacking in social tension. The behaviour was clearly sexual. In addition he once observed self-masturbation to ejaculation and the manual masturbation of companions.

Wrangham, theorizing tentatively from some physiological evidence from human subjects, suggests that masturbation may stimulate the secretion of testosterone and may occur when the latter falls below some threshold. He argues that young gelada males, living in all-male groups, suffer from sexual deprivation. Plausibly sexual behaviour between these males not only relieves this deprivation but might maintain higher testosterone levels in the participants than would otherwise be the case. Since aggressive animals often have higher testosterone levels than normal this might aid a male in persisting in attacks on harem males and thereby in gaining a harem. Such mutual sexual activity in creating relationships between males could also amount to a form of collaborative support in obtaining of harems. Wrangham comments: 'We may thus find the first evidence that so-called abnormal sexual behaviour may have a biological function'; but he points out that a number of issues need to be resolved. These bachelor males may not be more deprived of sexual outlets than are the harem owners themselves. This is because the oestrous periods of harem females tend to occur bunched together in time. At other seasons the male may entirely lack sexually active female companions. Dunbar (personal communication) has then observed males masturbating. Again, the frequency of masturbation is perhaps highest among older males recently defeated by a newcomer male who has taken over the sexual role in his harem. In other words, we are still uncertain about the extent of self- or mutual masturbation and the circumstances under which its occurrence is high. Certainly much touching of the penises, penile erection, and display occur between young male geladas and the behaviour is commonly used in greeting behaviour. Wrangham con-

cludes that an understanding of these relationships awaits renewed
field study.

Sexual 'predators' and herd cycles in geladas
The function of herd formation in open-country primates has been a
topic of considerable debate. A prime theme has been the argument
that group formation is often of survival value to individuals in gaining
a social cover from predation (p. 52). Someone else is more likely to be
eaten if I keep near to other people. Certainly the troops of *Papio*
baboons are important as a means of deterring predators, and solitary
animals take considerable risks. In the montane life of the gelada
baboon today predation from village dogs occurs, especially on young
animals, and the geladas are clearly fearful of them. Predation by
humans and dogs together may be heavy in certain areas. Yet herd size
is not constant; it fluctuates in relation to environmental and social
conditions.

The parties in which gelada herds move vary seasonally in size
(Crook 1966; Dunbar 1977). In the arid part of the year the parties are
smaller, they travel faster, and they congregate primarily at patches
where food is locally abundant. My observations were made mostly in
areas dominated by agriculture where the effects of seasonality could
have been especially pronounced. In the gelada's natural habitat the
Dunbars did not find an extreme seasonality in food availability,
especially since geladas could switch from grass to rhizomes and bulbs
as the key dry-season diet. Furthermore, while party size varies, the
local density of animals does not. This might mean that while direct
competition for resources is reduced by the decrease in group size, the
indirect competition remains unaffected.

Wrangham, after a short period of ecological work, remarked that
'herd formation clearly involves costs even at the beginning of the wet
season, when a grazing animal should have the best food supply of the
year'. He found that harem males in herds had to walk farther per day
to nourish themselves than did members of a lone all-male group.
Much of this extra travel is due to social interactions between harems.
Solitary feeding also has its cost, since the animal cannot then locate
food by congregating at food sites discovered by others. In the early dry
season, gelada resources are especially patchily distributed; gregariousness probably enables the baboons to gain rapid access to patches
rich in food. Herd formation may then come about in response to the
distribution patterns of rich food in patches. But patches are rapidly
exhausted by large herds, so that a smaller party size would reduce
competition when patches were least rich (Dunbar 1977). This takes us
back to explanations similar to those suggested for the variation in
group size early in these studies (Crook and Gartlan 1966) but these do

not account for the massive gregariousness of the species under optimum conditions when a more even dispersion of the population would reduce the costs of foraging.

Wrangham suggests an interesting and novel solution to this problem. If a harem is travelling alone and encounters an all-male group, the male then faces the risk that adult males from the group will attack him and usurp his reproductive role. A harem travelling with others is not only less likely to be the one attacked but, at least at the onset of the bachelors' approach, the male can count on the participation of other harem males in 'yelping chases' that deter the attackers. In addition the loud cries of harem males probably alert others to the presence of non-reproductive males and this may result in collaborative defence in driving them away. In sum, the association with other harems function in sexual defence in a way that is closely analogous to defence against predators. Herd formation provides three advantages: information about the presence of potential rivals, the assistance of fellow male reproductives in collective harem defence, and a reduced probability of any particular harem being chosen as a target for an attack or harassment. On the other side of course the line-up of young males is equally formidable. The patterning of relationships between individuals in these groups needs much further study.

How do the male reproductives of the 'gerontocracy' withstand the co-operative attacks of the young males? How often are harems formed by gradual means and how often by frontal attack? When does it pay a young male to remain with his companions operating a preferred strategy of delayed takeover? When is the pay-off to the young male greater in a gradual formation of a two-male team and a co-operative defence of a mating–rearing unit? How closely related are young males to the harem owners they join or defeat? A whole variety of subtle strategies are available. They concern fine judgements about the time spent in the non-reproductive phase versus time spent in collaborative reproduction and they also concern subtle choices of companion at all times. The topic is an attractive one for the application of games theory and mathematical modelling but, more important, we need more field data.

The demographic contexts for these events also influence their patterning. The Dunbars found that the structure of their study population in Ethiopia differed in 1974–5 from that of 1971–2. Although the age–sex composition and total number of animals present were similar in the two periods the number of reproductive units had decreased between the studies with a corresponding increase in mean unit size. As fewer males 'owned' harems, the all-male groups had increased in size and contained older males. This coincided with a greater frequency of direct attacks in harem takeovers.

Such shifts could be based upon periodic differences in population composition. Because there is a two-year birth interval and because females are in reproductive synchrony, the birth-rate is not constant from year to year. More individuals therefore enter the population in some years than in others. Furthermore, since males become sexually mature later than females, a smaller male proportion may be entering the reproductive population in some years than in others.

Females tend to remain in their natal units, which thereby increase gradually in size. At the same time more and more males are accumulating in all-male groups. Once an imbalance occurs between the number of males waiting to acquire units and the number of units that can be taken over or entered, the system could go into a series of oscillations which would be self-perpetuating, at least for some time. The excess males must wait until large enough units have been generated through the maturation of female offspring. Once this point has been reached there will be a rapid reduction in the number of non-reproductive males, and the large units will be broken up into a number of smaller ones, in part through takeovers and in part through fission of units containing followers. The result of this stage of the process is a large number of small units which the remaining young bachelors will be unable to enter. The cycle will then gradually repeat itself. All-male groups subject to a resistant collection of small stable harems led by assertive young adults may become relatively nomadic and move to areas where the population cycle is in a different phase and contains larger and less stable harems. (For additional ecological studies on gelada see Kawai 1978.)

Kinship in monkeys and apes
Recent research is demonstrating that kin relations are important determinants of relationship patterns in monkey groups. This is especially apparent from studies of troops of Japanese and rhesus macaques. Troops are composed of both sexes, but, whereas young males normally emigrate, females remain to comprise the core of the unit. These females interact with one another in ways that accord with their matrilineal descent. Descendants of sisters interact positively with descendants of mother or grandmother more than they do with those of aunts or great-aunts. Furthermore, when these groups split the division occurs between the lineages descended from particular females that began the matrilines. Lineages of descent from a female ancestor are thus prime substructures composing a macaque troop.

Some primates live in patrilineal rather than matrilineal descent groups. Here males stay with their male kin as adults and females move into new groups at adolescence. Examples are fewer, it seems, than for matrilines but include spider monkeys, the red colobus, chimpanzees, and also the hamadryas baboon when movements between clans rather than in and out of harems is considered.

Wrangham (personal communication) has recently sought to explain the basis for these two types of lineage system by focusing on the consequences of intrasexual competition. One might expect females to compete for rich food sources, for these are important to them in gaining nutrition for child-bearing and lactation. He argues that matrilineal troops of primates arise where the preferred primary foods such as ripe fruits occur in clumps, necessitating competition, and that coalitions of female kin increase the feeding possibilities for related individuals (cf. Seyfarth 1976 and above p. 75). Matriline coalitions also utilize secondary food sources such as leaves and unripe fruits and the species have digestive mechanisms for detoxifying the latter. These secondary resources are so abundant, however, that competition rarely arises for them and they thus constitute a reserve when primary resources are few.

Wrangham thinks that where there are no secondary resources, competition for the main resource may get so high that solitary feeding becomes essential. This appears to be true of chimpanzees (under poor food conditions), orang-utans, and spider monkeys which show neither coalition formation nor matrilines. In other species where patrilinearity has been suggested, food resources may again show important contrasts from those of matrilines. Nagel (1973) has shown that in the area exploited by hamadrayas baboons in the Awash valley there are no fruiting trees such as figs or tamarinds which by comparison constitute primary sources in the near-by *P. anubis* baboon area. Competition for clumped items seems less in hamadrayas, and there is plenty of low-quality food available. Group formation may be due here to the collaboration of males in defence against rivals, so that male relationships become the main factor influencing the dispersion of females.

Wrangham's theory remains tentative but if it stands up to further investigation it suggests that humans were primordially patrilineal. No apes are matrilineal and humans and apes share physiological characteristics restricting diets to high quality foods. The parallelism between man and gelada may perhaps also be supported by this developing line of thought. Matrilineal descent systems seem to develop only occasionally in human cultures and to be associated with female ownership of primary resources such as land (see p. 205).

Summary
(1) The mammals are classified into a number of orders: carnivores, insectivores, and Cetacea, for example. Man belongs to the primates, which also includes monkeys of various kinds and the apes. All these mammalian orders stem from small insectivorous animals that inha-

bited the forests while the dinosaurs were still living. A special innovation in both mammals and birds was homoiothermy, warm-bloodedness, which allows a constantly high level of activity that is not dependent upon the temperature of the environment. It also allows the colonization of environments that would otherwise be too severe. Clearly mammals and birds were equipped to radiate evolutionarily in places where cold-blooded creatures could not flourish.

(2) Primitive primates are quite like the early insectivores. The little mouse lemur of Madagascar lives in small groups in which each female owns a territory and lives in a tree cavity or hole somewhere within it. Overlapping the largely contiguous female territories are those of males which mate with the females in their area. Males and females thus live in largely separate systems only integrated through the overlap in range. Since many males are excluded from the area where the females are, there is competition between young upstarts and older territory-owners for access to the areas of females. Young animals usually do not get territories containing females for some time. This type of social system is very like that of many insectivores and seems to be a starting-point from which other primate societies probably developed.

(3) Survey of primate societies shows that the several grades correlate with certain ecological circumstances. Forest fruit-eaters live diurnally in small family parties usually with a single reproductive male. In both forest and savannah large parties with many males develop, especially among ground-dwellers subject to terrestrial predation. In certain open-country baboons and some other animals 'harems' appear in herds or moving in separate ranges. A great deal of discussion has focused on the adaptive significance of these societal structures. Earlier views were based largely on correlations between social structure and ecological factors. Modern studies of this kind can take into account many fine-grained features of both the physical and the social environment. Studies where ecological variation or other contrasts within the range of a study population occurs can also be cited as evidence for the influence of one ecological factor or another. Coupled with this approach is an argument from the axioms of sociobiological theory that attempt to explain the evolution of social structure in terms of the fitness that accrues to an individual living in it. These arguments can then be tested by studies in the field of either an observational or an experimental nature.

(4) Man is derived from an ancestor that he holds in common with the existing great apes. The likely lines of descent are under continuous debate as new information from fossils or new inferences from other data or fresh theoretical axioms arise. The fossil finds at present available are too few to settle debates. I present here some recent views on the subject.

(5) It is now clear that hominoids emerged in East Africa, presumably showing behaviour similar to but diverging from that of other ape-like creatures. Similarities to chimpanzees must have included many expressions of emotionality and emotional control, complex communication, and vegetarianism combined with some hunting for meat organized among young males. The strongly structured social organization of man with close bonds between particular males and females is not, however, a chimpanzee characteristic. It is found to a degree in gorillas but a closer similarity occurs in baboons. Their parallel evolution to man in a comparable habitat is thus of special interest.

(6) The parallels between man and baboons include the following: a complex and structured group life, status hierarchies, the formation in some species of long-term polygamous bonds between males and females, the division of societies into reproductive groups and non-reproductive 'surplus males', competition between males for access to females, collaboration between males in their various competitions, and in some cases intergenerational male collaboration in the maintenance of breeding units. Recent work has demonstrated the existence of both matrilineal and patrilineal kinship associations.

(7) The hierarchical structures of baboons seem to be evolutionary beneficial to their members in terms of the maximization of their inclusive fitnesses. The same appears to apply to the strategies of individuals involved in reciprocal collaboration. Different types of societal structure containing 'harems' are related to contrasting ecological conditions and social pressures arising from competition. Gelada and hamadryas baboons are shown to have especially complex social systems analysable in terms of their ecological context and interior social stresses. The replacement by a newcomer of the male harem owner in the gelada is not accompanied by his expulsion. He remains to look after his own infants and strikes a 'bargain' with the newcomer so that, while he remains sexually inactive, he assists his victorious opponent in preventing yet further take-overs of the unit.

(8) The males in the bachelor groups of gelada may show homosexual behaviour. This sexual activity does not prevent competition for females and the eventual acquisition of a harem. Indeed the homosexual activity might plausibly have an endocrinal effect in priming males for heterosexual activity.

(9) Competition between old males with harems and younger ones without them involves co-operation between males on both sides. The mutual assistance of harem owners in driving off non-reproductive males may be the basis of herd formation in the gelada baboon. A complex relationship between a co-operative reproductive gerontocracy and an equally complex group of co-operating bachelors results in

oscillations in group size and composition. Male geladas seem to have different strategies for obtaining reproductive females depending on the state of the population. This socio-demographic complexity seems to foreshadow that of man.

(10) Recent research reveals the importance of kinship and lineage in non-human primates. Matrilines and patrilines appear to be associated with differing feeding ecologies and foraging strategies. Man appears to be descended from patrilineal ancestors.

5 The ascent of humanity

> The art of reinventing the past is the oldest and
> boldest of arts. It creates a world out of next to
> nothing and peoples it with men and women who
> vanished practically without trace millions of years
> ago. A few hundred skull and skeleton fragments,
> about a thousand tons of stone and bone and
> roughly a hundred sites constitute more or less all
> the evidence we have of the emergence of humanity.
> On the other hand our knowledge of primate
> societies is based on ... some ... thirty com-
> munities.
>
> S. Moscovici 1976

From ape to man

We do not lack bold interpreters who attempt broadly based syntheses,
often highly speculative, utilizing studies from many disparate fields.
All evolutionary theory is necessarily synthetic and in the construction
of evolutionary models for man the need for wide-ranging integration of
fact and idea is paramount. Mere guesswork is not enough. Experienced appraisal and mature scholarship are essential: this is no field for
amateurs to play with. The implications for our practical understanding of ourselves are too great for us to tolerate romantic irresponsibility,
however popular such accounts may be.

Clifford Jolly (1970), an important theoretician of contemporary
physical anthropology, has this to say.

The nature of an evolutionary model, concerned with unique events, is such
that it cannot be tested experimentally. Its major test lies in its plausibility,
especially in its ability to account for the data of comparative anatomy,
behaviour and the fossil record inclusively, comprehensively and with a
minimum of sub-hypotheses. It should also provide predictions which are in
theory testable, as with a more complete fossil record, thus enabling discussion
to move forward from mere assertion and counter assertion. An evolutionary
model which is designed to account for nothing beyond the data from which it
is derived, may be entertaining, but has about as much scientific value as the
Just so stories.

In evolutionary modelling many suggestions are plausible, yet they
often fail to convince because they are insufficiently comprehensive and
are not backed by an adequate examination of contingent facts. Often
only a few of the elements of the hominid complex are examined and the

end-product is explained in teleological rather than developmental terms. The causal factors invoked in such theories, especially those concerning behavioural themes, are often such as to make the hypotheses untestable even in comparative study.

The main materials, apart from the actual fossil evidence, currently available for a re-evaluation of evolutionary models of man have been presented in outline in the preceding chapters and can now be summarized in Table 5.1. In recent years the rapid expansion in evolutionary ethology and in our comprehension of social dynamics in chimpanzee and baboon societies has added depth to the studies available for synthesis. The accumulation of palaeontological and palaeo-ecological information remains steady, but, although the emphasis in theories based on physical findings shifts with detailed analysis, the changes here are less dramatic.

Perhaps the most important emphasis is the integrative role played by the new theory of social evolution that stems from Hamilton's analysis of the principles of inclusive fitness and Trivers's studies of the role of parental investment in determining the variety of rearing behaviour under contrasting sociological conditions (Chapter 3). Individuals are understood to be operating strategies that maximize their fitness with respect to protection from predation, foraging, mating, rearing, and the achievement of social positions that provide good opportunities for mating and rearing. The variety of outcomes is enormous, and surveys of the range of behaviour shown in the more diverse mammalian orders illustrate the power of ecology in moulding the social structure of collectivities of individuals through the differential reproduction of the fitter representatives of successive generations (Eisenberg 1966; Crook 1970a, c; Wilson 1975; Barasch 1977). Social complexity arises particularly in species where the performance of co-operative activities enhances the inclusive fitness of the participants. Complexity increases both at the communicational level and in terms of the structuring of relationships. This has happened especially in the carnivores, where hunting skills of a collaborative kind have evolved several times, and in primates where hand-to-eye subtlety in relation to movement in trees combines with the need to 'equilibrate' behaviour to lessen social conflict that is potentially damaging to the reproductive success of individuals living in troops. Social intelligence may have evolved in more than one way and is based on a need to show behavioural flexibility, often in fluctuating environmental or social circumstances where rapid adaptation and interaction with others is a major component of fitness.

The tight structuring of social units in open-country primates is particularly apparent in comparative study and has led to social systems in which the activities of the two sexes are closely entwined in a

TABLE 5.1

Materials for an evolutionary modelling of protohominid – hominid behaviour

Principles of evolutionary ethology	Comparative social ethology of mammals	Primate–protohominid fossil record	Pongid social ethology	Baboon social ethology and societal structuring
Neo-Darwinian theory of natural selection	Mammalian evolution from the insectivores	Fossil genealogy and dating	The apes as forest specialists	Socio-ecology of multi-male and uni-male reproductive units
Contemporary population genetics	Adaptive radiations within mammalian orders	Palaeo-ecology and fossil adaptive radiation	Dietary adaptations of the great apes	Cycles in the population dynamics of reproductive units
Theory of inclusive fitness in social evolution and kin selection	Socio-ecological factors in adaptive radiation	Dietary adaptation expressed in changes in dentition	Spatial dispersion and social relations as functions of foraging ecology	Subadult male exclusion, especially in uni-male social structures
Sexual selection and its role in differential parental investment in social structuring	Strategies for maximizing the inclusive fitness of individuals (a) Anti-predation (b) Foraging (c) Mating (d) Rearing (e) Social competition	Skeletal changes, ranging, and foraging Bipedalism	Sexual relations in the chimpanzee society. Social separation of the sexes	Dominance and status ranking in both sexes
Theory of reciprocal altruism	Advanced social organization in carnivores and primates	Neoteny and hetero-chronic changes in development Cranial changes	Social equilibration and emotional control Collaborative hunting of males Food-sharing	Male co-operation in defence and in sexual competition Reciprocating altruism as a basis for male co-operations in several contexts

Bonds, compatibility, rules, and relationships. Species-typical societal structures

Intergenerational conflict in sexual succession

Homosexuality as a possible strategy maintaining competitive fitness between males

Intergenerational co-operation and the stability of reproductive units

Development of ape language and spatial awareness

Development of long-term mother–child attachment as a context for cognitive development cohering pattern of continuing relationships. This is a prime feature distinguishing, for example, the savannah baboons from the forest-dwelling chimpanzees which are in other respects so similar in their behaviour to humans. Tight structuring of social life entails competition for limiting commodities, including the reproductive spouse. The strategies of the two sexes differ in the resolution of these tensions along lines that accord with a sociobiological theory of wide application. Co-operation of two kinds, nepotistic altruism in relation to kin and the reciprocating altruism of regular troop companions, emerges as a prime aspect of the social dynamics of such groups. We have seen also that the exclusion of young males from reproductive units promotes marked intergenerational conflict that leads to a more-or-less permanent confrontation between a collaborating 'gerontocracy' and equally collaborative groups of young males. The complexity is compounded by resolutions of such conflict whereby dominant young and knowledgeable elders combine in intergenerational collaboration aimed at maximizing the reproductive success of both. Such complexities have the nature of bargains. Clearly there is enough material here to suggest a diversity of routes to man.

Theories based on behavioural or sociological considerations derived from research on contemporary primates can be anchored historically only if they can be connected to a means of sequencing and dating. This is possible only by relating this material to the fossil record. The comparative anatomy of fossils needs to be interpreted functionally in such a way that the strategies for maintaining the inclusive fitness of bygone individuals can be reasonably inferred and related to the possible social structures that are correlated with them. In this way data from living primates can be fitted to data from fossils and an evolutionary sequence of behavioural and mental characteristics be reconstructed.

The most provocative of such recent models is that proposed by Jolly in 1970. He had inherited from earlier writers the notion that the prime characteristics of humanity formed a 'mutually reinforcing positive feedback system'. This is to say that each separate character facilitated the emergence of its functional correlates in an autocatalytic manner, so that what was emerging was a cascade of features each forming an element of a functional whole. Walking on two legs (bipedalism) has the effect of freeing the hands for making and using artefacts. Tools and weapons replace the teeth in many tasks and there is thus a reduction in anterior teeth and a flattening of the face that correlates with the increased use of facial musculature in non-verbal communication. The freeing of the hands itself is important in the manipulation of helpless babies that need a long period of learning to acquire the newly developed material culture. While the interrelations fascinate, the origin of the complex remains obscure. One of the prime problems is to determine what set the positive, self-enhancing, feedback process in motion.

Many authors have argued that the development of a manual manipulation of foods and later of tools facilitated and perhaps determined the emergence of an upright posture and bipedalism. The advantage of increased height for vigilance and all-round observation of the environment is underlined by the many animals that employ upright sitting or standing postures for just this purpose. In addition, canines and the anterior teeth are reduced since they are no longer positively selected for tasks, including aggression, for which the hands now function more effectively. Unfortunately for this argument, chimpanzees already show well-developed tool use but have neither a full bipedalism nor a reduction of canines and incisors. Indeed, these teeth in chimpanzees are larger than those of the gorilla which rarely use artefacts at all. Other arguments can be dismissed in similar ways.

A basic proposition in all these views is the assumption that the main line of development in early hominid evolution was the enhancement of meat-eating and hunting as a means of increasing protein intake in 'open-country adaptation'. Hunting calls for weaponry, hand use of weapons and tools, upright posture for observation, and bipedalism for running. The hunting behaviour of chimpanzees is exemplified as a part-way development of the human complex. However, the actual behaviour of the chimpanzee does not suggest the selective forces that may have influenced man. Jolly points out that hunting chimpanzees use their hands; no weapons, no bipedalism. Their incisors are used in dismembering and tearing. Hunting by chimpanzees thus does not predict weapon use or bipedalism. Chimps run fast using their knuckles in part support in movement. In other words, chimpanzee-type hunting is a specific mode of life and does not predict the emergence of man-type hunting. It is a parallel development, not an ancestral condition.

Jolly then put forward an alternative explanation. The rapid development of man-type hunting occurred late, in the Pleistocene. This suggested that rather than a direct post-pongid evolution of carnivorous behaviour, Man spent a long period adapted to a different diet. During this period he would have accumulated those features (pre-adaptations) that allowed a rapid emergence of a hunting complex unique to the species when environmental changes made such a move strategically advantageous.

Jolly now turned to an argument by analogy and related the whole anatomical complex of the early (Villafranchian) hominids to those of the gelada and gelada fossil-forms (*Theropithecus*) about which he has written an authoritative monograph (Jolly 1972). He compared the features by which early hominids differed from the chimpanzee with the features distinguishing *Theropithecus* from the other baboons of the genus *Papio*. He discovered remarkable resemblances between the hominid and the *Theropithecus* 'adaptive complexes' which suggested to him that these animals show a convergent evolution in adaptation to grassland habitat. The details of his analysis are complex and his account is necessarily written for fellow-experts. The gist of his position is this.

The main resemblances between gelada and human history lie in changes in dentition. An increase in molars and a decrease in incisor proportions strongly suggest a diet containing small objects that need grinding rather than tearing. Certainly, as Crook and Aldrich-Blake (1968) discovered in Ethiopia, the gelada feeds mostly on grass seeds, roots, or bulbs, while the *Papio* baboons eat larger objects, usually fruit, and use their incisors more in their preparation. For such an animal as the gelada 'each unit of tooth-material allotted genetically to a molar will bring a greater return in food processed than a unit allotted to an incisor . . . selection should favour the genotype which determines the incisors at the smallest size consistent with their residual function' (Jolly 1970). Canine reduction appears dependent upon the same shifts.

There are, however, differences in molar structure between the hominids and the therapithecines. Whereas the latter mince and mash grassblades and rhizomes, the former have molars like mills that are particularly valuable in crushing small seeds, hard berries, and especially cereals. From all this it seemed to Jolly that the dryopithecines destined for hominization gradually exploited, or were forced by circumstance to exploit, grassland savannah in which small hard fruits and seeds of grasses constituted the main resources. In particular, lake and river flood-plains would have provided the appropriate ecology. Judging from modern geladas, such hominids would have shown a flexible herd-forming potential with a harem-type reproductive system.

How could the protohominid seed-eaters of Jolly's stage 1 evolve to the meat-eaters of his stage 2? Jolly argued that the intricate co-ordination of hand movements involved in the selection of small dietary objects such as seeds and in the elaborate manipulation of grass stems led to a manual dexterity and a predisposition for handling objects that facilitated the preparation of artefacts. Upright sitting on developed ischial callosities is a gelada feature to which human bottoms may be a parallel. Grassland encourages bipedal standing for observation, whether of predators or male rivals. In such a set of features incisor reduction is now correlated with bipedal sitting and standing and the great development of manual dexterity.

Hunting arose from this, rather than the chimpanzee adaptive com-

plex, in ways already suggested by numerous authors. We may imagine
that the dryapithecine apes may already, like the chimpanzee and *Papio*
baboons, have had some disposition for catching and eating small
animals, including mammals encountered while foraging. Climatic
shifts of the type described in Kortlandt's summary (see p. 66) would
favour an increase in seasonality, necessitating an increase in hunting
during periods of the year when the vegetable diet was in short supply.
Some reversal of the dental changes favouring an increase in incisal
breadth for meat-tearing then occurred. When Jolly refers to the actual
fossil record he suggests that the early 'robust' form of the
australopithecine 'man–apes' belongs to his stage 1 seed-eater complex
and the later 'gracile' forms (e.g. *Homo habilis*, etc.), may represent a
stage close to the establishment of his stage 2.

Jolly's solution to the jigsaw puzzle has not gone unchallenged. In a
closely argued critique, Szalay (1975) accuses him of 'squeezing the
apparent adaptations of probably bipedal, long hind-limbed protohominids with a different feeding mechanism into the model of
quadrapedal, long-armed grass-feeding geladas'. Such perhaps is the
fate of any argument by analogy. The distinctiveness of the species
compared keeps resisting the argument by asserting the independence
of the differences and the limits of inference. The substance of Szalay's
objection goes back once more to the details of dental anatomy. Sadly,
in the end, there is little else to which we can return.

The changes in anterior dentition shown in the pongid–hominid
transition, argues Szalay, need not be explained by the notion of
functional loss. While the importance of the molars remains
undoubted, the fact that the canines resemble incisors suggests a
positive selection for the development of effective incisors rather than a
negative selection based upon character reduction. Furthermore, it is
not certain that the canine–incisor line of hominids has shown an
overall reduction at all. The increased incisors of Jolly's stage 2 may
have been wrongly dated and actually present earlier. Szalay argues
that the hominid line has shown an increased emphasis on incisors from
the beginning, although their form, including the incisiform canine not
seen in gelada, differs from the anterior teeth of apes. Furthermore
there is some inconsistency in Jolly's argument. Geladas eat the same
diet as his protohominids are supposed to have done, yet their dental
apparatus is different. Geladas do chew up and swallow grass seeds, yet
their cheek teeth differ from those of hominids. The implication is that
dietary differences were more important than their possible similarities
and that the anatomical contrasts suggest a radical divergence in
foraging and diet rather than a convergence.

Szalay concludes that the development of a long incisor line including the canine has an important functional significance. Arguing from

ape descent rather than by the baboon analogy, he points out that the incisors are important in tearing and that their increased importance in protohominids could be linked with an increased role in dismembering carcasses and ripping meat off bones. Chimpanzees do not use their canines in killing; hands are used instead, and so the reduction in canines is not critical to the kill. Prior to the development of tools the incisors would have been a vital means of obtaining meat. If this were so then the shift to meat-eating may have occurred gradually in open savannah and not only in grasslands. It would probably have included a prime strategy of foraging for carcasses left by other carnivores, since at first actual killing would have been limited to small prey.

We may attempt to assimilate these arguments. It seems likely that a long transitional period occurred during which the shift from a vegetarian to a meat diet gradually developed. Jolly's stage 1 may then be reinterpreted as a long transitional period rather than as a specifically geladaform socio-ecological level. During this period we may imagine the following changes occurring:

(1) Increased seasonality and a more arid climate would have presented woodland dryopithecine apes with a food resource problem. An increase in hunting small game, already available as an option (as in chimpanzees), would have met the need for an adequate protein diet.

(2) The collection and eating of fruits, berries, and cereals would not have ceased. As with modern hunter–gatherers, these resources would have formed the staple diet for much of the year. However, the need for meat would have led to an increased efficiency in obtaining it. This must have been sufficiently important to have affected the incisors in both sexes in spite of pressures for sexual dimorphism in other aspects of anatomy.

(3) Hands were already effective in the manufacture and use of tools by the chimpanzee. Hunting for small game was manual, and no doubt co-operative. The search for larger carcasses necessitated long-distance travel for which the heavy time and energy costs were recompensed by the value of the find.

(4) Large cadavers are difficult to cut up and dismember. Tool-making therefore focused very much on the preparation of cutting tools, both small and large, to facilitate these tasks. In this way the first material evidence of such cultures appeared.

(5) Social interactions at the carcass probably resembled those excitable assemblies among chimpanzees gathering in fruiting trees. Carcass location certainly involves the same temporal-spatial uncertainties and the need for the transfer of information so that kin may benefit. Finding carcasses implies ranging and search as well as a visual monitoring of the activities of carni-

vores likely to have killed recently. It seems probable from the chimpanzee evidence that parties of young males may have played key roles in 'search and locate' missions of some degree of danger to themselves. Rapid assemblage of parties at carcasses may also have prevented neighbouring human groups from attempting to take them over or fighting for them.

(6) Danger from predators and competitors alike would have encouraged means of protection. The gradual development of club and spear carrying, of movement in coherent parties, perhaps with leadership and effective communication, may have arisen initially as defence for parties of such scavengers against both the large carnivores that killed the prey in the first place and against other competing human groups.

(7) The carrying of weapons for defence would quickly lead to their use in offence. The sooner the kill is located the more the meat and the better its condition. It follows that the scavengers would seek to find and descend upon a new kill as soon as possible, using clubs to drive off the original predators. If these were lions or hyaenas it seems that the attack must have been made in strength, for these animals would not have given up their booty easily. Sticks, stones, clubs, spears, and a tremendous creation of noise would have been the main means. Noise too would have assembled other individuals including women. The total co-operative impact must have been sufficiently dramatic to have given the killers a fearful surprise with which they were unable to deal.

(8) The use of weapons in offence would in times of shortage have allowed raiding parties to enter the home ranges of other human groups and attempt to acquire their resources. Nothing of course is known of the ranging habits of such early protohominid groups. Ranges were probably very large and undefended, but a conventional allocation of areas among residential groups may already have developed.

(9) Such raids may not have been limited to acquiring food. Quite quickly weapons could have been used to obtain additional mates. Warfare probably began early as an extension of competition between groups for several kinds of commodity required in the fulfilment of individual strategies.

One can see that during this gradual transition bipedalism would have been of great importance. Not only does it free the hands more effectively for weapon use than does knuckle walking but the gain in height for all-round and continuous observation would have been vital. The development of a long loping stride combines effective long-distance travelling capacity with sufficient speed. Such anatomical adaptations have far-reaching effects. They could not have developed overnight and imply a long period of evolutionary change. For example, man's nakedness was most plausibly originally an adaptation to the temperature regulation necessitated by long-distance travel and sweating (Newman 1970). The sexual significance of naked skin in tactile courtship is thus probably a secondary corollary of these changes in diet and foraging strategy.

Stage 1 in the ascent of the human species was thus most plausibly based upon the emergence of a vegetarian—scavenging mode of life rather than upon a specific cereal-eating phase. Such a hypothesis accounts for the uniqueness of the hominid transition and relies equally upon the argument by analogy and that by descent. As with Jolly's model it establishes the set of pre-adaptations essential to stage 2 in which the foraging behaviour of hominids focused more exclusively on the hunting of big game rather than small game and in which scavenging was largely if not completely abandoned.

The hominid evolutionary line was of course an entirely distinct one, stemming from a common dryopithecine ape stock with chimps and gorillas. It adapted with a unique omnivorous diet to seasonal savannah habitats. The increased emphasis on scavenging meant a pattern of resource opportunities in space and time necessitating skilled performance in exploitation. By contrast, the geladas' total absence of interest in meat emphasizes the specialization of its cereal dietary adaptations and its lack of that flexibility that the hominids doubtless inherited, as did the chimpanzees, from the dryopithecine ancestors. The value of the hominid–gelada comparison remains in an emphasis on the ways in which arid savannah moulds primate social systems to form uni-male reproductive units out of the multi-male units of other types, be they *Papio* or chimpanzee-like. The emphasis on bonded mateships is crucial, I believe, to understanding the origin of human socio-sexual life and the chimpanzee offers no clues here. The gorilla, the least arboreal of the great apes, however, does, for here we find a regular association between a male reproductive and several females in distinct groups.

The unique social evolution of hominids would seem to have started then with a terrestrial dryopithecine ancestor which, like the gorilla, developed a uni-male reproductive social unit, probably in response to a combination of selection pressures resembling those responsible for harems in other primates.

On the baboon analogy the most likely factors involved in the historical sequence responsible for such a change seem to be as follows.

(1) Patchy ecological resources that are best exploited by small parties reduce the size of troops or herds in which multi-male rearing associations usually occur.

(2) Sexual competition partitions these relatively small parties among adult reproductive males in such a way that one male becomes the alpha male of each party.

(3) Party size becomes calibrated in relation to male competition and the sexual satisfaction of females. The optimum size may therefore express the sociosexual forces in play rather than the most effective foraging party in relation to an individual member's acquisition of food.

(4) An effect of sexual selection in this situation is to enhance male size and physical power. A reduction in the number of such big animals in each group to 1 or 2 has the effect of allowing proportionately more food to go to females rearing young.

(5) Under good feeding conditions or under harassment from rival parties, small human groups probably assembled together and undertook co-operative activities often in relation to their mutual protection or in aggression against other groups.

In the gorilla the especially large size of the grey-back male protects the group from possible predation as well as from interference from other males. His ferocious charges enhance his protective potency and actual combat between males is evidently avoided for it rarely occurs in nature. The larger and more powerful build of male over female humans may plausibly be attributed to the same cause. Apes do not show the extreme disparity in the onset of puberty shown by the two sexes in baboons and this, together with a lack of sexual jealousy, as shown by the gorilla, suggests that the exclusion of young male reproductives from the polygynous family unit was not as pronounced as in the hamadryas and the gelada baboons. This would have made the development of intergenerational co-operation easier.

The bonding of adult reproductives to their families suggests that the burden of collective hunting fell more on to younger males than is the case in the chimpanzee, and that young males would have formed groups of consistent composition for their own protection. This would then have made them ideal adventurers for exploring the new scavenging and hunting niche. Females would have retained throughout the important capacity for gathering vegetable foods. In relating these changes to the fossil record it seems likely that *Ramapithecus* of the Middle Miocene, some 14 million years ago, was largely vegetarian but that the scavenging way of life became well established with the emergence of early australopithecines in the Pliocene. With the gracile australopithecines of the late Pliocene, around 3 million years ago, we may imagine hunting to have become the mode of life that led directly to man.

The origin of the family: a context for mother–infant attachment

We have argued that the reproductive unit of the human ancestor seems most plausibly to have contained a single male as the focus for the sexual activities of several females. The word 'family' simply designates the specifically human type of one-male reproductive and rearing group highly subject to cultural variation in its adult composition and rules of relationship. Throughout the course of its duration the prime behaviours that occur within the family are to do with the rearing of children by one or more females, with or without some degree of male participation.

By analogy with other terrestrial primates, the dispersion of females in small groups may have been the original source of the family; a dispersion made essential by a patchy distribution of food resources in the ecology of origin. Given a seasonality in the density of dietary items the separate groups may well have concentrated in areas of food abundance, not only because of that abundance itself, but because an increase in numbers reduced individual risk from predation and from attack by other human groups. Males dispersed among the female reproductives would have sought to exclude young reproductive males and to protect their mates and their young both from predators and from the violent attentions of reproductive bachelors seeking to obtain access to females. Evidence from other mammals suggests that such an event could possibly end with a slaughter of children to speed up the onset of insemination by a successful rival and consequently the rearing of *his* children by females (see p. 82). The father's attention would have tended for the most part to be directed outwards against possible interference with the rearing of his children, and different family men may have collaborated in ensuring protection. The establishment of a collective refuge or homestead for several families would increase the possibilities of protection and such a site would have been placed within easy reach of the main foraging areas of a home range. The family thus becomes a 'household'.

Child-rearing among humans is a long process. Children are closely dependent on their mother or a substitute parent for about ten years. The male would therefore increase his inclusive fitness if his bonding with one or more females and their children remains firm and if he assists in rearing them or at least in providing for them. D. Morris and others have argued that a number of features unique to human sexual physiology operate to maintain strong bonds. The main characteristics are:

  (1) Non-seasonal sexuality so that women not bearing children are available for and willing to enjoy intercourse in a relatively unrestricted manner at any time.

(2) The development of enhanced signals of sexual attractiveness, breasts, beards etc., and sensitive erogenous zones that increase the somaesthetic pleasure in love-making. The result is an emphasis on foreplay and diversity in sexual activity that again enhances bond maintenance, since a degree of novelty and inventiveness as well as reciprocal habituation is essential for the full development of sexual pleasure.

(3) The hairlessness of the human body and the sensitivity of the skin are likewise associated with this trend, although the former may be primarily an adaptation to thermoregulation (Newman 1970).

(4) The long duration of these bonds and their location in a 'household' may be a partial explanation for the changes in digestive physiology that produce a more-or-less daily bowel movement rather than the greater frequency seen in other primates. This reduction in the fouling of a home base reduces health hazards and was probably associated early on with defaecation away from the living quarters.

The exact composition of the human family varies greatly and is clearly an environmentally labile social characteristic responsive to ecological and economic pressures. For example, polyandry is found in certain ecological circumstances where the labour to maintain subsistence demands additional males in a household and, as a good sociobiologist might expect, a wife in these circumstances commonly marries two brothers or sometimes more (e.g. Goldstein 1971; Aziz 1978; Crook in press a, b on Tibetan polyandry).

The central feature of family life is the attachment between mother and child. This is highly stable and even when human 'aunting' behaviour means that children are cared for to some degree collectively, the primary link remains strong. This has been emphasized recently by studies of mothers in Israeli kibbutzim where an equality between the sexes in participation in labouring tasks was considered to be an ideal. Women recently began to express a need for more intimate contact with their own babies and this has produced a reduction in the creche system of child care that was an inevitable concomitant of egalitarian policies.

Bowlby (1969, 1973) has argued that the evolutionary significance of stable attachment behaviour between women and their infants lies in the protection from predation that this provides for the infant. This explanation, of course, may be applied to mother–infant bonding in any animal species in which it occurs. Yet there are animals that lay eggs and leave them without care to chance and fortune. Because such young have no nutritional needs supplied by the parent it seems evident that a physiological tie between parent and infant by which the infant is nutritionally dependent is a primary condition for the association, for which protection from predation secondarily follows. The two functions are commonly present together although there are a few species of birds in which the care given to hatching the eggs is later followed by protective behaviour, sometimes in creches (as with the ostrich), even when the young seem fully able to fend for themselves nutritionally. In these examples parental behaviour may aid the young in the discovery of the food items. In the case of the oyster catcher, the exploitation of shellfish by young is copied from the feeding style adopted by the parent and it is presumably transmitted by imitative learning. Human infants, like oyster catchers, learn in the company of their parents. One cannot argue, however, that such a consequence necessarily implies natural selection for this particular effect of the association. In the case of the human species the question requires further thought.

Compared with other primates the human child's dependency on the mother is closely associated with its relatively underdeveloped condition at birth. The human adult indeed exhibits a considerable number of anatomical features that are the result of the developmental retention of foetal characters into adult life (Gould 1977). The evolution of such a retention is known as neoteny. As early as 1926 the Dutch anthropologist L. Bolk was pointing out that adult humans are foetalized forms compared to the adults of other primates. Some of the characteristics in question are the retention of cranial flexure typical of babies in the womb, long neck, forward position of the foramen magnum, no brow ridges or cranial crests, thin skull bones, flat face, large brain case relative to face size, small teeth with late eruption, hairlessness, low birth-weight, and small size at birth and particularly the retarded closure of the cranial sutures. These features are discussed at length by Montagu (1960, 1962a, b). He points out particularly that the closure of the cranial sutures which coincides with the ending of brain growth begins in apes within the first few weeks of life. In man it is delayed until the 27th year! The human brain continues growing until the 20th year but the greater part of growth occurs during the first five. He remarks 'It is of considerable interest to note that there is a close correlation between the duration of the early learning period of man and the growth of the brain'. Certainly when sutures do close in childhood preventing brain growth the result is mental retardation. Man thus preserves a rate of brain growth and continued development of a foetal type well into adulthood and his brain has a growth rate and development in excess of that of an infant-ape brain long after the latter has ceased to grow. Sir Arthur Keith (1948) had argued that this extended period of brain growth through the development of an individual, when the greatest amount of social learning is happening, was an essential condition for the appearance of the human mind.

Possibly the small size of the human baby at birth is due to the evolutionary changes in the female pelvis consequent upon the assumption of the bipedal stance. In addition the slow development of the head until birth is important since it allows an easier passage of the birth canal. Bipedalism in relation to ecological changes may therefore have initiated a degree of neoteny that proved to have survival value in reducing mortality rates at birth. It seems likely that these retentions of neural plasticity, of skull flexibility, and other skull characteristics associated with the large amount of growth of the brain (77 per cent) after delivery may have provoked subsequent and partially consequential shifts in the nature of maternal care.

The underdeveloped condition of the neonate and the prolonged period of post-natal maturation are associated with long pregnancy, a long nursing period, and a post-weaning period of close attachment, during which the infant remains dependent on the mother. Montagu has discussed the extended period of pregnancy in human primates, arguing that the longer the single offspring is preserved in the womb the more leisurely its development can be. A foetus, he says, is on the whole better nourished and less exposed to danger than a newborn infant, and under the conditions of life of early man such a prolongation of intrauterine life would have been of great advantage. 'Genes, therefore, favouring such a prolongation of intrauterine development by a slowing down of the rate of foetal development would gradually have been established by natural selection.' Even when birth does come the human primate is still in a very underdeveloped condition.

Montagu also provides interesting evidence that the extent and patterning of foetalization is different in contrasted human races. Neotenous characters by which mongoloids differ from caucasoids include less body hair, larger brain-case and brain, broader face, flat nose, epicanthic fold, and so on. Negroids and Bushmen-Hottentot (*sic*) have yet a further list of differential neoteny from that of caucasoids. The varieties of human beings seem thus to express major discrepancies in the extent of neoteny in different races. These contrasts could arise as environmental adaptations. The retention of the broad face, flat nose, and epicanthic fold could thus be related to the arid, dusty, windy environment of central Asia where people of Mongolian stock evolved. The genetic factors that caused these contrasts may also effect other features of the child's association with the mother, and an extensive analysis of contrasts in child-rearing between different peoples might provide greater understanding of ethnic personality contrasts. The fact that personality contrasts between peoples may have some foundation in biological differentiation may not be popular, but research on such topics will be a necessary development of contemporary work on mother–infant attachment and its consequences in later life.

These arguments are summarized in Fig. 5.1 which shows the inter-dependent and successive changes that may plausibly have followed from the evolution of bipedalism. It is important to note that the genetic factors selected in this sequence have their differentiating effects at several stages of an individual's life during which social learning may also be occurring. Maturational development and socialization thus go hand in hand throughout the phase of mother–infant attachment.

We can see then that attachment behaviour is a consequence of a cascade of evolutionary events that are consequent upon (1) an anatomical adaptation to ecological change, (2) differential evolution-

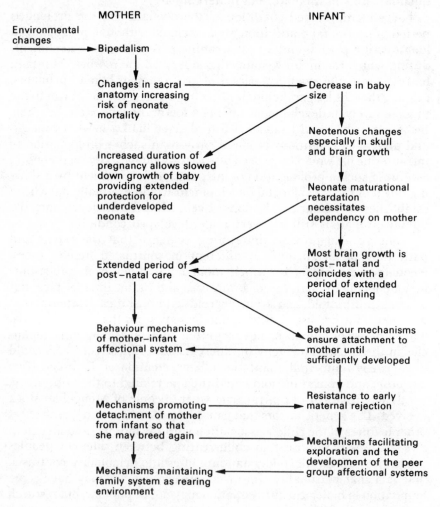

FIG. 5.1. The probable evolutionary cascade determining the emergence of early affectional systems and family life in man.

ary adjustments in the anatomy of the baby functioning in the reduction of infant mortality, and (3) compensatory adjustments in maternal
care to allow the child to grow during a longer period of dependency.
Attachment of baby to mother and vice versa seem also to have evolved
to ensure an appropriate social environment in which the interactions
essential for the development of intellectual functions, and later social
relations, can develop; for without them these structurally 'retarded'
young primates could never become psychologically adult human
beings. The evolutionary changes that increase the length of maternal
'nutrition' in its widest sense therefore seem to be the primary ones,
although they are correlated closely with the overall protection that
care provides for the undeveloped baby in the family environment. We
have already argued that protection against predators in these family
units is mostly the responsibility of the male.

The mother–neonate attachment is an essential basis for postnatal
development and, in both monkeys and humans, severe disturbance
results from a disruption of this phase. The subsequent extension of the
attachment into a less close parent–child relationship continuing into
adolescence also has several evolutionary consequences:

(1) It provides a secure and known social environment in which the
child can learn the numerous cultural skills that have developed
so rapidly in post-Pliocene humans. Without this base, socialization and consequent reproduction would probably not occur.
It is therefore advantageous in terms of inclusive fitness to both
child and parent to see that this educational phase provides
optimal learning opportunities for the child.

(2) The child can provide assistance to the parents in numerous
tasks associated with child-rearing and associated domesticities.

(3) The child in its relations with peers can learn the rules for
reciprocating altruism that govern the course of this process in
his group.

Recent laboratory research on infra-human primates strongly supports the view that the prime biological significance of attachment
behaviour is that it allows the performance of transactions essential for
the cognitive development of the child without which it would neither
survive nor reproduce. Mason and Berkson (1975) separated
laboratory-raised rhesus monkeys from their mothers at birth and
placed them with artificial mothers covered with cloth as surrogates. In
one group the surrogate mothers moved about irregularly in a manner
that necessitated frequent responses from the infant. In another group
the 'mother' was motionless. The mobile 'mother' seemed to supply
many of the features of normal social interaction, and the young
monkeys pounced on it, pursued it, and wrestled with it. The results
showed clearly that when the monkeys raised with the mobile surro-

gates reached two years they showed greater attention to other monkeys in social tests and tackled more problems in problem-solving situations (although not with greater success) than did those raised with static surrogates. At a later age the only young monkeys to show affective sexual behaviour came from the 'mobile' group. These results extended earlier research which had showed that laboratory monkeys that had been born in the wild were more socially competent, more alert, and better able to cope with problem situations than laboratory monkeys reared with surrogates from birth in individual cages.

Mason has continued this line of inquiry with an experiment in which young monkeys are reared with bitches (not *by* bitches). The monkeys attach and the dogs appear to enjoy their company without being maternal. Comparing 'dog-reared' monkeys with 'surrogate-reared' monkeys again shows that in general the experience of an active mobile mother surrogate, not essentially maternal in behaviour, provokes greater alertness and a greater capacity to cope with problems and social situations than is found in more deprived animals. Mason (1979) writes of these continuing studies:

These results provide convincing evidence that the rhesus monkeys' characteristic ways of coping with novel situations are profoundly affected by the nature of its relations with the attachment of figure . . . [which] . . . has a kind of paradigmatic quality: it serves the developing individual as its first exemplar of what the larger world is like and exerts a powerful influence on how it is prepared to deal with it.

Stationary surrogates provide few opportunities for the monkey 'to learn that the events going on around him are amenable to his control' (Mason 1979). The prime feature of the mobiles and the dogs was that they allowed the monkey to respond, stimulated it to do so, and promoted the performance of motor games. Transactions became possible and upon the results of these the alert 'attitudes' and effective coping skills seem to depend.

A similar finding has been reported by J. S. Watson (1971) for human babies. Infants learnt to control a mobile suspended above their cribs and responded to its movements with smiling and cooing. Given a moving mobile controlled by a device operated independently from the babies' movements and on a fixed schedule, the babies learnt that they could not stimulate it; its movements then failed to produce smiling and cooing. When both groups were later tested with a new free-response mobile, only those who had experienced one before learnt to control it.

The occurrence of interactions of this kind in which the infant can initiate responses to which it can in turn respond are basic to interpersonal transactions. The mother's presence provides a vital context for the child's social development and allows it to establish a basis of expectations that guide its subsequent social explorations (see also Chapters 10 and 11).

Mechanisms reinforcing the later attachment systems of affection that bind both infra-human and human relationships at successive life stages are likewise highly likely to have been selected for their significance in ensuring the cultural adaptation of a child to its society, without which reproduction and a maintenance of individual inclusive fitness would be impossible.

Harlow and Harlow (1965) have written of these systems that each one system develops through its own maturational stages and differs in the underlying variables which produce and control its particular response-patterns. Typically the maturational stages overlap. These five affectional systems are: (1) the infant–mother affectional system, (2) the mother–infant system, (3) the infant–infant, age-mate or peer-affectional system, (4) the sexual and heterosexual affectional system, and (5) the paternal affectional system. These systems find expression especially within the family, which seems to be the essential social structure for the development of a biologically effective human person.

Big-game hunters

No doubt the killing of big game emerged as a product of ecological change but it could not have occurred without a preadaptive set of behavioural features. It probably developed locally at first, in regions where a dependence upon a meat diet was more obligatory than in others. Woodland hominids at a scavenging phase in their history may well have coexisted with pure vegetarians in forests and developed hunters in arid lands. It was the expansion of the latter in Africa that promoted the emergence of ways of life geared primarily to big game. In this development man paralleled the original carnivores. The killing of prey larger in size than an individual predator is accomplished only by elaborate and refined collaboration. Among the various carnivores that practice such social skills the following traits have emerged (Schaller 1972):

(1) Co-ordination of action within a group, often with some division of labour.
(2) Food-sharing and often transport to the den.
(3) Elaborate communication of affect and intention.
(4) Subtle equilibration of behaviour control in relation both to the behaviour of the prey and to that of collaborators.
(5) Hierarchical social structuring of the hunting group.

These features were doubtless well developed during the evolution of scavenging by raiding the kills of other carnivores (p. 100). The ability to frighten off the big cats and groups of hyaenas already implies effective collaboration. It remained but a short step from the use of weapons in raiding kills to the use of the same or similar weapons in direct attacks upon the meat-bearing species themselves. Once this step was taken man became a carnivorous predator in his own right. Not only had he by then attained effective means of preventing predation upon himself but he entered into direct competition with the top predators themselves. This step thus took man to a commanding position at the top of the ecological pyramid. This position was furthermore easily maintained, for his carnivory was not exclusive. He still relied heavily on vegetarian subsistence in a majority of habitats while acquiring the potential to invade areas where only meat eating could support a human population. The development of clothing to assist natural homoiothermy allowed him to occupy even the colder regions of the temperate zone.

The fact that it is male members of the chimpanzee community that collaborate in hunting, often under the direction of a particular individual, strongly suggests a similar source for big-game-hunting parties in hominids. Certainly sociobiological considerations make this likely. The risk-taking disposition of young males, originating in their need to compete with older males sexually, also finds expression in an active outward exploratory tendency. Young males are not passively excluded from the 'centre' of a primate unit; they often consociate, explore in groups, and innovate new activities spontaneously. One can therefore imagine that their acceptance of life strategies that put them at higher risk than females and reproductive males may be related to an outward search for units into which to mate—as the gelada example (p. 82) suggests. Such animals would be especially well equipped to form the basis of hunting teams.

This argument needs further thought. Chimpanzee hunters are not exclusively young male animals nor is their behaviour divorced from that of other community members. The hunters do not, however, share meat voluntarily (see p. 71) and only the claims of other individuals ensure its distribution. If, then, in open country, the males of protohominids were distinctly allocated to age–class units comprising non-reproductives, there is no particular reason why they should seek to distribute meat among individuals other than co-operative companions. If meat was an especially valuable energy source they would clearly gain in physical strength over non-hunting reproductive males, and hence replace them more easily. Could this be so?

The protohominids in dry country must have acquired by this stage a mating system involving the bonding of a male with one or several females. Such a mating system implies the exclusion of young male reproductives from mating. Teams of young killer males would present a threat to harem-holders, old or young, and the development of collaborative male hunting skills would seem at first to shift the political balance in intergenerational conflict firmly in the direction of youth. It is immediately clear, however, that an increase in the ability of young males to displace reproductive males from their harems also increases the risk of the same thing threatening any successful young individual or group, especially if a tiring contest has preceded the event. We saw in the gelada example how the striking of a reproductive 'bargain' between representatives of the two generations tends to secure the reproductive roles of both and to provide a socially more secure environment for the mothers. If the killer teams did no more than feed themselves on meat without assisting other animals, they would gain little in terms of inclusive fitness.

If we are right in identifying the pioneer killers as young males, then we have to find some way whereby such behaviour enhances their inclusive fitness. Historically, their behaviour did not lead to an ecological separation of the generations but rather to a new and integrated system of resource exploitation.

Young males have the vigour and the outward impetus but they lack the experience accumulated by the older males. Effective hunting of large well-defended prey requires expertise above all, and expertise is acquired either through the dangerous process of trial and error or, less dangerously, through the acquisition of information under tuition. We may therefore imagine that an intergenerational bargain of the gelada type (p. 82) might very rapidly have been struck in protohominid development. Young males trade their risk-taking vigour for the older animals' information by safeguarding the reproductive 'rights' of the latter and by helping to supply meat. Such reciprocal bargains are likely to be struck between close relatives, and would moreover enable the older male to leave his women and to participate at times in the hunt. In this way he could not only provide direct tuition but also ensure a supply of meat for his own wives.

We have here an evolutionary 'inversion', as Moscovici calls it. The earlier separation and exclusion of young males from the reproductive unit is now replaced by their reintegration into the reproductive social matrix by virtue of their contribution to the feeding economy. The precise process whereby this occurred may never be known and a number of pathways are plausible. Certainly such an integration would have been facilitated by the appearance of patrilineal ancestors early in protohominid life (see pp. 87 and 166).

Neither in the chimpanzee nor in baboons (except possibly in the hamadryas, p. 80) is there an explicit social linkage of father with son, although further research may reveal geneaological links between collaborating males. In lions, however, we do know that the two collaborative males of a pride are half-brothers. In the harem life of baboons the son departs at puberty but there is as yet little evidence as to whether his return to a harem for mating purposes has direct associations with kinship. While the value of outbreeding would probably tend to discourage a return to very close relatives, among protohominids one way of ensuring an intergenerational transfer of information about hunting would be to establish a father–son relationship that endured beyond the son's puberty. Such an association would furthermore entail an establishment of a patrilineal kinship system.

An alternative aid to information transfer would be for the son to defer reproductive activity voluntarily for a period during which he received paternal tuition. That this is possible is shown by the way in which young male hamadryas defer sexual relationships in favour of establishing bonds with females that are as yet too young for sex (p. 80). In this way they can remain in a harem without exciting an owner's 'jealousy'. (It would of course be unreasonable to expect hunting tuition among humans to be given to small boys in the field prior to puberty, for boys of that age would not be strong enough to participate in actual hunts. None the less from an early age small boys play hunting games.)

Another possibility is for the father to guarantee a sexual future for the son either on his attaining puberty or after a period of deferred sexuality. He could, however, do this only as a result of a bargain with the members of other family units. The males of such units could, as a result of reciprocating altruism, agree to exchange daughters to enable their respective sons to enjoy sexual experience. Such an exchange between mutually admiring but largely unrelated males would secure the supply of meat for their units at the cost of tuition and give the closely related females in each harem an assured succession for their daughters. Such a process would to a large extent remove the risks of inbreeding and provide the basis for a strong social integration of relationships within a clan.

The experience of the older males will be especially important in groups that depend upon social skills, not only in the hunt but also in the regulation of relationships including intergenerational sexual succession. Their knowledge will enable them to predict the behaviour of younger men and to circumvent risk to their social positions by adjusting their behaviour in advance of a potential crisis. We have seen that the organization of the gelada herd, with its collaboration of older male reproductives in defence against the all-male groups (p. 85), is at least in part a response to 'sexual predation' from within the community and possibly also from young male groups travelling into the area from outside. The complex behavioural equilibration required in hunting will also play a role in defence against sexual predation. A co-operative defence by older males, all of whom have themselves once been young, must present a formidable barrier to the young adventurers.

Frontal attack is, however, only one of the means whereby geleda males acquire mates. The formation of a two-male team is an exercise in intergenerational tolerance and collaboration that allows the transfer of daughters to young males without strife. The problem here is to prise the daughters away from their mothers. It seems likely that, faced by effective defence against sexual assaults on harems, young hominid males would opt for less risky strategies involving an intercalation of their behaviour with that of reproductive males rather than the high-gain but reproductively dangerous take-over tactics.

Again, in geladas, the actual shift in male sexual responsibilities within a reproductive unit is very largely determined by female sexual and social satisfaction. As Dunbar and Dunbar (1975) have pointed out, large harems comprise a body of females with lower reproductive output potential than those living in smaller harems. Males that continuously shed females to other males may retain female loyalty more effectively than those that choose a strategy of maximum harem size. The same may have been true for our putative protohominid harems. Very early on in their history it may have paid the males handsomely in terms of inclusive fitness to adopt strategies that limited the number of their wives and to hand on the surplus to young males, probably relatives, who were prepared to co-operate with them. If the harem male were strong, he could select the young male he wanted and even strike a bargain with other harem owners for an exchange of sons between them. This would precipitate the beginnings of a reciprocal kinship system of reproductive succession (Chapter 7).

The relations between the young non-reproductive male population and the reproductive population are regulated by two forces: the outward movement of sons from harems or families and the inward movement of bachelors seeking mates. The way in which these two forces relate in the life-trajectories of individuals describes the nature of the resolution that they have found for intergenerational sexual conflict. If sons were to retain a greater contact with their home units and participate temporarily rather than permanently in peer groups (as extensions of small-boy play-groups, for example; 'gangs'), a basis would be established for a complex set of reciprocating contracts. Some possibilities follow:

(1) Son inhibits most sexual activities within his home unit. Mother and sister are not 'identified' as potential sexual partners. Father permits son to remain within his sociosexual sphere on these terms.

(2) Father passes on to son information and instructions about hunting.

(3) Sons of several fathers play together. After puberty, being so far denied sexual access to young females, they might show homosexual affection for one another. The bonds so established could be vital for the close co-operative friendships and mutual loyalty that are essential in dangerous hunts. The hormonal effects of testosterone activation through mutual masturbation may provide the assertiveness essential to risk-taking adventures on the hunt as well as the maintenance of sexual appetite leading eventually to heterosexual behaviour (see p. 83).

(4) Fathers may periodically join sons on hunting expeditions and demonstrate the prowess and expertise needed for a successful outcome. Some fathers of unrivalled skill will acquire legendary fame and charisma for the young and thereby emerge as clan 'leaders'.

(5) Selection theory predicts that fathers will be interested in the reproductive success of their sons and daughters. Within the process outlined above fathers have the opportunity of comparing the vigour and skill (intelligence) of each others' sons. A father seeking fine brides will offer his son on a basis of the young man's significant features. Fathers who reciprocate can extend their interaction into the mutual evaluation of such stated or potential propositions.

(6) Mothers are equally concerned about the reproductive future of their offspring. The emphasis on hunting should not disguise the fact that the collection of vegetarian dietary items remains vital for communal nourishment. Gathering skills, although less complex than hunting skills, also need instruction and transmission, and mothers doubtless have especial knowledge about each others' daughters and their suitability for each others sons. Their influence on the paternal evaluations may often be decisive. I am not proposing here a harem-type organization of hamadryas-like male chauvinism. The male gelada is very much dependent upon the support of his females for the fulfilment of his life strategies. Female geladas, by their intrasexual co-operation, can change their mates, exclude their mates from interactions, and determine many features of harem life (see p. 81). The same was probably true of the social organization of early humanity.

We have outlined a number of plausible steps whereby a complex of reciprocal patterns of interaction ensured (i) a control of the socially disruptive effects of intergenerational conflict over sexual succession; (ii) the effective transmission of hunting skills and contractual sharing of food; and (iii) a patterning of son and daughter exchange aimed at a tactical maximization of reproductive success for both parties. These steps are a fulfilment of the potential that arose in the primate stock through the elaboration of reciprocating altruism within social congregations adapted to particular environmental contingencies. They also reveal the way in which nepotistic strategies operate at this level of social complexity and intertwine with reciprocation. Finally, the power of sexual competition and the differentiation of parental investment remains evident. Intra- and intersexual strife has great potential for disruption in social units that depend on co-operation for an effective exploitation of their environment. This omnipresent risk calls for elaborate skills in co-operative social management. The most recent research on chimpanzees and geladas shows how significant this is even at the level of non-human primate society. Our argument extrapolates from this to the very roots of human culture. One conclusion is inevitable. At no point is there a break in the autocatalytic advance of behavioural change. There is no point at which man emerges as a distinct entity operating with 'social' or 'cultural' mechanisms that are entirely separable from those of a 'biological' level. Sociobiological evolution means the historical development of the social expression of age-old biological strategies. As the complexity of sociality increases in response to phyletic elaboration and environmental constraints, cultural mechanisms emerge as 'enabling devices' for solving strategic problems at fresh, and more complex, levels of integration. These mechanisms depend upon a tremendous development of intelligence, learning capacity, and communication.

Summary
(1) We begin this chapter by examining those more plausible models of human social evolution that have attempted to relate information available from studies of fossils (physical anthropology), archaeology, and behaviour research on living primates. Clifford Jolly makes the point that we are concerned with the evolution of systems in which structural and behavioural characteristics are functionally interwoven in such a way that the evolution of one complex of traits often facilitates the emergence of another in what tends to become a kind of autocatalytic cascade. Thus bipedalism frees the hands, tool-use develops, complex tasks necessitate learning. Bipedalism also causes anatomical difficulties at birth so that babies are born in a very undeveloped condition. They need long-term care in which much learning then occurs.
(2) Jolly concluded that anatomical, dietary, and behavioural traits indicate that human evolution paralleled that of the gelada, early men were essentially seed-eaters that had developed harem-type social life under similar ecological pressures.
(3) Subsequently Szalay corrected Jolly's interpretation of dental

similarities between gelada and hominid fossils and therefore also the nature of the inference to social life. The present position argues that human protohominid ancestors were exposed to an arid climate in East Africa that lead to an increase in hunting small game to augment fruit gathering. The remains of kills of large carnivores became a source of food; tools in the form of cleavers and cutters were used in the dismembering of carcasses. Young males may well have played key roles in these developments, as in the chimpanzee.

(4) The use of weapons (stones, spears) in defence and in driving the original predators off carcasses conceivably led to their use in offence so that the direct killing of big prey began to develop. Clearly bipedalism was an important concommitant here.

(5) The archetypal family probably consisted of a small harem-type unit with a male and a few females. The origin of this social structure could well have paralleled that of the baboon harem with both social and ecological factors playing a role in the process. A number of especial features define the human case ensuring loyalty between spouses and the consequent maintenance of a secure psychological environment for the slowly developing but hyperintelligent child. Apart from bonding, family structure is actually quite a labile and adaptive thing that varies with socio-economic circumstances.

(6) The retention of foetal characteristics associated with the early birth of the human baby has important effects on its development. Human babies and their mothers are emotionally attached to one another. Attachment seems especially important not only for the infants security but also in ensuring an appropriate social environment for the programming of the child by learning. It is through this process that the human infant becomes a social being set within a specific culture.

(7) The attachment between mother and child is maintained while the brain continues its post-natal maturation. The transactions between mother and child, as actively initiated by baby as by mother, are the source whereby the cognitive abilities of the infant are brought into play and developed through a succession of stages. Neoteny, slow development with extended maternal care, mother–infant attachment, and social transactions are the sources of a distinctively human training in the use of adaptively variable behaviours through learning and, as we shall see later, of a social patterning that provides a personal control of emotional expression.

(8) These social and developmental traits were evolving hand in glove with a need for increased social efficiency in an early hunting that necessitated high intelligence to underpin tactical collaboration. In addition, if hunters were primarily young males, a potential sexual conflict between them and a gerontocracy of family men may well have

emerged. It seems likely that co-operation between members of families may have developed through arrangements whereby daughters were swapped for male services in the hunt. Intergenerational tensions could have been reduced to socially manageable levels through the development of friendly relations involving exchanges without sexual rivalry, between men of different age groups. Parallels with non-human primate society are used in an attempt to fill in some plausible detail.

6 The behavioural elaboration of hunting hominids: intelligence, language, and exchange

> And when the natural history of the mental operations shall have been written ... we shall more clearly realise that educability itself is a product of natural selection though the specific results acquired through cerebral modifications are not transmitted through heredity. It will, perhaps, also be realised that the instinctive foundations of social behaviour are, for us, somewhat out of date and have undergone but little change throughout the progress of civilisation.... The history of human progress has been mainly the history of man's higher educability, the products of which he has projected on to his environment. This educability remains on the average what it was a dozen generations ago; but the thought-woven tapestry of his surroundings is refashioned and improved by each succeeding generation.
>
> C. Lloyd Morgan 1909

The wider significance of hunting

The immense significance of hunting in human history becomes apparent when one considers the length of time human beings have spent doing it. 'The genus *Homo* has existed for some 600,000 years and agriculture has been important only during the last few thousand.... Even 6,000 years ago large parts of the worlds population were non-agricultural and the entire evolution of Man from the earliest populations of *Homo erectus* to existing races took place during the period in which man was a hunter' (Washburn and Lancaster 1968). Only for 1 per cent of human history have agricultural ways of life predominated and all major biological changes that led to modern man had occurred prior to the invention of farming. Hunting itself probably began before the genus *Homo* was fully formed. Australopithecines were probably effective if not very organized hunters, and throughout the long hunting period elaborations of method occurred. For example, fossil evidence indicates that only late in time did *Homo* utilize marine or river produce; stretches of water must have been major barriers to movement. 'Hunting', remark Washburn and Lancaster in their valuable study, 'is a way of life and the success of this adaptation (in its total social, technical and psychological dimensions) has dominated the course of evolution. . . . In a very real sense our intellect, interests, emotions and basic social life—all these are evolutionary products of the success of the hunting adaptation.' And since this adaptation was world-wide the 'unity of mankind' is a consequence of a communality in adaptation; *Homo sapiens* is in fundamental respects the same creature everywhere.

In this chapter we examine three basic themes in human evolutionary development. The enormous capacity of human beings for showing adaptively variable behaviour is due to the great increase in intelligence and learning ability shown by the species. This is enhanced through the development of language and intellectual operations in reflection, problem-solving, and planning. Intelligence is the base and language the means for the richness of social exchange upon which societal exploitation of the environment and the establishment of an homoeostatically balanced economy can be achieved.

Intelligence: the components of adaptively variable behaviour

Today it is almost a truism to argue that human beings owe their ascendancy in the animal kingdom to their intelligence, but in fact the origin of that intelligence, its precise nature and its evolution, is very poorly understood in spite of an enormous literature on the differences between individuals in tests designed to measure it. Intelligence, for the most part, is seen by psychologists as a trait or disposition which varies between species and individuals and which can be assessed by placing a target individual in a situation designed to elicit behaviour that allows measurement. Most tests of intelligence take the form of learning tasks revealing the manner, speed, and extent to which a subject can acquire new behaviour. Types of learning vary; habituation is the most primitive type of learning, while classical Pavlovian conditioning is also found in lowly animals. The ability to learn how to escape or find food through 'trial and error' emerges next and has been extensively examined as 'stimulus–response' learning in instrumental test situations such as the Skinner box. The ability to solve a problem by insight, as in the classic case of Wolfgang Köhlers' chimpanzees who, after reflection, piled up cases to reach bananas suspended above them, appears only in higher animals and seems to require at least some type of ideation. The problem is solved 'insightfully' in the head before a response is translated into action. The ability to extrapolate from one situation to another is a similar phenomenon (Kruschinsky 1965). Surveys of animal learning reveal that the complexity of performance of which animals are capable increases up the phylogenetic scale and culminates in man (Thorpe 1956; Bitterman 1965).

Studies of the natural history of intelligence were at one time popular. Romanes (1884), in particular, collected anecdotal material describing intelligent behaviour in animals. Controlled ethological observations of such events have, however, been rare. We do not know, for example, the frequency with which intelligent acts of different types are performed by any animal in the context of its daily life nor how frequently its behaviour leads it to encounter environmental or social problems that need an intelligent solution (Charlesworth 1979).

Intelligent behaviour has been defined as 'behaviour that is adaptively variable within the lifetime of the individual' (Stenhouse 1974) or as 'cognitively guided behaviour employed to deal with problems' (Charlesworth 1979). Earlier writers, associating the increase in the performance of intelligent behaviour with the enlargement of the human brain, have considered its significance in relation to tool-using and the management of fire as well as in hunting and have treated these adaptations to changing ecology as factors initiating the increase in human intelligence. Since 1947, however, the prevailing trend has been to see the development of human intelligence as contingent on the emergence of complex and co-operative social organizations (Dobzhansky and Montagu 1947; Chance and Mead 1953; Etkin 1954; Eiseley 1956; Montagu 1962a) and to associate it with the emergence of neo-cortical behavioural control and language skills.

The most careful attempt to put forward a theory of the evolution of intelligence is given by Stenhouse (1974). One of the problems in discussing this question is that intelligent behaviour is clearly not due to a single factor. In one study, for example, it was considered necessary to examine some 120 independently measurable abilities to describe human intelligence. Debate has raged over whether tests should be designed to measure some single factor of 'general intelligence' or a multiplicity of separate abilities. It seems clear that no satisfactory theory of the underlying process yet exists. Stenhouse was not deterred and he selected, after lengthy consideration, four main factors that contribute to the occurrence of intelligent behaviour. These were:

(1) A capacity *not* to respond automatically, 'instinctively', to a situation but to postpone, pause, or explore it with observation or variable behaviour: the so-called P factor.

(2) A memory store: if a new adaptive response is to be achieved some latent or insight learning must have occurred, for this to happen information storage is essential. This store is termed the C factor in Stenhouse's book.

(3) A capacity to abstract and generalize (the A factor), to see what

is common and contrasting between events, and to relate them together.

(4) The sensori-motor efficiency to carry out a newly perceived patterned response (the D factor) and exploration.

These factors resemble those established as components of 'biological intelligence' by W. C. Halstead (1956) in his controlled studies of decrements in performance shown by human subjects suffering impairment due to brain damage, especially frontal lobectomies. In addition, the three stages of cognitive development, described by Piaget from studies of growing children, suggest a developmental sequence attributable in part to the maturation of attributes like these. In Piaget's system the sensori-motor abilities develop first, followed by storage capacity and abstraction, and last of all by the capacity to delay responses.

Stenhouse's theory begins by considering the emergence of adaptively variable behaviour in simple animals. As species come to invade more complex and variable environments situations occur to which a rapid adaptation is required within the lifetime of an individual. The need here is for an ability to respond to short-term environmental changes with variations that will ensure both the maintenance of the physiological homoeostat and reproduction. This ability develops in animals whose genetically endowed innate behavioural responses are so far too rigid to cope with new or changing environments. Something faster, more flexible, and capable of continuous change is then required.

In classical ethological motivation theory a distinction is made between the appetitive and consummatory phases of an instinctive activity. In the former, the animal locates through search the appropriate circumstances that will release the consummatory act of the sequence: eating or copulation, say. Stenhouse argues that variable behaviour is characteristic of the appetitive phase, which can be extended by means of developments in the motivational machinery into long bursts of exploration during which the animal either acquires highly specific information or builds up general information which is stored as a 'map in the head' for use when it confronts a problem later on. The sensori-motor abilities are clearly a fundamental basis for acquiring new perceptual information and for testing out motor sequences in attempts at solving problems. The A and C factors refer to the cognitive capacity to interpret information categorically in a variety of ways and then to store it so that it is readily available for recall.

Stenhouse utilizes the physiological model of Sokolov (1960) as a description of the necessary machinery. Animals build up interior neuronal representations of their world and are constantly comparing these representations with incoming information. When a novel stimulus arrives, it stimulates an arousal response which leads to investigative activities that continue until the 'novelty' is no longer unfamiliar. The stimulus is then incorporated into the neuronal representation and forms a further basis for later comparisons of experience with the known. This approach has a wide applicability in psychological theory of the so-called cognitive-dissonance type (Festinger 1954) and is clearly an important aspect of what Piaget terms 'assimilation'.

An important component of exploration is the capacity to withhold virtually all alternative activities, except responses to danger, while it is in progress. This capacity to inhibit or withhold other competing responses is what Stenhouse means by his P factor and it is vital for gaining the information essential to abstraction and storage. The combined functioning of these components allows the performance of the less variable 'instinctive' acts within sequences which are now flexibly and progressively related to environmental change.

In applying this approach to primates Stenhouse suggests that adaptations to an active life in tree-tops provided the starting-point for primate intelligence, particularly through the enhancement of the A and D factors involved in effective footwork from twig to twig. The P factor is also significant in calculating jumps. But this takes us little further than squirrels unless we add the importance of all these factors to the regulation of social relations which are fully developed in all higher primates. In comparing arboreal lemurs with equally arboreal cercopithecid monkeys, it is in the added complexity of the social hierarchies of the latter that Alison Jolly (1966) sees the significance of their extra abilities in laboratory intelligence tests.

Standing and walking upright, initially perhaps to see over vegetation and to browse on fruits by an extended reach, seems to have been associated with scanning operations in which a delay between stimulus and reaction would be important. Yet it is the added complexity of hierarchically organized social life on the ground, and hence an immediacy of contact between individuals that arboreal living tends to preclude, that seems to have promoted the delay component (the P factor) into an especially important role.

Michael Chance (1962b) suggested that constant competition between primate males for sexual access to females necessitated a capacity for inhibiting sexual and aggressive responses which would otherwise maintain a social group in a constant state of uproar. While Chance was mistaken in following Zuckerman's (1932) suggestion that female monkeys provide 'constant mating provocation', his argument can be applied generally to the competition for access to resources of all kinds which occurs between and within both sexes. This includes access to companions for grooming sessions, co-operative reciprocation, and defence. Such equilibration of behaviour entails Stenhouse's delay factor, especially in the control of socially inappropriate aggressive and sexual responses. It 'demands of the individual an intensification of the control over its emotional responses, both facilitatory and inhibitory'. In the rapidly changing world of baboon social relations, for example, the variety of contrasting stimuli impinging at any one time is large and requires acts of decision of considerable social delicacy. Emotional responses that are simply 'acted out' are likely to be unsuccessful in the context of a particular strategy for which social subtlety in execution is essential. A fine example is Hans Kummer's (1968) study of the behaviour of male hamadryas baboons when introduced as singletons to an enclosure already containing a male with a female consort. The newcomer feigns ignorance of their presence and by careful avoidance manages to prevent a quarrel. But this is no mere matter of physical dominance, for when the males are taken out and their positions reversed, it is now the former 'owner' of the female who, irrespective of size, avoids contact.

Chance (1962b) postulated that the enlargement of the neocortex was an anatomical adaptation to the circumstances requiring an equilibrational response. Since the protohominids had developed a social complexity that required especial delicacy in interpersonal relations, this neurobehavioural development was doubtless, as the 'biosocial anthropologist' Robin Fox has put it (1967), 'an important pre-adaptation giving them a springboard from which to launch themselves via tools, hunting and language, into the truly human state'. The development of neocortical control over the limbic systems of emotional behaviour must have coincided also with the development of language. Here, too, the P factor is clearly important, for speech involves alternation between partners in long strings of vocalization. While one speaks the other inhibits responding and 'thinks up' a reply.

It is an interesting fact that dominant primates, whether baboons or chimpanzees, commonly demonstrate considerable emotional independence from the swirl of confrontations going on around them. This degree of detachment, a consequence of inhibition but without loss of acute social attention, makes for the appearance of confidence. The activities of such animals often proceed in an entirely self-motivated way without particular regard for those around them. This 'stance' may be of considerable social significance for other animals, providing indicators of the performer's social reliability, confidence, and history of successful strategy in the social competition that precedes the attainment of high rank. An animal that has attained high rank is commonly used for social support by others in distress and especially as a refuge when an individual is under attack. Furthermore, since hierarchies may be structured more by avoidance than assertion, the dominant animal tends to participate less in interactions; but when he does so, it is with considerable effect.

Dominant and confident individuals are commonly the focus for the attention of groups, especially those with some form of hierarchy. It seems likely that much of the activity of the group is organized by learnt and variable responses to the relationships, roles, and ranks within it perceived through patterns of attention related to these relationships. While actual interactions may sustain or cause changes in relationships, and hence in the extents to which individuals are attended, the attention-pattern within the group is very likely to play a part in the learning of their social position by juveniles. To a degree then, as Chance and Jolly (1970) suggest, the structure of the group is mediated by the attention-pattern itself, for this provides the information upon which potential actions can be assessed.

Such an 'attention structure' is also important in human society where individuals of high status showing characteristics of restraint and strength are often given especial attention at the level of interpersonal communication and in events reported in the media. These characteristics are components of 'charisma', the attribution of which to another is based on the deeply felt emotional needs of dependent individuals which are rarely consciously expressed (Larsen 1977; Chance 1977*a*). The postponement factor is likely to be an important trait underlying the reflective restraint of such leaders in both infra-human and human societies.

The P factor may also play an important role in mother–infant relations. A certain indifference correlating with efficient handling of a baby is characteristic of effective gorilla mothers. In discussing Schaller's (1963) observations, Stenhouse suggests that maternal effectiveness increases with practice in part through a postponement of hasty emotional responses. This calm reflective handling of infants is a factor that ensures close emotional bonds between mother and child because of the security such confidence supplies. It is also attractive to other infants with less secure mothers. 'The lengthening of the period of juvenile dependence, characteristic of the high primates and reaching its extreme development in the human lineage, would furnish increased opportunity for its [the P factor] selection and development. The conflicting requirements for encouraging independence yet maintaining control (discipline) in the juvenile during the lengthy period of dependence, would appear to enhance the premium on P factor withholding—"forbearance" it could . . . be called' (Stenhouse 1974, p. 150).

Creativity may also be a consequence of the operation of the postponement factor under conditions of frustration or anxiety aroused by social circumstances. The redirection or 'sublimation' of aggression involves a delay in behaviour which allows novel expressions of motivational compromise. Since subordinate competitors are motivated to replace their rivals, these occurrences may allow insights into new and devious strategies whereby such a change could be brought about. The calculation of probabilities determining which course of action a 'bachelor' gelada should take to optimize his success in attempts at gaining mates from harems involves just such niceties and implies considerable 'reflection' on the part of the animals, although self-critical conscious intent is not suggested.

The four factors regulating the nature of adaptively variable behaviour probably vary in 'strength' independently in different individuals. Such a multi-factorial theory certainly seems likely to do more justice to human variability than any unitary theory of intelligence. Stenhouse points out, for example, that a $C.a.P.d$ person might well be a disaffected intellectual, a $c.a.p.D$ a locally renowned sportsman or artist, a $C.A.P.d$ a fast creatively thinking intellectual, and a $C.a.P.D$ might be a person handicapped by inabilities to abstract whose creations thus lack coherence—a frustrated writer or artist, for example.

The Stenhouse approach boils down to an essentially simple position. The enhanced capacity to show adaptively variable behaviour in higher animals is due particularly to the development of increased abilities in 'logical' abstraction and generalization and the use of an effective memory store. These provide the animal with the means whereby the information coming from the senses can be matched with what the animal already knows, and expectancies, which lie at the root of an animals decision-making, formulated. The capacity to withhold too impetuous a response is of especial importance in complex social relations that involve the balancing of conflicting motivations within rapidly changing situations. Animals skilled in this art may well become the focus of social attention owing to their ability to manipulate others in ways that may provide mutual benefits. While memory and logic are based on the expansion of the association areas of the brain cortex, emotional inhibition is due to the increasing control of cortical functions over those of the limbic system responsible for 'emotional' behaviour. The role of emotional inhibition in the regulation of motivational ambivalence in reciprocating altruism is especially important. We may suspect, indeed, that an enhancement of the P factor in behavioural determination evolved in close association with the ability to show reciprocal behaviour. Indeed personal restraint among humans is often a sign of a well-developed social intelligence.

The origins of intellect and language

A major puzzle in understanding the mental abilities of both apes and humans concerns the extraordinary gap between the ability to solve intellectual problems and the apparent absence of occasions for its use. While chimps and gorillas can learn to use a simple language and to communicate quite well with humans, such skills are not apparent in the wild, where no evidence of linguistic skills has so far been obtained. Among simple human communities also, the tests set by village life and subsistence farming practices do not seem to call for the intellectual responses of which educated village children rapidly become capable. As Humphrey (1975) puts it, 'If, despite appearances, the important practical problems of living actually demand only relatively low-level intelligence for their solution, then there would be grounds for supposing that high-level creative intelligence is being wasted. Even Einstein could not get better than 100% at O level.' Few authors have attempted to unravel this problem. As we have seen, Alison Jolly argued that the more complex intelligence of higher primates when compared with lemurs is a function of their more elaborated social life; this, too, is the line that Humphrey takes: 'the chief role of creative intellect is to hold society together'.

The social lives of higher primates are all complex. They involve the rapid solving of moment-to-moment problems concerned ultimately with the satisfaction of homoeostatic needs and the achievement of biologically strategic goals within the context of a community. We already know that the communication systems of socializing mammals are more elaborate than those of more solitary ones. It seems reasonable to suppose, therefore, that the elaborated use of signal repertoires involves an emancipation from the simplicities of vocal emotional expression and the use of sound and gesture in intelligent manipulations of others. Social primates are required by the very nature of the system they create and maintain to be calculating beings.

They must be able to calculate the consequences of their own behaviour, to calculate the likely behaviour of others, to calculate the balance of advantage and loss—and all this in a context where the evidence on which their calculations are based is ephemeral, ambiguous and liable to change, not least as a consequence of their own actions . . . here at last the intellectual faculties required are of the highest order (Humphrey 1975).

Accumulated knowledge and its application in well-predicted circumstance is not enough. These animals apply concepts based on evaluations of shifting probabilities, and for this a considerable computing facility is needed.

It can be no accident that the vast expansion of the human brain coincided in time with the advent of the hunting–gathering way of life. The cranial capacity of chimpanzees ranges from 300 to 480 cm^3 and the mean value of eight Australiopithecine skulls is 464 cm^3, with the largest not exceeding 500 cm³. After this development was rapid. The mean size for four *Homo habilis* skulls is 657 cm³ and *Homo erectus* averages 978 cm³. The largest *H. erectus* skull out of nine is over 1,250 cm³, which overlaps the range of modern man (1,000–2,000 cm³ with a mean around 1,300 cm³) (Tobias 1967).

Evolutionarily minded anthropologists have often associated this increase in brain size, which remains remarkable even when the proportionate sizes of the bodies concerned are taken into account, with the appearance of tools. Chimpanzees, however, are effective at simple tool-making and use; and even an orang-utan in Bristol Zoo has been taught by Wright (1972) to make and use chipped-stone implements. The main increase in brain size concerns the frontal lobes, which are essentially association areas rather than regions used for the complex sensori-motor co-ordination necessary in the preparation of objects. Reynolds (1976) concludes '. . . the best brains in *Homo erectus* probably did not go in for either stone working or pyrotechnics. Most probably they worked on something that has left no trace—on Sociology. In fact, if I had the chance to re-name *Homo erectus*, then I would call him *Homo sociologicus*'. But if this is the case what then imposed the tremendous increase in social problems that elicited so epoch-making an anatomical response?

Wolves, hunting dogs, and other co-operatively hunting Carnivora do not differ particularly in overall intelligence nor show a major contrast in cranial morphology with bears, which are notoriously non-social. Differences in disposition are displayed, but not apparently in the traits we are considering. Among primates of the same taxonomic group, the Cercopithicoidea say, there seem to be no dramatic contrasts in IQ or brain proportions between the relatively asocial patas monkey and the gelada and hamadryas which lead such inordinately complex lives. I would argue that social complexity *alone* is an insufficient cause for the magnitude of the evolutionary change we are considering. It is within the specific conditions related to social elaboration in the hominids that we are more likely to trace a plausible answer.

Scavenging hominids take their origin in vegetarian forbears. Even though chimpanzees may be sufficiently predacious to have a considerable impact on the ecology of neighbouring species, the apes as a whole are clearly and fundamentally vegetarians. Certainly, this is the dietary point from which the dryopithecine apes began. Yet in what, in evolutionary terms, was a short space of time they incorporated a whole new way of resource exploitation into a life-style which yet retained a basic dependence on vegetarian resources gathered carefully from the surrounding bush. Humans are facultative carnivores and only under conditions of poor vegetable or cereal resources is it essential for them to augment their diet with meat. Meat can solve many dietary problems; it comes in bulk, rich in proteins and with fats already predigested, as one might say, from the vegetable condition. It can be dried and saved up against times of food shortage, and a little goes a long way. Given ecological conditions favouring or necessitating the taking of meat the hominids *learnt* to do so. Since humans, unlike the carnivores, lack an 'instinctual' equipment for slaughter of this sort the whole movement can be construed as basically a cultural change, much as the Japanese macaques discovered potato-washing as a cultural shift once they were provisioned with them on the beaches of a Japanese island.

In Japan it was the juveniles who first began the change, a fact that fits nicely with the suggestion that young males were the prime exploiters of the developing hunting niche. This is not to say that generations of hunting have not selected for dispositional traits in hominids that facilitate chasing and killing. The fundamental shift was none the less different in kind from the evolution of carnivorousness elsewhere in the mammals.

Learning to hunt big game required, as we have already discussed, not only co-operation but technical skills in military-style ventures necessitating precise informational integration and a command structure followed intuitively or imposed by convention. Above all it required a coding of information related to hunting and a capacity to transmit that information quickly and sometimes at long distance. It required language but not necessarily the specific type of language that humans have.

I suspect that, as in so many other aspects of hominid evolution, one shift in the advance to language precipitated another that facilitated the first, and so on along a long chain of mutually reinforcing contingencies. This cascading 'autocatalysis' of evolutionary development is especially relevant to the emergence of intellect and language, for they are indivisably associated. Intellect and language both require coded information for their elaboration. It is in the precision of their codification of perceptual knowledge that hominids show so dramatic an advance over the pongids and other primates; and the handling of the code required the 'hardware' of a cerebral computer. To pursue, perhaps at some risk, the analogy; language is the software of the cerebral computer. There are then two associated evolutionary problems; to account for the origin of the hardware on the one hand and the software on the other. But the crucial understanding will lie in an exact analysis of the specific relation between these two that characterizes man.

It was no accident that the rapid development of the brain coincided with the emergence of hunting. Let us be clear about this; hunting is a social process and not merely the effective throwing of spears. Language is an enabling device that ensures effective social participation in the chase, effective social control of food-sharing, and knowledge about who does what, with what, and when. The computer handles the calculations of probabilities in attacking the prey and also the wide range of interactions arising among the hunters themselves. As Humphrey has so well expressed it, the basic quality of the human intellect is transactional, and given the linguistic tools a progressive elaboration of transactions under varying ecological and social contingencies became possible.

Chimpanzees can make use of language, and this has been seen as another step to man, especially since some chimps at least become hunters. It might be wiser to see the chimpanzee's abilities as a separate, parallel achievement in its own right. The communicational system of chimps is not that of man and probably could not have given rise to it. Attempts to teach chimpanzees to talk have failed. The species lacks a vocal apparatus capable of producing the range of articulations required. However, the experiments conducted so far have required the animals to speak English, a language in which even those humans not knowing English have difficulty; had the researchers concocted a Ponghominoid Esperanto they might possibly have done better. Recent work has shown that using gestural and other manual expressions Chimpanzees can communicate with people and use a variety of intellectual constructs.

Washoe, a chimpanzee trained by the Gardners in American Sign Language (Amislan),† designed for the hard of hearing, first stressed words referring to relations; 'more' for example. Object words gradually emerged and Washoe began spontaneously to emit sequences of signs where the meaning was generally clear. In terms of conceptual content her utterances closely resembled those of a child, but her mistakes in word order suggested that she was imposing her own formula on the sentence structures she was given. Instead of utilizing

---

† American Sign Language is an elaborate system using manual, facial, and bodily gestures. Most of the signs utilize movements of the hand or hands. Each sign is a meaningful unit—a word or string of words in English. Humans do not perceive or remember the signs as discrete units. Rather, the manual signs can vary in shape, location, orientation, and movement. Studdert-Kennedy (1977) argues that the variation in the signs and their interpretation by perceivers is evidence for a duality of patterning akin to that in speech. In other words, the signs can be viewed as phonetic units which combine in ways that produce words (morphemes) according to a complex of distinctions between components that allows the construction of a syntax. The signs are linked to form utterances through a blending of signs: a hand may adopt the shape of a following sign before the preceding one has been completed. Signs are thus analogous to syllables in speech. It follows that in using Amislan Washoe achieves the cognitive competence of some human beings.

the agent–action–recipient form of her teachers' communications she
tended to emphasize her own social actions. Furthermore, Washoe,
unlike young children, never used questions or negatives. She appeared
to use word strings in ways that brought out personal interaction but
not in a way that encoded conceptual relationships as such. Semantic
association of words did not seem for her to develop into a truly
syntactical association. The difference between chimps and humans
therefore does not lie in cognitive ability as such but rather in the ability
to use patterns of words syntactically in the operation of general rules
that relate concepts.

Premack (1976), using a different system of communication, asked
his chimpanzee Sarah to tell him when two sentences were the same or
different. This is not unlike the systematic training that children receive
in acquiring language. Children can, however, infer syntactical patterns even when these are not fully explicit, an accomplishment that is
beyond the reach of chimpanzees.

The chimpanzee seems therefore to have a linguistic 'deep structure'
rooted in the expression of here-and-now personal interactions. Addi-
tions of words to strings are essentially intensifiers—to add emphasis
rather than new meaning. By contrast, human sentences include
specific references to an object or objects in such a way that syntax
builds up round that referent.

These contrasts between chimpanzees and humans make sense in
terms of the probable social contexts of their origins. Chimpanzee
social life, as Jane Goodall (1971) has described it, is full of elaborate
personal interchanges, mostly concerned with the regulation of the
strength of responses—social equilibration in fact. Although chimps do
use tools, object play is not especially pronounced in young animals.
Man, by contrast, emphasizes object play and object reference from the
beginning.

Research still in progress at Stanford University suggests that the
gorilla may be able to formulate a language closer to human usage.
Possibly this is due to the less temperamental character of gorillas when
compared with chimpanzees. Possibly the Gorilla, with a greater delay
component in its mental operations, is a more reflective animal and is
thus able to approximate more closely to human thought.

At Stanford, Koko, a young female gorilla, has also mastered the use
of Amislan. After 36 months of training she used 184 signs; by 4½ years
she used 222 signs spontaneously at least once a day on 15 days out of
30; and by 6½ years her total vocabulary was 645 signs, about 375 of
them being used regularly.

Koko has an IQ measured as for a human, of 85–95; which is only a
little below the average of comparable human children. She argues,
jokes, shows displeasure, swears, and lies. She corrects incorrect state-

ments and enjoys games of pretence. Her sign repertoire includes 'bad', 'image', 'understand', 'curious', 'idea', 'gentle', 'stupid', 'boring', and 'damn!' She conducts a monologue with herself when looking at a picture book in the absence of her trainer. She refers accurately to past interactions of an emotional nature with her trainer. She invents new names for unsigned objects and is now beginning to talk with a younger male gorilla, Michael, brought in as a companion, who is also becoming accomplished in Amislan. The most interesting aspect of her talk lies in her revealed awareness of her own identity and her capacity for empathy. Once she took a photograph of herself, identified herself in the subsequent picture and signed 'Love Camera'. In response to the question 'Are you an animal or a person?', she signed 'Fine animal gorilla'. When shown a picture of a smiling chimp she signed 'Teeth', indicating a recognition of the being in the picture and identification with it. Shown a horse with a bit in its mouth she signed 'sad'; when asked why, she signed 'teeth'. She hates baths and when shown a picture of another gorilla having a bath she signed 'Me cry there' (Patterson 1978).

These remarkable findings raise many questions. First, the precise differences in language usage between chimpanzee, gorilla, and human children need much further study. Secondly, the evidence for self-consciousness requires systematic examination as to extent and implications. This will become especially interesting when Michael and Koko begin extensive conversations, and perhaps, in due course, converse with their own children. Thirdly, it raises the remote but tantalizing possibility that other advanced mammals might be able to acquire some linguistic ability if an appropriate sign language could be invented for them.†

Human language focuses especially upon the concept of an event, and words referring to objects are the pivot around which the event structure develops. If the use of tools, collaborative hunting, and complex social transactions are insufficient to explain the origin of human speech, what characteristic will do the trick? We need to identify the specific condition of early hominid social life that gave rise to an object reference system in communication of so marked a character.

---

† Although mirror experiments (p. 243) suggest that monkeys are not able to hold a clear self concept, this conclusion may be premature in the absence of an adequate research approach. Perhaps, after all, dogs and cats might be capable of some form of 'speech' with humans. Finally, the work raises an ethical issue. Koko is obviously as much a person as many a human child. What then are her rights? Are rights species-specific or are they dependent on a demonstration of being a person? And if so, what of apes in the wild who, like many a South American tribesman, face extinction through loss of habitat at the hands of human exploiters?

The answer almost certainly lies in the self-conscious use of property. The elaboration of a wide variety of tools for processes involved in self-protection, hunting, food-preparation, transport of materials, and building construction would mean that distinctions would have to be made between makers and users, between users and owners, between possessors and inheritors. In that some tools and goods are more valuable than others, their possession and use became immediately associated with social contrasts in rank and in role. Tools became part of the matrix of society, markers defining categories and boundaries in an increasingly complex societal organization. We can therefore suggest that a linguistic provision for the naming of both tools and people underlies the evolutionary development of reference in human language and the emergence of grammatical structuring that provides the context in which the name plays its part in a meaningful communication.

The language apparatus

Language functions primarily by the binding of object referents in space and time so that an internalized representation of an event may be constructed. Binding in space and time is brought about by the use of verbs and adverbs that place an object 'there' and 'then' or 'here' and 'now', or in other combinations of these. The tenses of the verb place an event in the past, present, or future, designate whether a probability or a certainty is involved or an obligation inferred, and show whether a named object is acting or an acted upon. These features, while varying immensely in the grammatical structuring that carries them, are virtually universal in human languages. They show clearly the function that language serves: an inner representation of events, either from the past or summoned up as future possibilities, in which the relations between objects and persons can be described and hence, in speech, precisely communicated. The task involves a very effective memory capacity with a system of recall. The expansion of the biological 'computer' to its human level seems to be without doubt the result of natural selection of brain structures that enhance these abilities (Dobzhansky and Montagu 1947).

The process whereby human speech evolved is proving to be an exceptionally difficult sequence to reconstruct, and work on speech behaviour bearing on this question has only just begun. This is one of those areas where experimental psychologists and ethologists are gaining much from their increasing interaction.

There are several distinguishable problems:
(1) The relationship between communication by gesture and communication by vocalization in the origin of language.

(2) The representation of events in the outside world in such a way that they are not only symbolized internally but their salient features can be encoded to enable a message to be transmitted.

(3) The problem of how far the brain is biologically prepared for language at birth in the form of inherited grammatical structures and specific susceptibilities to certain types of sounds.

(4) The actual encoding problem: how inner symbols are rendered into sounds that carry messages.

(5) The perceptual problem: how sounds are decoded and then reconstructed into the original message.

Somewhat paradoxically there is increasing evidence that vocalization *per se* was not the source of language development and that initially, at least, it had a relatively minor role to play. The importance of speech lies in the construction of messages for the auditory channel and not in the elaboration of language content, which is, however, its essential *raison d'être* (Hewes 1973). The work of Jean Piaget suggests that 'no form of knowledge . . . constitutes a simple copy of reality, because it always includes a process of assimilation to previous structures . . . and this is true from elementary sensori-motor behaviour right up to the higher logico-mathematical operations' (Piaget 1971, pp. 6–8). For Piaget, sensorimotor intelligence consists of a direct co-ordination of actions without any representation or thought. Any development from this fundamentally innate reactivity of lowly organisms comes about by the assimilation of new actions or acquired ones into the pre-existent 'schema'. At more advanced levels 'to know an object implies incorporating it into action schemata'. The same is true, it is argued, for the assimilation of new percepts into cognitive material, although in this case it implies the incorporation of new symbols into the current schemata of thought.

These internal schemata are representations of relationships between the sensory and motor activities of the nervous system. In a valuable discussion of this approach McNeill (1979) points out that any sentence in a story, say *The sun rose on the frozen scene. The men stopped their cars by the river*, represents an event, that is to say a set of actions which is not comprehensible to a listener unless he can relate them contextually and temporally to other actions. He goes on to argue that sensorimotor representations play a fundamental role in the programming and articulation of the contents of speech and in the form of the message itself. Different representations cluster around events such as causes, actions of a performer, state of the story, a person or location, and sometimes the subject as observer. Sensorimotor segments occur so often in speech that they can be called units in a syntax or 'syntagmata'. As a concept the syntagma, one unit of meaning pronounced in a single output, thus links the articulation of speech to its meaning. The way in which syntagmata combine resembles a developing hierarchy in which lower-order or later processes can be inserted into higher-order or established ones.

At the earliest levels of language development the action schemata may well have been quite literally schemes of action which could be interpreted when observed by others. The rapid developments of representational gestures would have converted mime (representation of an event not present in the here and now) into symbolization.

If then gesture was the basis of early linguistic communication how do we account for the involvement of the voice? Certainly manual communication by gesture can be developed into a complex system fully capable of replacing speech—as in the hand gesture conventions of languages for the deaf which, as we have seen, are fully employable in communication by the great apes. Protohominids could very well have operated a system of signals enabling them to interact in ways expressive of their needs in their environment. Certainly unacquainted deaf children can create a language between one another even when they have not been taught manual signs. They have been seen to combine signs into stable orders of preference. In normal persons gestures accompanying speech usually occur more or less synchronously with verbalizations representing the same sensorimotor content. It thus appears that communicative gesturing and speech output may be parts of a single process.

Hand movements may not be the only elements involved. Ekman's extensive studies of facial expressions have uncovered the extreme mobility and use of the facial musculature in conjunction with speech. One can imagine that at close quarters, with the hands engaged in domestic chores, facial movements could very well step in to replace the airy wave of some dismissive hand. Facial–visual communication allows communication at close quarters without major body movement and leaves the hands free for work. The early involvement of the voice would follow from involuntary movements of an interjectional nature, perhaps due to changes in breathing caused by surprise, tension, release of tension, the broken-up rhythm of laughter, and so on. The association between breath changes in stress and the origin of facial expression was originally discussed in works on the formation of mammalian facial communication patterns (Andrew 1963; van Hoof 1969; for a review see Vine 1970) and the idea is also likely to be valuable in this context too.

The association between facial expression, manual gesture, and elementary sounds in a system of primitive action representation could thus account for the early involvement of vocalization. Vocalization carries further, can be heard in the dark, and operates rapidly in one medium through a single channel; the auditory one. The enhancement of vocal language would seem to be based upon selection for an improved communicational efficiency superimposed upon the gestural basis which remains to fall back on. Referring to the development of language in individuals, McNeill points out the value of verbal play, as when children concoct sequences in long personal monologues without another person being present. Here verbalized action schemata can be combined and recombined in a highly exploratory way that is doubtless related to the interactions between the child and its mother. The accuracy of a child's utterance of a word varies. In interaction with its mother a child is not content merely to babble. Just as it is not content with a mobile that takes no account of its own movements, a child likes to 'control' its real mother. To achieve this the child seeks to produce sound variants that evoke maternal responses of a socially positive nature.

That the child intends to communicate has been demonstrated by Kaesermann (1977; see Foppa 1979). When a child's partner is instructed to indicate non-understanding by asking 'mhm?' after an utterance, the child starts to vary its sounds as if to improve meaningful contact. This tendency to vary sounds while in communication with an adult partner provides a selective process which attunes the child's utterances to the speech and meanings of the adult. In this way not only language but also dialect is acquired. Once again the vital importance of these early transactions with mother is emphasized.

The continuous sequence of short scenes in which mother and child stimulate and reinforce one another by means of physical actions and sounds forms the basic non-verbal transactions to which vocalization is gradually assimilated, not passively, but through the active modelling of the child's sounds on those of the mother whose behaviour provides the meaning. Action sequences and sounds are thus progressively assimilated both as behaviour and as cognitive constructs ('syntagmata').

Many detailed features of phonemes (speech sounds) have been analysed by sound spectrography which does the same for sound as frame-by-frame analysis does for film: minute contrasts in the phonetics of speech can be closely examined. In an extended discussion of such work, Marler (1979) points out the importance of the findings of universals across a wide range of cultures. For example, the timings of the onset of voiced sound in certain syllables are virtually the same in all cultures. There is a long list of similar features (Studdert-Kennedy 1977) and it appears that the basic constraints on patterns of vocalization are common to the whole species.

Marler (1976) has also wrestled with the fact that higher primates emit vocalizations that show subtle graduations within the same basic call. Such graded sounds could form the basis of a speech with a capacity for encoding symbols. For this to occur the grades of sound would have to be sufficiently precise as phonemes to carry the code and the perceptual apparatus of the receiver would have to be able to decode the relevant distinctions in the message.

Work with similar regularities in the calls of Japanese and pig-tailed macaques provides instructive information on the way in which different species may show contrasting abilities at recognizing certain sounds. Different types of coo-call, frequently used by Japanese macaques, were not easily recognized by the pig-tails even though the call as such occurs in their 'vocabulary'. Exhaustive training sessions eventually brought some experimental animals up to the Japanese macaques' level of performance indicating that they could make the distinctions but less easily. It seems that the 'Japanese macaques exhibit a special predisposition to process coo sounds in a particular way that parallels their apparent meanings' (Marler 1976). This might imply the operation of genetically based neural mechanisms that facilitate the perception of these calls rather than others, but this has yet to be established.

The human speech universals raise the same issue. Human beings could possess innately determined perceptual processes which, as neural structures in the brain, would greatly facilitate the formation and perception of language. Given a voice production that produces clear boundaries between functionally distinct phonemes, adult humans perceive such sounds as categories by reference to their boundaries. Infants are already sensitive to these same boundaries before they have learned any speech (Liberman 1979). It seems as if there are inbuilt filters for both the perception and the articulation of language. The operations of these filters create templates which both facilitate the recognition of language sounds and gradually come to govern the neuromuscular construction of sounds into strings forming the meaningful syntagmata of communication. Infant babbling must play a major role in language acquisition. These meaningless phonemes become shaped into the forms of a particular language and dialect through the child's interactions with a mother figure. The infant's task is to establish the links between what it hears as language and its own vocal 'gestures'. Auditory feedback from its own vocalizations guides its motor control over sound production, until the latter is finally captured by the patterns of speech of the mother (see also Studdert-Kennedy 1976).

In relation to language the human brain is in fact unique. Anatomical analyses of brain lesions responsible for aphasia have revealed specific areas, discovered by Broca and Wernicke in particular, that are involved in the production of language. Broca's area, located just in front of the cortical region responsible for the motor representation of the vocal cords, seemed to Wernicke to hold the rules by which language is coded into speech form. Wernicke's area, lying next to that responsible for the cortical representation of hearing, seems to be primarily involved in the recognition of patterns of spoken language (Geschwind 1970). Furthermore these features are particularly developed in the left cerebral hemisphere, so that the operations of language in writing and reading require information transfer via the corpus callosum. Cerebral dominance, a feature not known to occur in mammals other than man, is thus associated with the development of anatomical structures peculiarly associated with language (Masland 1972).

Based on many observations, it is generally concluded that human speech is a function of the neocortex, is restricted to highly specific areas and is lateralised to a dominant hemisphere usually on the left. Destruction of Wernicke's or Broca's areas in the left hemisphere or of the connections between these two areas uniformly produces major deficits in the comprehension or production of human speech. Lesions in other cortical areas or in the homologous areas in the right hemisphere produce either no speech defects or only transient deficits. In contrast, loci producing vocalisations in primates (other than Man) are equally distributed on the right and left sides of the brain (Robinson 1972).

While this quotation amply describes the specializations of the cortex with regard to language, it omits Robinson's additional examination of the role of limbic areas. These are concerned with vocalizations of an emotional valency that are not necessarily constructed in relation to grammar. These emotional sounds may be produced even by patients suffering from lesions in Broca's neocortical area. This is illustrated by Robinson's patient who, in addition to a major lesion of the left hemisphere involving the speech areas, was also a sufferer from manic-depressive psychosis. When manic, his speech faculty improved; under depression it diminished. Robinson suggests that human speech depends also upon an emotional system located in the limbic system which gives affect and nuance to the logical structure of utterances programmed cortically. This latter faculty is based in new 'circuitry' of the association areas and is largely independent of the phylogenetically older limbic structures that may be responsible for what Chance (p. 332) calls the 'agonic' and 'hedonic' modes of social interaction. In rational and logical discourse, the neocortical system is predominant. In times of emotional stress, however, the limbic system reclaims its old primacy and rational speech and thought are subordinated (Robinson 1972).

Speech is of course not solely the result of cerebral processes. The production of speech requires a talking apparatus, and here again man is unique. The production of graded signals in man has been greatly improved by the development of a specific set of anatomical conditions governing vocalization. In particular, the supra-laryngeal vocal tract acts as a sound filter in man because its shape can be changed by moving the tongue during the production of a sound. The shape of the pharynx constantly changes during the production of speech as the tongue moves forwards and backwards. These movements are vital for the formation of sounded consonants as well as vowels. Non-human primates lack the high degree of tongue mobility that is used by man for the production of a whole range of surds, labial, and dental consonants that combine to comprise the range of human language. It is indeed the precision of this graded signalling that allows the encoding of the vocabulary essential for reference and speech in our species. However rich the cognitive life of chimpanzees and gorillas may sometimes be, these animals remain biologically incapable of the specifically human mode of vocal discourse.

Figure 6.1 provides a summary of the possible sequences by which language is acquired ontogenetically and which may also represent a sequence of phylogenetic stages. Gestural motor patterns miming events are represented cognitively in sensorimotor structures. A simplification of gesture into signals with symbolic meaning is accompanied by the development of cognitive 'syntagmata'. In evolution, vocalization probably developed as the gestural language was largely replaced by signs in the facial–visual channel accompanied by vocalized breathing. This sequence is duplicated in mother–baby interaction; manual contact merges into facial–visual communication plus baby-talk. Human language has universal features both in the muscular and breathed controls of utterances and in the perceptual recognition of categories in graded sounds. It is likely that these have some neural basis, implying a genetic determination arising from natural selection of genes favouring language development. Languages and dialects are conventions acquired by learning. Infants have a strong predisposition to learn which is reinforced by social rewards from their mothers. Verbal play is an important component of practice and of speech creativity. The formal grammatical structure of language defines events in terms of time and place, allowing a rich development of the child's conceptual world.

Language allows man to construct plans and projects for action. Yet it also forms the basis for the construction of intellectual models of life processes that become whole systems of meaning whereby humans conceptualize their world of values and meanings. These conceptual models are largely based upon the elaboration of *metaphors* which guide and determine the way we view the world. An elaborated vocabulary is more than a list of names for objects and actions. It contains terms that stand in for processes that are described by reference to simpler, more easily comprehended ones. Jaynes (1976) writes: 'Consider the lan-

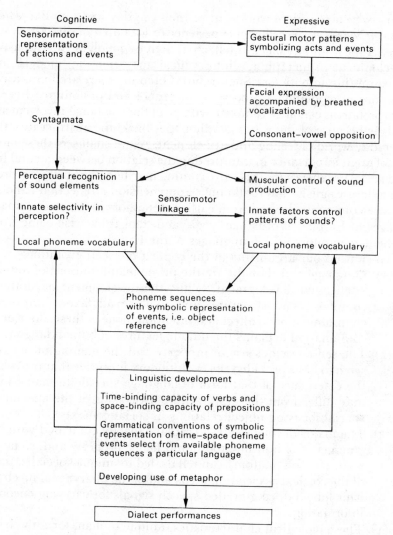

Fig. 6.1. Ontogenetic and phylogenetic progressions in the evolution of language.

guage we use to describe conscious processes. The most prominent group of words used to describe mental events are visual. We "see" solutions to problems the test of which may be "brilliant", and the person "brighter" and "clear-headed" as opposed to "dull".... These words are all metaphors and the mind–space to which they apply is a metaphor of actual space.'

Using words we 'grapple' with our problems seeking 'comprehension' as we 'mould' meanings for our use. Metaphors allow us to 'construct' a cognitive world out of the everyday and familiar when suitable words to describe an experience or idea are not directly available. Almost all advanced intellectual activity involves the extensive development of metaphor. Philosophical and scientific 'models' are based on this activity (see Snell 1960). Often too there are more ways than one of modelling a process by metaphor and profoundly diverse interpretations can arise complete with powerful emotional involvement. This is because of the way metaphor 'ties back' the abstract into the everyday world of feeling and attachment. As we shall see, these facts are of great importance in interpreting the relation between mental life and social organization. It is worth noting here how the abstract words of modern English, 'interpolation', 'apprehension', 'reflection', and so on, are commonly derived from earlier metaphors in the classical languages of Europe. Words like 'yoga' and 'taoist' likewise come from ancient metaphors in the languages of the East.

To sum up our arguments in the context of social evolution:

(1) Language and thought are the prime manifestations of human intellectual development. While the development of hunting, complex social structure, and tool-use all favour improved communication of affect and intention, none of these alone or in combination explains the unique features of human language.

(2) The self-conscious use of property and the naming of persons seem to have provided the evolutionary incentive that provoked the emergence of that form of language specific to man which may differ from the gestural linguistic skills of the apes in its special focus on object relations in social contexts.

(3) The major development of cranial capacity coincided with the emergence of hunting, tools, and hence property and, so far as studies of soft anatomy can tell us, led to unique specializations of the cortical association areas and of the pharyngeal mechanisms for producing graded speech signals for carrying encoded information.

(4) These biological characteristics, unique to man, form the basis of the subsequent societal development in our species.

(5) Language allows the internal representation of events by reference to objects and persons as if bound in space and time by grammatical constructs. The importance of this in representing past and future assemblies of events referring to relations between objects and persons is crucial for the development of civilization. The development of metaphor as a 'vehicle' for complex intellectual thought becomes the root of conceptual modelling.

Societal integration through exchange

Our discussion of the evolution of human society in the scavenging phase emphasized the tremendous importance of systems of reciprocating altruism. We have seen, too, how Trivers has emphasized their importance in the evolutionary development of the social organization of non-human primates and that these can be explained without contravention of Darwinian evolutionary principles. Certainly the baboons, especially the gelada, make use of reciprocation in several ways: for example, in giving aid to friends in socially competitive circumstances; possibly in homosexual behaviour between unmated males within 'bachelor groups'; between harem owners in defence against young male rivals; and between generations in the defence of two-male reproductive units.

All these reciprocations have a characteristic in common: there is a striking of 'bargains' in terms of behavioural response. There is a commitment to respond to one's 'friend' or 'colleague' in such a way that behavioural debts are paid. Without this commitment such a system could not be maintained and would lack a sociobiological explanation.

We can now see how such reciprocation would provide a firm basis for behavioural elaboration as soon as tools used as behavioural extensions began to play a key role in hominid interactions and became markers of users and owners. With the development of language and the naming of both objects and persons, reciprocating altruism would become represented internally in structures of thought and human beings, for the first time in animal life, could become conscious of the functioning of their own strategies. Language enables the logic of a strategy to be stated, examined, and developed. Here we can envisage the birth-pangs of morality and the loss of innocence. The book of Genesis is susceptible to a sociobiological interpretation.

A most significant historical development of reciprocating altruism occurred when the bargain was struck, not merely in terms of a reciprocation of acts, but also in terms of an exchange of tools, goods, and services. At this point human beings began to live not only within an ecology, but within an economy as well, an economy determined moreover by such conventions as wit might devise. And such conventions, while they could hardly be arbitrary in a belt-tightening ecology, none the less gave ample scope to cultural invention. Exchange, economy, culture, all take their source in the elaboration of reciprocation that language allowed.

Exchanges can occur between individuals in a variety of ways. A brief classification would suggest at least the following:

Intrasexual exchange—between members of the same sex
Intersexual exchange—between members of the opposite sex
Intergenerational exchange—between male or female parent and
                                          their sons or daughters

These three patterns may occur either within the family (intrafamil-
ial) or between families (interfamilial) of the same population deme or
group (intragroup) or they may occur between groups (intergroup).
Exchanges of the intergroup type may not, however, be specific to two
particular individuals. A group as a whole often contracts to exchange
articles with another. In this case the groups concerned are usually
represented by individuals who deal in their name. Exchanges may be
made in terms of raw materials, tools or weapons, products of manufacture or of the hunt, or in terms of some kind of service performed for
the benefit of a recipient. These services may involve the use of specialized implements or rare commodities. Services may also be of a social
nature, as in the arrangement of marriages and the exchange of brides.

The ecological context of a developing exchange economy remains a
crucial factor in determining its patterning and focus. The dispersion
system of the population will remain intimately correlated with the
ecological distribution of resources. Indeed, we here find ourselves
transversing themes already well argued with respect to non-linguistic
mammals (see Chapter 3). Hunter–gatherers will tend to require large
home ranges in arid areas and these ranges will tend to overlap greatly.
Defendability would be difficult and the location of limited water
sources would demand exploitation in common. A pattern of small
wide-ranging family units or kin groups is typical with a coming-
together for socialization at times of food abundance in a pattern
reminiscent of the chimpanzee. The regulation of socialization and
intergenerational competition requires ceremonial and rituals associated with marriage and the remembering of the dead.

In a richer ecology we can expect the home ranges of groups to be
smaller. Several families may opt to dwell together at a particular site
well protected from predatorial animals and the weather and defend-
able against other groups. Places such as caves often provided such
sites and could also become the locations where planning the hunt and
magical rites associated with ensuring the success of a hunt could be
practised and even pictured upon walls.

The occupation of a particular site entails a tendency to overexploit
the immediately surrounding area. As Hamilton and Watt (1970) have
put it, a 'central place system' is necessarily surrounded by a
biodeterioration zone, a zone of heavy exploitation, and then a less-
exploited zone further out. The biodeterioration zone is that area in
which the countryside is much modified by human activity itself, paths

interlace, vegetation is cut down, middens are exposed, and so on. The outer areas of exploitation may be far from the base and may be exploited to a degree by neighbouring groups. It seems that in a central place system, as in the more nomadic type, boundaries would not necessarily be defended owing to the high cost of patrolling them. In any case the population density of these early hominids was unlikely at first to have entailed great competition. As the numbers grew to match the supplies available, competition would have arisen.

Individuals living in relatively small groups with a core of close kin would have spent most of their time in the search for the resources that guarantee subsistence. The home base, whether permanent or seasonal, provides a focal point for the social life of the groups. This in-group activity expresses the basic life-strategies of each individual in interaction with his or her companions.

The coming-together of the social unit has a functional basis in primitive exchange. It is here that the daily nourishment for the group is assembled and redistributed. Gatherers bring in their vegetables, fruit, roots, and berries; hunters their meat. Where several families participate together resources are distributed and each family obtains its share. Within the family itself there is a further distribution between members with especial attention to the children. This then is the meal— a focus for sharing out commodities that sustain each group member.

We need to note here how different the human meal is from the crude relinquishing of excess resources between hunter chimpanzees (see p. 71). The contrast is explicable in terms of the major differences in social organization between chimpanzee and man. The formation of familial units with long-term bonded relationships between the male and his females is not a chimpanzee feature and among gorillas it is associated with evenly distributed and abundant food on forest floors. In man this basic structure has come to characterize the primary social association between the sexes and between parents and offspring, often living in areas of considerable dietary restriction. As we have seen, it is also the context for a primary division of labour in the maintenance of basic hunter–gatherer subsistence. The stronger, risk-taking males, especially perhaps youngsters of several families acting in common, become the providers of meat. The women, while taking care of the children, are the collectors of vegetable materials. This division of labour can function only in relation to the inclusive fitness of individuals if reciprocation between the sexes occurs and if their children, and those of related dependents, are given adequate nourishment. The human family as a rearing unit with associated kin is essentially a focus for nepotism as well as for a reciprocation of services between the sexes. The 'meal' expresses in a particularly compact event the operation of these ancient sociobiological principles.

Meals also allow exchanges of another sort. Information channelled through language is shared, the past reviewed, the present discussed, and the future planned. The meal is thus an occasion for information transfer. A hive of bees or a roost of birds may allow information about resources to pass from one individual to another. Language, however, gives this information transfer a precision found nowhere else. We can see, too, how meetings modelled on the meal, but now serving exclusively for communication, developed by a simple reduction of mastication in favour of talk. The modern committee meeting, with coffee and biscuits in the middle, is an obvious example.

Communication in which both past and future are present is the source of deliberation, reflection, and planning. These applications of language will find expression within the set of ideas by which the group understands its world and situation. Since such understanding is limited, it follows that the process is in terms of a belief system rather than an objective analysis of a modern type. Meals may come to embody rituals in which the past is expiated or the future coerced, and much of this will be based on a collective unconscious of limbic rather than cerebral origins.

As Morton (unpublished MS) in a survey of some of the implications of exchange, has written,

The practice of exchange is accompanied by the recognition of reciprocal obligations: credit, debt, theft and others—an act is carried out, or an object is given or taken, on the understanding that the other party has acted in a similar way in the past, or is expected to do so in the future. The recognition of reciprocal obligation extends outside the economic sphere to cover many aspects of human social activity; justice and revenge are two important developments in this respect, and property rights are closely bound up with reciprocal obligations. Group or individual ownership of property, in the sense of the prior right of use of tools and other articles by the manufacturers, need not necessarily imply the recognition of reciprocal obligations. But this recognition does add important new dimensions to the concept of property, by introducing norms for its transfer or disposal via reciprocal transactions. Acts of giving, receiving and taking acquire a new significance.

This new significance, we may add, includes a patterning of expectations that come increasingly to dominate human interactions. The very logic of human discourse, as Humphrey has stressed (p. 128), implies such expectations, for the very terms in which we speak are transactional. The meal, the forerunner of all collective bargaining, did much to mould language into its transactional shape, and the meal is a product of family life. Thought is rooted in our social nature, determines it, and is determined by it.

Summary

(1) Early in his evolutionary career man became a hunter. The success of this adaptation has dominated the course of his development and his cognitive capacities are probably due to the very large proportion of his history spent in this phase. Agriculture and industry occupy only a tiny and late fragment of the time man has existed on the planet.

(2) The major hunting adaptation of man concerns his capacity to show adaptively variable behaviour. This is due to a tremendous increase in his intelligence and learning ability. Intelligence is the base and language the means for the enormous richness of human social exchange upon which the structures of culture are built. Surveys of animal learning show that the complexity of behavioural acquisition and the ability to apply it insightfully increase up the animal scale and culminate in our own species.

(3) Intelligence produces adaptively variable behaviour within the lifetime of an individual. Recent scholars have argued for four main factors contributing to intelligence. These are a capacity to delay an instinctive response in favour of a pause for exploration, a memory store for acquired information, a capacity to abstract and generalize in the making of comparisons and in the exchange of propositions, and a sensorimotor capacity to carry out the acquired response. Intelligent behaviour probably originated in the interpolation of exploratory responses within appetitive behaviour that delayed the performance of consummatory acts of an innate sequence.

(4) In higher mammals living in complex societies it is important to delay the performance of a response to another so that some evaluation of its appropriateness and outcome may be made. A degree of motivational control through delayed responsiveness is considered to be of value under these circumstances and the 'equilibration' of emotional responding is a crucial development in cultural adaptation using applied intelligence. The enlargement of the neocortex in man may be a response to selection pressures favouring increased powers of equilibration and abstraction.

(5) These powers seem especially characteristic of individuals in social groups that acquire abilities in influencing others through the attention that is paid to them. Confidence, equilibrated emotional responding, and analytical intelligence seem to be factors involved in charisma in our own species and to be important also in good parenting of children. Intelligence is multifactorial and individuals probably differ greatly in the relative contributions of the four factors to their behaviour.

(6) In both human beings and chimpanzees intellectual capacity often seems to exceed the demands made upon it in terms of the frequency with which high-order activities are required. It seems likely however that the complexities of social transactions have been underestimated

and that it is in social living itself that human intelligence found both its origin and its prime utilization.

(7) Human social life is moreover closely bound up with the development of the hunting economy. The colossal expansion of the human brain coincided in time with the advent of the hunter–gatherer mode of life and continued to enlarge through most of the period dominated by this behaviour. Tool use and gregariousness are insufficient in themselves to account for the emergence of intelligence. Many sociable animals are not conspicuously more intelligent than their more solitary relatives. The origin of the human intellect must lie in the specific conditions of social elaboration in hunting hominids.

(8) Human beings are facultative carnivores; hunting skills have to be learned. The capture of large prey demands highly organized collaborative strategies of attack, pursuit, and kill in which groups of men act together in preplanned co-ordination and often under leadership. The hunting 'culture' required a coding of information relating to hunting and a capacity to transmit information rapidly and effectively between individuals. Language is the social enabling device that ensures the effective social participation required by hunting. Not only are the movements of the prey predicted but so also are the movements and relations between individual hunters and their family relatives.

(9) Chimpanzee language has given us some clues to the origins of speech but it is essentially a parallel development, a separate sort of language from our own, far more rooted in 'here-and-now' personal interaction than in references to objects and their relations. Human language binds events in space and time within a web of logical relations governed by grammar and metaphor.

(10) Probably the emergence of property, division of labour, and the concepts of inheritance and relatedness were all features that precipitated the development of the characteristically human language structure. Representation of events may originally have been far more gestural, speech emerging later. Sensorimotor intelligence, as Piaget termed it, may have preceded the emergence of a capacity to utilize logical propositions. The child acquires language mainly through transactions with mother involving gestures of many types including facial expression and eye contact as well as speech.

(11) Language is rooted in a unique brain structure imposing perceptual and motor constraints that are universal to the species and thus probably dependent upon genetic control. Language is based in biological hardware and dependent upon a cultural programme fed socially into the biocomputer early in life.

(12) Hunting, facilitated by language, resulted in the accumulation of local surpluses which allowed the development of primitive economies of exchange. We have already traced the origins of exchanges in the

sociobiology of reciprocal altruism. Exchange between related families is advantageous to both and the development of a network of exchange would easily develop from such a basis. The bargain in this form of reciprocating altruism is no longer a simple social or instrumental act but an exchange of tools, goods, supplies, and services. Economy is at this point emerging from socio-ecology and with it an elaborating set of conventions that form the rights and obligations of a community. The structure of a society practising an economic system of ecological exploitation will however remain controlled ultimately by the constraints imposed by ecological factors. An economy develops in relation to its exploitative capacity and the availability of resources either directly or through exchange.

(13) Social exchange began in the family meal when food was partitioned and information exchanged. The family meal was however not independent of the partitioning and exchanging process that went on between successful hunters. The use of token provisioning remains a social pivot in many circumstances in which human beings exchange information or resources.

7 Sociobiology and human social evolution

> Much of what passes for theory in studies of animal behaviour and sociobiology is semantic manoevering to obtain a maximum congruence of classifications. This process is useful but better described as concept formation. Real theory is postulational-deductive. To formulate it we first identify the parameters, then we define the relations between them as precisely as we can, and finally we construct models in order to relentlessly extend and to test the postulates . . . Its results are often nonobvious or even counterintuitive. The important thing is that they exceed the capacity of unaided intuition.
>
> Edward O. Wilson 1975

The new paradigm

Ethologists have always been aware that at least in principle their theories should be applicable to man (e.g. Thorpe 1962). Darwin had followed up his theory of natural selection with its direct application to humanity (1871), and as good evolutionists ethologists tend to take the same path. The result has been conflict; anthropologists, psychologists, and sociologists have almost universally responded to biological interpretations of key themes in these subjects with a protectionist alarm. Rather than engaging in effective debate they have for the most part merely rejected biological theories with assertions about their inapplicability to man.

There has been a reason for this: the systems of ideas basic to these sciences have been fundamentally opposed to evolutionary approaches and are based instead upon explanatory models that are rooted in assumptions resting in philosophical empiricism. Psychologists have assumed that all that is distinctively human rests upon the acquisition of behaviour through learning. This behaviourist assumption implies not only that there are no innate 'givens' in behaviour but that human beings can in principle learn to do or think anything. Anthropologists, in their version of this paradigm, assume that everything that is distinctively human is based upon cultural transmission through history, such transmission being itself dependent upon learning. The result of these twin sets of assumptions is that for the greater part of this century it has been impossible to relate biology to human social behaviour in spite of the obvious fact that human beings, like dogs and cats, were also organisms, phenotypical expressions of genotypes, individual collectivities of genes drawn from a species-specific pool. This has also meant that no theory purporting to account for human nature has been able to establish roots in theories explaining the animal kingdom. Man and beast have remained as rigorously separated as if special creation were still an effective theory in science.

The failure to respond to biological and specifically evolutionary initiatives was anchored in a series of profound misconceptions. First, the misuse of Darwinian ideas by social theorists early in the century, the so-called social Darwinists, and their implicit and sometimes explicit support of illiberal political doctrines in society, put the whole subject in bad odour, especially for those attracted by Marxism. Secondly, the *naïveté* of some early biologists' pronouncements could not possibly match the social scientists' awareness of the enormity of cultural diversity between human populations. Thirdly, the ecological adaptiveness of many cultural features was obscured through concentration on the details of human interaction, on myths and legends, without an appropriate analysis of the comparative economic bases of the social systems that support them. Lastly, the dependence of culture on language, which animals do not have, seemed to exclude effectively any consideration of social traits apart from those of cultural complexity. All this meant that the ecological relativity of human culture and the adaptive radiation of cultures in human history, together with the obvious parallels to adaptive radiation in the rest of the animal kingdom, went as unremarked as did the existence of human universals that clearly predicate a species-specific social structuring underlying cultural variance.

In the 1960s the renewal of research on the social lives of wild primates brought the theories of field ethologists within striking distance of man. The description of the adaptive radiation of primate societies and its correlation with ecology (Crook and Gartlan 1966) provoked social anthropologists in quest of a more fundamental theory to a vigorous reconsideration of evolutionary theory and comparative analysis in relation to human social history (e.g. DeVore 1971; Tiger and Fox 1966; Fox 1967).

Unfortunately at this stage ethology itself revealed a fundamental weakness. While making great advances in socio-ecology and showing again and again the adaptiveness of animal societies in relation to the environment, ethologists failed to anchor these demonstrations in an explicitly causal evolutionary theory. Niko Tinbergen experimentally verified the existence of selection pressures operating on behavioural traits in the field, but his conclusions were not yet related to population genetics. The outcome was a sudden outpouring of speculations that were very weakly based in actual evolutionary theory. These speculations, mostly consisting of elaborated advocacies of inspired guesswork, soon encountered difficulties. While the popular books of Lorenz (1963), Morris (1967), and Ardrey (1966) showed that biological explanations must be taken seriously in any debate about human social origins, the level of discourse remained that of dinner-table conversation. Sadly this meant that once again serious students underestimated the capacity of biological theories to contribute in this area of discourse.

Reynolds (1976), for example, in a scholarly work which treats in depth biological contributions to human behaviour, finally dismisses the claims of these writers on the grounds that

> We are now arguing against the idea that there is something within Man's nature or biogrammar that in some way structures his social dimensions. That may have been so up to the time when the species *Homo* first emerged, but now a very different and rather opposite situation prevails, namely that there is something in social structures and structures of thought that provides a more or less workable matrix for the physiology of the human nervous system. . . .

While Reynolds admitted that many human biological functions impose limits on human flexibility, he insisted that it is social structure operating through language and thought that patterns 'the biology of the individual by subjecting him to physiological stresses and strains'. This disjunction can be avoided by a careful examination of contemporary sociobiology.

It was the emphasis on the natural selection of the individual (Fisher, R. 1930; Williams 1966) as opposed to evolution by group selection (Wynne-Edwards 1962) that provoked theorists to attempt careful analyses of the evolutionary process responsible for altruistic behaviour. Since altruism is a major feature of primate and human behaviour, any successful theory of altruism was bound to make an impact on the social sciences. The theory that emerged (Chapter 3) has in fact revolutionized our comprehension of animal social behaviour, provided the underpinning of social ethology by population genetics which was so serious a lack, and now promises a biological basis for explanations of human social life. So radical a development is nothing less than a major shift in our comprehension of man.

A change of this order does not come about without opposition. In particular the anthropologist Sahlins (1977) has attempted to invalidate the whole sociobiological enterprise in anthropology, an endeavour undoubtedly fired by E. O. Wilson's excessive biological reductionism in his summary of sociobiological principles (Wilson 1975). Sophisticated sociobiologists are today well aware of the complexity of human life and the difficulty of applying Darwinian interpretations to it. Their successes so far, in my view, amply justify the endeavour. The debate is no longer concerned with the relevance of biology but with the complex ways in which biological and social information programme the behaviour of interacting individuals. To this we now turn.

Sociobiological theory applied to human society

No contemporary sociobiologist is arguing for a direct genetic determination of complex cultural attributes in man. Rather the developing theory emphasizes:

(1) the multiplicity of levels involved in the causation of human behaviour;

(2) that man's biological inheritance consists of broadly strategic guidelines that constrain what is acquired by learning within wide yet predetermined pathways;

(3) that man's prime evolved characteristic lies less in behaviour itself than in the capacity for novel adaptations and flexible responses to diverse situations;

(4) that the major biostrategy served by constraints on learning concerns reproductive effectiveness;

(5) that as a K-selected species a key aspect of reproduction involves nepotistic altruism and reciprocation between individuals and groups;

(6) that the unit of selection, as with other organisms, is primarily that of the individual;

(7) that warfare between groups sometimes produces group replacement or the reproductive subordination of one group to another so that a complex patterning of group and individual selection may be operating in our species (Lewontin 1970).

Animals adhere to evolved strategies of behaviour through the expression of motivational systems. We may therefore suppose that in Man a feeling of happiness is registered when behaviour is broadly within the guidelines that lead to the achievement of a biological goal of high inclusive fitness. Since motivational systems may sometimes operate in opposition we can argue that the optimization of an 'inclusive satisfaction' of an individual's behaviour will be in accordance with strategies that tend to maximize inclusive fitness. This proposition is a focus for much debate and must become a major area of research; the relation between personal contentment and strategies for maximizing inclusive fitness is at best often obscure and theoretically complex. For example, many motivational systems operate on the principle of reducing deviations from a position of homoeostasis to a point (the *Sollwert*) which is often more or less a state of rest. Biostrategies must set the *Sollwerts* of motivational systems in such a way that goals such as effective reproduction are achieved. The mechanisms involved here require much further analysis. In addition, social goals, for example self-esteem, are often associated with interactions that are by no means clearly related to differential reproduction. Whether there is in fact here an indirect connection with reproductive success or inclusive fitness requires careful examination.

The benefits received by an individual from his or her behaviour need *ultimately* to refer to inclusive fitness if sociobiological theory is to maintain its potency. Yet it is not supposed that this relation must be direct. Benefits on some *proximate* scale of motivational satisfaction may be only very indirectly associated with reproduction of self or relatives. The question as to what connections may exist between proximate systems of motivation (and the learning that occurs in relation to the emotional rewards provided by them) and the fulfilment of bio-strategies is the key problem area of human sociobiology.

Neither of the two leading contributors to this area (Alexander 1974, 1975, 1977; Trivers 1971, 1972, 1974) supposes that individuals are fully aware of the ultimate strategies that underlie their motivational needs and expressions. Indeed, a number of strategic devices—manipulation of children, cheating, marital infidelity—that tend to maximize inclusive fitness under certain circumstances may conflict with stated social propriety and with personal estimations of self-esteem. The task is one of balancing motivational promptings that might increase reproductive success against ethical values derived from social convention. This, indeed, is an area where we may suppose the reproductive strategy to act largely through unconscious promptings which are socially managed by the 'ego'. Freud's tripartite characterization of the human personality structure is thus given a renewed meaning. The id may be seen as representing those inclinations that are inadmissable to the super-ego but which tend to fulfil the strategic need to maximize reproductive efficacy. The 'unconscious' is thus no mere repository of traumatic memories acquired under conflict with the parent in early childhood. It is also the psychological space within which societally inadmissable inclinations of biostrategic origin exert an influence detectable in dreams, in irrational behaviour, and also in conscious, if socially dangerous, choices of personal interaction. It is in this area that differences in the biostrategies of the two sexes engender conflict between sexual partners and the attendant problem of their social and personal resolution. The origins of these mental complexities have a long history.

Contemporary sociobiology has no need to adopt an oversimplified model of man, nor to indulge in gross reductionism. It is essential to recognize that in studying human beings we are explicitly aware that the level of behavioural determination is unique in the animal kingdom.

The behavioural adaptation of primitive animals such as the reptiles is based on stereotyped innate patterns of response which have been very finely adjusted by natural selection to predictable details of each species' niche. In mammals, with the development of control over body temperature, the possibility of a wide radiation into less predictable, indeed sometimes highly variable, niches in the same environments emerged. The mammalian capacity to adapt to general ecological changes is also dependent on the emergence of learning capacities that modify behaviour adaptively with a flexibility of which no reptile is capable. Learning is often associated with elaborated societies in which evolutionary stable strategies for social cohesion, altruism, and reciprocation have emerged. Clearly a high level of social intelligence has been attained.

Between the non-human primates and man a further cognitive emergence occurred which, although based on earlier mammalian mechanisms, is unique. The main features of this new level of cognitive organization, which will be studied in detail in later chapters are:

(1) A capacity to represent events to oneself not only through sensorimotor memory and imagery but by symbols utilized in thought.

(2) A capacity to invent and follow complex and variable rules of behaviour in the elaboration of techniques and social skills.

(3) A capacity to experience oneself as an agent, and to form cognitive constructs that 'identify' that 'self' as an agent.

(4) A capacity to apprehend intuitively another person's current experiential state and so to empathize with him or her.

(5) A capacity to interact richly with other people by maintaining an 'identity' that relates to the apprehended 'identity' of another.

(6) A capacity to develop criteria for action (values) that determine choice when alternative lines of action become conceivable in a social situation.

(7) A capacity which projects one's value-loaded representation of the perceived world back on to reality. Reality is thus experienced as coloured by the values that determine an individual's social action within it. This projection then becomes subject to validation by companions. A consensus of ideas in a group comes to form their system of beliefs or 'ideology' that both 'explains' their human predicament and legitimizes their solutions to it.

(8) These powers comprise a process by which the individual relates to his environment and especially to his social companions by reference to a knowledge of self. The system as a whole is called the individual's 'self-process' (Horrocks and Jackson 1972).

Figure 7.1 represents the successive adaptations of three representative animal categories, reptile, mammal, and man, to three environ-

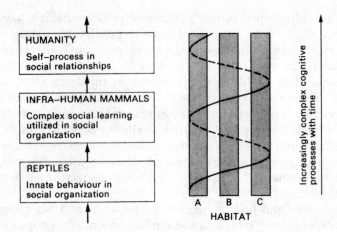

Fig. 7.1. The evolutionary spiral from reptiles to man showing adaptive radiation across three habitats and the progressive emergence of cognitive means of adaptation at successive levels.

ments and the emergence at three separate levels of successively more complex cognitive processes resulting in mastery over the more variable features of the environments occupied. Cognitive processes emerge with increased complexity as life extends itself as a result of the evolutionary process. We need not assume that the spiral has stopped moving yet.

In Man selection has clearly operated less on the details of behaviour patterns but more on the improvement and development of cognitive capacity. This capacity is capable of managing the enormous range of environmental and societal contingencies with which human beings have to deal. Yet it also operates within a species-specific set of behavioural constraints that provide the 'universals' of human social life. It is the discovery and analysis of these universals that has been the main support for developing a sociobiology of man. These we shall now examine, returning in Chapter 9 to a detailed study of the 'self-process'.

Species universals in man

Reproduction

The societal organization within which human reproduction occurs conforms to expectations aroused by the comparative study of mammals. The human sexes are mildly dimorphic with an emphasis on greater physical strength (but not necessarily on greater vigour, efficiency, or durability) in the male. Such characteristics in mammals are generally associated with a degree of polygyny which is also a characteristic of most human societies. Humans are bonding creatures, and men and women form sexual alliances of long duration. The human sex bonds parallel those of harem-forming baboons, and nowhere in our species does there exist either the sort of loose promiscuity typical of the chimpanzee or the totally strict monogamy of the gibbon. Human sexual *relationships* are thus far from arbitrary. While polygynous unions occur in the majority of human societies, monogamous ones are now perhaps the most generally common, for usually only a minority of wealthy men can afford a second wife. Marriage, in this broad sense, is thus universal in our species. Unusual systems, such as the polyandry of Tibet, are specific adjustments to unusual social and economic circumstances (see Goldstein 1971; Aziz 1978; and below p. 216).

Polygyny in mammals is associated, as Trivers (1972) has shown, with differential parental involvement in rearing children and with subtly contrasting reproductive strategies. Male human primates in general may be expected to maximize their reproductive success by adding females to their families whenever economically possible and to court and mate women other than their spouses, especially perhaps if the care of subsequent children can be guaranteed. A woman, by contrast, is likely to be more concerned with maintaining her husband's interest in caring for her and her children. Women in polygynous households are thus likely to be competitive and to prefer monogamy if possible. These sociobiological expectations are broadly born out by a consideration of human sexual relationships. Where an ethic of marital fidelity forms part of a societal system of legitimation one may expect males sometimes to 'cheat', a 'double standard' to arise in a proportion of families, and problems of sexual guilt and marital reparation to occur.

The human marriage system is also associated with a number of obsessive male concerns:

(1) male control over the exchange of women as commodities in kinship systems (Lévi-Strauss 1969);
(2) male purchase of wives (bride price);
(3) male concern with the chastity of wives on marriage;
(4) greater concern over female than over male adultery in many societies;
(5) a widespread conviction that men should be sexually experienced at marriage but women should be virgins;
(6) the greater age of males on marrying.

This imbalance in the sexual concerns of men and women and the imposition of male anxieties on females through their greater physical strength individually and collectively can be explained sociobiologically. While a woman can be in no doubt about the fact that her child is hers, a man may almost always be subject either to reasonable or unreasonable doubt. He can be fooled into believing himself a father when he is not. Clearly to invest in rearing a child that is not his own is to lower his inclusive fitness considerably. Selection is likely to have operated in all primates with polygynous reproductive systems to produce mechanisms or susceptabilities that reduce the possibility of male cuckoldry. The listed features of male obsession in human societies all seem related to this fact. Control over the sexual behaviour of women is the way men insure their reproductive investments.

The greater age of males on marriage can be explained in terms of reproductive potential. A young virgin clearly has greater potential than an older woman, while an older male is likely to have greater protective expertise, social influence, and possibly wealth to offer the would-be mother of children.

The contemporary development of women's 'liberation' from these and other sexually based constraints needs to be related to this sociobiological background; not, however, with any assertion as to the rightness or wrongness of human biology. The development of the modern means for self-control of fertility means that for the first time in history women have become free to decide whether they wish to be mothers or not. The need to negotiate new patterns of relationship freed from the old double standard, and based both upon the freedom of women and the technical feasibility of determining who is father to whom, is clearly apparent so long as sexual behaviour is related to strategies rooted in considerations of inclusive fitness. Having become aware of the biohistorical origins of our marital systems we are yet free to plan alternatives with different genetic implications. We are not bound by the past; yet cannot foretell in exactly what ways inheritance constrains possible futures (see also p. 222).

Dominance and prestige
The contrasting biostrategies of men and women are related not only to differences in physical strength but also to a supposed psychological and social dominance of men over women. In fact this matter is complex, and the ways in which men and women influence one another have been far more subtle throughout history than either chauvinist male or liberationist female writers usually allow. There can be little doubt that the greater aggressiveness of men socially is based on endocrine contrasts between the sexes and that, as for many other male mammals, male aggression serves in sexual competition: in the acquisition of a mate or mates and in the preservation of his investment against the risk of cuckoldry. Women are by no means passive participants in this process and have their own biological and social interests at stake.

Jerome Barkov (1975) derives human systems of status and prestige from the dominance hierarchies of infrahuman primates. He argues that 'natural selection has transformed our ancestors' general primate tendency to strive for high social rank into a need to maintain self-esteem . . . the main way in which we strive to maintain our self-esteem is by seeking prestige'.

It has long been doubted how far dominance hierarchies are actually the result of a *striving* for high social rank. The issue is further muddled by associating such a striving with the idea from Chance and Jolly (1970) that rank order arises out of the attention paid by subordinates towards more dominant individuals of a group. Social ranking and attention structure in monkey groups result from competitive encounters for commodities and for access to preferred companions (see p. 75). The hierarchy is the result of aggressive interactions but is not necessarily the consequence of differential striving for status as such. In fact several observers, especially Rowell (1972), have argued that the social positions of individual monkeys are maintained more by the avoidance of subordinates than by the threats of aggressors. In a recent review Deag (1977) uses data from wild barbary macaques to show that hierarchies can be the outcome of both assertion and avoidance but that the actual differentiation of rank in a group may be related to the degree of competition within it.

The idea of 'striving' for high social rank suggests an unvarying motivation for the consequences of persistent challenges that arise, particularly when a young male is seeking mates in a group into which he has transferred, or when social access to a preferred grooming partner is persistently denied to a female. In discussing the adaptive significance of these behaviours Deag argues that the behaviour used in approach—avoidance and other agonistic interactions can be assessed by its contribution to the performer's fitness. The hierarchy is a summation of numerous interactions. Advantages to the winner of an aggressive interaction which may lead to higher rank may include: (a) access to food or water; (b) increased feeding efficiency; (c) ability to intercede in fights involving kin; (d) priority of access to receptive females; and (e) freedom to participate in social interactions. A loser can minimize his loss of fitness by retreating before injury, not indulging in repeated contests which he will lose and not challenging older animals until strong enough to do so. Given a long life it may pay an individual to avoid conflict when young or weak or in an unfavourable social setting. A rise in rank may come about through ageing, through a change in the group, or through deliberate exertion to gain access to mates. Although not all studies confirm the finding, it is probably true that on average sexually assertive males who win access to females are also the ones who in repeated trials have emerged as the most dominant.

It follows that natural selection favours those performances of an individual that in agonistic situations produce the optimum trade-off, ultimately expressible in terms of inclusive fitness. In the gelada baboon, for example, the timing of an aggressive attempt at acquiring a harem from another male is related to one or another of several strategies and the outcome depends upon the responses of the females (p. 82). It is probably true, as Barkov argues, that at no point in human evolution was social hierarchy not manifested, but it remains simplistic to say that 'If human and non-human social dominance have . . . been continuous, they must necessarily be homologous.' New processes may well have emerged in man that make the connection tenuous. Indeed, Barkov's further argument implies that this is so.

This argument hinges around the model of motivation implied for the maintenance of self-esteem in humans. Barkov derives it directly from a 'drive' to dominate. 'With the development of a sense of self, our ancestors' primate tendency to seek high social rank would have been transformed. . . . The social dominance imperative would have taken the form of an imperative to evaluate the self as higher in rank than others: to evaluate the self as higher than others is to maintain self esteem'. Can these higher-order cognitive categories be derived simply from a motivation to dominate?

Human beings are of course often highly competitive and social rank, as in infrahuman primates, may be a product of agonistic behaviour. In man such competition is conducted through ritual and display rather than through direct conflict. Has natural selection had anything to do with these behaviours? Behaviour that maintains self-esteem may certainly be said to maintain or enhance inclusive fitness simply because it is also associated with good mental health, while low self-esteem is associated with social ineptness, negative attitudes to others, and illusions concerning one's own status (LeVine 1973). Effective reproductive behaviour and family life may be denied those for whom low self-esteem is damaging. In addition, high social status has in many societies been clearly associated with easy access to women, large polygynous families, and sometimes, as in the case of the Emperor of China, an unlimited and potentially reproductive harem. Such cases may not be typical, and in considering them in this way several distinct social processes may easily be confounded.

Prestige may rest on many diverse criteria, as Barkov points out. Some criteria, such as a knowledge of the Koran, for example, are by no means necessarily associated with reproductive success nor are they necessarily dependent upon overt competition. Social comparison is certainly an evaluative process but not necessarily always a competitive one. Individuals of high status, furthermore, are not necessarily always envied, for some of them carry great burdens of responsibility. High prestige undoubtedly confers some social advantages but there are also costs in the form of restrictions on individual action. Although having a Pope in the family may have effects on other relatives, and hence bear biological fruits through an indirect nepotism, the costs of ministerial indiscretions in the bedroom may be high, as numerous scandals show. While human beings often contest for satisfaction in terms of visions of personal esteem, the maximization of dominance does not necessarily relate to biological fitness.

Indeed in human affairs the ability to manoeuvre social situations and to influence affairs often depends less upon gross dominance and assertiveness than upon a subtlety of motivational equilibration that sometimes attributes personal success to another in order to achieve a result. Odysseus rather than Achilles was the strategist who brought about the fall of Troy. While Achilles in his aggressive assertion died young, Odysseus went on to make the voyage that was at once a journey in the world and into himself. In man it is the subtlety with which assertion is expressed rather than dominance itself which is socially significant. While both rest upon the same psychophysiological system as that of other primates, it is in the self-reflective control of personal expression that the especially human traits are found.

Incest avoidance and kinship systems
Incest taboos are an almost universal feature of human sexuality. There is a simple biological explanation for this. There is ample evidence to show that inbreeding between close relatives leads to both a reduced fertility and a lowered viability of offspring. Many mechanisms have been evolved in animals to reduce inbreeding and the human avoidance of incest seems to be one of them. The variety of prohibitions regarding the degree of relatedness tolerated for marital partners is, however, enormous.

Outbreeding exposes fewer deleterious genes in the offspring, whereas a degree of successful inbreeding promotes a larger proportion of one's own genes in subsequent generations. Alexander (1977) argues for an optimum balance at about the first-cousin level (Fig. 7.2). This corresponds in fact to the approximate distance in relationship between spouses preferred in many human societies. Alexander suggests that the preferred level of relationship tends to be greater when distant cousins are available and close when heritable resources lose their value as a result of extensive partition. Nomads with few resources that are inherited are expected to marry further out than farmers or titled families.

The application of a cost–benefit analysis from a biological (genetic) standpoint is both feasible and is required in any study of complex human marital systems. It seems likely that such systems exist to balance the cultural and biological advantages of nepotism against the

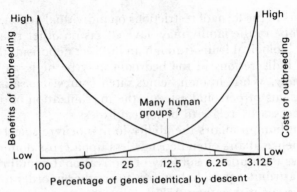

FIG. 7.2. The relationship between the benefits and costs of outbreeding. It is inferred that they tend to balance near the level of first cousins in most human societies.

need for an appropriate degree of outbreeding to maximize inclusive fitness. Needless to say, both the partners and the relatives of both partners will be interested in securing an optimum outcome.

Figure 7.3 depicts Alexander's (1977) chart of potential relationships between an individual (ego) and genetic relatives that can enhance inclusive fitness through nepotistic alliance. 'Reproduction will be maximised when the benefits from egocentric activities and reciprocal transactions maximally exceed their costs, and when their benefits are channeled to the closest relatives with the greatest ability to use the benefits to maximise the reproduction of their relatives in their turn.' In Man nepotistic altruism to children and relatives' children generalizes to include reciprocity between relatives, including distant ones, and finally reciprocity between non-relatives encoded in the conventions of particular societies. Each individual is thus situated within a complex web of interpersonal transactions which, to the degree to which they benefit an individual's reproduction in terms of predicting his inclusive fitness, can be considered in terms of genetic costs and benefits. The kinship, marital, and resource exchange systems of human societies are all likely to have genetic effects interpretable in terms of nepotistic and reciprocal altruism. Of particular significance for an individual's inclusive fitness is the marital system which governs how his or her children reproduce. The kinship systems are the means whereby human societies regulate marital choice under rules of material inheritance which, in that resources bear heavily upon reproduction over generations, are not at all irrelevant to considerations of fitness.

Now it is precisely this proposition that the anthropologist Sahlins has set out to destroy (Sahlins 1977). He provides detailed examples of how the stated kin relationships of human groups fail to correspond to genetic relationships. Thus a descent system may identify the son of a man's brother as a person belonging to the clan of descendants from an ancestor while excluding the son of a sister. Alternatively, in a different society where matrilineal descent operates, a sister's son may be a man's own proper heir. Kinship terminology and descent systems are symbolizations of the social order within which people behave and, in Sahlins' view, these symbolizations are unrelated to biological inheritance.

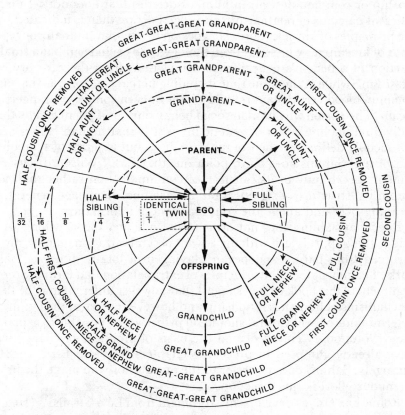

FIG. 7.3. Genetic relatives potentially available to an individual 'ego' for reproductively self-serving nepotism. Arrows indicate likely net flows of benefits. Half the genes of parent and offspring are identical by immediate descent. Other relationships are averages. Dotted lines indicate closest relatives other than ego, thus the most likely alternative sources of nepotistic benefits. Widths of lines indicate likely relative flows of benefits to or from ego, based on the combination of genetic relatedness and ability of recipients to use the benefits in reproduction. Extreme lateral relatives are less likely to be encountered or identified because of social or geographic distance, extreme vertical relatives because of their separation in time. Double-headed arrows indicate relatives whose statuses in regard to need of benefits or ability to use them to reproduce, and ability to give benefits, are doubtful owing to the uncertainty of age relationships of the individuals involved. (Thus, one's second cousin may be much younger, much older, or about the same age; one's sibling, on the other hand, is much more likely to be of comparable age.) Relatives on the right side of the diagram are those resulting from monogamous marriages; polygyny results in relatives indicated on the left. (From Alexandev 1977.)

The apparent arbitrariness of kinship systems and their symbolic roots leads Sahlins to a rigorous separation of biology and society. His is a return to Kroeber's old theme (1917) which split biology from the social sciences. Sahlins asserts that 'there is not a single system of marriage, post-marital residence, family organization, interpersonal kinship or common descent in human societies that does not set up a different calculus of relationship and social action than is indicated by the principles of kin selection'. He goes on to say that 'human conceptions of kinship may be so far from biology as to exclude all but a small fraction of a person's genealogical connections from the category of 'close kin', while at the same time including in that category, as sharing common blood very distant related people or even complete strangers'. Again 'The reason why human social behaviour is not organized by the individual maximization of genetic interest is that human beings are not socially defined by their organic qualities but in terms of symbolic attributes.' Sahlins goes on to point out that E. O. Wilson discusses human speech only in its function of communication rather than as within its 'structure of signification' or meaning. Language generates meaning over and above the conveyancing of information.

But what Sahlins does not do is to provide any theory which will bridge this gap. It is as if with the advent of symbolization man became divorced from nature and began playing in a totally different 'ball park'. I cannot agree. The principles of extrapolation that form the root argument of this book (p. 11) suggest that however different may be the mechanisms of human relationship and however powerful the cultural determinants of behaviour it should, in principle, be possible to explain their evolutionary emergence on the basis of processes of change we have already glimpsed in preceding chapters (see also Etter 1978). Strangely, Sahlins does not refer to the one author who made the first strenuous effort is this direction.

Robin Fox (1972) develops his argument from Lévi-Strauss's (1949) work on elementary kinship systems. Whereas all primates have ecologies, only the human primate has a self-governing economy based on things and activities that can be exchanged. Our considerations of the roles of the sexes in protohominids, with males performing hunting and competing for women, suggested that sexual selection had been important in creating a harem type of mating and rearing system. If this argument holds then Fox is probably right in suggesting that property exchange between harems led into an exchange of daughters. Such an exchange preserves the family structure as a descent unit without the inbreeding that would follow from incest and, furthermore, promotes alliances with other families which as a result of the exchange also contain one's kin. The dominant influence of males in such a system arises from the sexual selection of male dominance characteristics in socio-ecological adaptations; characteristics which assure the female of protection from predators, from harassment from other males while she raises her young, of high-protein food from scavenging and hunting. The reason why females do not do these things lies in their biological specializations for breeding. The relations of the sexes are co-adapted to function in an effective mating–rearing unit of biological advantage to both in the original environment of adaptedness.

The assumption that polygyny was a primitive hominid condition provides an explanation for the shortages of women that necessitate exchange. As Fox puts it polygyny ensures that there will always be males in the society who are dependent on other males for gifts of women. In man social conventions produce relatively fixed patterns of assignment of mates. It is this that is called a kinship system. Fox puts it bluntly: 'The simian formula aims at controlling the females of the group for the sexual purposes of the dominant males; the human formula aims at controlling the females of the group in order to exchange them for females of other groups. The change is from consanguine females as objects of use to consanguine females as object of exchange.'

There is another important effect of establishing a kin system of marital exchange. The advance to the human condition seems to have entailed a stabilization of descent from the harem male. By regulating the intermarriage of their sons and daughters and by establishing a lineage of descent, two harem males increase the probability that their genes will be safely passed into later generations by assuring their children of viable matings. In the gelada, where kinship rules are not yet known, males move into groups of young related females so that with the adoption of a fixed residence a matrilocal matrilineal system of descent would, if humans resembled geladas, be a likely outcome. If the primordial male hominid returned, however, to his parental group in the manner of hamadryas baboons (p. 80) a patrilocal and patrilineal system of descent would be established. Such elementary kinship systems would function within an economic system of alliance and exchange providing an optimum insurance for stable genetic transmission from generation to generation. The outcome is an increased predictability of individual satisfaction rather clearly related to plausible means of maintaining inclusive genetic fitness.

Dunbar's work on the gelada (p. 82) suggested that as the harems increased in size so they began to become unstable with a reduced reproductive success per female. The exchange of early hominid females between groups could have been based upon a similar demographically induced and socially managed pressure for:

(1) family groups to undergo regulation as to their size;
(2) sexual satisfaction for younger members of both sexes;

(3) control of reciprocal exchanges through alliance of older males;
(4) effective control of younger males by a male geronotocracy.

In the 1950s anthropologists thought that the basic mode of organization among most hunter–gatherers was a simple type of patrilocal exchange. Bands of small size (50–100) were seen as controlling territories hunted over by groups of closely related men. Girls were married out to men of different groups and a wife went to live with the husband. Such a system would lead to a symbolization of the exchange pattern in the concepts of patrilineal descent expressed in terms of lineage in the language of the group. The Shoshoni Indians of Nevada in fact lived very much in this manner (Steward 1955). If a spouse died his or her surviving sibling was expected if possible to marry the widow or widower. The families united in this pattern of exchange often grouped together seasonally when food resources were rich enough to allow it.

This simple patrilocal and patrilineal system of mutual exchange poses no problem for sociobiological theory. One husband–wife unit exchanges daughters with another and attempts to persist in that pattern even when mortalities occur. Clearly by exchanging mutual relatives of close genetic kin each reproductive unit is 'caring for' some of the other units' relatives. There is thus a *reciprocating nepotistic arrangement* between the groups concerned. Could it be that more complex systems are all derivatives of such an arrangement? It should be noted that a matrilocal matrilineal system of exchange, although expressed in quite contrary myth and legend, would sustain the same reciprocating nepotism as the one we have described.

Simple hypotheses will not carry us far in this field. As Keesing's (1975) most valuable account of such problems points out, recent studies of hunter–gatherers reveal a great diversity of band groups with much mobility between bands. For example the !Kung bushman bands contain a cluster of families, some of which are 'extended' by the continuing presence of married children and their families. Bands are not exogamous by rule and some marriages occur within the band, although not within a nuclear family or between close kin. A husband resides with his bride's father doing 'bride service' until two or three children are born to him. Such marriage occurs before puberty of the bride and this may mean an eight-year period in the father-in-law's group. After that the husband may choose to remain or to return. In either case it seems that the conditions for a reciprocating nepotism are fulfilled.

In so-called 'complex' systems the marital rule is only *negative* (i.e. a prohibition on some associations but no specification) whereas in 'elementary' systems it is *positive* and who one may marry is laid down in rules. In indirect-exchange systems some women move from group A to group B, B women go to C, and so on round a loop. Here exchanges are not reciprocal, but the genetic flow is none the less directional around the exchanging elements in the loop. The function of dividing wife-givers from wife-takers is related to intergroup dominance whereby the givers are beholden to the takers and where the latter tend to acquire most women and other goods.

A number of such systems are described by Sahlins himself in his book '*Tribesmen*' (1968). An interesting variant is the patrilateral form of cross-cousin marriage (father's sister's daughter). Here women are transferred in opposite directions in succeeding generations, thereby setting up a genetic oscillation between lineages (Figs. 7.4 and 7.5).

One of the main strategies of chiefdom organization in tribes is the 'conical clan'. This system comprises a ranked and segmented descent group.

'Genealogical seniority is the first rule of rank and it holds throughout the clan: individuals of the same lineage are graded by their respective distance from the lineage founder. . . . Priority goes to the first born son of first born sons and a different rank is ascribable to every member of the clan, precisely in proportion to his genealogical distance from the senior line (Sahlins 1968).

In such a system dominance and prestige have a genealogical base which transmits through first-born sons, necessarily establishing thereby a covert antagonism between parents and later-born sons and between brothers. This is exactly the sort of situation envisaged in Trivers's (1974) ideas on parent–child conflict. Under conditions of severe economic competition the system tends to ensure descent at least through the senior line.

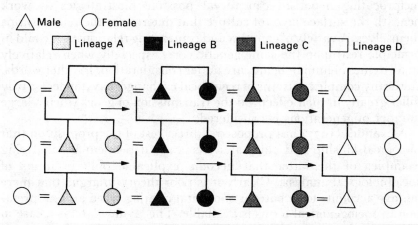

FIG. 7.4. The flow of women between lineages in the case of mother's brother's daughter marriage. (After Sahlins 1968.)

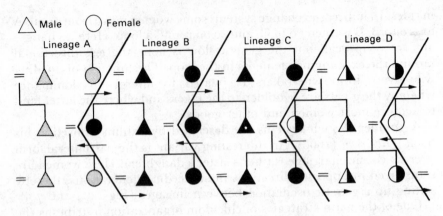

FIG. 7.5. Flow of women between lineages in the case of patrilateral cross-cousin marriages. These flows illustrate the movement of genes within closed population units and hence the genetic relevance of genealogical systems and kinship terms. (After Sahlins 1968.)

Fox's main point is that in complex cases elementary principles of direct and indirect exchange may be operating within the same system with one type of exchange being generated by the rules of the other. Complex sets of relationships can be erected on the very simple basis of exchanging sisters, daughters, or neices; principles of operation well within the reach of our protohominid ancestors. The main results of all these systems seem to be the allocation of control over the rules for exchange and inheritance to the older males, hence a gerontocracy and the perpetuation of alliance systems over long periods of time.

It remains for research to clarify whether or not the principle of reciprocating nepotism can reveal possible biostrategies at work beneath the surface layer of culture that determines the relationships themselves. A variety of complex and contrasting relationships could in principle rest upon the same genetic core, especially when relatively small demes of human beings are under consideration. In other words, culturally complex patterns of reciprocal exchange may not necessarily differ greatly in their effects on the transmission of genes when a large number of generations is considered.

Alexander (1977) has proposed a direct test of the proposition that biological kinship and cultural systems are dependent by analysing examples of the latter that become explicable only in terms of sociobiological analysis. Clearly it is poor theory to argue that mere fantasy accounts for a pattern of marital relating when an interpretation in sociogenetical terms is available. The 'avunculate' is a case in point.

Many cultures attribute the paternal role not to the genetic father of a child but to an uncle, specifically to the mother's brother and not to the father's brother. The dispensation of benefits and the responsibilities for the child's welfare are carried by this individual, who thus occupies a crucial role in the transactions and relationships of such societies. If this were simply due to some fantasy then its regular occurrence in many societies lacks effective explanation. There is, however, an interesting explanation in biological terms. We have already seen how widespread the social psychological effects of low confidence in paternity can be. This social system seems to enshrine that doubt in a particular way by linking genealogy to a descent system.

The children of a man's full sister are on average one-quarter like him in identical genes while those of a half sister are one-eighth like him. By contrast, the children of a spouse are either one-half related to the father if sired by him but not at all (or extremely remotely) related if sired by another man not a close relative. In societal situations where a man's paternity may be doubted, his sister's offspring (i.e. his nephews and neices) may become of greater importance to his maintenance of inclusive fitness than do his spouse's offspring. To the child a maternal uncle is then more appropriately a donor of benefits than is an actual (supposed) father in the form of mother's husband. It follows then that where (1) adult brothers are available to aid sisters offspring and (2) a low confidence in paternity exists an institutionalization of the 'avunculate' is predictable. In both general surveys of human societies (Murdock 1967) and in some detailed cases quoted by Alexander these conditions are fulfilled and the relevance of biological genealogy to kinship systems is therefore sustained.

Current research projects are in fact suggesting that the sociobiological approach to kinship is the most meaningful interpretation available: that patterns of relationship reflect degrees of biological relatedness and that humans favour kin over individuals of unknown degrees of relatedness in ways that maximize inclusive fitness. The renowned study of the ferocious Yanamamö indians of the upper Amazon by Napoleon Chagnon (1968a, b) has yielded a computer data bank that permits a close testing of such hypotheses. Chagnon's most recent analyses (1978) can be summarized as follows:

(1) Fights between villages take the form of displays that can escalate into real conflict. Disputes are usually between males over women. When sides are taken in a dispute they usually result in a teaming-up of individuals according to the closeness of genealogical relationship with each disputant. The relationships are well recorded in the awareness and language of the people.

(2) When a village has increased in numbers to a certain size conflicts over women increase in frequency and eventually lead to a division of the village by 'fissioning'; one party moves to grow

gardens elsewhere in the forest. Calculations of the average relatedness of villagers before and after fissioning show that after a fission the inhabitants of the small resulting settlements are more closely related than was the average relatedness of the population prior to fissioning. In other words the split has occurred between closely related factions or biological lineages. Fissioning is thus 'biological' and is not due to some process unrelated to kinship association.

(3) The Yanamamö are a patrilineal society and it is ultimately the men who decide who is to marry who among their sons and daughters. It is male quarrelling also that determines patterns of fissioning. Reproductive success varies enormously between male villagers but much less so between women. In fact, although more males than females enter the adult population, fewer of them actually reproduce when compared to the proportion of women that do so.

(4) Competition between men is vigorous and is focused upon reproductive success, in brief, headmen acquire more wives than other men and thereby sire proportionately more children. There is also a trend for headship to be passed intergenerationally down lineages with the effect that some men, through the success of their children and grandchildren, may produce many more descendents than others. This finding confirms strikingly the theory that the headmen's behaviour maintains and increases inclusive fitness. Indeed, it is doing so to a prodigious degree. Chagnon reports that in seven villages three-quarters of all the residents were descended in some way from the same man.

(5) After fissioning, a village tends to show a simple structure in which women are exchanged between two parties. As villages grow, exchange becomes complex and disputes increase because of this. Fissioning thus decreases antagonism through a simplification of exchange problems and in a way that increases the relatedness of the individuals involved.

(6) It is interesting to find trends suggesting that men who marry individuals related to them produce more offspring than those who marry individuals of unknown relationship. Marriage with cross-cousins here is successful both socially and biologically.

In another study, this time from Iran, Irons (1978) shows that the fertility rates of the Yomut Turkmen, a nomadic people living by mixed agriculture and herding but now shifting to technologically organized agriculture, vary with social well-being. Wealthier families provide environments in which individuals enjoy better chances of survival and reproduction than in poorer families. Wealthy males produce more children because they marry young, remarry quickly if a wife dies, and are more often polygynous as they get older than are poorer males. Competition for wealth thus translates into reproductive competition with effects on the inclusive fitness of individuals.

Research by Barkov (1978c) in Muslim Hausa villages of northern Nigeria suggests sociobiological explanations for psychological traits associated with personal relations. Muslim Hausa value emotional inhibition while non-Muslim Maguzawa Hausa do not and are relatively indifferent to emotional expression. Barkov expected Muslim Hausa who score high on measures of inhibitedness to reproduce more than those Muslims in their society that did not. As a control he expected highly inhibited Maguzawa to show no significant differences in reproductive success from those who were uninhibited. The results, at least with respect to reproductive success over a limited period, appear to satisfy his expectations.

Another general question concerns whether incest avoidance can be explained solely by cultural rules or whether something more fundamental is involved (Westermarck 1891). Bischoff (1975) argues that culturally imposed rules merely enhance motivational tendencies that are present as part of inherited strategies in any case. So far as brother–sister incest is concerned, this view is supported by natural experiments that have arisen as a result of cultural patterning ideologically imposed on inhabitants of certain Israeli kibbutzim. Here boys and girls have been raised in groups as intimately as if they were brothers and sisters. Although there are no barriers of biological kinship or taboo in operation, men and women from the same rearing groups do not marry. The records of thousands of marriages show that children from the same groups, although eligible for marriage, are not attracted to one another. This suggests that the normal close intimacy of young brothers and sisters produces a form of familiarity that effectively prevents mutual sexual attraction at a later age. The Israeli children were 'tricked' into feeling they were brothers and sisters and the mechanism that prevents attraction within a family became operative even among adults who were not biological kin (Shefer 1971).

During most of human evolution most children in a family would have been close in age: in modern families, where children can differ greatly in age or be reared largely in separation from one another, one would expect incestuous attraction to be in evidence. A study of such relations may be valuable. In fact, among the people of Taiwan some unrelated boys and girls may be 'wed' as children and then reared together. Many more problems in marital consummation befall these young people than do couples who marry normally (Wolf 1970).

In some human groups biological kinship is in no way invoked in the kinship terminology, for 'kin' may be defined simply in terms of group membership even when genealogical relationship as such is well understood. In those human populations where group replacement occurs to the extent of favouring some genes over others, the genetic significance of group membership may become as important to a member as are patterns of mating and exchange in other societies. Caspari (1972) has argued that slight genetic variations do arise between groups even when direct exchange is practised so that a gene pool may contain several contrasting sections. Where small groups are particularly susceptible to elimination an emphasis on group membership and a removal of potentially divisive kin relations may be valuable for individuals in that it increases the survival of the group as such. Arguing from experiments by Lewontin, Caspari points out that selection at the small-group level may well have occurred early in human history when groups were small and inbreeding strong. This would have been especially so during the expansion phase of human history when man was a colonizing species invading new and diverse habitats. Whether such an argument can be helpful in understanding contemporary human groups with non-genealogical kinship terminology remains to be seen and requires evaluation.

I conclude that the diversification of human kinship systems and their mediation by symbolization does not preclude the application of the kinship theory of sociobiology to them. Social ties may enlarge in response to ecological or economic pressures so that fictive or adoptive kinship networks arise. Symbolic extensions of kinship can serve to broaden the range of social ties and to readjust local groups according to pressures of demography and ecology (Keesing 1975). We can see that from genealogically defined kinship systems a variety of ecologically adaptive developments might occur with a greater emphasis on intergroup rather than upon interindividual relationship. This would mean that the family unit's functions within the group's distribution of resources may become in some cases of greater moment than the strict maintenance of genealogical preference. We may thus expect close correlations between societal systems and human ecology.

Much of the problem presented by Sahlins's rejection of sociobiological initiatives in attempts at understanding kinship systems stems from his exclusive emphasis on the symbolization of relationships in kinship terminology. He thus attempts to account for complex social processes entirely in terms of the ideology of the people concerned: that set of concepts regarding relationships roles and rules that legitimates the behaviour of a people. Such explanations of behaviour at the face-to-face level and in terms of the experience of the participants are called 'emic'. Emic propositions can be invalidated only by further descriptions of beliefs, etc. that differ from earlier ones. Emic description cannot, however, amount to causal explanation at any level other than the reasons people attribute to their own actions.

In contrast to emic studies are explanations by 'disinterested' observers or experimentalists which are dependent upon distinctions judged appropriate by a community of scientific observers. Such explanations are called 'etic' (Harris 1968, p. 576). Etic theory can be falsified through the dismissal of hypotheses by independent observers.

The attempt to explain certain cultural phenomena through recourse to sociobiological theory is etic. The propositions are in principle falsifiable through a failure to relate fact and theory. So far such propositions are proving heuristic and Sahlins's alarmist rejections seem unjustified.

Dangers arise, however, when etic theories of a highly reductionist kind eliminate the consideration of emic material. Certain models of human interaction concentrate entirely on the process itself without examining the quality of the personal aspects. In such studies the *meaning* of what is said and the meaning of such meanings to the people concerned often remains unanalysed. Sociobiologists can avoid the charge of reductionism by retaining an awareness of the multiplicity of levels responsible for human action. The understanding of the cultural variance that patterns face-to-face interaction requires emic study; but this cannot eliminate the need for the fundamental analysis that sociobiology can now begin to supply.

Reciprocity, alliance, and conflict

Alexander (1975) has examined Sahlins's (1965) detailed account of human reciprocity in the light of contemporary evolutionary theory and finds a convincing fit. Reciprocity depends upon mutual returns of benefit.

Returns, in an evolutionary sense, mean returns to one's genotype or increased reproduction, either through one's own phenotype or through the phenotypes of genetic relatives. From this beginning one ought to be able to calculate precisely the conditions under which particular acts of beneficence should cause the genetic backgrounds to spread.

What, for example, in a given population of interactions is the variance in cost-benefit ratios of particular acts given to particular recipients? What is the variation in expense to a beneficent individual depending on ecological and social circumstances? What is the cost of beneficence at different life stages—juvenile, adult reproductive, old animal, and between the sexes?

To augment inclusive fitness a return may be made directly, through benefits to an organism's own offspring, or indirectly to those of its other relatives. Benefits to non-relatives need likewise to be returned to relatives, and the lower the relationship the larger the benefit required. Can these ideas find application to the human situation?

Sahlins's (1965) model distinguishes between three classes of human reciprocity: 'generalized', 'balanced', and 'negative'. *Generalized reciprocity* is more-or-less altruistic in principle and consists in gifts, sharings, hospitalities, kinship dues, *noblesse oblige*, and so on. There are no clear contractual boundaries to generalized reciprocity, and the expectation of returns is indefinite. The strongly altruistic element means that the failure to reciprocate does not stop the receiving of benefits for a long time. Sahlins locates this generalized reciprocity in the household and within close lineages in a village. As Alexander points out, this is the equivalent of sociobiological nepotism arising through kin selection. 'Sahlins is telling the evolutionists that their expectations are fulfilled to an astonishing degree in primitive human societies.' As we have seen Sahlins (1977) was later to reject this idea thoroughly, although not on the grounds of his study of reciprocity.

Reciprocity depends upon a socially organizing principle involving kinship systems that pattern the genealogical relationships of individuals. However close this parallel must seem, it is important to realize that the benefit of the behaviour operates through immediate increases in the inclusive *psychological satisfaction* of an individual within the system. Whether it subsequently entails an increase in the inclusive reproductive fitness of the individual remains uncertain, but the issue is at least in principle a testable one.

Balanced reciprocity involves transactions of exchange within rather clearly defined contractual boundaries. It is more to do with economic association than with personal relationships of individuals. Here the behaviour depends upon the flow of material resources, while in the case of generalized reciprocity it is contingent upon close familial or clan relationship. The striking of these exchange bargains is thus not closely associated with relatedness, but is restricted within the relatively small geographical area of a tribe or of a people who regularly sustain trading relations. The behaviour is not contingent upon close kin relations and, although returns to self may sometimes be allowed to accrue to a relative, the system is not readily translated in terms of biological nepotism. Here, however, the alternative sociobiological approach of Trivers in terms of reciprocal altruism may provide an explanation. The transactions between these individuals are contractual and entail obligations of the sort that have been demonstrated for baboons (Packer 1977). In addition, the genetic relatedness of the individuals concerned is usually quite close, if only because of the restricted area over which it occurs. Cheating may occur within this system but the discovery of cheating here leads to immediate costs to the cheater.

Negative reciprocity is the attempt to maximize gain with minimal reciprocation. It begins with haggling and ends with exploitation. Reciprocity here is essentially in terms of the feud and depends in large degree on the expectation of cheating. It occurs mainly outside tribal borders and is rarely conducted among close relatives. Approbation for success in negative reciprocity depends on the loser being a stranger or better still an enemy. In general, strangers and enemies are not relatives in any close sense.

Alexander (1974) has gone on to suggest that group living in humans is, as in many other species, largely a response to predation; but here predation is conceived as emanating from other humans—theft, the cattle raid, warfare in fact; an argument strikingly similar to the case for 'sexual predation' in geladas (p. 85). One may also argue that, where resources are distributed in such a way that the home refuge is based geographically within the resource area, attacks will be made from afar upon the home base itself, for here the probability of plunder is at a maximum.

Hamilton (1975) has also considered the sociobiology of warfare from the viewpoint of population genetics and in some elegant theorizing demonstrated that war is most likely between the most geographically distant and least genetically related groups of accessible fellow human beings; a condition apparently well met in certain primitive peoples such as the Maring of New Guinea and the Yanomamö of South America (Harris 1974).

Damage to non-relatives has two results: the accumulation of resources to one's self and one's relatives, and, if it is associated with the slaughter of opponents, a marked reduction in competition. The other benefits of war are also clear. The killing of males and the acquisition of females increases the breeding potential of the male victors and, since the captive women will bear their relatives' children, the women of the victorious group may not be entirely opposed to them through jealousy. The acquisition of resources and land also allows the increase of population that follows from affluence and the absence of competition. A tribe that engages successfully in a series of wars is practising out-group elimination and is increasing its genetic representation in the succeeding generations. The capture of women means, however, that we are not here considering a biological group selection in which the genes of whole groups replace on another. The losers' genes remain represented as a result of cross-breeding. Where women are also eliminated, then true group selection may be operating. This appears to be very rare in history and the arguments for true group selection carry little weight.

A good example of expansion by warfare is provided by the Tiv people of Nigeria, who, by the repeated formation of alliance and coalitions, came to dominate a wide area politically and to predominate in the population. Alexander (1971, 1975) believes that this principle of group incorporation with replacement is of prime importance in the history of human expansion. Furthermore, in areas of scarcity, it may well have included cannibalism so that warfare became literally a form of intraspecific predation. The 'dehumanization' of the opponent, so important a factor in the history of human cruelty and prejudice, presumably played a role here. Once the enemy was seen as prey the whole range of hunting skills became available in warfare. In extreme cases the gains may have been both meat and women. Perhaps the fantasy that relates eating and the joys of sex is not entirely unrelated to human history.

The psychobiology of reciprocation

The importance of reciprocating altruism is unquestioned. There is little doubt that the prerequisites for the evolution of behavioural reciprocation were present in early hominid populations: long life, low dispersal, small mutually dependent and stable social groups, and a long period of parental care. While there is no evidence concerning the genetic basis of reciprocating altruism in humans, it seems certain that selection has favoured genetic factors that underlie the motivational system of reciprocal behaviour. Trivers (1971) proposed that a complex regulating system provides the motivational basis for the expression of the genetic strategy involved. The system rests on a number of interrelated propositions:

(1) The system is established by the offering of some service to a stanger by a donor. To behave in this way is to proffer friendship. Children in fact seem to respond to strangers rather than familiars with approaches of this type.

(2) Friendship is established when a recipient responds to a donor with reciprocation. This happens when a liking by the donor is reciprocated by a liking of the donor by the partner, who responds in an expected friendly manner. We have already seen how in baboons reciprocating alliances are the equivalent of human friendship (p. 76).

(3) Once friendship is established it is possible for one partner to exploit the 'goodwill' of the other, by cheating on his obligations. A compensatory motivational system involves a monitoring of returns so that under certain conditions indignation at the absence of expected reciprocations will appear. This indignation, which lies at the root of concepts of fair play and social obligation, will prevent the exploited altruist from continuing to perform altruistic acts. In so far as the indignation is aggressive it threatens the cheater with the loss of a friend and the reduction

of aid. In extreme cases the cheater may also expect an attack and injury.

(4) The cheater, before or after being the recipient of indignation, is likely to experience the dissonance between his behaviour and that of his willing friend as guilt. Guilt has to do with a person's self-evaluation, whereas if an individual's behaviour becomes publicly known and judged he may also experience shame.

(5) In either case a way to restore the *status quo ante* is to offer reparation which may well have to exceed in benefit the costs of former cheating.

(6) The cost–benefit analysis of these implicitly contractual relationships seems justified from social psychological studies reviewed by Trivers. In general it seems that the greater the need state of the recipient the greater the probability of his reciprocation. The greater the cost to the donor the greater the gratitude and sense of obligation of the recipient.

(7) The giving of an altruistic act and the forgiving of cheating will be related to experiences of sympathy which imply a degree of comprehension of another's condition.

Cheating may be subtle, as when an individual mimics reparative behaviour which is actually inauthentic. Awareness of such potential will lead to problems of trust in human relations. The balance between trust and suspicion is likely to be a fine one and individual tendencies are much affected by experience in relationships characterized by varying degrees of reciprocation or exploitation (see Figure 7.6).

Genetic control of such a complex system of behaviour is obviously not at all direct. In all probability the elaboration of the basic system already apparent in baboons is contingent upon the development of human powers of self-awareness, introjection, and projection which allow for a complex awareness of the state of play in a reciprocating partnership. The advanced level of human performance is thus related to the emergence of the self-process (see Chapters 10–12).

Reciprocation occurs in a number of contexts. Friendships may be close and personal, creating intimacies as intricate as those between kindred, or they may be confined to practical matters of commerce or partnership in a common endeavour. The same basic system seems to be operative in each case. Individuals within a given culture are likely to have a refined ability to detect and to perform at an appropriate level of reciprocity in accordance with (1) the level of genetic relatedness; (2) the level of familial relatedness; (3) the level of relationship through projects commercial or otherwise; and (4) membership of an in-group versus an out-group.

As we have seen, individuals of low or no genetic relatedness and from societally different groups living at a distance (geographically or

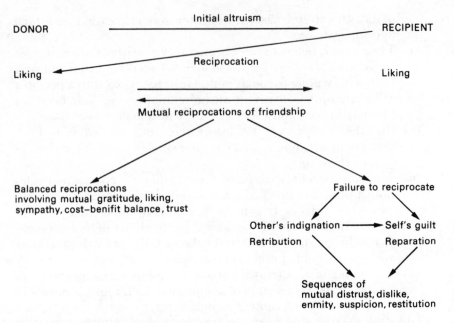

FIG. 7.6. An outline of the motivational system underlying human reciprocal altruism.

socially) are likely to show negative rather than positive reciprocity. Meetings between such persons will begin with high levels of distrust and will require special effort to convince those concerned that an overture of friendship is being made. The anxieties of strangers in foreign lands are not without foundation, one suspects, and cultures of xenophyllic tendencies, such as the Greek, are likely to stem from long familiarity with trading at a distance, travel, curiosity based on the advantages of being informed from afar, and a wide diaspora of kindred.

Marital and parent–child relations
Special cases of reciprocation arise in marital and in parent-offspring relations. The biostrategies of the actors in these relationships are asymmetrical, as Trivers (1972) has shown, and the possibilities of mutual exploitation are therefore additionally complex. Examples arise at a number of levels. The problem of the double standard in the sexual relationships of men and women is often especially acute and occasions deep feelings of frustration, indignation, necessitating reparation if not retribution on both sides. The negotiation of a happy relationship for both parties is especially difficult in modern Western culture where conventional rules are largely broken down and individual hedonism marked.

Where a biological advantage is taken through deceit and a rationalization of cultural values, the social discrepancy may well be repressed and the underlying biological strategy operating only through the 'unconscious'. Alexander (1975) makes this argument explicit in cases where the maximization of reproductive success is balanced against social constraint.

Consider two monogamous pairs . . . living in close proximity for some reason that represents reproductive advantage for both couples. If any resources are limited, any of the four individuals gains by securing for himself or his mate or both a disproportionate share. The profit . . . will depend on the likelihood and significance of the risk to them of breaking up or reducing the effectiveness of the co-operation.

Likewise if one male can cheat the other so that he fathers the children of both women he has clearly gained reproductively. Females can also gain by retaining a husband's favours and care irrespective of paternity.

Selfish motivations are often in conflict with the need to stabilize those social relations that provide a protective environment for an individual's activities. It seems that the explicit statement of social values in contractual ethics is underlain by strong contrary motivations that, aimed at a selfish maximization of reproductive benefit, would undermine them. These contrary motivations are denied in order that social relations may be preserved. 'Selection has probably worked against the understanding of such selfish motivations becoming a part of human consciousness or perhaps even being easily acceptable.' While this may be true of each separate actor, the fact of socially irresponsible acts of reproductive maximization is the root of much story-telling, gossip, and humour. Consciousness of another's unconscious is a joke. Motivationally speaking, however, all these behaviours are implicit expressions of an ambivalence that is plausibly based on the consequences of an evolutionary compromise.

Similar ambivalence in the parent–child relationship requires examination in terms of the maximization of self-interest by both parties. Trivers (1974) sees this ambivalence as a consequence of strategies by the two parties aimed at (1) giving and receiving adequate parental care and (2) the parent's weaning of the child as soon as possible in order to breed again *versus* maximization by the child of the reception of parental care to enhance the child's own eventual reproductive potential, perhaps even through the suppression of that of the parent. The outcomes have costs and benefits that are theoretically expressible in the language of inclusive fitness. In summarizing his theory Trivers argues that parent and offspring are expected 'to disagree over how long the period of parental investment should last, over the amount of parental investment that should be given and over the altruistic and egotistic tendencies of the offspring as these effect other relatives'. In general, parent–offspring conflict is expected to increase during the period of parental care, and offspring are expected to employ psychological weapons in order to compete with their parents. Conflict may also extend to the adult reproductive role of the offspring: under certain unusual social conditions parents may indeed mould an offspring, against its better interests, into a permanent non-reproductive. There seems little doubt that some such theory as this is required to account for features of parent–child relations in many animals and its extension to man is plausible.

Applying the theory to man, we find that parents are expected to train their children to behave with greater altruism towards their parents and with less egoism than would be to their own reproductive benefit. The children, especially as puberty and psychological independence approaches, may be expected to resist such pressure. The altruists' ethics of responsibility, decency, fair play, and self-denial have, in this perspective, consequences that may not be in the biological interests of the child. Parental manipulation of children, supposedly in the children's interest, may in fact be a form of deceit which the children in their turn may be expected to penetrate.

Freud discussed at length the relations between child and parent that are based on degrees of mutual suspicion. The ancient Greek theatre represented these fears in a powerful drama. Oedipus is the son of a king who, because of dire predictions at birth, is supposedly done away with as a young child. In fact, reared by shepherds, he eventually encounters his father by accident. A quarrel occurs and he kills him. Subsequently he meets and marries his mother, thereby taking over his father's role and position. Freud named the boy's distrust of his father the Oedipal complex. Oedipal feelings in relation to fathers and other authority figures are undoubtedly powerful between younger and older men and may well rest upon subliminal realizations that the father's concern with producing further children threatens the amount of care a child can receive from his mother. These hints remain suggestive. It would be unwise to seek too close a parallel between sociobiological and Freudian argument. One of the main points of the original story is that Oedipus is unaware of the social and genetic relationships of the figures he encounters in later life. The need to realize the hidden themes in personal existence is a clear message in the play, together with the point that such realization is likely to have powerful effects.

The anthropologist, Marten de Vries, has recently reconsidered examples of human infanticide from a sociobiological viewpoint (see also p. 214). The killing of her offspring by a mother is explicable in theory when an attempt to raise the child is likely to lead to failure after an expensive investment. It would be wiser to cut her losses early and to attempt to raise another child under better conditions later.

De Vries (1979) presents evidence that seriously questions the common assumption in Western culture that a mother's response to her newborn is one of instant attachment and inevitable rapture. Many mothers know very well that this is often far from their personal experience, which was highly ambivalent until they developed feelings of love for the child. Many mothers have experienced deep feelings of guilt on account of their inability to fulfil a culturally prescribed expectation.

Studies of child-rearing in 'primitive' cultures reveal that infanticide, especially female infanticide, is quite common. In addition it is common for a mother to attempt to raise only one twin. Infanticide for congenitally defective offspring is also well documented. De Vries argues that shortly after delivery women commonly feel distant from the newborn and the onset of nurturant feelings is delayed in order that they may evaluate the child. Evaluation leads either to mothering once the child is accepted or to abandonment if it is rejected.

Evaluation of the child's prospects will occur within an ecology of cultural meanings. A mother is not envisaged as estimating a child's ability to contribute directly to her inclusive fitness. Rather she may choose it if she sees it as physically well-formed and healthy and if she rates the present economic and social status of her family and the potential aid she can draw upon in her society to be adequate to rear it successfully. There can be little doubt that maternal acceptance of deformed babies in our present culture is due to the fact that society as a whole contributes greatly to rearing such children. Under such circumstances mothers have in fact come to delegate their authority to choose a child's fate to the doctor who, except when a mother's life is threatened, will usually allow the child to survive. Mothers thus fail to make a real choice simply because the possibility of making such a choice is culturally denied. Needless to say, modern abortion practices and birth control tend to eliminate the need for making such choices. The point de Vries makes is that a period of uncertainty and ambivalence may be a natural sequel to childbirth and that mothers need not feel guilty about it.

Sociobiology and law

We have argued that just as chimpanzee groups enlarge at food sources in ways that may enable males to defeat ranging groups of territorial opponents and to acquire more females, so the coming together of human groups at kills could have had a similar effect. In addition, the fact that human groups are distributed over land of varying productivity and with differing amounts of resources encourages tendencies to raid, to supplant, or to eliminate opposing groups in warfare with or without the capture of women. The increase in power (population size, resource availability, breeding potential, educational system, etc.) by one group is likely to be matched by another (Alexander and Borgia 1978). In this way cultural and sociopolitical history is driven by a steady growth in cultural and economic complexity due on the one hand to technological innovations in resource exploitation and on the other to competition between groups (see Chapter 8).

Even on a simple scale the management of relationships between groups, whether kindred or commercial units, is attended by conflict and distrust. The adoption of conventional codes of behaviour does much to increase the predictability of behaviour between individuals in commonly understood social settings, to regularize transactions in the formality of etiquette, and to provide sanctions against the cheater. These codes become 'law' and transgression becomes 'crime'. While some laws and crimes are at first sight largely arbitrary, one can read into them the necessity for regulations of conduct that reduce internal discord and increase the means of resistance to external threat and the means for co-ordinated aggression in economic expansion. Complex cultural systems had doubtless very simple sociobiological beginnings.

Laws will work in the long term only if the majority perceive in them benefits that are advantageous. Law which ensures group integrity in the face of potential internal chaos or external threat is likely to be perceived in this way. However, since competition is a necessary expression of the biological maximization of inclusive fitness, it is not to be expected that laws can be finite. Essentially they regulate the extent to which competition for inclusive psychological satisfaction can proceed without costs that exceed the benefits of societal control. Ultimately it is expected that these cost–benefit ratios refer to reproductive advantages.

The control of law may, however, fall into various hands. There will be a tendency for those who control the administration of justice to ensure that it acts to their maximum benefit. The converse arises when internal competition must be regulated to circumvent an external threat. Law is then imposed for the collective good of all. A similar justification for the repression of deviance arises when a faction in society is believed to be acting in such a way as to disturb the *status quo* or to threaten internal weakness at a time of external threat. Pressures arise within social structures as individuals identify with one set of policies or another that are believed to improve or maximize personal benefits. Contradictions between the value systems of factions in human societies generate the social pressures that are the subject of the historian (see also Chapter 14).

To illustrate the relevance of sociobiological theory to law, Alexander (1977) considers the relation between reproductive competition and law-breaking. Sexual competition and the taking of risks in sexual adventure are manifestly more apparent in males than in female humans. Law-breaking is correspondingly more common in the male population. Law-breaking furthermore is especially frequent in technological societies around the ages 17–22 years, which are precisely the years when warrior tribesmen suffer the highest mortality in military adventures. These years also normally precede marriage and the transition to being an upholder of law rather than a law-breaker.

In addition, it is well known that socially and economically disadvantaged groups show the highest incidence of young male law-breakers. Alexander assumes that male ability to increase personal affluence and influence are factors that influence the marital choices of desirable young women. Men will endeavour by fair means or foul to increase their desirability in this respect. One strategy for the disadvantaged male is to utilize his natural masculinity as an advertisement of desirability, thus shifting the emphasis from affluence and influence to physical vigour and virility. Machismo and braggadocio are thus exhibited, often in minor defiance of law and accepted behaviour, to show off personal valour that is unrelated to circumstances. Such vigour is indeed often attractive to women, if not in a potential marriage-partner at least in an exciting affair!

Alexander argues therefore that male law-breaking is associated with reproductive opportunity which in turn is related to personal socio-economic desirability. It is concentrated among men who are young, lack affluence and influence, and are often members of minority groups or disadvantaged factions of society. 'It is an obvious corollary that some law to equalise the possibilities of individual men of all classes and origins of "climbing the ladder of affluence"—at least in terms of personal capabilities—would provide the most reliable way of reducing the problem of overcrowding in prisons.' Needless to say, given the facts of sociosexual competition in human populations, the likelihood of such an equalization is remote indeed. The social psychology of historical processes suggests an ever-present necessity to balance social cohesion against individual competitiveness. Such a balance implies the acceptance of a considerable renunciation of egotism in social conduct. The proportion of individuals able to adopt such ethics and the extent of their influence in society has varied and continues to vary greatly and in ways that depend upon the *de facto* management of government and ideological fashion of the time. These related socio-economic circumstances influence the relations between groups and to these we shall later return (see pp. 390–4).

Generation gap, gerontocracy, and ethics

Human societies, like those of the gelada baboon, are processes operating through time. Many laws will be concerned with regulating the transfer of power between generations.

What happens then to an individual when life is prolonged beyond the period of effective reproduction? Sociobiological theory would predict a fairly rapid expression of deleterious genes and death, unless there were some gain in terms of biological fitness accruing to a longer extension of life. Since any such gain in fitness could no longer be due to the production of offspring it could only be owing to the aiding of one's existing children or other kin. Recalling the retention of older males in gelada reproductive units and their behaviour in aiding the new male and their own offspring, we can suggest that male humans would have been selected for longevity if their presence helped the survival of their young or of their grandchildren. This could result from protection and care, the provision of information, or social influence due to a charismatic effect enhancing the survival and reproduction of relatives. In many peoples, grandparents do indeed play such roles.

The move from being a father to a grandfather may involve a considerable change in social roles, entailing a shift from reproductive behaviour to one emphasizing care. Grandfathers are as closely related to their children's children as these children are to their uncles. One would therefore expect grandparents to be as altruistic towards their grandchildren as uncles are to their nephews and nieces. Indeed, they may be better altruists than the parents, for they are no longer concerned with their own reproduction. We may argue therefore that the grandfather's prime concern in life will tend to be expressed in an altruism towards many grandchildren and this might develop in opposition to parental inclinations regarding their children.

So far as the grandparents themselves are concerned, their behaviour is likely to reflect a reorganization of their ego structures in the direction of a renunciation of egotism, the development of less restricted capacities for giving aid, and a less urgent sense of self-identity. This relaxation, the 'wisdom' of the elderly, can become a cause for the attribution to them of charisma, particularly among genetic kin.

The charisma attributed to certain elderly people is based upon their helping roles and it gives them political influence. Their altruistic ethic is likely to find expression in their politics. Gerontocratic social structures will tend to favour nepotism with old men showing a wider range of altruistic behaviours to a greater span of recipients than do younger men. Such social structures should also favour the emergence of altruistic religious systems. The greater egotism of the young will tend to produce a generation 'gap' but, since with increasing age each individual eventually shifts to the strategy of the older age-group, the stability of the structure may be maintained over long periods. Furthermore, those who are not successful in reproduction may choose roles in the gerontocratic structure even when young, thus possibly replacing lost reproductive opportunities by the increased care given to kin. Monks are a good example, especially perhaps in old Tibet where most of them came from local families in mutual economic dependence upon the monastery (see also p. 216).

The extent to which individuals in a human social structure come to emphasize reproductive maximization, personal power, and the expansion of the political and economic influence of self and close kin is perhaps related to socio-economic circumstances similar to those producing r or K selection in animal populations. Under r conditions of resource availability, including those that encourage colonial expansion, exploratory and entrepreneurial 'warfare' against neighbours might be expected with a stress on high birthrate and an egocentric life-style without much emphasis on the wisdom of the elderly. The Vikings may provide an example. By contrast, under K selective circumstances with a large population living under conditions of finite plenty, there will be in the ethics of the people an emphasis on collectivity, on power in the service of others, on the resolution of conflict without combat, and on nepotistic values generally. There may also be a greater degree of introversion related to richer self-understanding and social control. In such a society old men will often be revered and egotism will be depreciated. Filial piety will be stressed. The traditional Chinese village provides a good example.

The development of large-scale political organizations (Chapter 8) derives most probably, as Alexander has argued, from the need to balance the power of influential neighbours. The consequence is the development of laws for maintaining internal cohesion and regulating external relations through some code of inter-state conduct. Clearly in such a sequence there is a tendency to delegate social decisions to a collective responsibility rather than to base them in actions that are purely selfish or nepotistic. The small size of families in modern states localizes nepotism within groups that are small as compared with the extensive nepotism of extended families in primitive kingdoms and chiefdoms. Personal altruism with respect to society at large is conducted in the expectation of reciprocity from the collectivity of the people, either in individual responses or through contracts undertaken with representatives of the 'government of the people' (Alexander 1978). The role of reciprocity in large states is thus codified in law and greatly exceeds in influence that of purely nepotistic behaviour. There will, however, tend to be some conflict between the two so that legal restrictions on nepotism, monopoly, etc. are consequences of elaborate societal organization.

Large-scale states with tight legal control over resource acquisition, personal behaviour in relation to reproduction, and the role of families in the control of socio-economic influence provide a further close analogy to K ecological circumstances in their effect on personal behaviour and patterns of relationship. It seems likely that in history the legitimation of the complex reciprocities of political structures took the form of ethics rooted in religious propositions enunciated and maintained by a priestly gerontocratic structure. The origin of the major world religions with an emphasis on reciprocal altruism occurred in states whose economies were moving towards the K end of an r–K continuum (India, China, Rome) and whose interior politics were increasingly dominated by legalism. The ethics of ego-transcendance by way of reciprocal altruism may thus have historical origins that are not divorced from socio-ecological and biological considerations.

Sociobiology and culture

The power of the sociobiological paradigm is that it provides a fundamental explanatory approach to major species-wide characteristics of humanity: male and female reproductive strategies, the incest taboo, kinship and descent systems, intergroup aggression, intragroup cohesion by way of reciprocal altruism, legal sanctions on behaviour, and the evolution of ethics. The explanation effectively relates man to behavioural evolution in the animal kingdom generally and thus for the first time anchors the study of society in evolutionary biology.

It is vital to realize, however, that explanations in terms of population genetics do not in the least explain the enormous variance in the cultural manifestations of these specifically human behaviours. Sociobiology explains why human behaviour is not arbitrary, why it is structured in a broadly characteristic way wherever people are, but it does not proceed to reduce all descriptions of individual human action to biological causation. Sociobiology is concerned with the boundaries of the framework of human action and not with the here-and-now causation of personal events. The two leading theorists attempting to apply sociobiology to man, Trivers and Alexander, have attempted to make this position explicit, for it has been a cause of much misunderstanding.

The etic explanation of human action offered here supposes that the biostrategies of the human species operate in large measure unconsciously. Men and women interpret their behaviour in terms of propositions generated by learning to relate the apparent causes and effects of their actions and emotions. These systems of interpretation are culturally variable and increase in sophistication in civilizations where education and research are vigorously pursued. Such interpretive systems are closely related to the means of subsistence whereby a group exploits its habitat. Culture is not therefore something arbitrary; rather it is rooted in ecological and economic necessities. The discovering of new means of exploiting the habitat initiates new forms of socio-economy, which in turn affects the way in which people interpret the world and regulate their lives within it. Cultural evolution thus comprises a historical process that provides human beings with the sociological environment within which the basic biological strategies of the species are worked out. It is to this process and its relation to sociobiological premises that we turn in the next chapter.

Summary
(1) The attempts by evolutionary ethologists to advance Darwinian explanations for human social life have been usually resisted by anthropologists and psychologists alike. Until research on social behaviour on wild primates brought forward evidence and theories of extrapolation that could not be ignored, the subject failed to develop.
(2) The neo-Darwinian analysis of altruism in primates and other animals produced a theory of behaviour change based fundamentally in population genetics and selection theory. This sociobiological orientation is theoretically strong enough to provide a new paradigm in the comprehension of human nature.
(3) The contemporary sociobiologist is arguing that human behaviour and meaningful action is controlled by interacting processes on a multiplicity of levels. The interactions between these levels are far from understood but the explanatory framework is strong. Man's biological inheritance comprises strategic guidelines that constrain the acquisition of behaviour within broad pathways limited by the boundaries set by our motivational systems. Evolution has primarily stressed the development of flexibility in man and the development of powers of adjustment to social change. The underlying strategy concerns reproductive effectiveness and that of relatives over generations. Human beings are not conscious that they bear biostrategies within them but are capable of constructing culturally determined explanations of themselves and of social action. The evolved capacity of self-awareness is the root of human intersubjectivity upon which culture depends. Scientific research uncovers the biological basis as well as the structure of the social matrix and thereby brings them into consciousness.
(4) The evidence favouring the new paradigm consists mainly in the realization that there are species-wide universals in human conduct and that action is in certain crucial respects not culturally arbitrary. This can only imply that constraints in ontogeny are operating throughout the species and that these are determined by biological factors operating in dimly understood ways in development.

(5) A consideration of such universals leads to a discussion of the following themes:

(a) Humans form sexual alliances through bonding and are not promiscuous. A degree of polygyny as in many mammals is common. Polygyny is related to contrasting reproductive strategies in the two sexes aimed at the enhancement of inclusive fitness. Many of the features that characterize sexual relations in man concern the male fear of losing his genetic investment through cuckoldry. By contrast a woman can rarely doubt that her baby is biologically hers. The male fear in this respect is the origin of many aspects of male control over women through the structure of marital systems.

(b) Male dominance and prestige also find their roots in male competitiveness and defence of mates. But influence in social affairs is less a matter of brute dominance than of the use of the evolved human capacity for motivational control in relating self concerns to those of others in the competitive manipulation of affairs. High prestige may often have a biological advantage through direct or indirect nepotism and male prestige may also be advantageous to related women. Social prestige does not necessarily have direct biological consequences; especially when it accrues through roles played in the reciprocation of systems of exchange the connection may be remote.

(c) Incest avoidance is balanced against a degree of inbreeding which in nepotism enhances fitness. Inbreeding is usually limited within degrees of relationship at about the first-cousin level. A lengthy consideration of kinship systems leads to the view that they are based upon elaborations of systems of marital exchange that control for inbreeding and encourage reciprocal nepotism between the intermarrying factions. While further research is needed it does seem that kinship systems are of genealogical and hence genetic relevance. Cases where kinship terminology is non-genealogical seem to arise where an emphasis on communal action has become especially enhanced and where group cohesion is of more significance than family distinction. A consideration of brother's-sister's-son's marriage in the 'avunculate' confirms the relevance of a sociobiological approach as do Chagnon's findings in recent research on the Yanamamö.

(d) Differing degrees of reciprocity between groups of people studied by anthropologists fit expectations from sociobiological theory Negative reciprocity (i.e. exploitation) increases with distance in genetic relatedness so that war is more probable between distant groups when exchange and intermarriage between them is least.

(e) The psychology of reciprocation comprises a complex system of behaviours with emotional concomitants. This system has been evolved, it seems, as a unique human process governing the balance between trust and distrust in reciprocation. Cheating is always a possibility in reciprocation and means of detecting the cheater are of significance to the would-be altruist who expects exchange (see Fig. 7.6).

(f) The connection between expectations of reciprocation and actual behaviour becomes complex in marital and child–parent relationships where the biostrategies of the participants are different. Marital and parent–child problems are rooted in the ambivalence inherent in this divergence. Selfish strategies are likely to express themselves here via the promptings of the unconscious mind since their admittance to consciousness would induce conflict with the stated intentions of reciprocation in feeling characteristic of the marital and parent–child 'contract'.

(g) Increase in social complexity results from technological advances in the exploitation of the environment and in measures of defence against enemies. Societal regulation becomes codified in laws which regularize transactions, increase predictability in exchange, and provide sanctions against the cheater. The control of complex state machinery entails a great increase in the reciprocal behaviour through which social organization is managed. Social rather than biological goals will be the main focus of individuals' lives and the biological effects of role playing in terms of differential fitness become difficult to detect.

(h) Elder individuals are more likely to promote altruistic action than more selfish younger persons. This sociobiologically based proposition, together with the fact that in most historical societies the elders represent stores of vital information, may explain the importance of gerontocracies in many governmental and religious organizations that influence people's lives through an imposition of altruistic ethics.

(i) Ethics of cultures are likely to be related to their economic base in the exploitation of their ecologies. In particular K economics are likely to be associated with religious systems emphasizing reciprocal altruism. The ethics of ego transcendance by way of reciprocal altruism may have historical origins that are not divorced from ecological and biological considerations.

(6) The tentative explanation of human conduct that stems from the sociobiological paradigm relates man to behavioural and social evolution in the animal kingdom generally and thus for the first time anchors the study of society in evolutionary biology through a fundamental

theory. None the less the enormous variety of cultural processes cannot be interpreted solely by sociobiological explanation. Cultures express the attempts of individuals to find meaning in their lives and to produce collectively systems of meaning that make life comprehensible and legitimize action. The capacity to construct interpretative systems rests in the advanced cognitive capacities of man which have evolved in relation to a need to represent social relations in language. The study of what people say in accounting for their actions (emic theory) gives an understanding of the processes of culture while sociobiological theorizing gives an insight into the ultimate meaning of culture itself (etic theory).

(7) Cultural evolution comprises the historical process which provides the sociological environment within which the basic biological strategies of the species find varied expression.

8 Societal evolution

History is the endless expression of the wrong way of
living.
                    Lawrence Durrell (Radio interview 1978)

Evolution of society

Three provisions seem to have been required for the extraordinary
radiation of the human species into almost every ecological region of
the planet and for the successive emergence of even more complex
socio-economic structures. These provisions were:
  (1) the complex balance between nepotistic and reciprocating altru-
       ism characteristic of human family units living in multifamilial
       groups.
  (2) the emergence of the capacity for coping with the complex
       information governing reciprocation, property, and descent
       through the evolution of intellect and language.
  (3) the transmission of sanctions regarding roles and rules in social
       structure from one generation to another together with the
       acquisition of novel technologies and the education of young in
       the skills required.
Given these capacities, human groups responded to competition
between themselves for resources and influence by a radiation into
areas requiring differential cultural adjustment and by an increase in
the complexity of their internal organization that assisted in the maintenance of the balance of power.

In anthropology, as in psychology, the evolutionary approach as
characterized by the sweeping speculations of the nineteenth century
lacked repute and had lain dormant until after the Second World War.
Functionalism, the detailed study of societal structure, had been foremost in the minds of the leaders of the subject. Yet, in much the same
way as the accumulation of animal forms had led first to taxonomy and
then into evolutionary theory, it gradually became clear that sufficient
evidence had accumulated to merit a new look at the process of change
in human society.

By 1952 Radcliffe-Brown, foremost of the British functionalists, was
able to argue that social evolution, like organic evolution, could be
defined by two features.

There has been a process by which, from a small number of forms of social
structure, many different forms have arisen in the cause of history; that is,

there has been a process of diversification. Secondly, throughout this process more complex forms of social structures have developed out of, or replaced, simpler forms.

Here then at the heart of social anthropology we find the evolutionary principles of radiation and emergence. The major problem in fact is to cope with the immense array of social and cultural structures described by anthropologists; simple statement is smothered by variance, and too close an examination of detail precludes a view of the forest from among the trees. The way forward can only be to sail boldly between Scylla and Charybdis with numerous cautionary asides.

We are concerned here with the way in which the dispersion patterns of human populations and their mating–rearing systems have moulded themselves to varying ecologies and changed through time (Forde 1934; Child 1951; Service 1962; Shapiro 1960; Clark and Piggott 1965; Krader 1968; Parsons 1966). We can detect here a direct continuity with our discussion of birds and mammals. There too we examined adaptations to the physical milieu (flocks, foraging systems, predator protection) and the formation of mating–rearing units resulting from social selection; always with the realization that the pattern of the latter was related to ecological circumstance, its form constrained by the exigencies of environmental exploitation (Chapter 3).

Among human beings the firm crystallization of the domestic group as the context for mating and rearing and as the unit, in primitive societies at least, for resource acquisition means that we have here an elementary social base both for societal structuring and for personal life. The family, in its many forms, provides the social unit within which the lives of men and women have their origin and support. One can see, looking back, how among the higher mammals similar basic units emerged through the confluence of mating and rearing functions within a single societal structure (Chapters 3, 4, 5).

Men and women are born and reared in the familial domestic unit. On attaining maturity they may move to other 'extended' familial units or create a new 'nuclear' unit of husband and wife (or wives). From this base, wherein the affectional needs of man, woman, and child are to varying degrees met, individuals participate in wider networks of relationships specialized for functions within the system of ecological exploitations. Such suprafamilial structures are built upon kin relations, lineages of descent sodalities of either sex, age-grade associations, and educational or initiatory groupings. They are concerned with obtaining and distributing material resources, with defence or offence against other groups, and with the distribution or restriction of information. They are also concerned with the preservation and transfer of social and material influence or power.

Members of families face two directions: inwards towards the personal relationship of the 'home' and outwards towards the shifting sands of continual negotiation with the outside world. These thus constitute two realms of human action with their interface within the individual himself (Fig. 8.1). The unit in evolutionary sociology, as in biology, is the person.

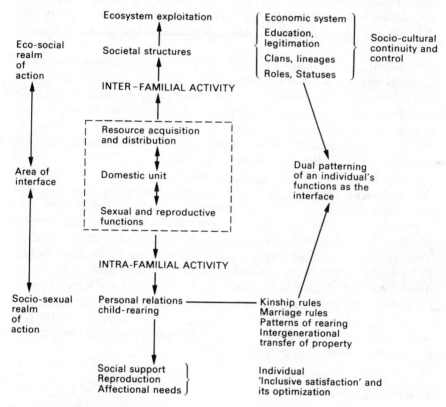

FIG. 8.1. The elemental base of societal structuring in man: the inter- and intra-group activity of the domestic unit.

The sequence of societal evolution comprises successive waves of adaptive radiation based on increasingly efficient exploitation of the environment. Hunting and gathering—basically a collecting mode of living—preceded the Neolithic agricultural revolution, which was based on an agriculture that was at first dependent on the digging stick and later on the use of the plough and draught animals. Later again, as productivity per man increased, the surplus available for redistribution became channelled through a nexus of market towns; with the emergence of trade routes, the focal point of a region became the city.

At each of these levels, hunter-gatherer, agriculturalist, and the early urban–rural states, the radiation of social form in contrasting environments was very considerable. For this reason anthropologists are understandably wary of careless generalization. Furthermore, it is not possible to take any one people (hunters, say) as representative of the level, since the variance at that level precludes typical identification. A current tendency to treat the Bushmen, for example, as if they were in some way *the* hunter–gatherers is most misleading, for in fact their way of life at the sites studied in the Kalahari desert is a quite eco-specific one.

Similarly, to list social structures as primitive or modern might be taken to imply a scale of primitiveness to the people themselves. The fine detail of hunter–gatherer life, the elaboration of complex skills and co-operation, all reveal a capacity for an intellectual life which can emerge into contemporary competence as soon as education is provided. An intelligent Neolithic man, Socrates, and Bertrand Russell could in principle have conversed together.

While it is true that the first phases of our biosocial development coincided with the emergence of hunter–gathering life, this was at a very early epoch. By the time contemporary hunter–gatherers had emerged, the human biological material had reached its present plateau. It is doubtful whether human beings have changed their average levels of attainment in intelligence and creativity since the late Palaeolithic. The difference between these historical periods lies in the development of skills and intellectual practices that are handed on by education and then transformed successively in each generation.†

With these cautions in mind we can none the less see a progression in societal elaboration both in the archaeological record and through the comparative studies of extant peoples.

Hunter–gatherers

Hunter–gatherers have existed since the Palaeolithic, although very few people still follow this way of life. The main contemporary populations are the Eskimos, the Bushmen of southern Africa, and the Aborigines of Australia, all of whom are adapted to desert conditions. In addition there are the pygmies of central Africa and the Semaing in Malaya, both in tropical forest, and other minor groups now amounting in total to only 0·001 per cent of the world's population. By

---

† In this context the vexed question of racial contrasts in ability remains completely open in the absence of any effective means of measurement. Indeed, even the desirability of bothering to measure whatever small contrasts in variance may exist is in doubt. Differences between peoples are far more intelligibly examined in terms of constraints on development and expression imposed by societal forms and cultural practices.

comparison in the year 10000 BC all the world's population was hunter–gatherer. A full list of peoples recorded as hunter–gatherers since the rise of modern ethnography is given by Lee and DeVore (1968) but many of these have since adopted agriculture or become otherwise acculturated.

So far as the acquisition of meat protein is concerned, hunter–gatherers, live in a coarse-grained environment. They occupy large ranges exploited in common by groups that are not in themselves kinship units. Individuals may to some extent change bands and hence their home ranges. In general there is little warfare and individual property vests solely in personal items of equipment. Individuals are not specialized for given tasks but each can undertake when required many of the subsistence activities of the group. This does not mean, however, that individual differences in skills are not significant. They are, and, as Service (1962) pointed out, the 'individuation' of a person around the complex of his or her skills is marked. Separated discrete roles in an intercalating social structure are not found here, however. The society is very egalitarian and head men provide 'influence' rather than leadership and authority. The gift is an important means of societal integration.

Hunter–gatherers live in a wide range of habitats that rarely provide them with more than a bare subsistence. Some of their supernaturalist ideologies are clearly related to the control of resources. Thus the pygmies have a no-man's-land deep in the forest which is the property of a god. Such a place becomes not only a nature reserve but also acts as a buffer against shortage by providing an area where food animals can multiply and so reduce the risks of over-exploitation.

A rare development of a society upon a hunting base occurred on the north-west coast of America, where the riches of the sea and the salmon runs in rivers provided an excess of resources. This enabled wealth to accumulate in villages, where 'big-men' became especially influential. Here the rivalry of gift-giving became institutionalized in 'potlatch', great occasions in which a big-man would attempt to outbid all rivals in the 'generosity' of his giving. But not all villages were rich, especially those inland from the coast, and Harris (1974) has suggested that the ceremonies originally had an important function in the redistribution of resources over a wide area.

Agriculturists

The full range of one-time hunter–gathering societies will never be known, for as soon as cultivation and husbandry appeared these dispersed peoples were unable to resist the power and resources of farmers and herders. The agricultural revolution gave the Neolithic tribes a supremacy, for control over food production also yielded a cultural superiority. The discovery of farming amounted to an ecological release. Hunters had reached some sort of equilibrium with their resources, as they do still today, and hence lived under a way of life determined by K circumstances (p. 45), but as soon as cereals and vegetables could be grown and animals domesticated for food the frequent surpluses enabled the population to increase and produced modes of life suited at first to a more or less r economy. Neolithic techniques equipped people to transform their environments, and for the first time the pressures of subsistence ecology yielded to the year-round projects of farmed land. This expansive phase led to the conversion of almost all suitable areas of the world into farmland; at first in the Near East exploited by a mixed economy of several domesticated animals with crops, and then, in an adaptive radiation, spreading out into specialized systems closely related to the habitat of occupation.

The tropical areas of the Congo, Amazonia, and Oceania produce a rich variety of foods in abundance, and if the soil is left fallow for long enough it recovers after use. In these areas slash-and-burn (swidden) agriculture is practised within a complex cycle of activities related to the use and recovery of the land.

Mixed farming in the temperate zones gradually developed into the methods of intensive agriculture using the plough, which appeared first in the alluvial areas of Mesopotamia and Egypt. For intensive farming in dry areas great irrigation works are needed, and tribal society was replaced by the development of small states. Without their organizing power the work required for maintaining the irrigation systems would have been impossible.

Pastoral nomadism was a relatively late development, probably depending upon an increase of populations in areas bordering the great steppes of Asia and Africa. Furthermore, it required not only the extensive domestication of the flock animals from which most requirements of life come, but also the use of riding animals and the emergence of a complex herding technology. Pastoral nomads always exist in an uneasy relationship with the farming communities that border their lands. A mutual exchange of products is vital to both but the relative poverty, equestrian prowess, and mobility of the nomads encourages raiding and, under circumstances of integrated leadership, to wars of conquest (such as those of the Mongols and Islam). Vast areas have fallen under the rule of conquering nomads throughout Old World history as repeated movements emerged from the central Asian 'cradle'.

The history of tribal organization begins with a dispersion of loose units barely distinguishable from the 'bands' of hunter–gatherers and ends in chiefdoms already heralding the emergence of states. Examples still exist today, although the speed of acculturation into the citizenry of twentieth-century states is proceeding at a rapid rate. Service (1962) classified the successive levels of societal organization into 'bands' at the hunter–gatherer level leading subsequently into 'tribes', a term also used by Sahlins (1968), and thence via 'chiefdoms' to 'states'. While I use these terms loosely here it should be emphasized that Service himself later abandoned their strict usage in defining a sequence: it is now apparent that European colonialism and the expansion of the post-colonial United States both directly and indirectly induced societal changes in primitive peoples beyond those that would have occurred otherwise.

For example the arming of some North American tribes (for example, the Iroquois) and the acquisition of horses by others led to expansionist war-making confederacies that reduced neighbouring tribes to hide-away groups living in poverty in very restricted ecological niches; yet these same peoples had previously followed similar modes of life that were more or less in equilibrium with their habitat and well adjusted to one another. Similar changes were induced throughout Africa by Arab and European slave-trading and by the Spaniards and Portuguese in Central and South America. Anthropologists have commonly studied the shattered remnants of these 'artificially' differentiated peoples, thereby making sequential reconstruction of earlier societal development difficult. Terms like 'bands', 'chiefdom', and 'primitive state' may be useful in classifying the results of these studies but are by no means reliable in extrapolating from extant to extinct stages. Service accepts as useful to extrapolation the 'egalitarian society' out of which grew the 'hierarchical society', which became replaced in only a few instances in the world by the empire state, the 'archaic civilization'. Within these stages an increasing societal complexity seems evident, even when we allow for reversals of evolution by regression to simpler conditions in adversity. The invention of agriculture certainly introduced a new principle, the inheritance of land, and the necessity for organizing such inheritance from one generation to another.

Tribes and chiefdoms

The so called 'segmentary tribe' of elementary agriculturists is sharply divided into independent local communities that are rarely of more than a few hundred people. These may consist of compact villages surrounded by agricultural land, or an 'open community' of scattered homesteads. Such units may comprise well-defined descent groups of common lineage or a loose network of purely local kindred. Whatever the organization of kinship, each village or district throughout a tribal area will be organized structurally in the same way; each is functionally equivalent, producing the subsistence requirements essential for the life of its inhabitants.

In these 'segments' there are two types of influential person; the official headman whose position is passed by descent or by custom to the oldest man and the 'big-man' entrepreneur whose charisma, personal initiative, and wealth gain him local pre-eminence. The headman as a 'duly constituted authority' has a merely official power which in segmented tribes means relatively little, for in communities of close kinsman things tend to run themselves. The headman, as spokesman and master of ceremonies, has few of the special privileges that at later stages of societal evolution accrue to those in powerful administrative roles. The 'big-man', by contrast, appropriates into himself a subservience of others inducing compliance—'a fisher of men, by the strength of his personality, by his persuasiveness, perhaps by the pressure of his wealth, which puts people under obligation . . . and constrains their circumspection' (Sahlins 1968). Here is the origin of those chiefs and warlords who have so dominated history, especially when, as constituted leaders, they also combine in one person the authority of headship.

The small-scale, localized network of economically independent units is connected by patterns of exchange, common language, and ritual rather than by any governing coherence. In times of threat people come together to resist enemies. Trade for produce that is usable as gifts in internal peacemaking is an important element in inter-tribal relations.

The 'chiefdom', by virtue of more centralized power and social control, overcomes the limitations of dispersion and loose interdependence but not without cost to the lives of individuals. Chiefdoms, unlike hunter–gathering bands or segmental tribes, are ranked societies with a hierarchial arrangement erected within a kinship structure, which is not yet, however, a division into classes. The 'conical clan', whereby the first-born sons of first-born sons rank highest by a rule of primogeniture, places authority and power in the senior lineage (Fig. 8.2). Political organization thus comes to be imposed upon a distribution of communities. While work for daily subsistence is organized segmentally much as before, the political authority can now call out large numbers of distant kin from the lower lineages for building communal projects such as irrigation works, temples, or palaces. Furthermore, the storage of taxed goods against hard times becomes a possibility, and may be an important communal advantage even if much of it is siphoned off for the maintenance of high-born lineages at relatively luxurious standards of life. Clearly, too, in a chiefdom begins a division of labour with courtly officials and executives emerging as the administrators of the governing power of the chief.

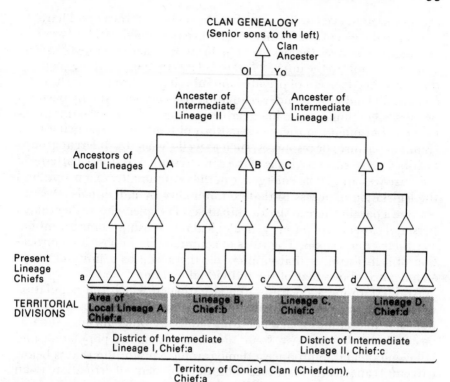

FIG. 8.2. Sahlins's schematic model of chiefdom integrated on conical clan lines. (After Sahlins 1968.)

The chiefdom has integration and a capacity to master the means to defend itself or to embark on territorial expansion. Ultimately it is not the emergence of chiefs that is important, but rather the development of an integrating administrative authority that can coerce individuals into the service of the chiefdom as a political unit. The development of such units has come about in many ways dependent on differing ecological circumstance but the trend seems clear enough, leading directly into the emergence of elementary states.

The formation of states

The relation between private property and communal ownership undergoes important changes throughout the sequence we have just described. Godelier (1979) points out that whereas rights to the tools, habitations, and the wherewithal of subsistence are commonly inalienable, the right to do what one will with one's land is always circumscribed by considerations of the public good. Individuals are never free to misuse land (contemporary industrial pollution is the noteworthy exception) and, even in the case of rulers such as an Inca or a Pharaoh, the implied concept was rather of an office personifying the power of a dominant class over the people. The local occupier remained answerable in principle to the interests of that class. In many farming societies there is a dual concept of private land inheritable through kinship and communal land usable under regulation by everyone. Among pastoral peoples a goup may have inalienable grazing rights over certain pasturages, but often too there is a pattern of temporal sequencing over common pastures or resources, such as wells, whereby different groups or tribes make successive use of the same resource. In these patterns of land use we can see the emergence of the communality of a people and the legislation of access to that communality by individuals. We can also see a parallel here in the kinship ideas of peoples who, rather than a personal closeness of purely genealogical relationship, come to emphasize their group as kin. The rules of communality impose a reciprocation of self-restraints that emphasizes the group as a unity of social significance above that of the individual or family.

Arable farming soon leads to a situation in which the population reaches the carrying capacity of the land. When possibilities of emigration or exploitation of neighbouring lands by other means (such as pastoralism) do not exist, some means of regulating population and fallowing of land to produce a demographic equilibrium that is below carrying capacity is essential. The development of irrigation is an example of how a release from K conditions of existence is attained, for it allows the intensive exploitation of areas as huge as the alluvia of great rivers. Under the new r condition a massive population is built up until a new level of equilibrium is attained by disaster or design.

The routes to the formation of states have been variously related to the gross ecology of the environment and have not always and at all stages involved a tyranny from the top. Republican states have always been a viable alternative but, perhaps sadly for the rights of individuals, rarely the predominant one. The development of intensive farming in the alluvium of the Mesopotamian rivers depended not only on the plough, but more especially on the availability of labour and governmental control over that labour for major works of irrigation. Controlled irrigation allows continuous agriculture and the crop yields relative to arable land are greater. Since fertility of soil is more easily maintained it is no longer essential to maintain large areas of uncultivated land in reserve.

Major undertakings in irrigation tend to correlate with centralized political systems and account for the emergence of imperial governments from the limited states of a petty chiefdom kind. Babylon, Pharaonic Egypt, ancient Peru, and China all seem good examples of this principle (Wittfogel 1957). Such states all had an elaborated bureaucratic system of government under the aegis of an imperial 'lineage'. Entry to the bureaucracy in China was, however, by way of a competitive examination that cut across the principle of hierarchy and led the way to a greater communality of at least the upper classes. Capital cities for the administration of the empire and the control of the distribution of resources develop together with transport systems, roads, and vehicles. Mining emerges as a basis for new products, increasing technical efficiency at all levels. The emphasis is on a cybernetically ordered economy anchored in the controlled exploitation of an ecological base regulated so far as possible to avoid over-exploitation. Communicational efficiency with records in writing becomes vital. The activities of the labouring forces are regulated by cycles of action, control over which is made customary and 'legitimized' through the elaboration of state myths and rituals. These 'substantiate' the abstraction of the state through performance, and participation in them constitutes acceptance of the ruling regime and its imperatives in the form of its gods (Rappaport 1978). To transgress the ethos of the state is in effect to set at risk its whole structure of socio-economically based exploitation of natural ecology and thus to incur societal rejection and punishment—even death. The government in a real sense represents the people's interests in that without it the whole system would collapse. In the end, government, however remote, remains answerable to the people. The Chinese emperor held only the mandate of heaven; when heaven refused to collaborate his time was short. The state system often survived only to the extent that it was renewable, adjustable, and innovational. An open programme may be the only means to survival. History is littered with the memorials of states whose structures became too closed.

In these sequences we have seen how kin-regulated subsistence economies were replaced by an increasing emphasis on communal activity. These were ruled at first by dominant lineages but developed into systems where bureaucracies not based on the kinship affiliations of individuals control the whole. While the division of labour into administrative cadres and the work-force produces castes or classes, and while dynasties of families may rule and intermarry at the upper levels, the process is gradually in a direction away from nepotism and towards a hierarchy of merit and competence irrespective of kin. Indeed, this shift is often the point at which an openness is introduced into a system made stale and maladaptive through cultural inbreeding based on class convention. High rank as a reward for proven competence becomes a criterion for prestige replacing the older nepotisms of primogeniture and delegation. Even in modern states the uneasy balance between these two strands in social control remain much in evidence.

Ecology and culture

'La vie sociale, sous toutes ses formes, morale, réligieuse, juridique etc. est fonction de son substrat materiel, qu'elle varie avec ce substrat, c'est à dire avec la masse, la densité, la forme et la composition des groupements humains.'

Thus Mauss (1950), from a firm socio-ecological viewpoint, stated the fundamental premise of this section. His main evidence had been derived from the clear dependence of Eskimo ritual life and community structure upon the annual alternation between a congregation at limited sites in winter, where seal and walrus approach a coastline and the water remains for a long time free of ice, and a spring dispersion along the coasts as the animals spread away. Summer hunting of reindeer on high pasturage and the pursuit of salmon likewise disperse the human population far and wide until cold weather signals once more a return to their winter quarters.

One of the most detailed discussions of the socio-ecological approach in anthropology is provided by Maitland-Bradfield (1973). Let us examine two of the sets of correlations he established.

Ecological radiation in the social systems of West Africa

The speakers of Western Sudanic languages are found widespread throughout the vast area of West Africa south of the Sahara. This area is split into two main ecological zones, already familiar to the reader from our consideration of adaptive radiation in weaver birds and baboons. To the north lies the highly seasonal, semi-arid savannah belt, while to the south we find the forested zone with less marked annual variation in its productivity. In the savannah the people speak one of three or four languages, each occurring in a vast block of countryside extending north–south from desert to forest edge. In the forest, by contrast, linguistic differentiation has proceeded to such a marked degree that distinct tongues unintelligible to outsiders may be confined in places to groups of a few thousand individuals. The local fragmentation of the basic linguistic elements common to the whole area is thus greatest in the forest, indicating the more highly localized and isolated nature of the forest communities.

In the savannah the farmers plant seed in 'fields' to grow millet as the staple to their diet. There is an intensive agricultural cycle with the labour provided by men. The land use is extensive, for productivity is poor and each settlement of bunched houses stands in its own area of croft land. The landscape is covered with a scattering of small independent communities of extended families related within a patriarchal conical-clan structure and divided 'horizontally' into age–set associations.

In the forest the people plant roots and cuttings which grow abundantly according to a simple agricultural routine carried out by women. Hunting and gathering goes on in uncultivated land between small and scattered villages. There is a considerable interdependence of the people in food production and collection. Forest productivity is limited by poor soil and the need for long periods of fallowing after the use of land for crops. Small compact villages within an area of gardens set in the bush comprise a social adaptation to these constraints. Thus, while slash-and-burn methods have given way to more permanent agriculture among these people, the limitation on productivity none the less still controls their dispersion. Family life is patrilineal and there are village councils with headmen. A prime structural feature is the ramification of secret societies with elaborate spirit rituals.

In the savannah a homestead 'ages' in correspondence with the declining fertilities of the soil that surrounds it. Fields are gradually created further away from the biodeterioration zone around the house. Eventually the distance becomes too great; the settlement itself is then moved to a new area. Over-cultivation and bush fires are the main promoters of movement; formerly the life of a settlement seems to have ranged between seven and fourteen years. Among some peoples the use of manuring improves yield and reduces the need for periodic movement, thereby allowing a denser settlement on the land.

Dispersed settlements in savannah and compact villages in the forests are ways of adapting to the differing seasonality and productivity of the two areas. The more arid the savannah the more the labour of the people must be adjusted to maximizing productivity in the short rainy season and to food storage. The emphasis is on an r strategy of food production (p. 45) in the rains, and the dispersal of the settlement means that co-operation is relatively slight. By contrast, the less seasonal the forest the more even and distributed will be the productivity throughout the year and production is geared to a K strategy of maximizing efficiency. Although Maitland-Bradfield does not use the r and K terminology, these distinctions clearly underly his further argument.

In both areas, he argues, the shift from an original hunter–gathering way of life to an agricultural mode of subsistence provoked a stabilization of inheritance so that property and land are passed from generation to generation according to custom. These customs eventuate in descent lines or lineages which have their focus in plots of land functioning as the resource base of the group. As population increases to a ceiling imposed by the productivity potential of the region there are clear possibilities for conflict between lineages just as there are also needs for co-operative endeavours: local fieldworks, irrigation schemes, clearance, etc. In the savannah, agricultural land trails away into the Sahel where the population practises pastoralism rather than farming.

Here the nomads may pose severe problems for the settled farmers in the form of raiding in times of shortage. As a result there is a need for a societal integration so that lineages do not split into quarelling or even warring factions. The age–set structure, with an emphasis on the availability of young men as warriors either in defence or offence, is a means of integration, cutting across lineage affiliation in the savannah and providing a set of hierarchically ranked 'elders' who can influence the settlement of disputes. The social system is a response to ecological and demographic pressures.

In forest lands similar problems of integration arise but in a context of denser settlement and a more continuous interdependence of families in year-round production. Maitland-Bradfield argues that the secret societies with their cross-lineage membership and powerful social sanctions arising from the communal fear of the spirits of the ancestors, provide the means of coercion that integrates social units and prevents fissiparous tendencies from getting out of hand.

In both cases, social organization provides the means of coercion that gives a degree of security against social conflict and also the means for generating those forms of behaviour that can limit population once a region is inhabited at a maximum in relation to its productivity. These peoples lack governmental structures that provide a 'rule of law'; control is therefore by convention and is maintained by powerful coercion of a social psychological nature. To err socially is to be excluded. To be excluded is to be without kin; which, in such a society, is to be no one. The risk is rarely taken by an individual, and such communities usually disintegrate when the social process as a whole fails to balance the people's needs in relation to their productivity and the raw rules of ecological competition take over. As Sahlins (1968) puts it, 'warre', in the Hobbesian sense, is always in the background of their lives.

The Great Basin Indians and the Hopi pueblos

In a close study of the Shoshonean-speaking people of the Great Basin area of western North America Maitland-Bradfield not only establishes correlations between the social structure of related groups of people and their respective ecologies but also suggests a probable historical sequence of increasing socio-ecological complexity. From an original hunter–gathering mode of life agriculture developed to varying degrees according to the suitability of the local habitat. We may select three peoples from among Maitland-Bradfield's studies as particularly good examples of the process.

In the semidesert regions south of the Great Salt Lake a group of western Shoshoni called the Gosiute lived in a harsh landscape, constantly moving in small groups in search of food gathered in different places according to an annual cycle. Autumn was a period of abundance when the people were able to congregate, hold co-operative rabbit drives, and celebrate a simple festival including a ceremonial funeral for those who had died during the year's dispersal. In so dispersed a population (only 1 person per 41 km² in density) there was little interdependence between families nor many intergenerational obligations. Marriage produced a simple alliance between families with a trend to father's sister's daughter marriage. Residence was commonly independent with a tendency to patrilocality. Here, then, was a minimal need for societal integration and, rather, an emphasis on wide dispersion in a region of especially poor productivity.

The Northern Paiute of Owens Valley inhabited some watered mountain slopes of the eastern side of the Sierra Nevada. The perennial streams provided moisture for a year-round supply of edible plants, which were gathered by women from plots of land near the waters. In the northern part of the valley men owned plots for gathering, but in the south women, as the gatherers, held the rights over the land, which was not, however, used for agriculture. In so relatively stable an ecology settlements were permanent (population density of 1 person per 5 km²) with close ties between families and mutual co-operation in many aspects of work. Here there were repeated multiple unions between families but not yet the creation of clear lineages. Cross-cousin marriage and bilateral kinship system were the custom. Each village settlement was able to run its own autumn festival and to maintain a 'Sweat house' used in religious ceremonies and as a place where men, especially elders, came together. A headman directed communal food collection, rabbit drives, and ceremonial.

Further south larger rivers with alluvial fans provided conditions where agriculture became a possibility. The Hopi people still live in villages called 'pueblos' surrounded by fields and a yet wider area over which gathering and hunting is practised. The property rights over the agricultural land vest in women and one can see in this a continuity from the role of women as the prime plant-food gatherers, through ownership of gathering sites, to ownership of productive farmland itself. The fields are actually worked by men while women prepare food and perform domestic tasks. This is probably why the Hopi practise a strong matrilocal marriage pattern, perhaps an historical extension of simpler systems in which the newly married man does 'bride service' in his bride's 'house' before returning to his father's community (patrilocality) or becoming independent. Matrilocal residence, female land ownership, and male labour in agriculture result in a matrilineal kinship system that is reflected in a developed kinship terminology and a communal living in which there is a greater emphasis on membership of a lineage than upon the nuclear family unit. The lineage is the main context for social activities and cross-cousin marriage between lineages maintains a system of alliance.

As with the African peoples, Maitland-Bradfield sees in Hopi ceremonialism an important device for integrating these complex little societies. Once land-owning lineages crystallized out of the simpler arrangements such as those of the Shoshoni, the danger of disputes between lineages and the consequent disruption of the village presented itself. Obviously the danger would be particularly acute where the agricultural resources failed, for whatever reason, to provide a sufficiency for the populace. To secure both food and co-operation an elaborate annual cycle of religious festivals developed in which ceremonies, derived originally from Mayan sacrificial cults, were spiritualized into a gentle intercourse with gods concerned with assuring rain and corn, moisture, and germination. The development of male fraternities and the collaboration of males in running these ceremonies provided a vital integrative activity for each societal unit.

The Hopi never developed extensive irrigation, for this is not an ecologically viable system in an area where the riverine alluvia are small. As a consequence food can be scarce when poor rainfall coincides with a high population. Disputes may then occur which the ceremonial is unable to control. Beneath the calm regularity of Hopi life is an undertone of tension which sometimes splits the community along lineage lines, eventually causing the village to break up.

A prime theme in these African and the Amerindian studies is that cultural devices (age–sets, secret societies, co-operative religious ceremonialism) develop to facilitate societal integration, especially where the inheritance of land that varies in quality can periodically or continuously engender tension between the kin groups (lineages) that own and exploit it. One may suspect that, especially perhaps under marked K conditions where the carrying capacity of an area is more or less continuously about to be exceeded, the cultural devices available to such societies are insufficient to contain the social tension that shortage inevitably generates. When social tension erupts into open conflict two consequences follow: the population may be reduced through killings and displacement from land may allow the soil to recover from excessive agricultural exploitation. The winners furthermore may derive a direct benefit in the form of produce captured from the enemy.

The highly seasonal, land-extensive, societies of savannah, steppe, and Sahel illustrate the uneasy relation between nomad and farmer and the raiding and warring that is a feature of such regions. Here slaughter is often extreme; loss of life large. These are correlated with the seasonally associated r strategies of maximal food production in rearing animals followed by maintenance and storage. Among these peoples alliance and conquest followed by further alliance among victors has often given way to expansionist movements whenever territorial acquisition has led to the elimination or incorporation of less effectively organized peoples (see p. 175). In more tropical regions the carrying capacity is related in a more stable fashion to the pressure of numbers. A regular cycle of events can develop which tends to control both the numbers of people present (infant mortality practises, etc.) and to maintain a pattern of resource exploitation near an optimum. This result, a characteristic response to K conditions, is well exemplified in Rappaport's (1971) remarkable study of the Maring of New Guinea (see also Harris 1974).

Control of numbers in tropical forest societies

The life-style of the Maring involves a cycle of activities that lasts about 12 years. Let us enter it at the point where warfare between neighbouring villages has just ceased and the peace plant or 'rumbin' has been planted. So long as the rumbin remains in the earth, peace will prevail. The enemies' gardens have been destroyed, some of the women taken, and the remnants are away with their allies. Their gardens are left fallow and our group has retired to its village—to raise pigs and people in peace. Yam is cultivated in gardens which gradually expand with the population. Women do all the work, and after several years of plenitude 50 per cent of a woman's energy is spent in looking after the prolific ceremonial pigs which by now are damaging crops and fences. New gardens at greater distance and requiring more travel time are created; but the grumbling has started in earnest. Meanwhile owing to an emphasis on the value of the male, the women practise infanticide on girls at birth. The population is now well spread out and insecurity grows—the enemy may be back on their land. One day the men call up their allies, announce a huge festival in which almost all the pigs are slaughtered, every one is fed excessively, and old feuds are remembered. Allies pledge themselves to fight, challenges to the enemy are issued, the 'rumbin' uprooted, and a 'war' occurs. While the effects of lethal combat may be lessened by elders of allied parties remonstrating from the side-lines, the fighting can escalate seriously until a whole village is decimated, fields destroyed, and women taken for the breeding of sons. The cycle is associated with a complex mythology and ceremonialism that governs the whole, defines personal attitudes, and 'legitimates' war.

Both Rappaport and Harris point out that the sequence is geared to a number of ecological events. Cultural, societal, and ecological interactions are correlated in a set of interconnected cycles. At the cultural level the people describe themselves as holding the great pig slaughter to 'thank' the ancestors for help in peace and war. Pig meat regulates the relation between the living and the sacred dead. At the societal level the cycle comprises birth and rearing of children accompanied by female infanticide and later the elimination of at least some 'surplus' males in warfare for which they were raised and that settles old scores. At the ecological level the agricultural system of yam cultivation requires the periodic fallowing of used land so that a continuous expansion of the gardens into forests soon brings a community within reach of others. The carrying capacity of the land is then nearly reached. Since the area is not rich in natural proteins, the pigs provide a resource that grows readily in the forest conditions. This is allowed to increase until the numbers of animals threaten both gardens and the time–energy budget of the female labour force alike. The slaughter provides protein in excess just prior to warfare—at exactly the time when the strengthening effect of its consumption is most needed. In warfare some men are killed, losers' villages may be dispersed, and gardens burnt and laid fallow. The effect is to create an uneasy balance between the resources available from the habitat and the population. The males, whose investment in reproduction is least and who are societally expendable, become the individuals most subject to regulation in warfare; they are selectively reared because of their importance in achieving a victory. Victory assures the group of space for gardens and an unhampered agriculture.

The community is the critical unit in these exchanges and either survives or is dispersed according to its success in rearing able fighters, in supporting them and allies with pig meat, and in maintaining the lands upon which the subsistence base depends. The effect of the whole system is to maintain a population balance in relation to ecology. The Maring do not have the cultural capacity to create an overarching 'chiefdom' that could maintain some alternative system of regulation. No one unit has emerged as a master over a large territory, for the terrain is not sufficiently productive to allow an accumulation of surplus food upon which such power would depend.

An extreme version of such a socio-ecological mechanism mediated via culture might be found in the Yanamamö people of the Venezuelan–Brazilian jungle. The males are trained to be ferocious to an extraordinary degree and their whole life-style, including their domestic life, consists of a hectoring showing off between chauvinistic males quite prepared to go to the limit if events press them that far. Alliances between villages are shaky and the whole area is in a continuous 'Brownian movement' as communities expand, fight, disappear, bounce up again around new gardens, make allies, loose them, and so on. Here too is a major emphasis on the breeding of warriors because, although as with the Maring, the women provide most of the productive labour, the maintenance of the group is dependent on male strength in hand-to-hand combat. The renounced ethnographer of the Yanamamö, Napoleon Chagnon (1968), has shown that the fighting was due to competition for women and frequent fissioning of villages (see p. 169). Harris (1974) attempts a further ecological analysis. The people move so much, he argues, because forest protein obtained by hunting is in short supply and the villages are in competition. The gardens are not a cause for competition because the forest is so fertile—but meat is. The effect is combat, for which preferential male breeding (with female infanticide) is important. There is, however, little field evidence for this proposition and the role of ecology in the Yanamamö system remains unclear.

Harris also argued that the failure of the Yanamamö to make use of the protein resources available from a fishing way of life along big rivers was due to their historical origin as nomads; hunters and gatherers living far away from the rivers in scattered populations. The main riverine peoples were destroyed as a result of Brazilian and Venezuelan settlement and the expansion of the rubber trade; the only Indians to survive were 'foot' Indians whose nomadic life protected them from the guns and diseases of white men. Yanamamö still do not construct canoes nor fish, nor do they know how to manufacture stone axes for farming. Their agricultural practice is thus later than the Spanish conquest and their expansion follows the demise of the canoe Indians. The extent of their ferocity—the 'Waiteri' complex—varies with the location of the village. Those central to the tribal area show it to the greater extreme, while those on the periphery, which are apparently under less severe population pressure, show it least.

In many primitive societies warfare does seem to be an effective practice of population control by indirect means, not by slaughter so much as by the associated premium on raising non-reproductive males rather than potentially fertile females. The more numerous the males the stronger the force which a group with hand weapons can put into the field, and the more likely it is to hold ground against competitors. In a demographic survey of 600 primitive populations (Harris 1974) the average ratio of boys to girls was 150:100 and some had twice as many boys as girls. Among adults, however, the average ratio fell closer to unity, suggesting a higher death-rate for men than for women.

In such a system psychological, demographic, and economic variables are regulated in such a way that each class of variables is interdependent with the others. The system has arisen out of the interaction between the historical skills of the population, their means of ecological exploitation, and the carrying capacity and topography of the land.

Demographic regulation, ecodeterminism, and sociobiology

Recent estimates show that during the roughly 1-million-year span of hunter–gatherer life there was an increase in population to about 5 million. The agricultural revolution that began 10,000 years ago released population growth to around 100 million, whereupon there followed a much reduced growth over 5000 years to about 500 million. The dawn of the Industrial Revolution 300 years ago coincided with another spurt to 1000 million around 1850, rising rapidly to 4000 million today. The total number of human beings who have ever lived is about 70,000 million, and most of these have experienced life within the past thousand years. These figures are an impressive indication of demographic changes that coincide with release from ecological constraints by agricultural and industrial technological inventions. Even so the intervening constraints on population growth may have been partly intrinsic and not due directly to resource limitation. The species formerly exercised constraints on breeding as a result of high age of menarche, longer periods of adolescent infertility, long periods of lactation, and hence long birth intervals in addition to the socio-economic processes we have been discussing. This is still the case in some primitive societies today. In general, it seems that the suppression of ovulation and menstruation while the mother is breast feeding (lactational amenorrhoea) has acted as the prime constraint. Where cultural belief encourages short periods of breast feeding, extremely rapid birth-rates are at once achieved so long as nutrition is adequate. May (1978) cites data on the Hutterites, a white American religious group, who rapidly build up families of eleven or so with 2-year birth intervals. This compares dramatically with the restrained family of the !Kung Bushmen who produce about five children with four years between each birth. Again, by contrast, modern western women by practising contraception may only have two children between the age of 20 and 30 although they could produce as many as the Hutterites or even more. The relations between culturally induced biological constraints such as long-term lactation, socio-ecological devices such as the warfare cycle of the Maring, and the actual economy of ecological exploitation of a people need much further investigation.

It seems then that human populations are well able to 'evolve' systems of socio-ecological relationship that produce self-regulation of population, as Carr-Saunders suggested as long ago as 1922. The peoples concerned do not of course have an objective understanding of these cycles, which are none the less symbolized in the sequences of religious ceremonial events that accompany them, 'explain' them, and legitimate them. It seems clear that those groups that eventually perceived the essential relations between numbers and carrying-capacity and were able to represent them intuitively became able to avoid or reduce the very serious over-exploitation, stress, and bloodshed which would otherwise be their frequent fate. In many animals there is a relation between breeding density and territory that relates productivity to spacing. While no animal has evolved mechanisms for population regulation as such (cf. Wynne-Edwards 1962) a degree of regulation is often a consequence of territorial spacing and other social behaviours. It seems that an intuitive grasp of these relations allowed primitive peoples to stabilize their societal organization under K conditions to a remarkable degree before the arrival of superordinate governing authorities.

The ecological approach to the radiation of social forms in pre-civilized peoples is a powerful one and is likely to engender much further field research and re-examination of historical materials. One clear finding in Murdock's (1967) *Ethnographic atlas* is the high frequency of patrilineal descent systems. These seem to be widely represented in many ecologies and to represent the earliest type of descent lineage. Control of resource exploitation by men, the early development of property, and the need for male solidarity in warfare, taken together with the value of women in marital alliance, seem the main causal factors in an evolutionary sequence leading to patrilinearity. Matrilineal descent systems, by contrast, are very recent, having developed, it is believed, only since the development of tropical agriculture (maize in the Americas, yams and taro in the Pacific, root crops in Africa). As we saw for the Hopi pueblos, the development is associated with a major influence of women in the agricultural system.

Descent systems are susceptible to change in accordance with shifts in ecology or in the subsistence technology. Keesing (1975) expresses it thus:

> A shift in technology or a change in environment makes a change in the division of labour appropriate; the balance in the subsistence tasks performed by men and women changes. If the balance is in a direction that makes the existing pattern of postmarital residence maladaptive, the statistical frequencies of residence choices shifts and eventually the ideological 'rules' change.

Murdock, who founded this viewpoint, saw such structures as fairly stable, according to the extent to which the cultural and ideological adjustments resulting from shifts in residence rules and group compositions had been worked out. Shifts to matrilineal descent followed by a return to male predominance in the division of labour may lead to viri-patrilocal residence with a splitting of matrilineages and a decline in their importance. Lags in cultural adjustments to residence changes are commonly suggested as explanations for complex and obscure descent-systems of which many remain.

One feature that requires further examination is the extent to which change in ideological (religious) values can promote cultural change and constancy of ideological values can inhibit it—in both cases independently of ecological exploitation. It is important not to envisage cultural change as one-way response to economic history. The power of symbolization is great and a two-way traffic between the social patterning of labour and the cultural values of a society is highly likely. In addition, wherever a degree of ecological release is attained, the possibility of value-led shifts in cultural organization is increased.

The studies of human socio-ecology cited here are all fundamentally correlational. They reveal how environmental and social factors relate to one another in ways that reveal the functional significance of social acts. There is quite a literature now on this subject often concerned with functional analyses of quite limited cultural activities, for example the maize processing techniques in New World cultures (Katz, Hediger, and Valleroy 1974), the capture of trophy heads by the Mundurucu as a means of eliminating competing consumers of peccaries and tapir (Murphy 1960; Durham 1978) and the relation between foraging and spaced births in Bushman women (Blurton-Jones and Sibley 1978). As with correlational studies of avian or mammalian societies, the nature of the causal mechanisms that produce such functional behaviour often remains obscure and contrasting explanatory viewpoints are heavily contested. Theorists have tended to emphasize either those explanations of their institutions that are given by the people concerned themselves (i.e. emic explanation, p. 172) or to suggest a direct cultural adaptation to environment through the elimination of less 'satisfactory' cultural themes (Murdock 1956). The satisfactoriness of 'habits of action', 'cultural instructions' (Cloak 1975; see also p. 4) or 'memes' (Dawkins 1977) has rarely been described in terms of measurable criteria. Sufficiencies of metabolic requirements, energy, social homoeostasis or emotional satisfaction have all been suggested.

In this book we have been arguing (p. 153) that experiences of satisfaction are most plausibly related to the successful outcome of behaviours that are in evolutionary terms strategic. In other words cultural behaviour is held here to enhance evolutionary strategies for the maximization of an individuals inclusive fitness. This idea is further supported by Durham (1978) who argues that the persistence or elimination of a cultural trait depends on its effect on the differential survival or reproductive success of individual performers. He proposes that cultural traits, although acquired rather than genetically inherited, are none the less selected 'naturally' for their reproductive outcomes in sociocultural life. This idea does not of course require people to be conscious of the relation between an activity and its consequences (although they may be so). Explanations which people hold may more often be in the form of the myths that legitimate their behaviours.

An important effect of this general viewpoint is to focus attention on the consequences of individual behaviours in fulfilling cultural norms. Both stability and change in culture arise from the activities of individuals and the manner in which, as a single person or as a collective, they respond to hazards arising in time, resource problems, demographic problems, wars (Vayda and McCay 1978).

Such ideas as these also allow us to use sociobiological theory in broad attempts as explaining the structure of societies and hence also the mental structures of their members. Since selection may operate upon both the 'biological' and the 'cultural' instructions there is no longer a need to become endlessly bogged down in the nature–nurture controversy when attempting functional analyses. The causal determination of behaviour in terms of how genetic factors and acquired responses construct action sequences may be left to the specialist concerned (see Chapter 9).

Dickeman (1979) offers an attempt at synthesizing the descriptive social anthropology of agrarian patrilineal societies showing polygyny with sociobiological principles. Her approach is important not least because such societies and their transformations are so widespread as to suggest an origination in the evolutionary base from which much of human social organization stems. A brief account of her work so rich in detail and reference cannot do it justice here, but some awareness of its range and stimulation to anthropologists can be gained from a summary. These are Dickeman's main points:

(1) As postulated by Trivers (1972), female mammals are expected to control fertilizations by choosing those males most able to increase their reproductive success and that of their offspring; males by contrast should tend to exclude other males from reproduction to increase their own success in mating. Given that human males invest less in rearing children than women do and tend to mateships that are polygynous, it follows that men who possess resources, wealth, land, and prestige are likely to mate more women than those of less exalted means. Human polygyny is in fact normally associated positively with socio-economic status.

(2) This social fact is also commonly associated with patrilinearity (inheritance through father) and hence the formation of male lineages. In such societies women will tend to marry upwards to gain in socio-economic status, for this is likely to ensure the effective rearing of their children to reproductive adulthood in areas where life and family fortune are uncertain.

(3) Competition between men, by contrast, is likely to lead to gross differences in reproductive success and in wealth and social status. Many men move down the ladder of socio-economic status. The end-point lies in soldiering, banditry, or vagabondage, or alternatively to respected celibacy in a monastery or similar institution. Sometimes, men of low status are dependent on those of higher status for the provision of wives.

(4) Since the strategy of a woman would favour marrying up the social ladder, hypergyny as it is technically known, it follows that her family and close kin will endeavour to facilitate this move. Entry to the top of society, where there is least room for women, will be aided by provision of a large dowry. This functions in effect as a purchase of social position and potential reproductive success, leading to improved inclusive fitnesses for all close relatives involved. A dowry is thus a 'groom price'. By contrast, lower down the social ladder, a man may have to purchase his wife from among women potentially moving past him to higher realms. Bride price is then a common device to ensure a low-status male's reproduction. It also provides an index of his status relative to other potential grooms.

(5) Another feature of these systems is female infanticide, especially among the wealthy. An excess of women otherwise accumulates at the top, and boys rather than girls are there the commodity that can protect family inheritance in future generations and bring about its spread through colonization.

(6) The similarity of this system to those in other animals is marked. The Orians–Verner model of avian polygyny (p. 53) in which females prefer males with the more productive territories, even when these males are mated already, is a case in point. Men, as mammals, can be expected to show 'herding' behaviour to prevent other males mating the women they have collected. Dickeman suggests that devices such as claustration (shutting up women in harems), the wearing of garments that hide the body and face, and even the eyes, virginity testing, clitoridectomy, foot-binding, and marks of marriage such as the wedding ring are all means whereby males reduce the risk of cuckoldry. The human system includes a great paternal interest in the rearing of children as well as high rates of fertilization. The male's emphasis on his family unit and in practical nepotism is great.

(7) But even famous families usually last only a few generations in the majority of traditional agrarian societies. The reason for this lies both in ecological unpredictability whereby land and fortune can be suddenly lost in natural catastrophe, maladministration, or warfare and in the psychological deterioration of the

male descendent that is all too common a result of wealth and easy living. It follows that in ecologically uncontrolled environments there will be a rather rapid turnover of dominant lineages and renewed vigour at the top in successive generations. This vigour will come from males that are successful in competition and reach high socio-economic status under changing conditions. The male entrepeneur is a major asset to his family.

(8) The likelihood of survival for a patrilineal family is increased under more stable ecological circumstances. A firm socio-economic status with education of sons who will inherit efficiently also prolongs a family's life and influence. In stable societies with emigration as a possible option one may expect younger sons to go abroad 'to make their fortunes' while the family estate may pass by primogeniture to the elder.

(9) Male life-span is on average less than that of females and especially high rates of mortality are known to hit men in times of catastrophe. It follows that intense polygny in a relatively short life is a predictable male strategy for maximizing fitness. The rarity of male infanticide can be associated with the same function, since families will tend to favour males as prime inheritors and as possible colonizers in newly opened areas of opportunity.

The roles of males in enhancing the fitness of relatives on 'falling' out of the reproductive hierarchy is especially interesting and poses many problems for study. While many lives of 'expendable' males must end with little contribution made to their inclusive fitnesses, it seems to me that males may step sideways, as it were, into institutions that have major functions in society and within which their influence may affect the social well-being and reproduction of relatives. Successful generals, literati, ecclesiastics, and renowned celibates may have indirect influence on the welfare of those genetically related to them.

The socio-economic relations between villagers and monks in traditional Tibetan society is an interesting case in point. In some mountain valleys of Ladakh, which I visited in 1977, the social system remains intact and dominated by local monasteries. These were far from being feudal overlords, however: local families contributed a son to the monastery who, in return for food and familial resources contributed to the monastery, could in principle attain high rank in the ecclesiastical hierarchy. These monasteries administer the religious system that governs peoples lives and in large measure constitutes the social legitimation of village life. Access to the written word by way of a monk relative is significant in these largely illiterate communities where books have magical power and where their reading may influence the sense of well-being and hence the functioning of a monk's relatives. Men in administrative institutions may gain great power through asceticism and literacy and their influence on their more worldly relatives is not insignificant (see further p. 356).

Dickeman's theory is based upon a wide survey of evidence, some of which remains patchy and inconclusive. None the less it all points in the same direction and reveals a pattern in the social organization of agrarian economies clearly explicable within a broadly conceived sociobiological framework. We can in fact extend her approach to include a rare type of domestic arrangement. The work of Goldstein (1971, 1976) and Aziz (1978) provides the first account of a polyandrous marital system sufficiently quantified and developed for inclusion within a wider frame. These authors, following·the earlier studies of Prince Peter of Greece (1963), have studied the ecology and economy of certain village populations of southern Tibet and Himalayan Nepal.

Tibetan polyandry is fraternal; a set of brothers marries the same spouse and the children are raised in common under the same roof. Clearly a variety of arrangements are possible depending on the number and age range of the brothers and this variety is well documented in Aziz's account based on long familiarity with the one-time inhabitants of Ding-ri in southern Tibet who are now settled just over the border in Nepal and thus available for anthropological study. The brothers co-operate in running the farm which maintains the family in an environment exposed to all the seasonal problems of high altitudes, a short growing season, and a long hard winter necessitating storage. A rule of primogeniture ensures that estates are maintained and passed down from elder son to elder son. The offspring of each generation remain together so that, while the eldest brother has the nominal and executive power, the system is dependent on the transmission of land between generations of co-operating brothers living communally as groups. Traditionally one brother in a family becomes a monk, thereby relating the farming community to the literate body of non-reproductive ecclesiastics who comprise the legitimating authority for the social system. Unmarried women tend to be 'religious' but usually remain in a household as additional labour. Land, parents, relatives on the estate, goods, and often landless dependents form an indivisible, inalienable inherited unit of great durability and flexibility. Where brothers can be spared one may become a trader and earn additional wealth in ways other than farming; conversely in bad times or following deaths in a family a monk brother may return from his monastery and enter the productive and reproductive life of the community.

Aziz reveals that the polyandry obtaining in the Ding-ri area was particularly characteristic of agricultural peasant families who were mostly tenant farmers paying tithes from their inherited landholdings to the actual land owners. Polyandry was not found in the town central to the area among the merchants and officials who lived there. Here each son married his separate bride and the property was divided on the death of the father. Among the wealthy Tibetan aristocracy monogamy or in some cases polygny has prevailed (Stein 1962). This state of affairs appears to have characterized the country until the Communist take over and still remains a preferred way of life among Tibetans who remain in the highlands of Nepal. Once people leave the traditional subsistence economy there occur changes which have not yet been adequately surveyed.

In the Tibetan ecosystem the effects of polyandry are revealed from Goldstein's (1976) data from the village of Tsang in Limi, Nepal. Because of polyandry one-third of the males do not seek their own bride and 31 per cent of potentially reproductive women do not bear children in wedlock because of the marital exclusion resulting from polyandry. The mean number of children from married and non-married women in this village is 3·3 and 0·7 respectively and 38 per cent of the marriages are polyandrous. Goldstein argues that were the population to revert to monogamy there would be a sudden population increase of numbers some 16 per cent.

These high-altitude farmers are faced by particularly harsh conditions in which the potential yield is always small and hard won. There is always a labour shortage and a need for extra labour from the non-landed class of 'small-smoke' peasantry (Aziz 1978). There is thus a degree of tension between the perceived need to retain a strong labour potential and the tendency to leave the land for the monkhood or for trade. The polyandrous *domus* can be interpreted as a response to K selection between modes of subsistence in an ecology where the carrying capacity of the land is not only low but also subject to severe seasonal restrictions in productivity. There is a requirement for a strong labour force with a small number of dependents. Polyandrous households maximize the labour force while retaining an emphasis on the consanguinity of those involved in co-operative farming. They also control the number of dependents through the provision of only a single wife and her offspring.

A fascinating feature of the system is the emphasis it places on the quality of the woman chosen to be the wife. She is expected to be able to handle the interpersonal difficulties inherent in the marital arrangement. These wives in fact come from upper strata in the social system so that hypogamy (marriage down the social ladder) is an established feature of tenant farming life. The woman is consequently very much respected by her husbands and by their relatives. She commonly has a considerable degree of personal and economic freedom and is often the pivotal figure in the household. In conjunction with this, patrilinearity (so characteristic of the agrarian cultures with polygyny discussed by

Dickeman) is weakened and a bilateral reckoning of kinship well established in spite of the continued emphasis on primogeniture. A wife may share her bed with male relatives of her husband congenial to her but she may not do so with her own male relatives. Marriage is exogamous and a careful kin-reckoning on both sides of the family (paternal and maternal lines) guards against incest.

A town life with a cash economy does not impose the harsh subsistence conditions that constrains the lives of the peasantry. Without the economic constraint monogamy flourishes and traders and officials alike practise neither polyandry nor primogeniture. Their estates are divided between the several sons. Indeed it seems that families in which for whatever reason an ecological release is secured (entry to the land-owning class, widening trading interests, appointment as an official, etc.) show a tendency to monogamy (Goldstein 1976). Polyandry is rapidly disappearing from those parts of Ladakh most open to supplies and influence from India as a result of road construction and this shift seems likely to extend itself throughout the Himalayas (Crook in press *a*).

We can now place the emergence of the agrarian polyandrous *domus* within a widened version of Dickeman's theory of social structure. She assumes that in a basically rich agricultural ecology, in which competition between families leads to great differences in household wealth, security of tenure is none the less low due to climatic and political (social) instability. Under these recurrently *r* conditions competition is maximized. In Tibet the carrying capacity is very low necessitating a careful conservation of resources and maximization of labour potential to maintain the necessarily small population. The subsistence farmer has responded to this by developing a system that ensures the unbroken transmission of productive land from one generation of co-operating brothers to another and whose marital arrangement keeps population pressure low. The system has clear resemblances to those social units in birds and mammals where co-operative work is essential for the rearing of offspring under difficult conditions (Chapter 3).

The emphasis on the integrity of the estate is recognized among Tibetans as the prime reason for the polyandrous *domus*; to split an estate between the brothers would probably mean that the resulting set of monogamous families would be unable to maintain itself on the land. The sexual mores whereby male relatives of the husbands have access to the wife imply that the mean relatedness of relatives in successive generations remains high and of greater import than precise individually differentiated kinship links. The risk of inbreeding in small mountain communities is reduced by the awareness of relationships running back over several generations which is fostered by the bilateral kinship system and exogamous marriage.

The economic pressure on the peasantry is increased by tithes and work obligations imposed by the land owners. Their high income means that these families are not subject to the direct ecological constraints that affect the farmer's life. They are thus free to marry monogamously or even polygynously thus fitting the pattern described for Indian and Chinese extended families by Dickeman. The occurrence of polyandry among the land-holding peasantry can thus be interpreted in terms of a functional adaptation to ecological and social constraints. Release from constraint through changes in status or occupation or through a shift in the supply of resources through a modernized transportation system, leads to a move towards monogamy or polygyny. Indeed, were the aristocracy and upper-class land-owning families of Tibet as polygynous as Dickeman's theory would imply (and so far I have not located adequate data on this) then the practice of hypogamy in the polyandrous system of their tenant farmers could be explained as one way of relieving the accumulation of women at the top of society. Tibetan polyandry thus arose under the special conditions of a high altitude ecology which shifted the domicile and marital organization of the subsistence farmers out of the pattern characteristic of agriculturists in other Asian areas. Table 8.1 represents the Tibetan system as seen through the studies of Aziz and Goldstein. Comparative study in other areas will gradually complete this picture.

These formulations naturally remain speculative and more field work is needed to substantiate and complete them. Dickeman herself has made the modest disclaimer of producing a 'wandering melange of biological notions and historical and ethnographic tidbits'. I feel sure that her approach is the beginning of the application of ideas from evolutionary ethology to historical studies as well as being an important contribution to theory in biological anthropology. It will stimulate much work and thought.

Civilization and the modern era

The emergence of archaic civilizations depended upon the concentration in the city of control over the means of production. The development from a mere chiefdom entails the *institution* of laws and an order imposed upon a citizenry by officers of a government. The way in which this occurred differed in the great civilizations of the ancient world, and we may note again the relation between an ecology capable of supporting major irrigation schemes, intensive plough agriculture, the production of surplus agricultural goods, the emergence of trade, and the accumulation of power in the hands of merchant princes, ecclesiastical authorities, and other urban-based bodies. The institution of kingship was often associated with the need for a charismatic leader in times of war.

TABLE 8.1

Household organization and marital patterns in Tibetan society

Functional status	Basic economics	Way of life	Marital system	Mode of inheritance	Type of selection
Land-owning class: aristocrats, government officials	Inherited wealth, income from taxation, and obligatory services	Estate management Government	Monogamy or Polygyny	Extended family nepotism. Primogeniture restricted?	*r*
Traders	Cash flow exchange of goods	Travel itineracy accumulation of funds Business	Monogamy	Division of wealth among relatives	*r*
Land-holding tenant farmers	Subsistence agriculture Sale of excess where possible Little cash flow Obligations to land owner	Hard agricultural labour Pastoralism	Polyandry	Primogeniture Transmission of land holding rights to fraternal group of next generation.	*K*
Landless peasantry	Cash flow from casual labour, etc. 'Serfdom' in some cases	Itinerant labour, also crafts	Monogamy	Division of wealth among descendants	*r*

From Goldstein 1976; Aziz 1979.

We cannot here embark upon a full-scale history of civilization. Our aim is simply to delineate those circumstances that surround the evolution of the human person, to whom we must shortly return. But one or two further steps are perhaps permissible. The ecological approach to history has yet to be fully developed. The insights it can bring are considerable, for it emphasizes the fundamental relationships between demography and finite resources—the Malthusian equation—that are always present, and not less so today.

We have noted the uneasy balance between the nomad pastoralist and his farming neighbours. In central Asia, the vast areas inhabited by nomads were backed by the very ancient farmed and imperially controlled lands of China. It is not surprising that Asia has been the cradle of so many westward movements. Tribes came out of the centre where their numbers, exceeding the carrying capacity of the land, forced immigration upon them and where the power and stability of China for most of history (the Mongols excepted) precluded movements eastward. Europe was settled by successive waves of such peoples—Celts, Saxons, Huns—who also often spilled southwards into northern India. Such peoples, whose representatives now comprise the inhabitants of modern European states, eventually attained enough stability and power to resist further encroachment, and neither Mongol nor Turk reached far into the western parts of the subcontinent.

In subsequent history we can still trace the influence of numbers and resources. The colonialist expansion into North and South America and Australia may be read as a continuation of the westward movements that began in central Asia. The subjugation of much of the world under European empires coincided with the industrial revolution, which, like the agricultural revolution before it, secured a release from ecological constraint through the acquisition of new power through the application of machinery to mining coal and iron. The German attempt to gain an Asian *Lebensraum* was a further expression of this movement, of which the great territorial expansions of the USA and USSR are the contemporary residue.

The development of technological societies with legal systems based to varying degrees on democratic or socialist principles has entailed the rapid transformation of the old patrilineal feudal system that so often preceded it. We can see that modern societies have in large measure achieved a stability that rests upon the removal of the ecologically and socially based unpredictability of the agrarian world. This increased predictability and control of resource distribution is based upon two main factors; effective food production, storage and transport, which has yet to be perfected on a global scale; and legally imposed egalitarianism giving individuals much more equalized rights of access to resources that are crucial to family well-being. This second factor is achieved not so much through the elimination of competition and hierarchies of wealth, although this indeed has been the aim of communist social experimentation, but by taxation that redistributes wealth, educational benefits, and social opportunity. It is this rapid redistribution of money that limits the personal value of the old focus on the lineage, the extended family, and instead increases the value of purely personal initiatives and the maintenance of less expensive and more independent monogamous nuclear families. This emphasis turns away from investment in future generations and towards maximizing income and social opportunities for a small number of offspring. In effect a socio-economic K situation has replaced the unpredictability and recurrent r situations of the ancient regime. Many contemporary changes relate to these trends.

Socially mediated economic controls on family size lead to women seeking alternative activities and gainful employment outside the home. This is followed necessarily by demands for equal economic rights with men. Sex technology frees women from the imposition of male fears and allows them to control their own fertility. High divorce rates and family instability reflect these changes, as does the emphasis on the small family unit with shortened reproductive years.

Short (1976) has pointed out that the contemporary woman in the developed countries of the world experiences menarche at about 13 and menopause at 50. Between these years there occurs on average a mere 2-year break—contingent upon bearing two babies—in an otherwise incessant life of menstrual cycles. This compares with the !Kung hunter–gatherer woman with her 15 years of lactational amenorrhoea, 4 years of pregnancy, and only 4 years with the menstrual cycle. Modern women may thus spend as much as nine times longer in the menstrual cycle as do women of primitive societies; and presumably as did women of previous societies in earlier phases of history. This is clearly outside our evolutionary experience and besides the medical consequences (breast cancers, etc.) necessarily results in the great contemporary need, especially following the development and use of effective and reliable contraceptives, for women to discover new roles in society. Imitation of male roles and dramaturgy is not necessarily the answer, for biologically and physiologically women simply are not the same as men. There can be no doubt that within this century changes in Western society have raised severe identity problems for many women. Research has shown that women are more concerned about being liked than, on average, men are, and are consequently more concerned with self-presentation in social transactions. A woman's identity tends to be defined through her identifications with others upon whom she traditionally depends, notably through the husband. The capacity to attract men and her reputation among other women in the roles of wife and mother are traditionally the twin poles about which a woman's identity is built. In the light of our sociobiological and anthropological discussion this outcome is predictable from evolutionary ethology as well as being an outcome of social conditioning.

The contemporary situation demands a new and different response from women if they are not to experience severe alienation, especially in the middle years when sexual attractiveness has waned and the small brood has flown from the nest. In women gender identity and personal fulfilment often seem to work in opposite directions, for the traditional role has encouraged little autonomy except within a narrow sphere. Nowadays a woman is often confused by wishing to have a job, be a mother, be a wife, be a lover, freely relate to those who attract her, retain a husband, be economically independent, and yet the centre of a happy family all at once (Gavron 1966). The task of coming to terms with such contrary aspirations is not surprisingly a hard one (Crook 1973). Yet with the advent of the modern meritocracy the autonomous woman can in theory rise as high as she wishes in whatever status hierarchy she chooses. This will not, however, be achieved without experiencing personal conflict in her social, and especially her maternal, roles.

If men and women in this century are to understand each other better it seems clear that an answer lies in mutually acceptable changes in gender-role expectations. It is likely that endocrinological biases on behaviour give the woman stronger inclinations to home-making than is usual in men. Women are likely to shine in expressive communality, in creating atmospheres within which work or relaxation can be performed. On the other hand the greater assertiveness of men on average will tend to place them in positions of leadership. Yet these sets of gender attributes overlap enormously, and many men and women show abilities in both spheres. New emphases on collaboration in joint enterprises in this middle ground of shared competence, rather than the recollection of old fears and polarizations, are certainly required. The greater autonomy of women will increase a woman's sense of worth in a less sexually polarized society and a warmer feeling for sociable collaboration can enhance the softer and wiser side of masculinity.

Important attempts have been made by theorists of the 'mass society' to explain the relations between contemporary psychological issues and the emergence of the industrial society. Most writers on the mass society (Riesman 1954; May 1967; Berger and Luckman 1966; Homans 1974) argue that in the Middle Ages in Europe a single, generally accepted view of life and values stemmed from the cultural dominance of the Church which supervised the social process through ecclesiastical controls and ensured consensus in belief through a dogmatic theology that was often enforced through inquisitorial coercion. The Reformation, with its humanistic focus, shifted the emphasis to the formation of individual values and hence yielded a gradual fragmentation of the shared sense of universal truth. This historical shift removed the burden of personal integration from the Church and placed it firmly on the shoulders of the individuals concerned. The strain that these new-found identity problems produced is revealed in the appearance of subjectivism in the developing existentialist philosophies and in the birth of the science of psychology itself.

The industrial revolution produced a social split between the private experience of the home and the public experience of work. The working 'masses' operate collectively, for one man's work and behaviour is commonly merely the repetition of another's and roles may be occupied by successive individuals whose imprint in structure is quite impersonal; persons become human cogs in inhuman machines. In contrast to the necessarily personal involvement of the individual in agricultural labour, either on owned land or within a set of established arrangements on a patriarchically managed estate, industrial work produces a loss of the feeling of individuality in work, a growing conformity of personal expression and a maintenance of self-worth in the home rather than within work. As the home, too, becomes devalued by its separation from the place of labour the individual suffers and in alienation from his environment increasingly adheres to the lowest common aspects of conformity culture. There remains a yearning, albeit often unconscious, for a richer type of self-fulfilment. As May (1967) puts it, there is a tragic sense of life having lost significance. The very physicality of the industrial environment is abstract, mechanical, lacking the 'spirit of place' that comes from environmental contexts saturated with the architectural expressions of a past collective identity.

In the modern world universal literacy and open access to books and technical instruction removes power from the male *literati* who in traditional agrarian cultures could gain control of information flow and who, as the only scholars, were indispensible in the governance of public affairs. As literacy spreads a number of changes occur. Lévi-Strauss (1962) emphasizes the major shifts in mental climate that arise when analytical literature, universal reasoning, and explanation in the service of wealth and economic development become enshrined in the modern education system. The concrete science of doing is replaced by the abstract science of explaining and applying. Mythical thought and magical performance give way to scientific analyses and knowledge proclaimed through the demonstration of theses. 'Bricolage' leads to engineering, signs become concepts, and intuition, imagination, and fantasies of projected mental powers give way to practically applicable abstractions couched in the jargon of specialists. The non-temporal world of the peasant with its changeless round of the seasons becomes the structured time of history. Life gains in discrimination but looses the charm of immediacy. Literacy shifts the structuring of mind and value from action to thought and from inward experiencing to the outward projection and scansion of words and numbers (Goody 1977). The meritocracy of modern states, anchored in the literate and numerate skills that in high performance characterize only a few men and women, replaces the old male autocracy of feudal or mercantile wealth. The elaborate intellection of technological society easily loses contact with a base in earthy experience. This results in a sensation of personal and social fragility that is reaching alarming proportions.

The recent concern with ecology and pollution is a belated realization that beneath the surface of technology and business systems lies an ecopolitical bedrock. With no room for expansion, and with a population heading fast towards carrying capacity, the rapid depletion of the global stocks of oil upon which contemporary civilization depends poses a problem of adjustment of quite an unprecedented biosocial magnitude—yet one fully comprehensible in terms of ecology and demography. The prediction from these sciences is that social tension will mount and that, unless alternative sources of energy are found and means of global population control enforced, our civilization could relapse to a much simpler agriculturally based economy through a period of world-wide social upheaval, high mortality, and social and personal distress.

Summary
(1) The sequence of societal evolution comprises successive waves of adaptive radiation based upon increasingly efficient modes of exploiting the environment. Hunting and gathering gave way to Neolithic agriculture and this to agrarian societies using the plough. The urban–rural states crystallized when cities emerged as centres for exchange in areas producing agricultural surpluses and merchandise for commerce.
(2) The emergence of chiefdoms coincided with the development of centralized economics and required the development of an integrating administrative authority. As states enlarged the government became responsible for major projects in the public interest; irrigation, defence, and transportation for example. Kin-related subsistence management was thus progressively replaced by bureaucratic hierarchies with complex divisions of labour. The process is away from nepotism and towards the complex reciprocities inherent in a hierarchy based on individual merit and competence irrespective of kin.
(3) Studies of West African peoples and the Indians of the Great Basin area of North America illustrate the way in which agricultural practices, economics, and social complexity correlate with differing ecologi-

cal environments of exploitation. In particular female ownership of land, in some cases derived from the gathering grounds used by women, may lead to matrilineal kinship systems which are however not common in tribal societies. Systems of social legitimation, religious belief, and ceremonial enactments of myth are also related to ecology and develop to facilitate social integration.

(4) In tropical rain forest environments the increase in population can easily exceed the carrying capacity. Cyclical wars occur in some tribal peoples through the adherence to an almost ritualistic cycle of changes dependent upon a natural relation between numbers and the capacity of the environment. These sequences are rationalized in myths but function effectively as constraints on population growth through social means.

(5) Societal processes have been explained in terms of the operations of the legitimating myth, in terms of eco-determinism and in terms of the performance of biostrategies by the individuals comprising groups. The relation between these analytical approaches is only now becoming clarified.

(6) The occurrence of hypergyny in agrarian societies is shown to be explicable in terms of the maximization of inclusive fitness by individuals in intrasexual competition for positions of wealth and well being that yield reproductive success in unpredictable socio-economic circumstances. The asymmetry in reproductive strategy between the two sexes accounts for contrasting fates of men and women. Basically women are prone to rise in society and men to fall; or to sidestep into institutions of celibacy and influence. Under conditions of ecological release young men act as colonizers thus opening new opportunities for social expansion.

(7) The history of Europe was dominated in early times by repeated invasions and settlement by successive nomadic tribes spilling out from the central Asian cradle. The subsequent westward push, the development of empires, and the Russian expansion towards the east are all seen as continuations of those population movements. Stability has only recently come about and the development of modern societies reflects the removal of the ecologically and socially based unpredictability of the agrarian world.

(8) Post-industrial society is characterized by meritocratic bureaucracy rather than nepotism, the nuclear rather than the extended family, an egalitarian tax structure rather than a class based accumulation of wealth in an upper stratum of society, small rather than large family size, and an emphasis on education rather than the production of children. All these changes resemble social adaptation to K conditions in animal societies.

(9) In addition the gaining of reproductive control over their bodies

through contraception means that women are predominantly experiencing menstrual cycles rather than pregnancies and lactation during their reproductive years. The adjustment of women to new roles in society is associated with high divorce rates, rapid marital turnover and a widening of acceptable standards of sexual conduct and partnership.

(10) The spread of literacy and numeracy is associated with the emergence of a meritocracy of men and women replacing the scholarly male *literati* of former years. Mythical thought is replaced by science, imagination by analysis, the non-temporal world of the peasant by the structured time of urban daily routine. Inward experiencing is replaced by the outward projection and scansion of words. Such an objectifying mode of life tends to produce an experience of alienation from nature and a sense of lost contact with the real.

(11) Against this background the modern population faces the imminent threat of a major change in socio-ecology driven by the rapid depletion of fossil fuels which power our present global economy. A rude awakening from the technological over-confidence of the last century may or may not result in appropriate societal change within the tight time schedule that is predicted.

9 Worlds with meaning: the nature and significance of personal identity

> There is the sensual consciousness, enormous and potent; and then there is Mind. Mind is the function of abstraction from sensual experience and in abstraction it established another world of reality for Man.
>
> D. H. Lawrence 1978

What does it mean to be a human being? In previous chapters we have explored the extent to which primate societies, particularly those of chimpanzees and baboons, have evolved complex behaviours, communication patterns, and societal organization that come superficially close to the elaboration found in *Homo sapiens*. Then, in a direct examination of some aspects of primitive human societies, we found not only correlations between societal structure, behaviour, and ecology that demonstrate an adaptive process but, in addition, sequences of historical change that suggest the way in which social organizations and their legitimation through culture come to fit their ecological opportunities and to respond to competition. This approach furthermore seems to be well underpinned by modern evolutionary ethology which provides a link between the biology and sociology of man. We now turn from societal evolution to the problem of the unique cognitive attribute of man: the self-process.

Self in society

The self-process (Figs. 9.1 and 9.2) lies at the root of all human interaction and provides it with the special quality of projective intersubjectivity whereby one person can say that he knows what it is like to be another. The self-process converts the human organism into the human person. It is a species-wide universal and implies not only complex cognitive functions in adults but also an elaborate developmental process. It always operates within a complex social setting.

In Fig. 9.3 the organism is represented in the left-hand column of social organization as a participant in both a reproductive unit and in a wider societal frame. Both a human individual and a baboon may be placed in this way. In the right-hand column the individual person is depicted as a participant in a domestic family and within a wider frame of juridically and politically enforced rights and obligations. The per-

(1) Analytical processing of verbal and non-verbal information arising from a partner in interaction in order to relate it to past experience of transactions and to create an appropriate response.

(2) Through the experience of social rewards and punishments an individual repertoire of responses is formed. Gradually the individual comes to practise and confirm or replace various role performances in relation to others.

(3) Internally symbolized, these roles amount to identity constructs or opinions about a person's own nature. These constructs are upheld or cancelled through actual experience.

(4) Identity constructs have high emotional investments attached to them, especially since they determine an individual's sense of his own worth or self-esteem.

(5) Effective interaction with another requires at least sufficient self-esteem to permit a degree of autonomy in transaction. Without a degree of autonomy even achieved goals may be evaluated negatively.

(6) The capacity to relate a comprehension of another's intentions (emotional as well as objectively stated) to one's own hopes, fears, and purposes depends upon an ability to empathize. Acute observation of another combined with an imaginative capacity to feel oneself as the other lie at the root of empathy. The constructs arising from empathy are tested in the course of further interaction, directly or indirectly.

(7) With increasing experience the person's sense of self matures into an enduring structure of attitude and action with the capacity for imaginative intersubjectivity with others through speech and emotional expression. Growth in this capacity may continue throughout life unless defensive formations inhibit responsiveness to narrow channels (Chapter 11).

(8) The boundary to transactional possibility in Man is defined by the extent to which individuals learn to feel safe with patterns of interaction. Such security may relate to boundaries of motivational expression ultimately functioning in biostrategy; for the most part these boundaries are not reached and the possibilities of self-expression are confined by personal learning in an environment of cultural adaptation.

FIG. 9.1. The self process. Human transactions are mediated by a highly adaptable cognitive process unique to the species and which comprises the most elaborative cognitive apparatus in the animal kingdom. The main features are given here.

son is placed in a cultural matrix of meanings in a way that no animal can be. If we now fold the right-hand column of this figure over on to the left-hand side we achieve a representation of the human system in which cultural organization (meanings, propositions, ideas) is imposed upon and expresses societal organization. A comprehension of the human social system requires description in terms both of structure and in terms of the meaning that the structure has for people.

Figure 9.4 illustrates the process in which the individual person is involved and in which he or she is a participant. Starting at the bottom of the diagram the group size, composition, and way of life of his society is anchored within and adapted to the local ecology through a techno-

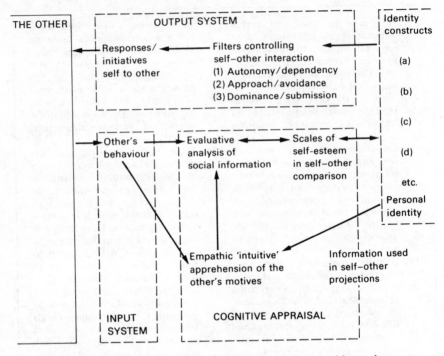

FIG. 9.2. The self-process of the human person in interaction with another.

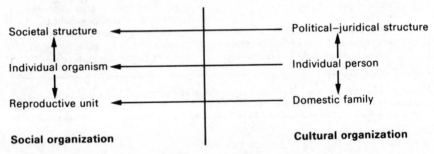

FIG. 9.3. Societal and cultural organization in human social systems.

logy of exploitation. As we have seen, this approach is basically that of Harris (1968) and provides an etic (p. 173) explanation of the sociocultural process based in ecological determinism. At the top of the figure we envisage the system of ideas, the ideology, whereby a people interpret and regulate their affairs. Here is the symbolization of nature and human relationships. A study of this system provides the emic (p. 172) explanation of the social process in terms of the reasons people give for their actions.

This figure expresses then the relation between two processes; it

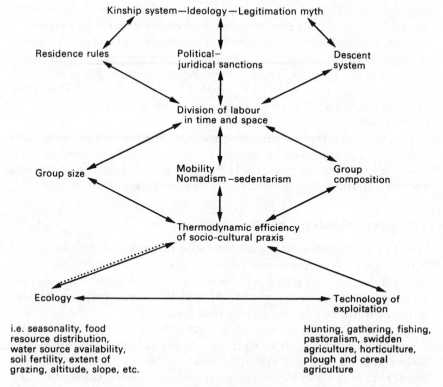

FIG. 9.4. A model of the sociocultural ecology of a tribal society.

depicts the interface between, on the one hand, the process of resource and energy acquisition upon which life depends and, on the other hand, the process of comprehension and justification whereby people make sense of their lives and to which they refer as a community. All means of resource acquisition and of reproductive relationship are ultimately processed through face-to-face transactions between individual persons who bring to their negotiations systems of self-justification which are utilized in assertions about the social legitimacy of their proposed actions. Explanations of the social process that ignore the meanings that individuals attribute to it are ultimately fragile, for they ignore the most characteristically human dimension in the whole scenario. Furthermore, it is not always the case that ecology determines the patterning of reasons; eloquently the modern misuse of ecology through over-exploitation and pollution shows how an ideology of commercial maximization can operate temporarily without reference to or respect for the ecological base.

The individual phenotype of the human species it not only the most recognizable unit upon which natural selection works; he or she is also the fundamental unit that creates the ideas vital to the patterning of transactions in human communities. Cultures are learnt by individual persons and transmitted through their activities from one generation to another. While symbolizations, rules, and formulations for behaviour can exist in the abstract like an ancient Egyptian ritual that is no longer performed, they require to be embodied in human beings before they can play roles in a social process. The social life is a reality only when it is performed.

The interpretation of what it *means to a person to be a person* is thus inevitably a prime focus for any evolutionary cognitive ethology. The ground of this inquiry is precisely the juncture of biological energetics and the interpretative hermeneutics of face-to-face transactions.

The psychobiology of the person

Freud began his discussion of this topic through his division of the person into three components; the biological source, energy, or 'libido' called the id; the ego that mediates between social convention and the undisciplined tendencies of the id; and the super-ego, the heavily introjected imperatives of society that confine the ego's mediation to narrow paths. We cannot normally mate as baboons do in public. And even baboons run into trouble if they do not calculate the social here and now of the moment correctly. Society demands controlled emotional expression and the ego is the mediator between convention and bodily delight.

In social psychology the functioning of the ego in this often difficult task has become so central a focus that there is a danger of forgetting the id and all its works. Freud and Jung both had interests in biology and, whatever the complexities of their hermeneutical investigations, never lost touch entirely with the body or its symbolism. By contrast Mead (1934) and Sullivan (1955), in their analyses of ego functions, tended to see persons purely as reflections of the social process. Today such an approach is all too easily represented in computer modelling that is often as facile as it is elegant. A developmental psychologist with evolutionary training is unlikely to let this social balloon rise quite so far.

How then can we conceive of the relations between biology and culture as expressed in the performances of persons? In a provocative article entitled 'Is a cultural ethology possible?' Cloak (1975) made a determined effort to break the dichotomizing logic that bedevils almost all thinking of the nature-nurture issue. It is virtually impossible to solve this question by the simple superimposition of social learning theory upon some quasi-ethological base. It is not the case that biologican structure 'comes first' and then the whole gamut of classical and operant conditioning, observational learning, and insight learning comes along and sits upon it as if upon a seat. The learning-theory assumption of a *tabula rasa* and of the explanatory power of the reinforcement concept is too embracing for so simple a solution to work. Some far more radical interpretation of acquired behaviour in relation to innate responsiveness is needed. Cloak's contribution was to point out that any neural organization that regularly responds to an environmental cue with a characteristic behaviour may be termed an 'instruction' irrespective of its origin.

In higher vertebrates, hierarchies of such basic instructions are inherited biologically as incompletely functional units. Additional 'instructions' are derived from experience and stored neurally as elements of acquired behaviour set within the framework of the innate instruction hierarchy. Cultural instructions have this character of filling in the spaces in an 'open programme' and are selected by use or disuse according to outcomes that are reinforced in relation to the overall function of the strategy in question. Reinforcement, then, is not independent of an 'underlying' strategy but guided by it. The acquisition of behaviour is constrained by the programme within which it is incorporated.

Cloak suggests that cultural instructions are more analogous to a virus or bacterial gene than to a gene of its bearer's own genome. They resemble parasites that have gained some control over the behaviour of the host within which they may live in symbiosis or which they may actively damage; as when a meshing of innate and acquired responses leads to behaviour that no longer operates effectively with respect to ultimate function. While these programmes are 'guided' they are none the less sufficiently open to allow deleterious instructions to enter. Many acquired instructions are derived from the long-established material culture (houses, pathways, agricultural and industrial technology, rights, obligations, shrines, and shibboleths) of a society which therefore acts as a transgenerational instruction store.

One problem with Cloak's analogy with computer programming is that it does not allow for the fact that cultural instructions can be extinguished and replaced by novel or modified ones, whereas the wired-in components of the programme are not so flexible. This of course is the whole significance of the 'open' programme. The existence of modifiability allows for rapid adaptation and speedy tracking of environmental shifts and changes. The open programme also allows for the accumulation of a vast hierarchy of alternative responses that entail sensitivity to many varying social situations. Social skills are built within such open programmes. The concept of an 'evolutionarily flexible strategy' (EFS) in which the proportion of the programme that remains open is large expresses this idea well.

As I have argued previously (Crook 1970*a*) the social environment may not only fill these 'open' portions of the programmes but may also direct the selection of the innate repertoire as well. Environmental and societal changes set up patterns of acquired behaviour which become the basis for elaborate traditions of interaction functioning within the guidelines of 'evolutionarily flexible strategies'. These traditions may in turn provide the contingencies which, over a longer time-scale, select for shifts in genetic constitution. These sets of causal factors are thus 'nested' within one another like Russian dolls and in a highly systemic manner.

Putting it another way, we may say that higher organisms present themselves to the world with biogrammatical frames for action within which sociogrammar is acquired from an existing material culture. And this culture, in so far as it is undergoing historical changes, can also produce successive recompositions of itself within the tolerance of the organism. Modern understanding of developmental processes supports such a viewpoint.

Using an idea derived from developmental processes in embryology (Waddington 1957), Bateson (1976) likens the development of behaviour to the movement of a ball rolling down a slope upon which its advance is directed by ridges and valleys. This 'epigenetic landscape' models the possibility that deflections from a path may be followed by a roll-back into the original valley so that different developmental pathways may lead to the common end-point. Such 'equifinality' may also be obtained when a valley curves round to rejoin that in which the ball was originally rolling. The point is that internal controls can regulate physical maturation in ways that allow for flexible runs to a finally equivalent state. Correspondingly, there are likely to be rules that allow for comparable flexibility in behavioural development and additional rules determining when switches from one developmental pattern to another occur. In particular, once a steady-state has been reached in one set of functions, self-modifying systems may shift to a new stage of development. Modern observers focus on both environmental cues and on developmental levels for explanation, rather than looking for a precise developmental chronology predetermined bodily in advance.

This approach also relates well to Jean Piaget's view that emergent properties in cognition are based on the assimilation of novelty within existing structure and that increasing cognitive complexity occurs in a set of stages each of which builds upon its predecessor. One can see that the intercalation of acquired instructions within open programmes would operate in the same way. Not all the cultural information that fills a biogrammatical frame may be advantageous but it is acquired from within a matrix of culturally determined alternatives that allow flexibility. The matrix itself is contingent upon ecological circumstances which may constrain the social expression of a community. Evolutionary flexible strategies allow effective subsistence and reproduction in a variety of circumstances and by a multiplicity of routes.

How open are human frames? Clearly if the biogrammar is elementary and behaviour almost entirely filled in by acquisition then the instruction set of practical interest to us is almost entirely cultural in origin. Is there a point at which the biological frame can be ignored? Many theorists who are not evolutionists have adopted this position—especially social learning theorists. The evidence is now moving the other way and at levels of investigation that are often quite distinct from one another. In particular there is the evidence for constraints on learning (Hinde and Stephenson-Hinde 1973), for language universals (see p. 134), for face-to-face species-wide rituals of communication in greetings, courtship, and agonistic contexts (Eibl-Eibesfelt 1970; Ekman 1973; Kendon and Ferber 1973), for innate non-verbal components of interaction sequences (Argyle and Kendon 1976), and for universals in mother–infant interaction; all these results imply a significant degree of biogrammatical guidance over behavioural acquisition through learning. It is doubtless significant that much of this guidance appears to arise in the cognitive realm and to be of especial importance in behavioural development.

As we have seen in Chapter 4, Kummer showed in a remarkable set of experiments that when he convened small groups of gelada baboons in enclosures the social relations that were generated between them followed a set of clear-cut rules. Thus, when a dyad of animals either unknown to one another or separated for several weeks was convened, their relationship went through a series of predictable steps that led to a state of mutual compatibility that could be modified in predictable ways by the addition of further animals.

Kummer writes that gelada baboons can build one-male groups similar to those of wild conspecifics even without the experience of such relationships in their ontogeny.

The mutual strangers seem to have a program for the social structure of their species, but they must learn, mainly by trial and error, to apply it to the set of individuals found in the new colony. . . . One would have expected that primates develop their bonds, intervene with others and choose their spatial arrangement more in dependence on individual preference and aversion than on principles based *only on sex and dominance status*. (Italics mine.)

It is most significant that the process whereby dyads, triads, and one-male groups convene out of the mutual introductions of strangers uses only simple components of social intercourse, i.e. the agonistic and sexual repertoire, the relative compatibility of same-sex and cross-sex partnering, intervention, and inhibition. The overall strategy of an individual in a small group is to maximize his or her sum of realized compatibilities while minimizing that sum in others. Furthermore, the rules governing these sequences are peculiar to the gelada as a species. Wild gelada groups are essentially the same as Kummer's experimental ones except that a history of kin and friendship relations is superimposed upon and probably obscures the 'non-historic structural principles' apparent in a convened group without such a tradition.

Hamadryas baboons differ from geladas in one crucial respect. A hamadryas male, unlike a male gelada, intervenes in fights between females and thus prevents dyads between females from developing. The result is a monopolization of female social interactions by the male so that a hamadryas sociometric diagram is a star clustered on the male rather than a chain figure typical of geladas. We are thus dealing with species-typical rules that govern the interactions between individuals in such a way that a characteristic societal configuration governed by typical sequences of events is a regular outcome when individuals find themselves together.

The point of all this is to ask whether there may be similar 'rules' for the formation of elementary social structures in man. Such rules would amount to a predictable sequence of compound 'instructions' in Cloak's sense, based within a limited number of evolutionary flexible strategies governing group formation and sexual relationships.

Let us take a glance at what such a set of rules might comprise. Supposing we were able to repeat Kummer's work but using humans, would we find regularities in behavioural sequences that lead to mutual compatibilities? When such compatibilities were established would we find recognizably human groups in accordance with the natural history of the species? Would differences between races be swamped by universal species-wide tendencies? Is there perhaps a biological blueprint for basic human relationships at the face-to-face level?

Using Kummer's style of formulation an intuitive listing of interaction rules governing the structuring of newly convened hominid groups *might* read as follows:

(1) Newly convened dyads go through several stages in which each member ascertains (a) the relative dominance and (b) the approachability (openness) of the other. Compatibility is reached when each member is comfortable with his or her position on dominance–submissiveness and approach–avoidance dimensions *vis-à-vis* the other.

(2) High dominance of both partners in a dyad reduces the probability of compatibility.

(3) Compatibility between two men is highest when the dominance contrasts between them are not great and both are approachable people.

(4) Compatibility between two women is highest when there is a perceptible and mutually acceptable dominance contrast between them and both are approachable people.

(5) Compatibility between a man and a woman is highest when there is a clear-cut and acceptable dominance distinction between them, usually with a dominant male preferred by both partners.

(6) In any group of several men status distinctions are established either by direct contrasts in dominance–submissiveness or by indexical behaviour representing tacit assumptions about positions on this scale relative to some value held in common.

(7) In such male groups compatibility is maintained by conversational or formal fictions that seemingly lower the status of dominants and raise those of the more submissive. Often, for effective communication to occur, social manipulation to attain a fictional equivalence on the scale in question is important if issues neutral to that scale are to be discussed. Among males high levels of mutual compatibility greatly assist the performance of co-operative endeavours; the primordial example is hunting.

(8) Complex decision-making in male groups is usually controlled by mediators of middle status (diplomats, Macchiavellians, trouble-shooters) whose satisfactions are task- rather than status-related. (Inclusive influence rather than dominance may be a good predictor of high levels of inclusive fitness.)

(9) In all-women groups compatibility is maintained by similar means but the generally higher level of approachability in women (who are less fearful of losing status) makes the manœuvring less fraught and the dominance gradient less steep.

(10) The introduction of a third person to a dyad produces an asymmetry in which two are usually more compatible than either is to a third. Effective intersubjectivity appears to be a face-to-face process, and three faces thus pose problems for continuity and stability. The compatibility of any two of the three commonly rises on the departure of the third.

(11) If sexuality is significant in an unstructured triad, competition between two of the same gender occurs until one is sociosexually de-skilled by whatever means by the other. Since men often employ face-saving devices, fictions disguising this outcome are commonly entertained. Since women are less anxious about status loss and mutual compatibility they may tend to indulge in a positive feedback that accentuates the outcome of their attempts at a sexual victory.

(12) Sexual competition and fear of cuckoldry leads men to attempt to control women and to seek their complicity in successive (promiscuous) or simultaneous (polygynous) sexual alliances. Where socio-economic conditions prescribe the opposite condition, matriachal or polyandrous societies may eventuate, but normally with males still playing important roles that enhance apparent prestige of individuals. Female-dominated societies are rare; patrilineal descent and the avunculate (p. 168) are common.

(13) If societal legislation prescribes relations between the sexes other, say, than those of strict monogamy, then suppression and repression operate to produce individuals compliant in forming economically or ecologically adapted social units.

(14) Societal prescription is commonly experienced as oppression, especially by the young, and high levels of emotional suppression produce deviance from the legitimate norms of behaviour. Different societies accept different degrees and kinds of deviance.

(15) Gender roles stem from personal preferences in styles of sexual and affectional performance which are programmed early in life (see below). While the norms of gender expression are probably distinctive of each sex, the range is wide and extensive overlap in the preferred modes of self-expression occur. Where societal legitimation narrows the range of expression that is acceptable deviance may be suppressed. Where deviance is more acceptable as a result of widening the acceptable standards of personal expression a 'permissive' situation arises in which a wide variance in role-taking can develop.

(16) There seems to be some oscillation in time between periods of maintaining rigid 'standards' of socio-sexual conduct and more relaxed ones. These shifts express periods of frustration followed by movements towards anarchy that eventually become socially alarming.

I claim no formal evidence for these suggestions. It is, however, striking that analysis of the personal characteristics of individuals that generate types of interactions can be placed in a circular or a 'circumplicial' arrangement based on a limited number of dimensions resembling those upon which Kummer based his rules for geladas (see also p. 80). In particular, the interplay between behaviour expression on dominance–submissiveness and approach–avoidance dimensions accounts for most interactions shown in the human species (strictly speaking this is known only for a Western research sample of the population). This suggests that social relating at the face-to-face level may rest upon a small number of underlying rules operating with thresholds determined by positions on a much smaller number of dimensions than seems intuitively likely. This is because the outcome of the interplay between factors can generate a bewildering variety of expressions that grade subtly from one to another. From an examination of the formal characteristics of human interaction, the social psychologist Roger Brown (1965) concluded that two major dimensions of interaction are almost universally present whenever one person meets another. These are the dimensions of *status* and *solidarity*. In the first we find individuals organizing their social relations in terms of perceived dominance or submission or in terms of superiority–inferiority in relation to some criteria for status. Possession of status often gives differential access to commodities, particular rights, and deferences, but also often to obligations as well. In the second dimension, degrees of personal closeness, affection, warmth, liking, or friendship are perceived and are used expressively or as guides in interactions.

Independent research on groups as diverse as army officers (Carter 1954), graduate students (Borgatta 1969), mothers and children (Schaeffer 1959), fathers and young children (Becker and Krug 1964) all reveal surprisingly similar prime dimensions of variance. Summarizing these researches, Carson (1969) affirmed that major portions of the interpersonal behaviour of human beings can be conceived as involving variations on two independent bipolar dimensions: dominance–submission and love–hate. It is important to realize that these findings are based on careful factor analyses of covariance between many measures in observational and experimental samples of people. We are not talking here in general hypothetical terms but about the results of rigorous analysis.

A useful model can be constructed by drawing up a hypothetical two-dimensional space utilizing our two dimensions as Cartesian coordinates with the point of intersection representing their psychological middle values. If the vertical axis represents the *status* dimension and the horizontal one *solidarity*, then we have four quadrants representing hostile dominance, friendly dominance, friendly submission, and hostile submission (Fig. 9.5). The model also includes the possibility of representing intensity or strength by placing the point of intersection of two measurements on the face of the circle.

The suggestion that interpersonal behaviour may be ordered 'circumplicially' in this way was originally made by Timothy Leary (1957) during the early, academically productive phase of his extraordinary career. Together with colleagues at the Kaiser Foundation in California he developed a framework which, although tenuous at the time, has since proved to have robust empirical foundations. Not every arrangement of a two-factor domain will produce a circle or 'circumplicial' arrangement of scores. This arises only when ratings of different behavioural traits can be arranged in such a way that adjacent ratings will be highly correlated, measures of more removed traits less so (but closely correlated to their neighbours), and further comparisons again more closely correlated (Swenson 1973, p. 179).

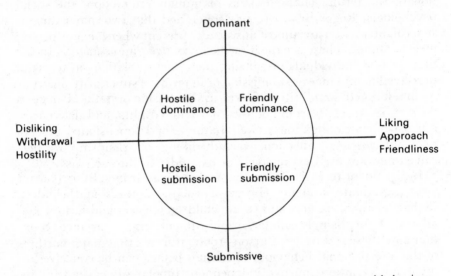

FIG. 9.5. Cartesian coordinates of status and solidarity in interpersonal behaviour.

Leary devised a circumplex of 16 categories resulting from a division into four parts of the quarter segments shown in Fig. 9.6. When neighbouring behaviours are paired the result is eight 'octants' which Leary used as the main basis for discussion. The name of each octant, competitive–narcissistic for example, is so constructed that the first name refers to the milder of the two expressions of the same behavioural trait. If we treat each of the 16 behaviours as a pattern which has become consolidated into a social stance, then we perceive that these stances are designed to preserve the security of the individual through eliciting those responses from others that are least threatening to him. A person's stance tends therefore to create the 'social environment of adaptedness' in which he or she feels able to function creatively with least anxiety. The stance is in fact a coping style comprised of both assertive coping behaviour that is related to reality and also defence mechanisms operating with varying degrees of selective inattention and obsessionalism. The stance is far from a simply passive security operation; it supplies the interpersonal domain within which a person interacts with his idea of what another's world 'should be'. How far this is related to a mutually negotiated reality depends on the openness of the two persons in interaction, the extent of their anxiety with respect to one another, and the 'games' (p. 294) they are habitually and situationally inclined to 'play'. In Fig. 9.6 each segment comprises a typical stance. The inner circle names the characteristic response such a person is likely to show in a wide range of social circumstances; the next circle shows the behaviour that his or her stance is designed to elicit in others; the next circle lists behaviours of a more extreme kind elicited more clearly under a degree of stress. The outer circle lists the octant names.

Leary shows that the elicitation of complimentarity operates in different ways on the two main dimensions. Complimentarity means reciprocity in the dominance–submissiveness dimension (i.e. domi-

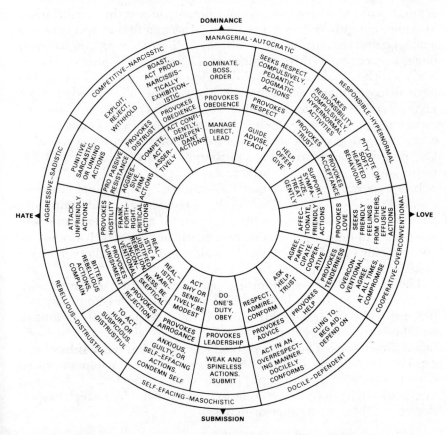

FIG. 9.6. The two-factor circumplex (dominance versus submission and hate versus love, i.e. avoid versus approach) with 16 distinct behaviour categories. Circle segments define qualitative contrasts in behaviour and distance from centre suggests strength. In the outer ring the 16 categories have been reduced to eight names defining overall dispositional traits; the first word indicates the less extreme form of the type. (After Leary 1957 and Carson 1969.)

nance induces submissiveness and vice versa) but, in the approach–withdrawal dimension, dislike or hostility generates a corresponding avoidance, while warmth and open-heartedness likewise tend to soften and make more friendly even an initially highly defended individual.

To illustrate the system consider meeting at a party a docile-independent individual who has been categorized as a member of this octant on account of his behaviour. He seems on first acquaintance to be unusually respectful and trusting of one's opinion. In response I begin to become somewhat expansive, suggest advice, tell little wisdom stories from a slightly inflated personal stance, and then begin to discover the other is becoming excessively clinging, wants to see me again, overholds in eye contact, and persists in lengthy conversation. Making an eventual excuse I refill my glass and find myself next to a man who proceeds to give me an uneasy feeling of having the conversational carpet removed from under me. I find myself outmanoeuvred when I wish to make a point mildly different from his and by trial and error discover that I can approach his world at all only when I am saying 'yes' to his ideas. Feeling slightly Machiavellian about my experiment, I move from this narcissist and meet a lively young woman whose warmth gives me feelings of having known her for years. Miss Co-operative–Conventional is a darling but sadly, after half an hour, seems to have surprisingly little to say.

It is important to realize that well-adjusted people quite normally respond to others in a way that produces comfortable conformity with another's stance yet leaves sufficient room for self-differentiation and assertion. An individual who is consistently and insistently occupying one and only one of the octants is certainly either a social psychologist doing an experiment or else a sick person.

The fact that such an immense potential for diverse transactions seems inherently based in combinations of tendencies from only two dimensions seems to support the idea that the universals of human social interaction may depend on some species-wide array of dispositional dimensions. The interpersonal effects are naturally subject to a great deal of cultural editing so that the communality of human experience is obscured by ethnographic diversity. The basis for human intersubjectivity may, however, lie in transactional rules which to some degree we share with other primates.

The self-process as a human universal

I am arguing that the most crucial evolutionary emergent in the phylogeny of human powers is the ability whereby the person conceives of himself as an active agent distinguishable as an entity from others and about which propositions can be entertained. It is of course this capacity that gives depth and meaning to human transactions and allows of their development within a given culture.

We know remarkably little about the evolutionary origins of the capacity to represent oneself to oneself as a self. Even advanced mammals interact with one another on a level of awareness that appears to lack this component, which evidently requires a cognitive apparatus present only in man and perhaps to a degree in the great apes. In an experiment with captive animals, Gallup (1970) provided rhesus monkeys and chimpanzees with mirrors in which they could observe their reflected images. Within each species two groups were anaesthetized and one of the groups received dabs of dye on cheek and ear while the control group did not. On awakening the animals observed their faces in mirrors. Chimpanzees used their reflections to touch their *own* noses, thus demonstrating an awareness that the image represented themselves and showed a change in their appearance. The rhesus monkeys failed to show this self-directed behaviour. Human infants can recognize themselves in this way at least by the age of 15 months (Lewis and Brooks 1977).

In human beings the ability to represent oneself to oneself makes it possible to learn about the relationship between bodily states of emotion and different experiences of identity. It is this connection that in turn allows an individual to express his own emotion to another and, further, eventually to appreciate the intentionality of another through empathy. The complex intersubjectivity of human relationships would be impossible without these abilities. How do we account for their evolution?

The roots of the self-process, an open programme gradually filled in through social learning, comprise, we shall argue, a prime species-specific characteristic of man. These roots are a product of organic evolution and yield abilities that function to optimize the inclusive fitnesses of individuals through subtly mediating the interactions essential to the maintenance of the human social environment and reproduction within it.

A key theme in this book has been that human evolution led first to the creation of a society characterized by nepotistic altruism which was then increasingly led by reciprocal altruism to a codification into ethical systems legitimating some patterns of social interaction and excluding others. We have seen in the work of Trivers and Alexander that there are sound biological arguments for a continuity of development from primate social evolution and that the mechanisms of natural selection are the most likely causes of human psychological evolution.

Given the emergence of a society of reciprocal transaction, a further evolutionary step became inevitable. The subtlety and potential range of these interactions required rapid processing and a speeding up of adaptive modification in relation to shifting interpersonal circumstances. We can see that an enhanced capacity for the retention of information and the ability to operate upon it logically in abstraction and generalization provided the intellectual power that met this need. In addition, the development of further abilities in delaying emotional response gave time for some ideational analysis of a situation. This provided the mechanisms for producing cognitively guided behaviour that was employed in dealing with problems and yielded adaptively variable behaviours in the lives of individuals (Chapter 6).

In human societies reciprocation has become of paramount importance in resource acquisition, in the maintenance of the domestic unit, in collaborative defence in relation to other groups, in developing new and adaptive technology in energy transformation, in medicine, and finally in the management of various forms of power holding through patterns of transgenerational succession. As Trivers has made clear, systems of reciprocation entail the possibility of exploitation by the cheater and produce a corresponding ability to detect non-reciprocation. This is a form of competition that leads to a progressive evolution of powers promoting subtlety in both interpersonal exploitation and in its detection and control (p. 176).

Much of human life concerns the formation and dissolution of partnerships. The emotional system of partnership entails balancing trust and distrust, which depends on processing information about the levels of reciprocation in progress. On the trust side of the system lie the complex feeling states of liking, sympathy, and gratitude, while on the side of distrust lie indignation and dislike, perhaps enmity. Reciprocal altruism would therefore seem to have brought about the natural selection of a means for ensuring the balance of relationships between potentially untrustworthy partners.

The faculty that monitors the state of play between partners is empathy; the ability to detect the intentionality of another through representing his emotional and cognitive cues to oneself as if they were one's own. This allows a person to stand in the place of another and thus to appreciate the nature of an ongoing relationship. The human ability to mimic emotional states and attitudes and thereby to present an inauthentic picture of oneself to another is clearly a further twist in the spiral of cheating and detection. Deception of various kinds lies deeply embedded in the structure of transactions, and its detection becomes correspondingly subtle. Non-verbal monitoring is especially developed here and functions largely independently of the assessment of the verbal propositions in an exchange.

The evolution of subtle empathic abilities is of value only if it correlates with an equally competent ability in discrimination between the states of mind of another and those of one's own. And this of course requires an ability to experience oneself as an agent in the world distinguishable from others. It is this ability that the mechanisms of the self-process accomplish in the formation of an identity structure. An autonomous identity is the secured base for interaction and emotional negotiation. Clearly a person who lacks autonomy is open to deception and manipulation as well as to experiencing major problems in achieving his own prospects. Autonomy is highly likely to yield achievements which may relate to advancements of one sort or another with the ultimate outcome in differential reproduction of self or relatives. It is not, however, essential that the autonomous person be explicitly aware of himself through intellectual introspection. The categorizations that underly his performance may remain implicit until social conditions arise that demand more explicit formulation in language (p. 264).

The development of autonomy is however by no means assured in human life; accidents of birth and upbringing can profoundly affect the development of individual identity so that the ways in which the open programmes of personal development are achieved vary enormously and the extent to which an effective maturity is reached is likewise problematical. There does seem, however, to be a consistent endeavour in every person to achieve or to complete a process of personal growth that leads to a perceived autonomy within the cultural frame of society. Persons whose rearing conditions have left them badly deprived of experiences that enhance identity-formation commonly invest great amounts of emotional energy and money in an endeavour to 'grow'. Growth is felt to have been accomplished not so much when some state of 'happiness' is achieved but rather when an individual's self-respect has been made firm by experiences in which his or her appropriate autonomy has been demonstrated.

The evolution of human psychological structure has been a process of autocatalytic advance much in the same way as human anatomy has developed. The self-process, I am arguing, is the refined end-product of a series of changes (Fig. 9.7) which began with the emergence of reproductive nepotism and reciprocal altruism in our primate ancestors. Without this evolution we would be unable to reflect upon our position in the world and to design solutions to personal and social problems. We are at first unconscious of the sources of our attitudes and feelings, but through study, scholarship, and reflection we are making ourselves conscious of them. The ability to do this with the apparatus that the evolutionary process has bequeathed us gives us such freedom as we have.

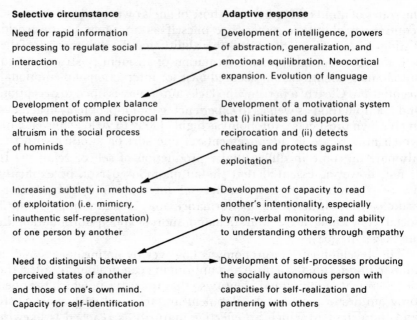

Selective circumstance	Adaptive response
Need for rapid information processing to regulate social interaction	Development of intelligence, powers of abstraction, generalization, and emotional equilibration. Neocortical expansion. Evolution of language
Development of complex balance between nepotism and reciprocal altruism in the social process of hominids	Development of a motivational system that (i) initiates and supports reciprocation and (ii) detects cheating and protects against exploitation
Increasing subtlety in methods of exploitation (i.e. mimicry, inauthentic self-representation) of one person by another	Development of capacity to read another's intentionality, especially by non-verbal monitoring, and ability to understanding others through empathy
Need to distinguish between perceived states of another and those of one's own mind. Capacity for self-identification	Development of self-processes producing the socially autonomous person with capacities for self-realization and partnering with others

FIG. 9.7. Autocatalytic stages in the evolution of the self-process.

The development of self through transaction

Whatever the involvement of biological determinants in the patterning of human interactions and the formation of relationships, human beings are not directly conscious of the processes involved any more than the instinctive sparrow has an awareness of the biological strategies it performs. Human beings are, however, remarkably conscious of themselves as agents in a social world and talk endlessly about it. This self-report can become the focus of study so that the processes of human inner life are themselves better understood. This is equivalent to adopting the emic position of the cultural anthropologist rather than the etic position of the biologist or ecologist of mind (see p. 172). We are only just beginning to infer the nature of the processes that underlie self, and a vital aspect of contemporary research concerns its development in ontogeny.

The root of contemporary western thinking on self lies in the distinction made by William James (1890) between the 'I' and the 'me'. James argued that, 'In its widest possible sense, a man's Me is the sum total of all he can call his.' This includes his body, possessions, ancestors, relations, reputations, profession, and bank account. He attributes values to these elements of his 'me' so that his self-esteem depends on his perception of the quality of these elements within a system of values that compares these items with those in the repertoire of other 'me's'. He has strong attachment to this 'me' which gives rise to degrees of elation or depression when the perceived quality changes in relation to his perceptions of others. The social 'me' rests on the recognition a man gets from his fellows, so that images from parents, friends, and work-mates all become constituents of the 'me'. A man largely regards himself as a product of other's views and is motivated to maintain or increase self-esteem by reference to a nexus of social perceptions. James's view of the me is thus the basis for a large literature on 'identity'.

James's 'I' is more difficult to describe. He says, 'It is that which at any moment is conscious, whereas me is only one of the things which it is conscious of'. This 'I', then, is the agent, the experiencer. James points out that while the 'I' has an experiential continuity it varies greatly with respect to its state. Indeed, the changeableness of these states suggests that there may be no actual 'I', no *substantial* or informa-tional entity. All one can have is a knowledge of the changing states of the 'I' and their relationships. To James, then, as for a Buddhist theorist, the 'I', as consciousness of self, is a stream of awareness that appropriates the material of thought in the construction of the idea of 'me'. 'The thoughts themselves,' to James, 'are the thinkers.' Now this view of the 'I' lies at the root of the psychology of states of consciousness that forms a pole of contemporary thinking counterbalancing analyses of the 'me' conceived as 'identity'. James's 'I' and 'me' are basic to investigations of consciousness and identity respectively. In this section we set out some contemporary thinking on identity. We shall consider consciousness later (Chapter 11).

'Identity' has been used to refer both to those attributes of an individual that maintain the consistency of his personal presentation in encounters with others and to the 'place' he occupies in a community. Here we are primarily interested in the first usage (de Levita 1965). Some authors (e.g. Horrocks and Jackson 1972), use the term 'self' or 'self-process' as virtually synonymous with identity and prefer to talk of 'identity constructs' for those ideas about the self used in the repre-sentation of social roles. Among the founding writers on the subject, G. H. Mead (1934) in particular developed an almost behaviourist approach. To him social acts are events through which an individual can learn the perspectives of others and incorporate these, and espe-cially the attitudes of 'significant others' (parents, siblings, close friends, transference figures, etc.), into his view of himself. Indeed, a person becomes such only through a progressively elaborated process of role-taking in relation to other people. Individuals not only conceive of themselves largely as others see them but also tend to act in accor-dance with the expectations that others may hold. Communication is a vital element in the development of the person and in the social control of personal behaviour. Mead's work has led on to Homans's (1961) view of the person as strongly influenced by a need for social approval, which, while obviously important, would seem to relegate individuals to somewhat passive and compliant roles in society. As we shall see, from the very beginning new-born children are strategists pursuing goals that end in autonomous action in the world. And strategy is first expressed in a child's relationship to its mother.

Clinical studies of the neonate and very young babies have tended to belong to one of two orientations: either (a) an emphasis on the influence of effects from constitutional maturation (the nativist view) or from the environmental context (the nurturist view); or (b) some form of interactional model in which an outcome is seen as a static product of the two. Were these models adequate to an explanation of the mother–infant relationship one should expect that one could predict the effects of development from one stage of life to another. For example, the influences of perinatal anoxia or premature birth might be expected to be found repeatedly in deficits in perceptual-motor, neurological, and cognitive functions at successively later ages. Surprisingly, in fact, the effects of 'trauma' of this sort tend to disappear with increasing age, a clear example of the developmental tendency to recover from deflections from normal trends and to focus on a terminal 'equifinality' (p. 239). Studies of the longitudinal effects of pre- and perinatal stress all point towards a rather rapid attenuation of effects attributable to these causes and a preponderance of the influence of familial and socio-economic factors. [Interestingly, for example, the ill effects of initial perinatal complications persist longer in families of lower socio-economic status, as an important study in modern Hawaii has shown (Werner, Bierman, and French 1971).]

Studies of battered babies (Spinetta and Rigler 1972) often reveal personality characteristics in the parents that differ from those of parents who do not batter children. Paradoxically, however, subsequent predictions that parents with such characteristics will batter babies are not borne out. Clearly there must be some combination of baby characteristics with parental ones that eventuate in battering. Sameroff (1975) remarks, 'Since abusing parents appear to be selective in the choice of the child they abuse, a missing element in the predictive equation for child abuse would seem to be characteristics specific to the child'. Sameroff goes on to point out that the characteristics of both child and parent are continuously and progressively varying. Static interactional models must therefore give way to a dynamic theory of developmental transaction in which the changing features of parent–child relating are examined in time.

A truly transactional model needs to stress the child's active engagement in attempts to organize and structure his world and the way in which his responsiveness and that of the parent are geared together in ways that have outcomes for *both*. Sameroff argues that personal deficiencies in children need to be regarded as products of a *continuous* malfunction in the styles of parent–child relating which prevent the child from organizing his world adaptively across time. Since self-correction through time seems to be a natural process in child development a continuing deficiency indicates a correspondingly active malfunctioning through time. This may be due to an initial maternal inadequacy that sets up a reciprocating pattern of progressive interactions of failure in relating, but it can equally well be due to sensorimotor disequilibria in the baby to which the mother, for whatever reason, fails to adapt herself. Sameroff gives a simple model of the sequential development of emotional disturbance in a child with coincident feelings of resentment and guilt in the mother. We could begin with many precipitating circumstances but, in Sameroff's example, the excessive anxiety of the mother before the birth is chosen. Her anxiety necessitates instrumental delivery, and perinatal complications and difficulties in feeding follow. The progressively frustrated child begins to become difficult for the anxious mother, whose increased diffidence gives positive feedback to the child's irritability. This in turn angers the mother, who resorts either to guilty resentment and pandering or aggressive and punishing routines. This vicious circle of events progresses in successive stages of mutually aggravating feedback through time. Such a model immediately suggests possible nodal points in the sequence where intervention by a pediatrician or therapist could be helpful and the sequence pushed in the direction of a better mutual accommodation (Fig. 9.8).

The emphasis in clinical reports of sequences such as these makes us focus on the symbiosis of mother and child in normal development. The patterning is always highly idiosyncratic, arising from the unique

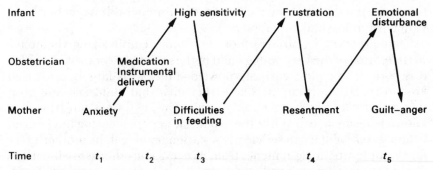

FIG. 9.8. Possible transaction sequence in a development of emotional disturbance. (After Sameroff 1975.)

attributes of the baby, which, in spite of the limitations of its repertoire, is a surprisingly perceptive, wilful, and demanding little individual. While an emphasis on the genius of the baby is a great shift from earlier assumptions that the baby was a passive reactor to parental stimulation, it remains equally inappropriate to ignore the dynamic quality of the parents' attitudes. These are expressed, for example, in mother's verbal reports, which can reveal the *reasons* why she does what she does.

Mothers behave according to the folk 'personality theory' they hold, and their knowledge, attitudes, prejudices, and awarenesses all determine their routines with their infants. These maternal 'cognitive sets' become crucial to any understanding as to why a child is growing up in the way it does. Indeed, since many of a mother's attitudes are socio-economically, class, or culturally based, some explanation of the deficits in infant recovery from perinatal complications may lie in enquiring into this aspect of her life (Parke 1977). Of course, we need not stop at the mother. Recent studies suggest that, in the contemporary West at least, the father plays a more important role in infant development than was formerly thought and his significance to the child can register long before it reaches the age of 6 or 7, when he emerges in any case as an important socializing agent for the child with respect to the extra-familial world (Parke 1978). Indeed, in modern clinical work with 'family-therapy', the whole constellation of interacting attitudes of family members is brought into play.

These studies and others focusing on the importance of interactions in time (Cairns 1972, 1976) suggest the need to supplement normative data on development with ideographic reporting that allows a perspective based on the idea of individual life-trajectories. Given that a 'search for meaning' is crucial in human life, the means whereby an individual creates meaning is highly dependent on precise and personally relevant events in a lifetime's development. Here we are considering childhood; but the principle extends to the whole of an individual life. The construction of explanatory models may be based in normative understanding but must allow for the innumerable deflections and variety of individual experience.

Contemporary research is more and more emphasizing the active participation of the very young child in the social network within which it is born. The child's earliest knowledge indeed is largely organized around social information. The earlier idea that children were born into a 'blooming buzzing mass of confusion', as James put it, is now known to be incorrect. While the neonate is poor in focusing its eyes and cannot track well, it can see clearly a stationary object, its mother's face for example, about eight inches from its eyes. The other sense functions are likewise well developed and operant conditioning in simple learning is possible from birth. Infants, for example, can learn to suck differentially in order to change the brightness of a photographic slide or other effects. Infants respond to face quality and distortions of it by 6 months, and even by 1 month a link is established between the mother's face and voice. Infants recognize strangers as early as 3 months. Certainly by the end of the first year the infant has the sensory ability and cognitive capacity to process large amounts of information about the social world in particular. When does the infant begin to conceive of itself as a self?

The conceptualization of self
Conceptions about self probably emerge gradually, and are contingent upon the integration of a number of concurrent processes. The infant learns by testing hypotheses which become increasingly complex with time and are related to the satisfaction of needs and curiosity. The child, as a motivated hypothesis-tester, must necessarily eventually come across the proposition of itself as an agent. We must proceed carefully here, however, for other advanced mammals are also hypothesis-testers and live in complex social worlds, yet seem to lack abilities of self-reference.

The first stage in the awareness of self is somatic, organized around kinaesthesis, proprioception, and other bodily cues. The infant soon discovers that external objects—especially those moving, vocalizing variable ones that are persons—are instrumental in relieving bodily stresses. Re-afferent feedback provides the child with its first evidence that an event may be contingent on its own performance. When it closes its eyes the world disappears. When it cries a face appears.

This 'contingency feedback' from the care-giver is, indeed, the main source of the child's initial experience of itself as an agent. Experiences that certain events are contingent on its own actions generate expectancies which come to differentiate the infant's own actions from those done to it by another. When an infant's demands are rewarded, he is in effect learning to become the controller of a simple social situation. The distinction between self-as-agent and other-as-respondent arises from the infant's own initiatives.

In a mirror experiment Lewis and Brooks (1978) presented infants of various ages up to 24 months with a reflecting surface behind which was placed a TV camera for recording their behaviour. After the introduction to the mirror the child's mother wiped its nose and in so doing placed some red dye upon it. Since mothers commonly wipe infants' noses no child responded to this treatment by touching its own nose. Infants were then brought to the mirror again and their behaviour recorded. Below 12 months almost no infant responded to the red mark as a result of observing itself in the mirror, but beyond this age there was a rapid development in nose-directed behaviour (25 per cent of 15–18-month-old infants, 75 per cent at 21–24 months). The children's responses to their bodies generally were also increased when their noses were marked, but this effect was not found to increase with age. In this experiment, responses to the face thus appear to be generally differentiated from those to the body.

In a further experiment infants were shown pictures of themselves as well as pictures of other people known or strange to them. Up to 21 months the infants did not discriminate between themselves and other infants. Self-labelling of the infant's own picture began at about 15 months, and by 22 months pronouns such as 'me' or 'mine' were being used. Thus, even prior to the use of pronouns or names the child uses differential labelling to mark its awareness of self as opposed to other children of similar age. A highly interesting finding was that, especially among girls, infants looked as much at their own pictures as at a stranger of the same sex but significantly less than at a stranger of the opposite sex. It seems as if responsivity to self and to the opposite sex begin to appear at about the same time. This is probably based in the awareness of the opposite sex as different, and reveals an early use of social categorization.

In further experiments, mirrors and TV playback were used to elicit the infants' responses to images that either respond contingently to the child's actions or do not do so. By 12 months children imitate video-tapes of themselves more than they do representations of other children. By 9 months infants are likely to show behaviour that is contingent to their mirror image (i.e. to play in response to it) and to show more of such behaviour in relation to self-image than to others. By 15 months infants distinguish between themselves on TV and other conditions.

Lewis and Brooks (1977, 1979) suggest that a simple rule may be operating here. Once an idea of what is 'me' is developing, then things like 'me' are to be approached while things not like 'me' are to be avoided. Operations based on a self–other comparison may be very important in the development of a child's social behaviour. The rule may play an especial role in peer relations and peer imitation. The use of older siblings in education may become very valuable. Work on other primates has shown that peers rather than adults are likely to rehabilitate isolate-reared and depressed monkeys. Another child may be a child's best therapist and assist it most in developing social relations.

The experience of oneself as a distinct entity and the conceptualization of such experiencing in words is doubtless preceded by a growing awareness of self (subjective self-consciousness, p. 313) which is not as yet separated in a clear contradistinction from others. The task is, after all, not an easy one for one cannot *see* oneself. The conceptual realization involves relating the process of self-awareness to contingencies in such a way that the concept 'this action produces x and this action–experience is me' arises. The concept of me is a reification resulting from the integration of numerous experiences of contingency.

The extent to which a child clearly differentiates its self from others increases with age and develops in relation to interactions with a caregiver. Duval and Wicklund (1972) suggest, for example (see Chapter 11), that the young child's tendency to act as if everyone else existed only as a support for its own processes is brought to a sudden end when a parent begins to contradict it or frustrate its intentions. Such experiences provide a clear insight into the distinctness of self versus other (see further p. 314).

Prior to the realization of 'me' as a concept, emotional states and expression are not clearly experienced as related to self. Indeed, Lewis and Brooks (1979) argue that an *emotional experience* as such does not occur prior to the linkage of self-awareness to an emotional state. Once an infant has discovered through experiences of agency and contingency that his awareness is focused within an experiencing body he can also learn to differentiate and locate feelings within himself. He can learn to label himself as cross or sad just as he can label himself as small or belonging to the male gender.

Consciousness of the awareness of self and consciousness that the quality of that awareness changes with emotional states are both contingent upon an ability to distance oneself from that awareness itself; a distancing that takes the form of conceptualization. The conception of oneself as a 'thing' results from the integration of many experiences and their extraction as conceptual units in a representational universe. Lewis and Brooks call this the 'categorical' self —the self as object—as opposed to 'existential' self-awareness that lacks categorization into concepts. Duval and Wicklund (p. 314) refer to the quality of the consciousness of these two conditions as objective and subjective respectively. The conceptualization that represents the categorical self forms the very root, not only of the self as agent, but of the functional social self in a world of others. It is the basis for evaluations of self-esteem.

Labelling the experiences of the self depends upon social experience. Ekman's (1973) study of facial expressions suggests that the expression and comprehension of at least some seven categories of emotion may be a human universal. The list includes happiness, fear, anger, sadness, disgust/contempt, surprise, and interest. The universality of these communicative expressions must indicate a degree of uniformity in the underlying emotional processes responsible for them. These fundamental emotions doubtless emerge naturally in the course of mother–child interaction and become labelled as part of the transactional process of language acquisition. More subtle labelling is doubtless socially determined, as Schachter and Singer (1962) suggest. Different qualities of arousal are evaluated and distinguished in the context of social events that give them meaning. Emotional labelling and reference to self is thus the result of an integration of internal and social stimulation in the context of an interactive performance in which I know myself to be an agent. For the child to be able to experience complex feeling states such as shame or guilt he must be able to incorporate the standards of others. Indeed, since these standards are largely cultural in origin, the extent to which a child experiences shame or guilt is culturally related. Mediterranean children are more likely to acquire shame, whereas northern Europeans are more familiar with guilt.

To conclude: the child's emerging sense of self is dependent upon the growth of its cognitive abilities in categorization, its experiences of contingency and agency in interaction with care-givers, and its experience of the emotional quality of its own conscious states. The human species has been well endowed with the basic powers that promote the conceptualization of self as agent, a cognitive construct that is fundamental to the operation of the self process and communication between self and other.

Attachment and 'The Game'
The expression of an emotion in animal and human behaviour commonly comprises a signal system that serves to induce a partner to remove or assist in removing the source of conflict that engenders the feelings. Pleasing affect is associated with the achievement of a sense of security near an attachment figure and in a familiar environment. In particular the 'relief' experienced following the cessation of thwarting is especially pleasing and signals the establishment of a 'consummatry situation'. A great variety of emotional conflicts is dependent upon the variety of possible sources of thwarting and innumerable gradations of intensity. Feelings can thus be gross or very subtle indeed. Novelty and exploration away from an attachment figure such as a parent is clearly pleasurably exciting for many young animals but rapidly switches to alarm if their surroundings are excessively strange or if the attachment figure disappears.

Many studies have been made of the anxiety induced by the removal of attachment figures for short or long periods. A number of primate species have been observed, and the results have much in common although they vary in ways that reflect 'rules' (pp. 80 and 235) governing the social system of the animals concerned (i.e. compare Hinde's work on rhesus monkeys with Kaufman's on bonnet and pigtail macaques in White 1974). Bowlby (1969, 1973) has described an initial protest stage of separation in human infants followed by an aggressive phase ending in 'despair' characterized by a cessation of activity and depression. Mothers may be rejected for some time after their return if the delay has been substantial. In humans the effects of long-term maternal separation may result in a number of long-term emotional or neurotic effects (Bowlby 1969, 1973; Ainsworth 1962) but these are often additionally associated with broken homes, distressed parental relationships, and poor institutional care with multiple separation experiences that may have greater significance in the long term than the early separations. Generally, however, research is beginning to suggest that children who have spent more than a week in hospital or who have repeatedly been in hospital before the age of five are more likely to show emotional disturbances in adolescence than others. Loss of a parent in infancy may also be associated with a predisposition to depression in later life. Different styles of mothering tend to yield emotional dispositions of certain types in their children. It is clear, however, that these outcomes also depend on other adult figures and peers whose friendship and warmth can often compensate to a degree for defective parenting.

A series of important studies with both non-human primate and human babies shows that the neonate and infant respond with an especial alertness and curiosity to situations in which a parent or substitute responds to their initiatives. Mason (1979) has shown how monkeys reared with automated mobile mothers or with bitches that responded to their activities showed signs of cognitive competence that were missing from more deprived individuals. The importance of 'meaningful' interactions between the human mother and child as a critical aid to cognitive development is great. Indeed, the child needs this type of responsive environment if it is to learn how to make an impact upon the objects that surround it. A young baby begins very early to associate environmental changes with its own movements and hence, through integration, to build up sensorimotor schemata that operate upon the world. The system is constructed through learning to compare feedback from muscle movements, with feedback from perceptions of change in the environment.

Papousek and Papousek (1979) in particular have experimented with operant procedures whereby the child can learn at a very early age to turn its head, switch on a slide, etc. for a simple reward. Elaborations of sequences, i.e. turning head twice to one side to obtain the visual reinforcement of a new slide, allow the child to discover rule-based behaviour. Following rules is then a guide to controlling the environmental response. The baby is, however, no passive rule-learner; it seeks to set up maternal behaviour that will produce cognitive rewards. The Papouseks demonstrate with a striking sequence of photographs that a baby in its mother's arms will gaze at its mother's face until eye contact is achieved. When this happens, the mother responds with a head-tilt smile and a verbal greeting. The baby then smiles and shows pleasure, which stimulates its mother further. By controlling eye contact the baby is able to control the mother's responsiveness. Experiments show that babies ignore mothers that behave in unpredictable ways; such mothers may then have difficulty in reconnecting with their babies. In addition, if the mother shuts her eyes the baby will stop trying to achieve eye contact and will begin to show distress, even though still warmly held in its mother's arms. In general, care-takers show a range of natural behaviours specifically related to contacting and alerting the baby (Fig. 9.9) which seem to function in assisting the cognitive development of the child.

---

(1) Caretaker presents herself/himself maximally to infant in all perceptual modalities.

(2) Caretaker presents predictable simple routines enabling infant to establish elementary categorizations of familiarity/novelty.

(3) Caretaker adapts to infant's restricted means of establishing personal contact.

(4) Caretaker shows naturally reflexive responses to baby behaviour which are often given without conscious deliberation.
Elements of these response patterns are:
  (a) Slow, clear enunciation of concrete 'baby talk'.
  (b) Speech of higher more variable pitch than adult speech.

(c) Repetition and modification in speech and non-verbal communication maintains maximum neonate alertness.
Consistency plus variation are the key to 'education' of the neonate.

(d) Eye contact elicits parental greeting behaviour.

(e) Imitative mirroring of a baby provides feedback with which it later discovers its own ability to imitate the adult.

These responses are part of the reciprocatory transactions whereby mother and infant relate together and mutually reinforce their attachment.

FIG. 9.9. Caretaker responses to newborn and infant humans that provide the primal interpersonal context for early cognitive growth. (After Papousek and Papousek 1978.)

We may argue that the human baby seeks not only contact-comfort as do young primates, but also that its initial explorations are centred upon its mother's face and perhaps especially in an eye-contact smile routine. The maintenance of this recurrent activity achieves both a sense of security and the excitement of early explorations of an interpersonal world. The child learns by the results of its initiatives that it too is an agent capable of a degree of control over others. Childrens' emotions are probably founded in the maintenance or thwarting of a growing cognitive control over their relating with others.

It is obvious that for the almost immobile, defenceless, and limited human baby its first cognitive development will be in the area of mutual responsiveness with its care-taker. In its 'environment of evolutionary adaptedness' this will clearly be the mother. Cognitive control over interaction is thus a vital part of the development of the baby's emotional life. Without control the baby experiences negative feelings. Genetically programmed responses to mother gradually change to a cognitively programmed control over input. The 'exploratory' drive of babies is directed towards cognitive discovery of this sort and it is significant that behaviour that elicits baby-contingent environmental responses does not habituate. It is replaced by sleep or rest as biorhythmicity dictates. A baby is most attentive to its mother's face immediately after a feed when its metabolic needs are satisfied. The period of socializing then leads naturally into sleep. Of course mothers do not spend their time automatically baby-talking and smiling at the pleasure of their infants. The reciprocal patterning of events becomes one of mutual negotiation. It is in this increasingly subtle interplay that mother and child come to guess where the other 'is at' and thus to develop rules that allow for mutual satisfaction. For the child this negotiation is the process of discovering how to behave intersubjectively through the establishment of 'rapport'.

The importance for cognitive development of styles of mother–infant interaction which support the initiatives of the infant is stressed in John S. Watson's fascinating studies of what he terms 'The Game'. He argues that when an infant perceives a stimulus it begins a process of 'contingency analysis'. That is to say it seeks to establish whether that stimulus is contingent upon something that it has done. When a contingency is understood the stimulus gains new meaning for the child and releases vigorous smiling and cooing. In fact the stimulus begins functioning.

In the first 2–3 months of life slow response recovery and short memory prohibit the infant from becoming aware of contingencies. Then one day someone, usually the prime care-giver, begins playing a game with him. For example, every time he bobs his head he gets his nose touched, or his belly is blown every time he jiggles his legs. Here is a clear stimulus, a quick response with a short recovery time, and ample repetition. The baby understands, smiles, and coos. His mother is pleased and repeats the game with variants. If the situation is unclear or ambiguous baby does not smile, indeed he may cry. The essence of the game is the clear-cut contingency between the baby's action and the care-taker's response. The smile and coo is probably an innate human response that links the baby and the care-taker together in a way that promotes the baby's understanding of the social world and, indeed, because of the importance of contingency in the discovery of self as agent, his awareness of himself.

Watson (1972) devised a wondrous mobile that when suspended above a baby's cot would start moving when the baby made certain movements on a sensitive pillow. Babies supplied with cots and mobiles behaved differently according to whether (a) movement of the mobile was contingent upon their own behaviour, (b) the mobile moved periodically but not in relation to the baby's movements, or (c) the mobile stayed still. Babies with contingent mobiles showed an increase in their responses over a 14-day period ending with 140 pillow responses per 10-min. session. Babies in the other conditions showed no such increase. The first condition was associated with a great flowering of smiling and cooing.

The game hypothesis states that the child engages in contingency games with mobiles or people because the behaviour establishes a link between its own initiatives and a responding, ultimately social, world. 'The game is *not* important to the infant because people play it, but rather people become important to the infant because they play the game.' And the smiling ensures that they do so.

Parental, social, or environmental responses that are contingent on the infant's own initiatives are experienced as rewarding, give the child pleasant feelings which are expressed in smiles, and also lead the child to seek further information about its world. A failure to influence parental responses is experienced negatively as frustration. A mother's further responses to these initial moves may either reward or punish the infant. Rewarding the child's happy response to its parent's responses to its initiatives is likely to enhance relating, to lead to feelings about its own actions as good, and to easy development of self control. It may be suspected that a longer-term outcome could be a high level of basic trust and a steady self-esteem. Punishment by over-disciplining mothers may by contrast lead to emotional conflict, ambivalence, and perhaps subsequently to a belief in self as a victim and as a possible retaliator. Children rewarded for suppressed behaviour resulting from a thwarting of their exploratory activity may perhaps show an equal ambivalence later of a confused and rejecting nature probably coupled with a low self-esteem. Furthermore, since such a child would have learnt that assertive initiatives meet with little response, it may abandon them in later life. Children punished for negative behaviour caused by thwarting may perhaps later become depressed, anxious, and believe themselves to be bad. Much research is needed before relations such as these can be clearly affirmed. It seems, however, as if this is the general trend of discovery (see also Chapter 10).

Interaction effects such as these may crop up in a complex variety of forms as the infant grows. Not only is its initiative affected, but its expectations of others will gradually take shape with consequent implications for an emergent self-definition. The context of these transactional styles is twofold. On the one hand biogrammatical rules probably confine possible developments so that extreme deviations are deflected back towards population norms. On the other hand, social convention, affecting mother and child alike, do much to determine the overall styles of affect-laden interaction between them. Emotions are named only later in life and children probably learn to define their range of affective experience by self-limitation and to discover by trial and error when an experience of another belongs to a category with which they can cope. Emotionality as self understanding is only gradually acquired as a system of meaning within which a child's transactions with others are carried on.

The life-trajectory: changing experiences of self

A person's experience of self is so much a social phenomenon, so much a responsive process, that we cannot imagine it to hold constant through an individual life, or indeed to be the same in different periods of history (p. 275). The person in creating meaning and initiative within meaning adapts to the developing conditions of life as he ages. Persons of differing epochs inherit from their forebears the insights into world and self that the forebears have had. In this section we examine the different stages of life and the dimensions that influence personal identity within them. To begin with we treat contemporary man; needless to say only he can be a subject for direct research (see further p. 273).

Erik Erikson, perhaps the most influential pioneer of identity theory, bases his work within the context of professional psychoanalysis. The developmental stages of a child's growth were divided by Freud according to the focal areas of the body that successively dominate motivation and expression. Thus the baby's oral phase (sucking, intake, and by derivation incorporation or taking of another into oneself) gives way to the anal phase (sphincter control, attitudes towards dirt and bodily products, cleanliness, tidiness and, if accentuated into adult life, an over-precision attended by anxiety in 'messy' circumstances), and ultimately the genital (sexual expression with, ideally, full emergence of sensual gratification which requires mutuality, give-and-take, and warmth with another). These phases overlie one another progressively rather than replacing one another, so that anal or oral 'characteristics' are often attributed by psychoanalysts to attitudes shown by adults. Erikson (1950) built up his set of stages upon these basic themes but in the form of sets of antitheses that indicate paths of development. In brief, Erikson argued that during the eight stages of development (infancy, early childhood, play age, school age, adolescence, young adult, adult, and maturity) different polarities were of concern in the formation and maintenance of identity.

In infancy, experiences with the mother establish the degree of basic trust a child has in itself. Mistrust arises from negative qualities in the maternal relationship, particularly when characterized by overcontrol, coldness, or dislike shown by the mother. Not only is warmth crucial to the emergence of self-trust but the mother needs to indicate that her actions are meaningfully directed and are not independent of the child's somatic and cognitive needs. An impairment in basic trust tends to result in a later tendency to inward withdrawal when difficulties arise; sadly such withdrawal prevents the individual from coming to terms with the risks that need to be experienced if trust is to achieved.

In early infancy the focus is on autonomy versus shame or doubt. This is the anal–urethral stage of psychosomatic development during which the effects of punitive or facilitative toilet training are established. Self-control may be achieved with a sense of autonomy and 'pride' that is crucial for the emergence of self-esteem. Conversely parental overcontrol provides a sense of inadequacy, of 'anal impotence', and provides the roots for a deep sense of inner shame within which one cannot be truly a master of oneself.

During play age the child undertakes initiatives, but if these go wrong in relation to the world of powerful adult figures then 'guilt' is the result. The child may then develop an anxious overcompensation—trying to get things right yet not knowing quite what is wrong. The result, argues Erikson, is a form of tireless initiative in which adults so affected see their worth entirely in terms of the social value of what they are going to do next and not in terms of being themselves irrespective of 'other-control'. The switch at this age from parents to other models such as firemen, train drivers, etc. allows superficial identifications which go with fantasy initiatives disassociated from the risk of guilt inducing conflict with a parent.

The period of sociosexual latency, school age, is deemed to be characterized by industry versus an inferiority, a phase in which the quality of action is valued and generates feelings of self-completion or inferiority.

The emergency of sexual potency in adolescence creates a welter of superimposed polarities which all crowd upon the child at the same time. The young person is often very preoccupied with how he or she appears in the eyes of others rather than with what he feels himself or herself to be. Erikson (1959) argues that at this time the ego values acquired in childhood consolidate into a sense of identity which is the 'accrued confidence that one's own ability to maintain inner sameness and continuity is matched by the sameness and continuity of one's meaning for others'. An impairment in the gradual development of these ego processes throughout childhood results in identity diffusion rather than identity accomplishment.

The diffusion syndrome commonly occurs between the ages of 16 and 24 when an individual is faced by choices that will in large measure determine the future trajectory of his life; for example, occupational choice, sports, with whom to be intimate, sex partners, and friendships. The results of such choices tend to crystallize an identity out of the many separate identifications that the young person carries. Diffusion produces a sense of inner inconsistency, of shame at inadequate self-definition and at a responsiveness that is easily overcontrolled by others, a lack of initiative and, in intimacy, a fear of loss of identity in an engulfment by the other. A tense reservation, caution about commitment, and a basic mistrust of the social world is the result.

At this age, too, there is little perspective with respect to time. Time seems endless, without characterizations. At its happiest this results in the glorious languor of youth when all is possible, everything is open, an omnicompetence in a world of summer afternoons. The opposite is the fear that time may bring change, that sleep and awakening are equally fraught with possibility, that life might actually be worth ending, that entry to the world of adulthood is overwhelming. Inability to concentrate, avoidance of both competition and sociability lead to a depressed view of self and life. Ideals and gender are likewise ill-defined and give rise to a profound existential doubt about oneself.

As a psychoanalyst, Erikson paid attention to the precipitating circumstances of identity diffusion in his young patients. He found a characteristic syndrome of maternal attitudes in which a pronounced awareness of social status and a mannered need to maintain a facade of wealth and happiness went with an intrusive form of affectional expression based on a hunger for approval and recognition.

Profound inner insecurity in these mothers' relations with their husbands produces jealousy at any sign that the child identifies with the father. The whole edifice rests upon a hidden sense of social vulnerability. Husbands in such marriages typically do not show the initiative at home which they do in their often successful fields of work. Their wives are allowed to dominate by default, to intrude emotionally into areas of the self that lack certainty, with the result that the man is an emotional captive by collusion or alternatively leads an elusive life of extra-domestic activities attempting now and again to 'make it up' in ostentatious displays of concern. Adolescents with such parents find nothing in either of them with which to identify in a way that provides either values or certainty. Tragically there are many such people in the middle-class society of the contemporary West and the alienated youngster is a paralysed victim of social inadequacy and in dire need of understanding, critical support, appropriate intimacy, and warmth.

In adulthood identity processes are concerned with degrees of withdrawal and outward creativity on the intellectual, artisan, and social levels. The later years of maturity focus on integrity, acceptance, and wisdom in the face of declining powers. Erikson characterizes the whole life-trajectory in terms of the self-process and in his brilliant handling of clinical material remains always close to life, avoiding the obscurity and abstractions of excessive theory. He is concerned with the acquisition of virtues: hope in infancy; confidence and assertive warmth in the young adult; creativity in the middle years; and acceptance and wisdom with advancing age. These virtues are expressions of self that convert those who are their bearers into exemplars. The virtues are accompanied by good feeling, by forms of equanimity. While some acquire them with grace and simplicity, others can only devoutly long for them. Their acquisition usually requires work and the existence of models is a spur to action. Virtuous persons are not necessarily successful as the worldly know success, but in their functional autonomy and self-understanding they are ultimately the only recipients of respect.

Self, attitude, and values

Horrocks and Jackson (1972) attempt a more formal presentation of the self-process with less focus on clinical constellations. They approach the issue as cognitive theorists and derive their viewpoint basically from that of Jean Piaget. The self, to these authors, is above all an organismic process whereby the individual derives and constructs *representations* that comprise interpretations of himself in a subjective world that seeks meaning. The individual *symbolizes* his mental and behavioural activities in such a way that he 'confers' a psychological entity upon the organism that is his body. *Functionally, the self-processes is the means by which the human organism becomes aware and understands itself as an incarnate being with a past history and a plausible future.* Self is also a process of positioning in time with an awareness of alternative possibilities themselves deliminated by the development under which it has gone.

We have here in fact an elegant definition of the biological function of the self. The human species is by nature cultural. Intersubjective culture is not something added to human nature; it is both the product and the means of human evolution, especially with respect to higher mental functioning. Collectively, self-processes in interaction are the cultural process subject to past history and present situational control and possessing a degree of openness towards the future.

Self operates by entertaining hypotheses about its own definition that produce identity constructs. These hypotheses are tested experientially through performance upon the social stage whereupon the risk of affirmation or negation by others is taken. The whole process is an aspect of cognition concerned with the personal discovery of the nature and logic of relations with objects. Cognition involves perceiving, recognizing, conceiving, relating, judging, and reasoning, all of which have a developmental history that has been the especial concern of Jean Piaget and his school. The conceptual system by which an individual interprets his world is dependent upon the level of cognitive manipulation that has become available to him through experience and education within a particular culture.

In major works, Jean Piaget has analysed cognitive development as a sequence of increasing differentiation through the development of multiple hierarchies of ideas. The process resembles that of a pianist who, once skilled, relegates elementary principles to stereotype and concentrates on the flow of the music. No longer does she seek for the positions of the notes; a phrase is read and streams forth upon the ear. Piaget, in common with other authors (e.g. Werner 1948) postulates a number of discrete stages in cognitive development in the child. They are four in number: the sensorimotor stage, the pre-operational thought stage, the concrete operations stage, and the stage of propositional or formal thought.

The child begins its development with a relatively small number of motor responses which may be developed rapidly as a result of assimilating new habits. Cognitive development, to Piaget, is purely a matter of the assimilation of new material into earlier cognitive structures, the most basic of which are the primordial sensorimotor mechanisms. Such an approach clearly has much in common with the ideas we have discussed (p. 233) on the development of sets of instructions in the expression of evolutionarily flexible strategies, and provides a valuable link to biological and phylogenetic thought on development.

Piaget is, however, not merely placing, as it were, a learning faculty between appetitive behaviour and a consummatory response. On the attainment of each level, a new set of analytical skills becomes available for a renewed understanding of the world on an entirely fresh level of cognitive integration. The world is worked over afresh with 'new eyes'. The levels emerge through the assimilation of material that meshes with biological growth to allow a switching in of entirely fresh kinds of insights in a developmental series.

In the pre-operational period (ages 2–7 approximately) symbolic thought appears whereby the complexity of actions remote in time and space can be added to these of immediate semantic relevance. The child is now developing rules for categorization, for identification and differentiation. But so far he has little ability to 'operate' with the concepts he forms. In the early part of this phase the child overlays a highly individual set of responses with a more general conceptualization of events. In the later part he can generalize more freely and operate with expectancies that are less bound to the immediate circumstances. The child can now refer to a self and relate it to current happenings.

During age 7–11 approximately the child develops the ability to conceptualize manipulations of objects and quantities. These concrete operations also allow the self to be interpreted both in the sense of an 'I' and a 'me'; it can now be experienced as an object and the testing of hypotheses about self begins.

In the final stage propositional operations become possible by which the child becomes capable of hypothetico-deductive reasoning; he can think in terms of objects or abstractions in probabilistic terms unrestricted by actual situations and can construct imaginary realities through inventing and examining propositions about the world. Whereas at the 'concrete' stage the child's thought was largely applied to tangible objects, once the stage of formal operations is reached he can think in terms of pure propositions or abstractions that are the mark of intellectual creativity. Conclusions from hypotheses without actual observation can now be drawn with a good chance of being right. This also means that the child can now attribute qualities to himself and implement them in role play, a kind of active hypothesis-testing in the social world.

An important aspect of the developing self-process concerns the way in which a child comes to distinguish its own subjectivity from that of others. Social interchange is the matrix of self-formation but early on the experience of self is closely bound up with experience of the world. Exteriorization, as Horrocks and Jackson call it, is a process whereby awareness is expanded over the world of others so that they are almost 'incorporated' within the world of the child. A resistance to such an intrusive process develops increasingly in the third stage, as the child becomes clearer about the relations between it and exterior objects and a surge of egocentricity often develops. The distinctive self as an entity with separate judgements, its own theories, its opposition to parents, is thus characteristic of early adolescence.

This 'narcissism' gradually relaxes as the young person realizes that the proper function of reflection lies in the prediction and interpretation of experience rather than in contradicting others. And so, with greater self-definition, the adolescent becomes able to appreciate the contrast between self and others and to form relationships in which the flow of mutual reflection is unhampered by self-absorption and each is open to the other. Naturally this ability develops slowly, for the self is very protective of its own concerns and perceived threats to esteem provoke a return to defensive closure which replaces the open-heartedness of inner security.

The self-process includes many emotional components, it is affect-laden. The responses a person makes to others are not merely the result of intellectual activity but are far more profoundly expressive of attitudes that develop through personal experience. Emotional life, about which we have much more to say later (Chapter 10), hinges upon a person's psychosomatic responsiveness to metabolic deflections from steady states. Some such deflections are richly rewarding, as when emotional expression with a loved companion yields affection, the ecstacy of touch and the oceanic plunge of orgasmic experience. Emotional confidence is infectious: others open towards those who understand and practise love. In another arena, threat and anxiety arise particularly in relation to the maintenance of self-esteem. Pride, shame, guilt, and remorse are states of mind that close the self from others and set up an emotional restlessness, an endeavour to resolve or escape a personal dilemma.

The structure of self is expressed to others by way of attitudes which are the result of an individual's emotional history in which defence has been balanced by more positive coping and the expression of values and ideals. A person is at one and the same time an ideal self enshrining the values of the individual he would like to be and an operational self that tests the perceptions that others have of him through the attempted activation of his ideals in roles he chooses to take.

Observation and identification with models form the basis for the creation of an ideal self a person would like to be. If he can behave in such a way that others confirm him in his ideal role then he will probably endeavour to improve his performance. Values, roles, and attitudes form an interdependent system subject to enhancement or depreciation according to a balance between social acceptance, self-esteem, and the need for autonomy (Fig. 9.10).

The performance of a role adopted from a model is often more a matter of style than the enactment of a cardboard social type. Indeed, the more the performance is typed the more the playing of the role suggests an over-identification, an excessive compensation for aspects of the self that are felt to be defective. Shifts in style are expressive of the meaning a person wishes to convey to others by the adoption of a role. A relaxed style implies attitudes of open concern, values directed towards others, and an abandonment of juvenile egocentricity. Such a person shows a self-confidence born of a tested personal security. The introjections from others have been successfully made his own. By contrast, tense anxious styles imply attitudes of self-protection and an absorption with some personal difficulty which, even if not already comprehended, will also be predominant in the meaning life has for the individual.

Everyone seeks to construct a meaning for his or her life that makes sense. Indeed, personal philosophies of life are likely to reveal attitudes and values that reflect in large measure an emotional history. The 'I' lives within a constructed world of meanings and is closely identified with them. If they are broken down a serious crisis is usually provoked.

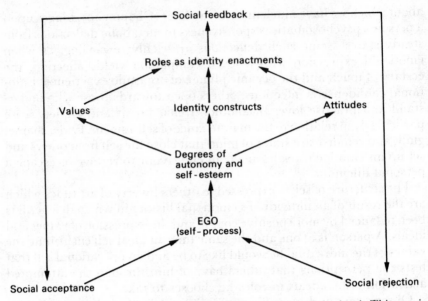

FIG. 9.10. The self-process as a hypothesis-testing activity of the 'ego'. This ego is referred to by the subject as the nominative 'I' or, by an exteriorization of viewpoint, as the accusative 'me'.

A person's 'identity hierarchy' is the total set of identities he or she entertains and may wish to perform. The incorporation of values means that the social system may not always satisfy one's need for an expression that maintains one's self-esteem. Conflicts between the practice of autonomy upon which inner esteem rests and the feedback concerning the public esteem in which one is held may then arise and promote internal discord.

Individual styles of expression are applied to performance within a societally prescribed role (nurse, doctor, housewife, social worker, husband) and degrees of fit vary from person to person. There are three modes of role-performance. *Role-taking* is the manifestation of an identity hypothesized by an individual. *Role-playing* is behaviour representing a performance within a societally defined situation. In this case a conflict between what one wishes to be and social pressure to conform to a type may arise. *Role-figmentation* is an acting-out of behaviour representing an unconscious wish to appear in a role that does not actually represent the subject's valued identity system. It is thus an autistic performance, for the meaning of the social feedback received is neither apprehended nor related to an awareness of self processes at all.

Rules, roles, and powers

Sequences of behaviour may be analysed according to their *causation* or according to the *reasons* for actions that individuals give to them. The first analysis is in terms of physiology or brain activity while the second is concerned with the meanings persons attribute to their activities. These meanings comprise the 'sociogrammar' of human activity.

The development of a capacity for objective self-awareness and description marks the boundary line between the animal and the human, the organism and the person, brain and mind. A whole new vocabulary comes into play in which subjective states are taken for granted and become, indeed, the very material for investigation. The conception of a person requires that an individual shows not only self-awareness but also the capacity to say what he is doing. Further, a necessary condition for having the concept of oneself as a person is that other people also recognize one as such. For this to happen a group of people must be able to know that each one of them has at least an idea as to what he is doing and can relate it to others.

Theorists such as Cooley, Mead, and Homans have emphasized interpretations of human behaviour in which individuals seek social approval and modify their role-performance to acquire it. Such a view fails to emphasize the significance which a sense of autonomy has for the meaning with which an individual invests his life. The study of self as a process places the emphasis upon formulating meanings for existence in which constructions of oneself are enacted in various ways as roles, internal dynamisms that seek selectively opportunities for self-definition, enhancement, and social adaptation. Roles are the means through which an individual tries out and assesses his constructions of self.

Rapidly changing social conditions and the continuous and irregular shifting of sands in ethical fashion present the individual with an almost continuous pressure to define, confirm, change, redefine, and reconfirm himself. Such cultural mobility in modern Western civilization is one cause for the popularity of 'encounter' in which, through participation in groups focusing on feelings and values, individuals can strengthen their grip on their sense of self and meaning in the world.

Harré and Secord (1972) in their important formulation of the post-behaviourist paradigm in social psychology argue that human transactions occur in relatively brief events to be called 'episodes'. An episode has some very interesting properties. First, what happens is usually relatively stereotyped, for interacting persons follow rules; secondly, the social stance of the interactants is normally well defined. People in episodes occupy roles. Rules and roles comprise the structure of meanings that people utilize in comprehending their social positions in actions involving one another. Some episodes are flexible, with each participant freely negotiating the roles and rules for that event in their lives, a situation which can also allow negotiation for rules for changing rules and roles. Other episodes are strongly structured by convention; they are liturgical or ritualistic in form and participants *act* their way through them with little negotiation as to how each may alter in the 'being with another' according to fluctuations in mood.

Individuals monitor their performance of roles and rules and compare themselves with the performances of others. Harré and Secord consider that the study of the reasons for an action in terms of an individual's conception of his rules and roles comprise the social scientific analogue of the study of physical causation in the life sciences.

Performances of rules and roles by human beings have an additional subtlety. Persons are capable of standing back from their performances, taking distance from their roles, even to the extent of subtly mocking their own performances and conveying that mockery to others. There is a sense here of an individual acting his own part rather than simply performing it. Irving Goffman has developed this idea of dramaturgy in social action with careful analyses of the complexities of meaning inherent in events that are apparently quite simple human episodes. The fact that people can exercise this higher order control allows them to superimpose important stylistic glosses on their performances which may convey to others, often differentially, very subtle yet precise nuances of meaning.

Roles, rules, and style are all aspects of the mutual manipulation of individuals in accordance with purposes, plans, and intentions, whether consciously deliberate or unconsciously operated as in Eric Berne's (1966) account of the neurotic 'games people play'.

As a result of differences in upbringing human beings show a tremendous range of individuality. While all normal individuals possess the power of speech and self-monitoring, other powers and liabilities are the direct result of acquiring capacities or deficiencies in ability to follow certain types of rule or occupy certain roles. Powers and liabilities refer to the readiness with which individuals may weep or show anger or trick another under certain circumstances. The idea depends on the individual showing differentiable states which to a degree come under his voluntary control. Harré and Secord argue that 'much of human life is seen as the exercise and circumvention and blocking of the exercise of powers or the activation of liabilities'.

In humans the main process that determines behaviour is self-direction according to the meaning an individual imputes to a situation. Self-direction and monitoring are little-studied aspects of psychology, and Harré and Secord admirably make them central to their explanatory system. The development of behaviour in this light they call ethogeny, which thus implies primarily a study of the out-comes of social interaction from birth onwards. Harré and Secord argue, however (p. 152), that ethology cannot play any role here. Ethology of animals is necessarily restricted to the study of overt behaviour and an analysis of meanings is precluded. In understanding people it is essential to consider what they say, and for this reason Harré and Secord distinguish between ethogeny and ethology as fields of study. Ethogeny relates more to phenomenology than to the behaviour description to which ethology is bound.

These distinctions are valid but of little interest to an evolutionist of mind. We have seen that the word 'mind', in so far as it means human mind, must refer to the cognitive properties of the person. The key question for an evolutionary cognitive ethologist therefore concerns how these properties develop both in phylogeny and in ontogeny.

The development of personal autonomy

Perhaps the most crucial developmental task in which a modern person is involved is the attainment of a sense of active responsibility for his performance in the social world. This responsibility involves relation-ships with others in the wide variety of societal settings in which an individual finds himself. It is in making himself accountable to others and to the institutions within which he functions that leads to attitudes conducive to leadership, instigation of initiatives, and social concern.

Some of us perform responsibly and in socially accepted ways entirely under the control of social expectancy and our needs for approval. Such behaviour is like a pack of cards, for it may collapse when changes in society, social values, or personal mischances in life arise. A much more important aspect of responsibility comes from within in a manner that is not necessarily conformist. This *interior responsi-bility*, as Horrocks and Jackson call it, involves the idea that each person takes care of himself, and endeavours to become the person he con-ceives himself to be. There is a drive here for inner consistency and a self-reliant satisfaction that is far beyond the forms of mere egocen-trism. The acquisition of this degree of autonomy depends upon an interiorized sense of self-esteem that is both realistic in relation to social convention and accepting of personal inadequacies and talents without a compensating self-pity on the one hand or inflation of self-worth on the other.

There can be no doubt that a fortunate upbringing greatly assists in the development of such an open type of self-esteem. Adolescents that are successful in acknowledging their strength and weaknesses appro-priately have an ability to be objective within their home environment and to make effective use of its resources. The parents are clearly the primary figures in assisting the development of such attitudes (Cernik and Thompson 1966). Coopersmith (1967) studied the factors conducive to self-esteem over eight years. Parental warmth, clearly defined family roles and limits, and parental behaviours that were respectful to the child were crucial and seemed to provide the affective feedback most useful during the child's construction of self through interaction.

The development of responsible autonomy has been described as the emergence of an inner 'locus of control' that governs the integrated function of the self-process (Phares 1976; Rotter, Chance, and Phares 1972). People differ in the extent to which they believe the outcomes of their behaviour are due to their own control and initiative or due to factors outside themselves. 'Internalists' are those who perceive the locus of control to be within themselves; 'externalists' 'believe' it to lie outside. Internalists often seem to be superior in their efforts at coping with themselves and with environmental pressures. They acquire more information, retain it, and use it more effectively than externalists, and are more effective generally in cognitive processing.

Children show this contrast in school, where internalists show higher achievement and a capacity to delay gratification. The expectancy of an internalist that he is 'in control' leads to greater reliance on his own judgements so that he is less easily influenced by others. Internalists have more initiative in social contexts, are less anxious, and are more critically adjusted to social norms.

A belief in ourselves as autonomous is thus a crucial emergent in the integration of the self. Research in this area now runs directly contrary to the behaviourist position of B. F. Skinner (1971) and certain other social learning theorists, who examined the self-process purely in terms of responses to social rewards and seem to imply that the autonomy of individuals is unreal.

Phares, in arguing that the 'myth' of freedom and autonomy is perhaps the more useful reality after all, provides evidence and opinion with which cognitive ethologists, I believe, must accord. Crucial to societal management is the intersubjective relating of people who have taken their self-process to an integrative level that affirms an optimistic belief in oneself, for from that belief stems a balanced warmth and concern for others.

These studies of the self-process demonstrate the extent to which human behaviour is determined by unique processes substantiating a distinct level of psychosocial existence. A number of recent philosophical writers align themselves with this viewpoint by emphasizing the especial character of human *action*. While the word 'behaviour' refers to the observable conduct of organismic activity and is thus available for objective analysis, the term 'action' refers to the meaning content of the behaviour. The actions of people in intersubjective relating are fully interpretable only by reference to their *intentionality* within a context of meaning (Harré and Secord 1972, following earlier writers). The attribution of an intention to a person carries with it the notion of an agent implicitly responsible for the behaviour expressed.

Shotter (1974), in an important essay on this topic, argues that studies in the social sphere of human life call for nothing less than a personalist approach (MacMurray 1957, 1961); this implies a place in the moral rather than the traditional natural sciences. I am fully in sympathy with Shotter's orientation but would argue that a developed evolutionary cognitive ethology will not be interested in old-fashioned boundaries such as these. Shotter himself argues that the mechanisms of the person arise from and within the natural mechanisms of the body. The relation between the two will become a focus for an integrated social science of the person towards which current studies of the self-process are clearly moving.

Action that involves a social intention becomes a matter of *negotiation* whereby the rules of relating are created as the process unfolds. 'While an event is to be explained by discovering its cause, an act is to be explained by *giving its reason*, by saying what the person was trying to do in performing it' (Shotter 1974, my italics). The significant understanding lies not in an appreciation of the goal-directed mechanisms of the beast but in 'the end proposed or intended by the person, not any actual end he may attain'. This is not to argue for any mysterious *élan vital* but simply to say that the behaviour of people is directed to perceived and socially *constructed* ends. The entertainment of a *project* allows for the construction of action through negotiation. The result must be in large measure indeterminate, for the outcome necessarily *emerges* as the negotiation proceeds. Individuals thus have the *power* (Harré and Secord 1972; Shotter 1974) to construct the future from a field of possibilities negotiated not at random but within a set of rules themselves often placed within a hierarchy of further rules. Individuals as natural, biological agents relate socially not in the overdetermined manner of all but perhaps the highest of other animals, but through the expression of the *powers* they have in relationship through a matching and sharing of intentions. Indeed it is through the expression of these powers that the evolutionary flexible strategies of human beings are themselves expressed.

Shotter goes on to point out that the attribution of a state of mind to another—joy, say—depends on experiencing what the other *shows* one as much as it does on what he says. Indeed what I show to you non-verbally may be 'correctly' interpreted by you even when I say something quite other—only to change my opinion later. The assessment of psychological states, contrary to much earlier thinking, is not at all private. It depends on the feelings we have in ourselves about the other, which can be tested for verisimilitude through an encounter, an entering into subjective contact, with the other. Humans seem to possess a natural ability to sense the mental states and intentionalities of others, much as one often 'feels' when someone is regarding intently the back of one's head. If Shotter is right about this, we have here another clue to the extraordinary extent to which man has evolved as an intersubjective animal.

Social intercourse resembles, then, a game in which some of the rules specific to the particular interaction must be created as one goes along. Even the meaning of sentences must be construed from utterances unique to a specific content.

Face-to-face conversations are not mediated solely by linguistic rules . . . rather . . . we continually monitor the construction of our expressions in rela- tion to our intended purpose. We can say that our natural powers present us with possible forms of expression . . . while our personal powers allow us to select among them the expressions whose meanings are appropriate to our purposes (Shotter 1974).

The meaning of discourse as a logical construction has to be completed by oneself and one's listener out of the influences exerted by the utterances that pass between.

Human action, the intersubjective relating of selves, is the realiza- tion of possibilities in a social exchange wherein real alternatives are present. An individual's powers are effective to the extent that his meanings are present in his actions, and to the extent to which he makes himself intelligible in intercourse with others. To perform this effec- tively demands an inward authority to represent oneself so; the respon- sibility for action that can come only through the emergence of personal autonomy.

The history of personal powers

Before closing this chapter we need to take up again a question raised earlier (p. 259). The structuring of the self-process is so profoundly social a phenomenon that people of differing epochs are highly likely to have categorized their worlds in radically different ways from modern man and even to have had qualitatively different types of identity and degrees of self-awareness. I left this question until the end of this chapter since it seemed essential to see what contemporary research had to say about modern people before attempting any reconstruction of past persons.

I am going to suggest here that the results of research on chimpanzee and gorilla categorization in their use of language, mirror experiments with apes and children, and studies of the development of self-awareness in infants all suggest that a capacity for a self-conceptualizing consciousness is an ancient, species-specific, human trait. We argued (p. 244) that this awareness is an essential concomitant of the processes of mutual evaluation through empathy in balancing trust and distrust in partnerships based in reciprocal altruism. It seems likely that the beginnings of such a capacity may well have been present in our protohominid ancestors. This does not however necessarily mean that early peoples practised that form of self critical and introspective self-examination that is so marked a feature of contemporary life and of paramount importance in the development of a modern person. Earlier peoples, while capable of self-conceptualization, may only gradually have learned to conceive themselves as selves. While the work of Erikson and others shows how vital this awareness is to contemporary individuals, such a critical importance may be purely a function of modern civilized society and not at all representative of earlier modes of identification.

The egalitarian mode of life in hunter–gathering communities does not provide a range of diverse role opportunities that is the root of identity variation in 'civilized' people. A person in such a society is born into a social position defined by birth order, sex, lineage, and other group categorizations. Since these social categories are fixed for him societally he simply grows into an identity that is as it were already assembled for him. The self-searching that goes with a choice of role is not a luxury in which hunter–gatherers or other tribesmen can indulge. This does not mean that an individual lacks character or distinction as an individual. Indeed his may be a very well marked personality taking pride in his accompgishments and social position. He will, moreover, be well aware of himself as an individual and grasp intuitively the essentials of empathic mutual evaluation involved in actions of reciprocal altruism. He may be an adventurer, a courageous hunter, inventive, and resolute. Yet he may perform all this in an unquestioning way, unaware of the conceptual categories that structure his life implicitly. His metaphorical constructions (p. 140) in discourse will be simple, earthy, reminiscent of events, and neither abstract nor explicit to himself. His life will be ruled by the myths that he and his fellows believe account for their way of life.

An important aspect of tribal life commonly consists in the enactment of ritual. Ritual, as defined by Rappaport (1978), is a performance of more-or-less invariant sequences of formal acts and utterances that have been handed down from one generation to another. The invariant components of the 'canon' of a ritual encode those aspects of the conceived cosmological and moral order that are felt to be eternal. Participation in a ritual provides an index of the adherence of an individual to the system of beliefs and hence it predicts his probable behaviour. While it does not perhaps indicate the precise nature of his belief or morality, it does reveal his subscription to the common 'rule' of a group and an obligation to abide by that rule. Rituals usually include a number of 'ultimate sacred propositions' as Rappaport describes them; utterances that assert ineffable truths. The core of the sacred, argues Rappaport, lies in the 'proposition' and not in a fact. These utterances give sanctity to the ritual which is controlled by hierarchs and used in the enforcement of social behaviours.

The sanctions of rituals could not carry weight, however, if they did not also invoke those strange experiences of the numinous that positively validate the claims of the ritual for a believer. The repetition of words which often have no material referents, are neither verifiable nor falsifiable but are simply taken as unquestionable, has great power to induce a sense of belonging. Perhaps this deeply emotional experience of contact with the 'divine' is derived, as Erikson (1966) suggests, from the feelings of the young infant for its mother. The experience of the numinous in nature may be a profoundly meaningful 'regression' in which the universe itself is not only understood as 'mother', which in a sense indeed it is, but also experienced as safe, comforting, all embracing. There is no doubt that verbal repetition or chant can induce an altered state of consciousness in which everyday concerns are transcended (Chapter 13). In that rituals commonly point both to the cosmic abstraction and to emotional experience it can be said that they give the 'conceptual . . . the power of the experiential and the experiential the guidance of the conceptual' (Rappaport 1978). From such roots the elaborate systems of meditation of more advanced civilizations may have developed (p. 356).

The cosmic idea that explains all without actually 'explaining' anything is thus a proposition which asserts a sacred 'beingness' into which believing individuals may then allow themselves to 'regress'. The 'vitality which the worshipper feels in the divine object is his own, projected upon what he takes to be other or "encompassing" '. The adaptiveness of ritual, Rappaport argues, lies in its ability to bring about the transcending of normal egoic consciousness in a social participation that, in the name of the divine, unifies the hearts of the people and reveals a wider truth, the value of belonging. These rituals in effect tend to regulate the relationship between non-introspecting humans and their social order which, as we have argued, is usually in some functional relationship with the socio-ecology of the population. Ancient and primitive peoples were not introspectively conscious of the meaning of their actions in the sense of having constructed an analytical theory about it, but they often did entertain notions that functioned socially, and ultimately ecologically, as if they had.

The same is probably true of self-understanding. It seems likely, for example, that the Homeric heroes had little inclination for any type of contemporary introspection. In a sense they lacked analytical consciousness; they apprehended rather than comprehended their actions. In the *Iliad* the heroes are guided or driven by bodily sensations, the belly, the breath, or the blood and in these physiological sensations the voices of their Gods speak often commandingly (Snell 1960). Jaynes (1976) argues that this type of mentality depended upon a cerebral activity that made much greater use of the right hemisphere than is the case in the analytically introspective people of later civilizations. It is indeed not implausible that a psyche dependent on intuitive, empathic understanding of others and of nature may have been much less lateralized or at least organized functionally in a different fashion from the cerebral structure guiding analytically verbalized action in modern people.

The great age of gods and liturgical rituals coincided with the emergence of the early civilizations dependent on massive collective labour for the construction of the irrigation upon which they depended. Jaynes argues that in the earliest of such societies, soon after the dawn of agriculture, the voices of great leaders came back to their immediate descendants as hallucinations and guided them. Later, such ancestral voices were projected into statues. The worship of statues became a ritual in which the voice of the God was heard in hallucinatory fantasy. The mentality that heard voices and was driven by them could have become an institutionalized form of consciousness in these early civilizations where conformity was enforced by the hierarchical social structure (p. 200). Lacking a history of self-conscious introspection the minds of simple people may well have been captured by such a system. Uncritically and often painfully living out their days, people of those epochs may have lost the relative independence of the egalitarian tribesmen, becoming more like ants than humans and locked within great systems of psychological servitude. The breakdown of this type of mentality probably came about when natural catastrophes, economic collapse, or warfare necessitated contacts with civilizations of differing beliefs and when increasing division of labour generated more interaction in cities.

Interstate trading and commercial enterprise eventually gave rise to an urban middle class. Here an economically dictated emphasis on entrepreneurial activity induced the birth of self-criticism in the interest of improved social skill. Introspection was born perhaps through an elaboration of language yielding appropriate metaphors for new experiences. Jaynes's (1976) book on this topic is a mine of fascinating information. While the reconstruction of mental history in this way requires a psychological archaeology yet to be developed, it is already clear that the human psyche has probably grown only slowly through several phases:

(1) The intuitive, non-analytical awareness of self as an agent capable of producing contingent acts by others. Intuitive non-verbal empathy becomes associated with this primitive sense of self in the regulation of interactions.

(2) A developed apprehension of self in relation to others and the world becomes the root of ritualized actions and conventionalized myths providing meaning and a sense of belonging.

(3) A need to develop more complex social skills in a world of wider horizons provokes increasing comprehension of the nature of the self that interacts with others. Introspective self-searching begins together with the development of metaphorical expressions appropriate to this new discourse.

The preoccupations of contemporary human beings with autonomy, self-development, and conscious intentionality are thus relatively recent. They began in the city states of Greece, India, and China at different dates and gradually spread throughout all civilized (city-based) peoples. Our research into the identity and the consciousness of contemporary urban citizens needs to be anchored in a wider comprehension of the mentality of primitive peoples and such literary evidence from past civilizations that remains.

These lines of thought make it clear how labile and socially responsive a thing human identification processes are. 'Identity' is not some inmutable property of the species but an often painfully constructed set of conceptualizations and attendant feelings that relate the individual to his transient experience of the world. While the capacity for identification is ancient, the form it takes has varied and self-critical insight into its nature and function is most probably a consequence of urban civilization. This must also mean that self-aware individuals of today are capable of initiating educational systems that can change the form of identification and self-consciousness in future generations.

Summary

(1) The self-process whereby an individual becomes aware of himself as an agent in the world converts the human organism into a person. Conceptually symbolized ideas of personal identity and roles in life have high emotional value especially since they determine an individuals sense of his own self-esteem in relating with others.

(2) For an individual to behave with appropriate levels of personal autonomy in his or her relations with others a sufficiency of self-esteem is essential. A dependent seeking for recognition and approval from others tends to delay or cripple the development of autonomy.

(3) Human interaction requires an ability to empathize, to feel oneself

as another, in order to evaluate where an individual stands emotionally during an on-going transaction. Empathy is also important in developing the trust upon which co-operation depends.

(4) The human individual is not only a gene carrier in his generation but also a unit of proposition creation in the patterning of his own cultural interactions with others. Culture is rooted in the human person's seeking for meaning through creating propositions.

(5) Biostrategic constraints on human learning and cultural behaviour almost certainly exist. These strategies are to be conceived as 'open' programmes, the greater part of which is acquired in interaction with other persons. The patterning of these actions seems to be constrained according to two main dimensions, dominance/submissiveness and approach/withdrawal, which differ in their manifestation in the two sexes in ways that relate to reproduction.

(6) The early coping skills of the child in relation to parental demands tend to emerge as social manipulations seemingly designed to evoke in others those behavioural stances with which an individual feels most safe. Generally dominant behaviour elicits submissiveness and vice versa. Approachability, by contrast, allows another to approach more easily, while avoidance creates the same tendency in another. The basis of human feelings in interaction may lie in transactional rules that are to a degree foreshadowed in other primates.

(7) Much of human life involves the formation and dissolution of partnerships. Since a partner can exploit another by deceit, individuals monitor their partnerships for reciprocity. The evolution of subtle empathic abilities upon which this system depends requires a competence in distinguishing one's own states of mind from those empathasized to be present in the other. Without this ability autonomous action is impossible. Autonomy is seen to be important in that it is plausibly the means whereby differential reproductive success via social advancement may be achieved.

(8) Contemporary Western individuals show persistent efforts to attain a consistent level of autonomous behaviour. The achievement of autonomy is by no means assured however. While babies are born with the tendency to initiate interactions with their mothers whereby they construct a sense of their own capacity to influence the social world, they are also easily alarmed by parental responses in which the emotional warmth upon which they depend for psychological growth is withdrawn.

(9) A child's emerging sense of self depends on the growth of its cognitive abilities in categorization, its awareness of its own capacity to influence others through taking initiatives and its experience of the emotional quality of its own conscious states.

(10) In contemporary Western adolescence the values acquired in

childhood consolidate into a sense of identity based upon a confidence that the way one presents oneself publicly is also the way in which one is seen. If this confidence fails to develop, argues Erikson, there emerges an inner inconsistency, a willingness to comply too easily with others, a lack of initiative and a fear of intimacy lest it should be overwhelming in the sense of causing one to act in ways unwished for in oneself. In later years the self-process focuses on creativity and inner poise.

(11) Modern adults in interaction observe a multiplicity of roles some of which they make their own. Those they enact confer psychological identities upon their organismic being. Most persons try to behave according to some ideal self or role acquired through admiring others taken as standards.

(12) Roles, rules, and styles in social interaction are all aspects of the mutual manipulation of individuals directed both towards personal security and the fulfilment of goals that are ultimately biostrategic. The performances of individuals in interaction often has an almost ritualized or dramaturgic quality even though learned during the acquisition of cultural norms.

(13) Research suggests that in modern society autonomous individuals who believe they are responsible for events contingent upon their actions tend to achieve more socially, to rely on themselves more, to show more initiative, less anxiety. They tend to be both more critical and better adjusted to social norms.

(14) In the environment of human evolutionary origin individuals with high confidence in themselves probably influenced others greatly. As we have seen in Chapter 7 such influential figures often have exceptionally high reproductive successes. Probably in early human history the achievement of autonomy was related to high inclusive fitness so that traits underlying the developmental trend to autonomous self-presentation may well have been positively selected.

(15) Yet such autonomy may not at first have been associated with explicit self-consciousness through introspection. The literatures of ancient peoples suggest a gradual development of the 'consciousness of self-consciousness' which is so characteristic of modern man. Research directed to a better understanding of the mentality of primitive peoples and the development of a 'psychological archaeology' are both needed before a wider comprehension of identification processes can emerge.

10 Troubled minds

Enlightenment is the leaving behind by Man of his
self-caused minority. Minority is the impossibility
of using one's own reason without the guidance of
another; . . . it is due not to lack of reasoning power
but to lack of decision and courage.

Kant 1748

Evolution and the 'unconscious'

One of the dangers of an open programme is that it may become filled
with junk. The troubled mind is a junk-filled mind, smothered by
undigested garbage. At some point along the way a mistake is made, a
wrong track taken. The end is a maze of confusion rather than the sunlit
uplands of clear self-perception. And yet, usually, the track taken seems
to have been a sensible one, a safer path. But safe paths avoid the
experiencing that leads to growth. Safe paths lead to choosing safer
paths again and the self gets locked up in its self-protection. In vain
attempts to gain the respect it would like to bolster its shaky-esteem the
troubled mind justifies itself with nonsense and may fail to grasp the
problem at its root: the problem is fear. How does all this come about?

The fact is that a mother is probably naturally ambivalent about her
child, and the child therefore has good reason sometimes to be afraid.
But since the newborn has yet to know itself these experiences remain
as primitive states not yet consciously realized, not easily incorporated
by a growing sense of a self that is rooted in optimistic explorations of
its own initiatives.

In his paper on parent–child conflict Trivers (1974) puts forward
several important ideas based on sociobiological theory (p. 78) which
undermine the accepted notion that mothers necessarily love their
babies. There are several cogent arguments for supposing that mothers
may sometimes have major reservations about giving care.

The neotenous human infant requires an especially lengthened
period of maternal care. The mother's investment is high and she has a
number of decisions to make that affect her overall reproductive success. The first decision is whether the newborn is fit to rear and whether
she can provide the care and circumstances needed to rear it. As we
have seen, the anthropologist de Vries considers that infanticide is a
natural option under certain circumstances (p. 180) and that mothers
intuitively evaluate their newborn children and their circumstances
before the development of attachment. Later the mother may decide to

reduce her care in order to produce a further child. Other reductions in care-giving may arise whenever competing circumstances attract the mother's attention. In the complex life of human beings these will be manifold.

Sociobiologically, a female mammal operates a strategy to ensure that her investment in one child is not so great as to preclude other investments that have effects on inclusive fitness. The infant mammal is correspondingly likely to show behaviour expressing a strategy that ensures its mother's attention, and preferably to a greater degree than to other children and siblings.

Under the varied conditions of human society with family conditions varying with respect to resources, number of children, age of parents, and relationship between parents, the baby may not necessarily arrive under optimum circumstances. The conditions for conflict with the primal caregiver are easily set.

The parent–child conflict as it expresses itself in moment-to-moment negotiation is a matter of each participant seeking an overall emotional satisfaction within which the presence of the other is included. Conflict arises whenever the timing of the helpless child's demands for attention (bodily discomfort, elimination, feeding, holding) and its needs for cleaning, suckling, bodily contact, etc. are in conflict with the mother's willingness to provide for them. The necessary deprivations and rejections of the weaning period and the arrival of a further child in the family, to which the mother must also attend, are circumstances in which a degree of rejection will be experienced by any child. The infant's inevitable frustration will be met with wise or unwise responses by the mother, and the child's frustration can generate destructive anger towards the parent which the child may well be afraid to express. The child's needs may in fact be satisfied only if he is 'good'; and being good means compliance with maternal demands. Compliance in turn means the inhibition of the aroused rejection, or at least muting its expression to the extent that the child stays in contact with mother. Compliance with a rejecting mother may, not without reason, be experienced as dangerous.

The child in fact expresses refined skills in 'equilibrating' (p. 124) its emotional needs to fit a social setting. Equilibration involves the inhibition of some tendencies to act or their replacement by others. Emotional equilibration is a pronounced feature of ape and human life and plays a major role in performances of reciprocal altruism. In the context of parent–child conflict it enables the child to retain contact with the mother and hence to maintain care. In the same way that we have argued that natural selection may have produced the motivational basis for complex reciprocation in human beings, so too does it seem likely that natural selection has enhanced the child's capacities for equilibration in the context of its relation with caregivers. It looks indeed as if a further key to the unique behavioural characteristics of man lies in an understanding of his biologically inherited capacity for suppression followed, in the case of cognized material experienced as so threatening as to risk the breakdown of the self, by an active repression whereby such material is prevented from appearing in consciousness. The possibility of its re-presentation is precluded by a process that is no mere forgetting or elimination, but rather an assertive denial that clearly indicates the threatening nature of the rejected material. This denial entails psychological work. Relaxation allows some of this material to present itself either in dreams or other flashes of awareness that may be very disturbing in that the self is momentarily unbalanced. The store of such repressed material is known as the 'unconscious'.

The idea of the 'unconscious' is one of the most difficult concepts in psychology. Intuitively appealing yet it explains very little. The mechanisms that operate when one argues that a person is behaving 'unconsciously' or 'with unconscious motives' are little understood. We mean of course that there is an observable discrepancy between a person's actions and the meaning he or she attributes to them. This discrepancy extends to the ambiguities necessarily present in such a person's value-system and philosophy of life. It is often intuitively easy to guess what the hidden motives may be, and a major personal clarification may come about when a therapist's client becomes able to incorporate new insights into his world of meanings in such a way that the discrepancy disappears. At one level the problem is cognitive, involving the clarification to oneself of motive and action. At another level the processes that precipitate such ignorance of oneself are clearly emotional in nature and not at all easily expressed in words. Indeed, they may have been established in the child before he could speak or was even conscious of himself as agent.

As the child grows he is faced with the necessity of balancing two contradictory tendencies within itself. On the one hand, for cognitive growth to occur, the child must orient himself to novelty and respond to it with exploration. So long as the child operates within the protective environment provided by his mother, anxiety is low and learning can proceed. When, on the other hand, a child's exploration takes him into worlds which arouse maternal rejection or punishment, anxiety is aroused in a strong form. Disapproval of the emergent self for the performance of the exploratory activity natural to its growth is especially productive of anxiety because the infant is dependent on mother for safe exploration. The mother's rejection arouses fear, not only of desertion but also, by implication, of developmental failure; for without the mother cognitive growth would be impossible. Parental disapproval thus produces anxiety which the child can resolve only through compromise.

Compromise takes the form of behavioural closure whereby the infant voluntarily restricts its activities within an arena acceptable to mother. The child thus adapts to its maternally imposed social environment through *defence* formation whereby he avoids, denies, or suppresses the emotional responses which, although natural reactions to frustration, are unacceptable to his mother. *Coping* with his mother produces that programme of behavioural responses which the child feels able to perform and thereby defines the initial *social environment of adaptedness* within which he can feel at ease with himself.

There is good reason to suppose that the emotional experiences that lead to the suppression of some patterns of responding and the enhancement of others are not forgotten. They remain as unclarified memories that are not incorporated cognitively into the rules whereby a person explains himself to himself. Since the basic root of closure is an experience of fear, it follows that stimuli that sufficiently resemble those of the original precipitating circumstances will tend to evoke fear again. Fear hurts; as an experience it is normally avoided. Hence, with no clear understanding as to why, a person comes to shy away from certain kinds of social experience.

Some authors attempt to dispose of the concept of 'the unconscious'. Yet the term refers usefully to those memories that were once attended to so vividly that they cannot be erased but which, because of the fear with which they were associated, triggered so much avoidance that they failed to be incorporated in the cognitive rules that construct the understanding of the self. In later life defence is not so much against the ancient memories as such, for they are in any case barely available without extensive psychological work; it consists rather in a failure to process information which tends to arouse anxiety and for which no rules of incorporation have been established. If some means of incorporation has developed the information may not simply be denied, as in selective forgetting, but distorted to allow at least some degree of assimilation by the self.

As the child grows, this process of coping closure continues, taking place within the frame of dispositional dimensions first discovered by Brown and developed by Leary and later authors (p. 239). It thus comes about that personality types seek to create for themselves social environments which do not arouse in them the fears of their primal experiences.

The roots of coping closure lie in the the child's ability to equilibrate its responses in relation to those of the parent. They are an adaptation enabling the child to grow within the constricting circumstances of its long-term dependency on mother. Every one of us shows a degree of such closure and, in so far as self becomes aware of its social frailty and continues its initiatives in spite of it, personal growth continues. It is when self fails to incorporate the information associated with the primal hurts that difficulties and a troubled mind arise. These processes are inevitable characteristics of being human, the evolved basis upon which the diversity of human personality rests.

The descriptive work of the great psychoanalysts, Freud and perhaps especially Jung, suggests that the repressed material as revealed in dreams, fantasies, and the evocative folk legends and fairy stories of primitive peoples is far from arbitrary, rather it tends to be patterned in a highly thematic way. Jung, more of a poet perhaps than a scientist, named these themes after the key figures that appeared in them and considered these 'archetypes' to evidence a 'collective unconscious' perhaps common to all mankind. Jung's intuition may be based on a universal responsiveness found in human affairs; each of us has a mother, a father, attempts to be a hero, seeks the wise man. These figures indeed reflect the organization of the human family and are the sources of information and expression needed to ensure personal growth. The vivid childhood memories of repression in the service of equilibration undoubtedly concern such figures seen cloudily through the eyes of the half-formed self.

These considerations suggest that most adult human beings actually comprehend few of their sources of action and impulse and are often far from knowing consciously what they are about; what we profess to know is usually a rationalization of what has impelled or directed us from within. If this is the case, and I believe it to be so, we can argue that there is in each one of us a great repository of themes that tend to guide behaviour and about which we have little understanding. The sources of these 'unconscious' activities seem to be at least threefold: first, as we have already argued (p. 154), there are likely to be some action tendencies related to innate biostrategies which, in given cultures or family situations, are not directly expressible and need to be moulded into some form of compromise with social reality. Secondly, the family bedrock common throughout humanity is likely to provide 'archetypal' themes that pattern unconscious expression. Thirdly, frustrating and traumatic experience in infancy occasions repression of natural anger due to the child's capacity to equilibrate its behaviour in relation to parental demands. The human being does not therefore show unconscious behaviour of only one origin. Indeed we may argue that the biostrategic material motivates, that the archetypal patterns give shape to responses and fantasies, and that the defence mechanisms select possible courses of action from those not eliminated by fear in infancy.

Part of the power of the unconscious is owing to the effects of infantile experience being incorporated at a stage of life when the brain is grossly underdeveloped. Indeed the lack of cortical material implies that much of the interpretive brain is not yet formed when infants experience their major problems with the mother. These experiences are thus laid down in the 'old brain', they tend to operate in isolation from behaviour based on later acquisitions and are not automatically connected with the interpretative activity of the cortex. Early experience is thus especially associated with the limbic system of the brain which has major influences on emotional life.

In his book *The dynamics of creation*, Storr (1972) emphasized that human beings face not only the developmental needs of adjustment to the physical and social environments but also a crucial need to balance this buried, motivationally powerful, inner world against the pressures of the outer one. He argued that much of human creativity in the sciences as well as in the arts reveals the manner in which individuals attempt to bring about this adjustment. The schizoid personality, which according to Kleinian psychoanalytic theory takes its origin from problems in the oral phase of infantile development, may seek reward in abstract ordering of the experienced world rather than in personal relating. Newton and Einstein would appear to be remarkable instances of this type of development. The writings of Kafka reveal the bewildering powerlessness of a child subject to inconsistent parenting. Detailed examination of such material has led psychoanalysts to see the creative process as essentially adaptive; it brings some order out of the chaos of the inner world, an order validated in part by the social rewards given to creativity of a high order and in part by its intrinsic satisfaction. The power of symbols seems to derive from the transformations of very early experiences as the interpretative mind attempts to integrate these ancient memories into adult life and a world of meaning. In science intense preoccupation with a logical 'scientific' problem may be resolved by an idea that emerges in dreams in an entirely symbolic form distant from the technical medium in which scientific discourse is maintained. In the case of art symbols may stand for themselves or undergo transformation depending on the culture of the time.

Research has established that we need to dream. It seems unlikely that the content of dreaming is nonsensical, as some hard-line psychologists have sought to maintain. Dreaming is likely to represent a core process whereby the world of outer representations is related to themes of early origin in individuals' lives. The creative power of the dream to settle problems in the work of both scientists and artists indicates its resolving power and the vital activity of unconscious material below the run of everyday conscious life.

The effects of different styles of mothering

Before asking in what way modern therapists seek to correct the cognitive imbalance of their clients we need to look at recent empirical studies of the development of troubled children. Although Freud argued much about early development, his ideas were essentially inferences from clinical interviews with adults and were subsequently interpreted with great insight. Bowlby has championed the direct study of the origins of disturbed behaviour in the family, emphasizing the role of mother as the primary caretaker. Although great debates focus on the relative roles of mothers and other caretakers there can be no doubt about Bowlby's immense influence on contemporary study, in particular his insistence on the evolutionary ethological approach.

The work of Emde and his colleagues (Emde, Gaensbauer, and Homas 1976) reveals that the integration of the baby's behavioural organization shows peaks at two nodal times in the first year. After each peak there is a period of consolidation in behaviour and in social relating. Each shift represents the achievement of a level of integration facilitating relationships with care-givers that is appropriate to the immediately subsequent phase of physical growth.

After two months there is a shift away from endogenous control. The baby sleeps less and is more wakeful. This is the time when the social smile emerges and the baby regards intently its mother's face. There is an upsurge of babbling and cooing and of exploration. The 'game', as Watson calls it (p. 257), with care-givers begins. It is also significant that after this age the child's learning abilities are much developed and the simple reflex responses of the neonate gradually disappear.

At between 7 and 9 months another developmental shift occurs and a new plateau of social orientation is achieved. There is a further increment in wakefulness at this time and the baby begins to differentiate between care-givers and strangers. In particular, fearfulness towards strangers develops. This differential response also heralds the *attachment* to a particular figure, usually the mother. This powerful preference for an attachment figure has developmental parallels in many species of mammals and birds. Indeed, as Bowlby has shown, this orientation of a baby to its mother may be considered to be the human analogue to imprinting in other animals.

This also is the age at which expressions of surprise, fear, and anger become differentiable in the child's response repertoire. Emde's model of infant emotionality suggests that prior to 2 months two dimensions, happiness–unhappiness (hedonic tone) and arousal, account for the observed measures of behaviour but that later an additional dimension related to the orientation of a baby's attention (inward or outward) becomes gradually apparent.

These studies of the developing emotional life of the child are vital to a comprehension of its interaction with its mother. An aspect of attachment is that alarming stimulation, injury, stress, or brief separations or rejections by the mother evoke approaches by the child to the mother. The natural termination of these approaches is bodily holding. This *contact comfort*, vital in most primate species, clearly has a number of biological functions. In particular it ensures that the baby is safe if it becomes important for the mother herself to flee, either from a possible predator or, more likely, from a human aggressor. Additionally, however, attachment ensures closeness to the mother for numerous care-giving functions, including the facilitation of cognitive development. Many selection pressures doubtless acted together in the evolution of this behaviour system.

Bowlby's main contribution concerned the effects of major separations from the mother of several weeks or months. Response to separation develops in three stages. In the first, *protest*, the child shows distress in an odd environment and clings to the parent when reunited. In the second, *despair*, the child is generally inactive, uninterested in the new environment, and on reunion shows clinging or else anger. In the final stage, *detachment*, the child is interested in its environment but rejects the parent on reunion. This rejection is often specific to the originally more favoured parent; the other parent may still be greeted warmly. In the home environment sudden bouts of anxious hostility are common even after short separations. Similar behaviour is known from rhesus monkeys (Hinde and Spencer-Booth 1969). Detached children may remain so for some time after reunion and may show anger as an initial response to the rejected parent before renewing more friendly relations.

Recent work shows that responses similar to those evoked by long-term separation may be expressed briefly after short separations. The extent to which they appear is, however, revealingly dependent on the quality of the child's relationship with its mother.

A test of the quality of the parent–infant bond has been devised by Ainsworth and Wittig (1969) in which the baby is exposed to a 'strange situation' including the presence of an unknown person and a short separation from its caretaker. The baby's behaviour on the care-taker's return is studied. In a later study, Mary Main (1980) reported on individual differences in response to the strange situation. A key dimension is the extent to which the infants avoid their mothers on their return, a behaviour regarded by Main as indicating that the infant is experiencing an inner conflict.

In Main's sample of American white children, over three-quarters of the babies responded to the mother's return by approach, reaching towards her, smiling and vocalizing, or crying. Approach is the most typical response. A substantial minority of babies are little disturbed by parental departure and may be friendly to the stranger, but show avoidance rather than approach to the mother when she returns even though they may have approached her happily earlier. One-fifth of the sample failed to greet mother on return, some failed to look at her, some turned away after looking, and some actually crawled or walked away. Often, when picked up, these babies attempted to get away or otherwise resist physical approaches being made by the mother. Avoidant babies are called type-A babies; approachers are type B; and there is a third, minority group, C, who show extreme clinging to the mother, excessive distress on separation, and generally fearful disturbance. On reunion they show both comfort-seeking and angry resistance.

Avoidant infants often show blank facial expressions on reunion and tend to pay attention to their toys or other objects. Yet this attention is incomplete and studies of heart-rate fail to show the deceleration at this time which is the usual accompaniment of attention. Avoidant babies and infants also show a number of other characteristics. For example, if the stranger tries to make friends, the child, although seemingly open to the approach, avoids at the last moment. In addition, if an adult actor shows distressed crying in their presence, they show no sign of concern but go on playing with their toys. For type-B infants, by contrast, the sight of a distressed adult evokes focused attention, a serious absorbed facial expression, and every sign of concern indicating the beginnings of empathy. Avoidant infants are highly specific in their avoidance, displaying it to one parent while anxiously approaching the other.

All evidence points to the conclusion that type-A and type-B babies are equally cuddly as newborn babies. Avoidance at 1 year of age in one child and not in another is thus a matter of differential development. Avoidance or approach seem to be responses to modes of parental care that differ in style although not necessarily in consciously expressed intentions. It seems that avoidant babies have inherited difficult mothers.

It is at once apparent that by avoiding its mother the infant cuts itself off from learningful experiences and also denies the mother opportunities for sharing her concern with her child. Gaze avoidance is an early manifestation of such behaviour in the home environment and is a well-known component in infant autism. Gaze avoidance is in fact about the only way in which a human baby can 'cut-off' (Chance 1962a) unpleasing stimulation. These responses occur even in children born deaf and blind and are thus not dependent upon the actual visual modality but rather upon the system of interpersonal contact as a whole.

A number of authors argue that gaze aversion is a mechanism for dealing with stress by modulating arousal, including an increased heart-rate, and that it allows for the possibility of re-engagement with the other which an 'all-or-none' response such as crying might preclude. Avoidant behaviour is perhaps a means of retaining control under emotional pressure and is thus part of an emotional 'coping skill'. We have already argued for the importance of face-to-face gaze in the most basic initiatives of the mother–baby 'game' and for its consequent importance for social learning (p. 256). It seems therefore that an infant employing gaze aversion as 'cut-off' may be severely damaging its psychosocial and cognitive development whenever the behaviour becomes habitual.

During these tests the occurrence of anger towards objects representing the absent parent and the occurrence of temper tantrums on the parent's return suggested to Main that the chief emotional state with which the child is coping is anger against the parent resulting from the deprivation from contact comfort. Independent evidence of the baby's aggression is found in acts of violence which have been recorded only from babies that are subsequently classified as avoidant. Such infants may, for example, hit the mother's chair after she has left it. They also show a variety of odd activities, including stereotyped behaviours such as staring or rocking, self-slapping, or hair- and ear-pulling. All these, ethologically, are displacement activities and are exactly the type of behaviour that is associated with motivational conflict in other animals.

In humans as in other primates maternal reproof, rebuttal, punishment, or hostility is met by the infant with a persistent attempt to get near the mother. The fact must be that infants are built behaviourally in this way because, evolutionarily speaking, no one else is likely to give them the support they need. In any case punishment is normally a short-term situation which can lead to a return of comfort. When the infant attempts to remain close to a rejecting parent, however, a situation arises that is highly loaded with both attraction and fear and is specific to primary attachment figures (and, in adulthood, to their transference representatives). Most mothers reject their children only briefly, so that such events are simply part of the parent–child transaction and contribute to socialization. The fact is, however, that a proportion of human mothers actually dislike physical contact with their infants and manage to convey their distaste to the child. If, in addition, the child is actively rejected when it needs contact comfort the child's approach—withdrawal conflict is then unsolvable. As Main puts it, 'The conflict is now serious, deep, and non-verbal. A single movement on the part of the mother, intended to drive the child from her, at least initially brings him anxiously towards her—yet he cannot contact her, although only contact will terminate the activity of the system.' We are in the realm of a pre-verbal 'double bind' of a basic kind dependent, as it evidently is, on the frustration of the child's innate seeking for maternal contact.

Bowlby (1973) has argued that anger is the inevitable outcome of such frustration, yet the destructiveness of fully expressed anger would, at least in the child's fantasy, literally remove the inadequate mother from the child's world. As the mother's behaviour is persistent, being part of her character structure, the rejected child begins to show an equally persistent suppressed aggression owing to the unrelieved frustration in its most fundamental relationship. A strong avoidance of the mother may then develop and become firmly consolidated; furthermore, similar patterns of resentment are likely to appear in the company of persons who in some respect resemble the mother. Young infants with such an experience of mothering may well reject rather than approach their mothers after short separations. Type-A infants thus appear to be products of a particular type of mothering about which the mothers themselves will be quite unaware.

The dislike of physical contact by mothers of avoidant babies is normally obvious. Main writes, 'some have tended to hold the babies awkwardly or rigidly if at all, and may arch away from the baby if he becomes too intimate with them while held; some at sometime actively reject the baby's initiations of contact. One mother pulled back and said angrily, 'stop it'; another turned her face away immediately . . .; another yelled "Don't touch me!"; and another shoved the baby's head down into the crib until he stopped trying to get up.'

Research indicates further features of the 'character armour' (Reich 1949) shown by these defective mothers. They tend to be compulsive, mechanical, rigid in attitude and responsiveness. Facial expressiveness is generally lacking. Main refers to an 'impression of almost eerie sweetness' and a sort of hypnotic charm about some of these women who seemed especially resolved to inhibit all expression of their angry disgust at physical contact.

Conclusions about the directionality of causation in this mother–infant dilemma need care. The transactional model (p. 248) shows that not all babies are born neutral. Some are 'difficult' from birth and require all the resources a mother can bring to child-rearing. It seems especially likely that the type-C babies with their excessive dependency may well be of this type. To some extent 'difficult' type-A babies may precipitate the negative responses of their mothers. None the less, the regularity of the association of the type-A babies with a particular type of maternal behaviour does suggest that it is the mother's cold lack of responsiveness that elicits the avoidant responses of the baby.

This research is of fundamental interest and deserves maximum development. In the first place we seem to have discovered in this primal mother–infant conflict one root of certain types of character formation. The process seems to be an almost inevitable consequence of the evolved structure of the human motivational system in young children. As in other animals the 'cut-off' serves here to maintain proximity when the expression of approach is impossible and the expression of open hostility is even more liable to evoke parental rejection. Avoidance arises proximately from a switch in behaviour when two motivational tendencies in opposition cancel one another out. The structuring of motivational systems in this way seems to have an ultimate explanation in that selection favours the maintenance of proximity at all costs, even to an unfriendly mother. Avoidance by controlling the expression of anger achieves this and ensures the child at least a physical security.

It seems likely that the proportion of contact-avoiding mothers in a population varies from culture to culture. In particular, the findings of Klaus and Karin Grossmann (personal communication) in north Germany show a significantly higher number of avoidant babies than in the American sample. This suggests a possible cultural involvement whereby maternal attitudes about strictness in upbringing and emotional control, generally more marked in Germany than in the USA, play a role in reinforcing the effects of a character armour acquired from precisely this emphasis in the mother's own rearing. It does not require clinical experience to guess that A and B, and even C types of behaviour are traceable in adults. It could be that the initial emotional experience of an accepting or a rejecting mother, with all the subtle grades of maternal anxiety and caring interposed, tends to produce a relatively fixed character structure and may endure into adulthood. In a given culture such traits will tend to effect values and conventions of child-raising and family atmosphere in ways that will legitimate the very practices that produced the problem.

It seems plausible that powerful intergenerational effects may be in operation here whereby patterns of emotional control in infancy predispose to certain character structures in adulthood, which in turn impose the same or similar dispositions on the next generation. These sobering thoughts are to some extent lightened by the realization that not all children of the same family turn out the same way and that the father's influence may compensate for maternal negativities. How far these effects are general within whole families awaits further study, as do the ethnic and socio-economic concomitants that may be associated with differing proportions of type-A and type-B babies in a population. Do we have here perhaps the beginnings of a better understanding of ethnic or national character? What will be the results of further research of this kind in other countries, in Greece, Japan, Russia? A fascinating line of inquiry lies open before us.

If we assume for the moment that avoidant infants are likely to become avoidant adults we must also assume that this will be an effect of an enduring style of parent–child relationship throughout upbringing. Exposure to adults of different disposition, to friends, and numerous accidents of life may alter the life trajectory of an individual enormously. There seems little doubt, however, that an avoidant person acquires troubles that an open-hearted taker of initiatives may avoid.

Among the difficulties faced by the avoidant child is the fact that it can no longer influence the social responses of the most significant person in its life. We have already seen how important stimulation that is contingent upon an infant's own initiatives is for its cognitive growth. In particular social experience contingent on a child's own initiatives is likely to play a major role in the acquisition of important social skills. To the extent that individuals becomes avoidant so also do they tend to deny themselves the experiences upon which social relationships are based.

Some animal experiments throw light on the likely consequences of such a situation. John Watson (1977) reviewed studies that show that if animals are exposed to aversive stimulation which they cannot control (electric shocks, say) then in an experiment in which they could rapidly learn to terminate the experience by jumping a barrier they fail to learn to escape. By contrast animals that are not exposed to such aversive stimulation learn to escape very easily. The experimental animals have here acquired a 'learned helplessness' through the 'interference effect' of exposure to stimulation they cannot control. Seligman (1975) argues forcefully that the same concepts apply to human beings. Indeed, even uncontrollable events of short duration may have a major interference effect on learning if their significance to a person is great; the loss of a loved one, for example. Furthermore the perception of one's inability to control events may undermine life-supporting behaviours and have damaging psychosomatic consequences. Seligman finally argues that depression itself may be viewed as a severe form of the 'interference effect' and may arise through a perceived inability to control events. In a curious addition to the theory Watson also notes that even positive stimulation *if it is not contingent on a child's initiatives* can promote a learned helplessness. Indeed, maternal smothering with good things or excessive affection may be as damaging as rejection. Seligman ends with an important rule. 'To the degree that uncontrollable events occur, either traumatic or positive, depression will be predisposed and ego-strength undermined. To the degree that controllable events occur, a sense of mastery and resistance to depression will result.' The vital importance of developmental processes that aid the development of personal autonomy is made vividly apparent here. Not only is a requisite degree of autonomy essential for a sense of personal well-being, but it seems very likely that helplessness and dependency have throughout history been associated with poor social and reproductive success.

Yet, as we have seen, the effects of cold mothering are more complex than this. The child is not only to a degree 'depressed' but also angry and likely to express this socially in later life. The angry avoidant individual may be brilliantly successful as the world knows but potentially dangerous to himself and others. A society dominated by such individuals, as Reich (1945) in various ways has also suggested, can be a danger to the world.

The social context of neurosis

Early ideas on the social structuring of the self (Cooley 1902; Mead 1934) came together with psychoanalytic interpretations of the range of human character in the work of Harry Stack Sullivan (1955). Much of the contemporary formulation of psychiatric and personality theory finds its first expression in Sullivan's work. As a practising psychiatrist he was naturally particularly involved in the study of clinical cases and his firm avowal of the importance of interpersonal relationships in the formation of both benign and malignant character structure led to a profound reinterpretation of much psychopathology as a product of defective communication in family life. Outside pathological material the same principles apply to the formation and maintenance of everyone of us.

Sullivan argued that if the relations between a child and other people follow a benevolent course and the child's need for support and exploration is fulfilled, then human development takes a constructive path promoting realistic intimacy and social creativity. On the other hand if the interactions are fraught with fear and anxiety, development takes a path that is both narrowed and confined by the precise nature of that anxiety. An individual's experience of interaction in the world consists of *tensions* with respect to needs and anxieties and *energy transformations* whereby an event happens either physically or psychologically so that an individual's action relieves the preceding tension. Tensions rest fundamentally on the requirement for satisfaction of specific needs and on the maintenance of inner security. To Sullivan, any experienced threat to the security of an individual, especially to that of the self, elicits anxiety which is rooted fundamentally in parental and social disapproval of the person presented to the world. To Sullivan anxiety has always to do with other people.

Individuals develop relatively enduring patterns of energy transformations which comprise their character structure. These patterns Sullivan called *dynamisms*. The concept implies an affect-laden habit that is of crucial importance for the maintenance of the self in that it functions to reduce or constrain tension. Elementary dynamisms are simple physiological or physical responses, but complex dynamisms are constructed out of elaborate patterns of responsiveness originally made to key people in early life—significant others. Dynamisms exist in relation to needs which in turn have a hierarchical organization which changes both with life circumstances and as a result of personal growth. In many ways Sullivan's notion foreshadowed those of Fritz Perls and Abraham Maslow, father figures of the grass-roots growth movement of the late 1960s and early 1970s.

Sullivan's identification of the key role of anxiety in character formation led him to propose that a great many behaviours are 'masking operations' that partially relieve or substitute for its expression. Anger allows release of tension which, although it may not remove the source of anxiety, does remove its experience. The fear of the anxiety-promoting object is destroyed by anger almost as effectively as if the object itself has been violently removed. Anger as a form of assertion can raise self-esteem and enable the subject to observe its fear and the fearful object or person more realistically.

Selective inattention (suppression) and dissociation (repression) are Sullivanian terms for their Freudian equivalents (in parentheses). They are means of defence from anxiety by denial. Similar mechanisms are sublimation and obsessionalism. Guilt is a rationalization of anxiety that is expressive of an individual's sense of failure to live up to his ideal self. Pride is a cover for insecurity and is based on over-valuation of traits that may be the result of fantasy. Shame is a sense of failure to live up to the standards of some significant other person or reference group.

These matters deal with intrapersonal processes. In interpersonal relating the presence of anxiety will clearly produce defence mechanisms that distort personal expression to another. Communication may thus become easily impeded so that one member of a couple may not clearly understand what the other means because their messages are confused. In particular, messages regarding affect are often presented at a non-verbal postural level that may contradict what is being said. The stage is thereby set for misunderstanding and mistrust. When this develops between persons who are psychologically dependent upon one another we have all the ingredients for emergent, socially induced, neurosis. As we have seen (p. 241), the characterization of a person (Carson 1969) tends to comprise an interactional style that provokes a complementary and hence safe pattern of responding in a companion. A normal individual is a mix of fixity and flexibility according to a position on a limited number of dimensions.

One development associated with the idea that interpersonal

behaviour is designed to elicit complementary responses is the 'exchange theory' of social interaction which is attributable particularly to Thibaut and Kelley (1959) and G. C. Homans (1961), who writes: 'The open secret of human exchange is to give the other man behaviour that is more valuable to him than it is costly to you and to get from him behaviour that is more valuable to you than it is costly to him.' One detects here in a blatant form the capitalistic ethos of the American business school. Trivializing as this approach may be, with its basis in Skinnerian operant conditioning and its failure to consider phenomenalistic self-report as meaningful in human action, it can often be employed quite effectively in behavioural prediction. Relationship-formation is said to go through the stages of sampling (among possible friends), bargaining, commitment, and institutionalization. Intimacy is the result of emotional bargaining, institutionalization is the societal structuring of an intimacy, say, by marriage. Mutual reinforcement undoubtedly plays a vital role in the formation and maintenance of relationship, but the emphasis on behaviour rather than on mutual explorations of intersubjectivity and personal meaning, together with the crude metaphors of the market-place, clearly locate exchange theory in the *Zeitgeist* to which it belongs. We do not have to express the facts of human relationship in this idiom (see further Swenson 1973, p. 248).

A more subtle approach, using the full complexity of verbal reports from both 'normal' and 'clinically' interviewed subjects, is the social games analysis of Eric Berne (1966) which lies at the root of his therapeutic system known as transactional analysis. Based fundamentally in a popularized transliteration of Freud for the masses, Berne's analysis conceives the individual's personality structure as due to internal biological programming (cf. the id), probability programming arising from personal experience (cf. the ego), and external programming arising from social rules (cf. the super-ego). The 'phenomena' of mental life and personal interaction involve transactions between the fluctuating 'ego states' of the partners. There are three: the 'child' state, the 'adult' state, and the 'parent' state, which again have characteristics of the tripartite structure of personality in Freud. The 'child' is the spontaneous, fun-loving, irresponsible, and ultimately irrepressible part of each of us. The 'parent' is the introjected authoritarianism of one's own father/mother parentage. The 'adult' is the reasonable, reflective, reality-oriented ego state in which social experience is utilized in constructive attempts at interpersonal problem solutions. Transactions between people are conducted between ego states. A transaction between two persons consists of 'strokes' (a regrettable term with devitalizing overtones) which reveal the ego state of the individual. An interaction between two 'adults' would be reflective, possibly critical but constructive. Two 'parents' are likely to agree, Lorenzian fashion, on the appalling character of the rising generation, and two 'children' may well spend their time giggling over some delicious prank while consuming too much whisky from a great-aunt's cocktail cabinet.

Another type of transaction occurs when 'parent' of individual A interacts with 'child' of B. The result is likely to generate some heat as the authoritarian, possible pompous, condescending attitude of A impinges on the rebellious and possibly youthfully narcissistic B. A consistent 'adult' (A) can enter pleasantly into the fun of the child or the ponderous anxiety of the parent without being drawn into it, and one consequence may be a shift in B's ego state to that of the 'adult' condition.

Crossed transactions find the participants in real trouble. They occur when a respondent replies in a different ego state from that addressed. In a crossed transaction communication usually has to be broken off until a shift in ego state occurs. Co-operation is not possible, for example, in:

A ('adult'): 'Could you lend me £5? I was too late in getting to the bank today.'

B ('parent'): 'You're always too slow in anything practical. Why do you expect me to manage your affairs?'

More complex transactions arise when apparently adult verbal transactions are underlain by non-verbal parent–child crossed transactions. The result is not surprisingly a great deal of misunderstanding and emotional frustration.

Berne elaborated the transactional idea into the concept of 'games people play'. These are habitual manoeuvres with a socio-psychological pay-off, usually strongly loaded with suppressed emotion. An example is 'If it weren't for you', commonly played by married couples. It requires a dominant and a submissive player in which one or the other manages to place the blame for his or her personal inadequacy upon the other. 'Kick me' is a masochist's game in which he seeks out others who persecute him. 'Now I have got you, you son of a bitch' is a game in which A manoeuvres B into a position in which B unsuspectingly appears to play a trick on A, which A then publicly discloses. 'Rapo' is the sex game by which women attract men and arouse their passions, only to become strict moralists at the last moment. The result may be to their disaster. 'Look how hard I've tried' is a game a partner in some married couples may try to play with the spouse's therapist. Berne's popularity and current influence on therapy is considerable but it remains unclear how effective the approach is. Full of gimmicky novel-sounding names for well-known intrapersonal conditions his work has had less appeal to serious students of the interpersonal process. It does, however, illustrate the complex confusions and covert intentions present in many relationship situations. Insight into the nature of his life 'script' and socially distorting games often helps a confused individual to order his patterns of relating in ways that are socially more effective.

The most important contribution of studies of interpersonal processes remains in the area of psychobiology from which, having been based on the work of Sullivan, it originally came. Research on the families of schizophrenics reveals recurrent patterns of transactions involving a rejection of the child by the mother, and a disinterested father emotionally estranged from her. The curious feature of many of these distorted families is that they are none the less often stable, although unsatisfactory for all members (Lederer and Jackson 1968). In such families no explicit agreement is reached on who is in control in what situation, and any attempt to define roles within the family is immediately sabotaged by another member. It is as if any asserted position by anyone is a challenge or threat to someone else and the resulting transactions comprise patterns of mutual denial so that no clear outcome is ever permitted.

In the schizogenic family the future patient is commonly exposed to overt instructions on one level that are simultaneously cancelled or made impossible by contradictory information, often expressed non-verbally:

'Mum, may I go out to the cinema tonight?'
'Well, dear, um—of course you may but you know your father is not too well and hasn't earned anything this month. You know how he worries when you are out in the wet . . . such dark evenings now.'

Or

'Hello Mum. [Kisses her as she enters room, whereupon she stiffens.]
'So you like your old Mum then—do you?'
'Of course I do—you know I do Mum.' [Said looking down and punching one hand lightly into the other or biting his nails.]

The result of persistent transactions of this type is that the patient, and probably other members of the family as well, have little clear idea of who they are or what their nearest and dearest *really* feel for them. Where such a family script is written into a child's emergent self-process there is, at the least, a prescription for extensive dissociation and narrowed copying skills. At worst a weakened ego takes refuge in some past identification unrelated to current realities and, as this consolidates through repetition, dynamics develop that lack any real contact with an already virtually indefinable family situation. People who cannot get away from one another, who are mutually dependent, who consistently deny one another's perceived realities, and proffer conditional likings of a paradoxical or contradictory kind eventually drive each other mad (Bateson, Jackson, Haley, and Weakland 1956; Haley 1959).

Research on family dynamics has contributed much to our understanding of poor mental health and neurosis. Schizophrenia is a multiplex condition and physiological effects contribute to its causation, but family dynamics research has thrown light on situations in which no one has the ego-strength or the intelligence to attempt to redefine a situation that involves mutual and habitual self-cancellation.

The study of human interactions as such has taken us a long way in recent years. As Watzlawick, Beavin, and Jackson (1967) argue, human beings, except when totally alone, are never actually outside the communicational medium. Birdwhistell (1959) argued that individuals never really communicate. What they do is to become part of communication. Engagement in communication may be more or less explicit but so long as a person is in frame with another he cannot be outside communication. Students of interaction are not so much interested in the ontogenetic origins of behaviour, in whether individuals are conscious or unconscious of the implications of their actions or in the precise precipitation of events in causal sequences within a multiplex system; they focus instead on the *effect* of a 'stroke' on other people. These actions elicit responses irrespective of the extent to which they are consciously comprehended. They are elements in the social game which, whether schizogenic or normagenic, is the continually present fact of the intersubjective communicational medium. 'Play' varies in intensity, in focus, and in skill, but some kind of play is perhaps always in progress. Ultimately what is of interest is the intentionality of the player, the intention of an action within his world of meaning.

Watzlawick *et al.* (1967) demonstrate in their interaction analysis of George and Martha's vicious dialogue in *Who's afraid of Virginia Woolf?* (Albee 1962) that the apparent complexity of the emotional content of their communication almost conceals the narrowed stereotype of their interactional style. This stabilized relationship is locked within a mutually destructive circle from which neither interactant has the courage or insight to break free. The excuse for their harrowing togetherness is the myth of their relationship with their son, which sets a limit on the extent of their mutual ferocity. As if in some psychological potlatch ceremony (p. 195), such families are continuously creating and destroying their assets under the controlling influence of some mutually held rationale: 'We must stay together because of the children [ma, old father, the neighbours, etc.].' Such systems are likely to change only when time or circumstance breaks the structure and the about-to-be-freed collusionists face with fear the possibility of that freedom.

Personal growth and contemporary psychotherapy

The security operations of the emerging self have their effects at many levels. Within the communicational continuum an individual's stance is shown as much in his posture, his mannerisms, his eye energy, and his use of hands and gesture as in his conversational manner and content. The 'character' of an individual is patterned not only into his conduct but into his body itself in the form of a maintained muscular tonus that in the course of time produces 'character armour'; bodily distortion that inhibits self-expression as effectively, because made concrete, as the psychic controls on emotion (Reich 1949). Depth psychology, whether of Freudian, Jungian, or Reichian inspiration, seeks to probe those personal processes that, at the interactional level, are expressed in the restrictive roles adopted in social 'games'.

The person, as a product of the primal family scene, learns physical means of emotional control (angry violence, tears) that become literally embedded in the musculature and in a tight control of the autonomic nervous system. The work of release from interactional stereotypes thus involves far more than a degree of intellectual insight into what games one may be playing and their plausible history. It remains true that therapy in depth requires a genuinely experienced recovery of feelings associated with those crucial themes in family relating that established the inhibiting dynamism in the first place. Such a re-experiencing is carried through in the knowledge that the outcome is no longer pre-determined and that learning to choose alternative ways of relating is possible. Re-experience of traumata may evoke discrete events perceived as crucial to an individual or thematic material endured perhaps over many years. The task of the therapist is to facilitate the expression of the 'authentic' emotions associated with recall so that the emotional truth rather than the protective dynamism is the focus of the relived experience. The extent and depth of the experiental therapy required for opening up new options within the psyche varies, but most methods involve (a) the abreactive re-experiencing of negative emotion; (b) the discovery that such emotional expression is deeply relieving of long-term tensions, even to the extent of a gradual muscular relaxation in body armour; and (c) insight, not only into the general historical causality of a condition, but, more important, into the way in which, through transference, present-day orientations and attitudes to others are expressions of the original fears.

One of the most remarkable facts about people is a tendency to self-righting. Therapists can usually work with the assumption that the self seeks clarity, poise, and intimacy. It is as if the negative effects of childhood repression are mere deflections which, as in any epigenetic process, are set to return to more desirable goal states as soon as conditions allow. The 'recovery of the repressed', as Freud termed it, may be a painful process in which deep resistance is encountered but it is a commonly desired one. The key obstruction is an unwillingness to risk the psychological discomfort involved, which primarily concerns hurtful decrements in self-esteem. Those involved in personal growth, with or without a therapist, soon discover however that the uncovering of emotional pretence, hurtful as it may be to pride, yields the sense of discovery, of truth knowing and of opportunity that is the beginning of a profound and pleasurable self-reconstruction.

Anyone glancing today for the first time at the field of psychotherapy might well be overcome with confusion and dismay. Not only is there deep disunity among psychiatrists working with individuals whose troubled minds arise at least in part from organic defects (Clare 1976), but systems of counselling or therapy for the merely worried are legion, many of them clamouring for attention in an unseemly and clearly commercially motivated advocacy. There is an all-too-common trend for some whizz-kid therapist to present a gloss on Freud and other classic approaches, to write a best-selling and highly gimmicky book which gains interest, adherents, and clients, and then to establish a system of therapy or 'personal growth' with a hierarchy, expensive training courses for would-be practitioners, and big-sell packaging in various forms of advertisement to attract a sizeable slice of a middle-class, well-to-do, clientele. There is something unseemly about the whole business that seems to stem from the capitalist ethic in American medicine. This does not mean that an important new understanding is not developing. It simply means that no one therapeutic system is likely to possess an exclusive truth nor need its claims be taken too seriously.

This attitude to modern therapy is supported by the few critical studies made to differentiate between the effects of contrasting systems. Research in this area is notoriously difficult but evidence (Lieberman, Yalom, and Miles 1973) points to one conclusion: it is the person of the therapist and the way he presents himself to clients that counts and not the specific technique he is practising. This has vital significance for training: it means that no amount of skill and technique will substitute for the personal growth of the therapist himself. He must have done his own 'work'. This also suggests that modern therapists who have tested the therapeutic value of their activities are free to use techniques and skills eclectically from the range available and that subscription to one school or another is inessential.

There is one line of thought that has emerged with great clarity in the last decade and that is the theory of therapy associated with Carl Rogers and Frederick Perls and their respective therapeutic methods. In this section of the chapter we shall consider the theory of the troubled mind their work supports, its value in the practice of therapy, and its relationship to evolutionary ethology. To begin we need a little history.

Although Freud's original theory emphasized the conflict between an individual's libidinous nature and the social world, he later came to focus more on the negative aspects interior to the self and to believe that these too were rooted in a biological given—a death instinct. This fundamentally non-Darwinian idea has found no long-term support, and it gave rise to Wilhelm Reich's rebuttal of Freud and a fresh emphasis on the strength of societal control over emotional, and especially sexual, behaviour. The effects of the frustration and coercion of infantile sexuality, Reich believed, led to major distortions of the personality expressed in the armouring of body musculature and character alike and to repressive sadistic attitudes towards these affectionate few who had fully realized their genital character. These distortions he referred to as the 'emotional plague'. Reich's emphasis on sexual freedom was revolutionary in his time and had tragic consequences for him. It drew attention strongly to the origin of neurosis in the social frustration of natural development and played an important role in generating the sexual permissiveness and greater tolerance of emotional expression of today. It also gave rise to important techniques of 'body work' or bioenergetics in which physical expression of deeply inhibited emotions is facilitated by a range of exercises focusing especially on deep breathing. The consequence is a reappearance of powerful feeling that had been long denied.

In the 1960s, in a different more 'permissive' climate of opinion and following the development of 'ego' schools of psychoanalysis, Abraham Maslow (1962, 1964) re-expressed the person-versus-society conflict in a new way. He realized that the lives of outstanding individuals known to him simply could not be explained by the social learning theory approaches of his time with their emphasis on basic need-satisfaction, or 'deficiency motivation' as he called it. These individuals were bent on self-discovery, on self-expression. And they put the value of being authentically themselves above that of any conformity with the values of others. It was possible for these 'self-actualizing' people to experience life without the closure to experience that living according to the value of others entails. They were capable of greater personal involvement and commitment largely by virtue of the fact that choices were less frightening. By accepting a degree of fear these individuals were able to grow and extend themselves. Self-actualizers were not only more open to others, to ideas, to the world, than most but were also more autonomous. They were also more than usually capable of deep inner experiences, 'peak experiences' indicative of self-integration. The secret to all this was a style of fearlessness and a focus on 'being' rather than 'becoming' somebody. In Maslow's work the emphasis on sexuality has gone; instead the self-actualizer is the opposite of the alienated, emotionally impoverished conformist to the conventions of family, class, and race who has yet to experience the difference between self as self and 'self as how others want you to be'. Maslow had a great influence on a whole generation who, in revolt against middle-class values, set out themselves on a search for self-actualization and, with great courage, often found it.

Carl Rogers's own life is a vivid demonstration of self-actualization. Homans (1974) writes that Rogers grew up in a rural environment that imposed harsh religious ideals enforced by strong parental authority. Rogers at first accepted these ideals but, while training for the ministry at a theological college in New York, began increasingly to question them. He created his own discussion group to work through his vocational conflict over both the behavioural injunctions of religious idealism and also the truth claims of religious doctrine. Hoping to find an environment with greater freedom of thought he turned to training in psychology, where he was exposed to Freud's teachings and their authoritarian influence in psychological medicine. As he developed as a therapist and clinician he found more and more that the static imposition of doctrine, as in the case of religion, grossly impeded those styles of unhampered thought that not only enable research to proceed but also allow more effective, because more personal, therapy.

This experience led Rogers to focus closely upon the way in which personal development is moulded by the value and meaning that an individual's behaviour has for significant others in his life. Where the regard with which a young person is held by father, mother, or teacher is made conditional upon the fulfilment of certain expectations then a pressure to conform is establismed that may run counter to intuitions and needs that are closer to the young person's heart. When an independent stance is experienced as too anxiety-laden, young people incorporate the attitudes of others as their own. Making positive regard conditional on the fulfilment of parental wishes has enormous power to coerce a child away from the fulfilment of his natural inclinations. In Rogerian thought this power is the major factor responsible for character-distortion. The conditions set by a father, say, for showing love to a son are called the *conditions of worth* which the child must fulfil if he is to receive his father's positive regard, warmth, and friendship. Later on the conditions become the internal controls of action which the son uses when judging the worth of his own behaviour and feelings.

It follows that when direct experience, either of situational origin or of a natural impulse arising from within, challenges a self-perception based upon a condition of worth the individual will feel deeply threatened and will show *defence* to protect a self-structure originally derived from others. Distortion and denial of the experience then arises and its meaning is not assimilated. Defence is a form of coping that prevents the development of an inconsistent self-concept, possibly leading to fragmentation and anxiety. The loss of positive regard from others and, worse, of positive regard for oneself is profoundly productive of fear and the threat yields anxiety in abundance.

Self-structures based on introjected conditions of worth are rigid, cannot receive contrary experiences and, since these arise frequently in this diverse world, become closed, blocked, and narrowly assertive. Rogers argues that in childhood the need for positive regard is so strong that the child typically chooses to live for this at the expense of falsifying his or her actual personal experience and motivation. He argues that the imposition of this choice arises from the natural yet tragic developmental course of infancy and accounts for 'the basic estrangement in Man'.

What has been denied here is the 'natural organismic valuing of experience' which would allow bodily and emotional expression unimpeded by the controls imposed by fear. Needless to say we have here a continuum from those individuals subject to gross distortion in infancy to those who were fortunate in having parents able to give the child regard for itself with relatively few conditions. For example, parents who encourage their children's sexual self-expression without attempting to define it too firmly in advance would be doing a good job in this light; and their children would probably avoid the 'emotional plague'.

The young person's ongoing experiences of life are assimilated by the developing self-structure to the degree to which they are not filtered out by conditions of worth. An individual fully open to experience selects information for assimilation according to the processes of his own organism as a functioning ethogenic unit. The organism has the property, argues Rogers, for naturally evaluating experience that guides the person towards the satisfaction of needs and the development (actualization) of a self-structure of meanings that enables the adult to develop continually through the successive stages of life. The open organism is an exploratory one, so that as life continues there is always the new to be assimilated. Personal growth in principle never stops. Furthermore the open individual finds joy in novelty, in exploration and, as his self-structure achieves a degree of integration, this adventure will naturally include increasing awareness of an inner life. Self-actualization leads naturally, then, to deeper experiences of being, acute identity experiences recognized as 'peaks' of realization (Maslow 1962) which encourages yet further adventure.

'Fritz' Perls came to California after training as an orthodox analyst in Europe and a rich acquaintance with the psychodrama of Moreno; a technique in which clients literally act out their troubles on a stage and themselves play different roles in their own drama. The full expression of the introjected parts of oneself, 'voices', became a key element in Perls's developing method. In California Perls was also influenced by the Zen buddhist emphasis on direct 'here and now' experience. Perls, like Rogers, focused on the introjection of inauthentic 'voices' and encouraged them to 'speak' experientially to one another in dramatically vivid sessions in which the seated client engages himself in an inner psychodrama. Perls argued that inhibited emotional expression sought release in performance which terminated when the gestalt or wholeness of the felt-meaningfulness of a state of mind had been fully enacted. The self then moved naturally to the formation of another gestalt. Gestalt formation is often inhibited by introjections and it is in the working through of dialogue between introjection and authenticity that therapy occurs.

A crucial concept in Rogers's work, which has parallels in Perls's too, is the idea that openness is the opposite of defensiveness and that its presence is detected by the appearance of certain qualities (Pearson 1974). Openness allows an individual to receive affective cues that feel risky. Defence produces an avoidance of such cues. In reaction to cues the open person responds in a way that reveals a unity in his affective and cognitive processing of them. He feels and thinks congruently. The closed person by contrast intellectualizes, rationalizes, or ruminates interactively around the topic, all of which expressions are aspects of a denial that the experience has any relevance for him. The open person experiences himself as the locus in which the feeling happens and accepts responsibility for that; the closed person by contrast attributes the feeling to another or to a situation: 'You make me angry', or 'This rain is so depressing'. The open person is willing to go into the experience, to work through it, to process it with awareness of its personal and social implications, and to allow it to flow into its consequences or reach a natural (gestalt) closure. The closed person prevaricates, blocks, and is left with an incapacity to respond effectively or autonomously. 'Unfinished business' remains which will crop up again.

Evidence favouring these theoretical positions is based not only upon clinical observation itself but also on evaluative studies independent of the clinical setting. An interesting classification of the stages of ego formation that illustrates the tactics involved in keeping out of trouble and the gradual discovery of autonomy is provided by Loevinger (1966) (see Table 10.1). Each stage consist of injunctions to self listed as ways of self-control. The role of anxiety in regulating behaviour and in filtering both experience and responsivity is evident. Block (1971) found that these stages worked well in longitudinal studies of young men and women passing from adolescence to adulthood although he pointed out that the last stage was a rare one. Block also showed that there were marked associations between the personal character of his respondents and the personalities of their parents. A 'benign' family is required for an easier passage through the stages of personal growth. A malignant one more or less stops it.

TABLE 10.1
Loevinger's stages of ego development

Stage	Control paradigm
1. Impulse–ridden	'Better control myself, otherwise someone will *hurt* me.'
2. Opportunistic	'Better control myself, otherwise someone will *dominate* me.'
3. Conformist	'Better control myself, otherwise someone will *shame* me.'
4. Conscientious	'Better control myself, otherwise *someone else* will be hurt, dominated, shamed, or made guilty and then *I* will feel guilty.'
5. Autonomous	'Better control my excessive conscientiousness, otherwise I will be held back from achieving competency.'
6. Integrated	Reconciliation with the unattainable, achievement of a sense of integrated identity. Self-actualizing values leading to individuation.

The essence of therapy in both Rogers's and Perls's systems is listening. Indeed in Rogers's 'client-centred therapy' it is the central process. The listening is, however, to be carried through by a person unequivocally demonstrating *'unconditional regard'*. It is this attitude that is fundamental for therapy to occur, for it is the very opposite of the attitude that created conditions of worth and hence an attitude that facilitates an opening of the person to 'risky' self-experiencing. The emotional and cognitive assimilation of risky experiencing is aided by the therapist reflecting to the client exactly what he senses him to be saying. Badly done this becomes a parrot-like echoing; well done it affirms the client's experience and at the same time intensifies his awareness of it. Both the experience itself and the relief from the dread of disapproval tell the client that it is not only safe but pleasurable to proceed. The essence of the skill is very close empathic attention by the therapist without preconceptions or analytical interpretation as to what he is to say. Interpretation is of course possible outside the therapy session just as any objectification of an interpersonal process is possible, but it is not part of therapy itself. The difference between Rogerian therapy and traditional Freudian therapy lies not so much in the client's task (bringing up his moment-to-moment feelings and cognitions) but in the warmth of the therapist's unconditional attention beside him or before him, not sitting behind him in non-commital silence.

Perls's work assumes precise listening also, but a gestalt therapist is more interactive. He or she may aim to frustrate the operations of the introjected voices so that an experience of visceral and sensory conflict is fully blown into awareness. The failure to escape ends in an authentic expression of the client's self. When the ground has been well prepared, the insight into the falsity of the introjected voice is a powerful agent for change. The gestalt therapist's repertoire also includes many game-like structures which likewise provoke the client into an experience of his nature unfiltered by notions of how he ought to be.

In both cases the sense of self open to one's own visceral and sensory responding (organismic valuing) provides a feeling of emotional truth. The assumption of such a position of authenticity is experienced as of inestimable value and the client begins to undo his own conditioning. The focus ceases to be upon himself as a social product: he is aware of himself as a process open to the world and capable of responding freely to it.

The role adopted by the therapist in both these systems is essentially that of the 'good parent'. The good parent values his or her child unconditionally and supports its own personal growth. I remember once when I had been having difficulties through illness at school I talked about it with my father. I was troubled and he said to me, 'Well, have you done the best you can?' I thought about this and answered, 'Yes—I have.' 'Well then,' said my father, 'there is nothing else you can do about it, is there?' At the time I found this enormously supportive. My father in that event was a good parent to me. I felt able to return to school knowing that I had the strength of his acceptance behind me. Admittedly a gestalt therapist is more pushing and inventive than this but his role is the same, always to support and even to provoke the client's authentic self. As Perls put it, the direction is from 'other-support' to 'self-support'. He had not read the Zen Masters for nothing.

The key assumption in these theoretical interpretations of therapy is that the person has undergone a deflection or distortion in development but that in most cases there remains a powerful, partially obscured motivation to undo the blocks and rigidities and to emerge as a self free from conditions of worth. Often a person is far from aware of the pressures for change within himself. They 'well up' in frightening shape at odd moments and the 'ego' is so busily employed in correcting the imbalance in favour of inauthenticity that it may take time before the individual can consciously reorganize himself in a new direction. Jung's concept of personal individuation and the idea of self-actualization, as well as such themes as buddhist enlightenment, all point to the same socially suppressed force for growth in individuals. To differing degrees the individual has to go against his internalized voices and perhaps also against those voices really present out there in his social world. This causes pain, especially when two or more people, as in many types of marriage, are tied together in a collusion to protect each other's inauthenticity. Growth hurts, but often occurs even when the ego wills otherwise. 'It happened in spite of me' is a common remark made more in awe than disapproval!

Evolutionary cognitive ethology as a basis for therapeutic theory

Theories of therapy do not ask why human beings have this property of equifinality in the development of personal autonomy. Some of the sociobiological themes we have been considering in this book may help to anchor theories of therapy in an evolutionary ethology of the human self-processes. We have presented a case for thinking that the self-process is an evolutionary consequence of the emphasis in primate evolution on social transactions involving reciprocal altruism. Since the altruist is open to exploitation, selection favoured the emergence of the capacity to estimate the likely outcome of interpersonal relating in order to balance the mutual advantages of the interactions. This entailed evolution of the human capacity for self-consciousness based upon an integration of experiences of contingency and agency (pp. 224, 251, and 315). In parent–child conflict the person of the undeveloped child is open to exploitation. The human biogrammar is so open a programme that there is a risk of incorporating a sociogrammar of introjected voices that work fundamentally for the well-being of others instead of for oneself. Since parental pressures produce controls on sexual activity that have been designed to protect adult males from cuckoldry, to control the sexual exploits of sons in ways advantageous to parents, and to so coerce daughters that they became chattels in a marriage market, it seems highly likely that parents' coercion is not only designed to meet their own emotional needs but is, at a more fundamental level, expressive of their evolved strategies for enhancing inclusive fitness.

The long-term dependency of the child places it at risk in responding to such coercion with expressions of personal assertion and hence self-validation. We may wonder why in fact young humans do not simply adopt their parents' schemata and conform. It would seem to be less trouble. The answer seems to lie in the notion that an excessive introjection of parental values has several disadvantages: (a) it maintains social dependency and reduces the opportunities for learning about behavioural contingency and self-as-agent that will ensure a balance of advantages in reciprocal activities with others; (b) it allows parental manipulation that may be contrary to a person's social or reproductive success; and (c) it reduces the likelihood of a flexible and assertive response to social change and transgenerational succession. It follows that the person is likely to show a tendency towards rejection of parental values in adolescence and a new assertion of his or her own authority as a reproductive organism engaged in 'collaborative competition' (Crook 1971) with other humans.

Why then do parents not encourage the personal growth of their children? This would seem a biologically wise thing to do if it ensures their own children's reproductive welfare. The answer of course is that that is what parents think they *are* doing; and some indeed actually succeed in doing so.

Human parents rationalize their biostrategies in terms of sociostrategies and speak not in terms of long-term reproductive success but rather in terms of wealth, prestige, and lineage. Only where inheritance is concerned does reproduction come to play a role in the foreground. Of course, to any one generation, it is difficult to predict reproductive success in subsequent generations in any other terms.

Given the facts of, (a) childhood dependency, (b) the openness of human programmes in development, and (c) the crucial role of the individual organism in ensuring genetic continuity (and hence as a unit of selection), it seems likely that parents may behave with more or less conditional regard depending on the predictable outcome for the child in the years of its adulthood.

The economic viability of families and systems of marital inheritance are relative to prevailing economic circumstances. Given socioecological security, cultures containing fixed rules for social order are apt to preserve themselves over long time courses. It may then be advantageous for young people to receive a firm education in the emotional control relevant for the maintenance of a particular cultural morality. It can be predicted that in cultures of this kind there will be a heavily conditional and indoctrinating rearing system and that the subsequent coping closure (p. 282) of the offspring will ensure a rigid social regularity in the next generation. Within the confines of such a system conformists will do well socially and reproductively, but non-conformists will be penalized as victims of the local 'emotional plague'. (Note that non-conformist younger sons may do well as colonizers while conformist elder sons may do well under primogeniture. The social and familial pattern needs careful examination.)

Under circumstances of low socio-ecological security, culture values may shift to an emphasis on individuality, enterprise, initiative, and exploration—a 'frontier spirit' in fact. It may then be the case that an emphasis on enterprise in childhood lessens the conditionality of the regard in which they are held and favours a greater acceptance of the 'child of nature'. In other words, the fact that some populations contain more 'benign' families than others may well be related to socio-economic and cultural factors.

It may have been the case that under conditions of difficulty, such as those which probably obtained during the millennia when the hunter–gatherers were spreading over the globe, the value of assertive auto-nomy in the competitive collaboration that maintained communities was high. We have as a consequence inherited a tendency towards the development of autonomy in adulthood irrespective of the necessary compromise that a dependent childhood requires. The individual necessarily develops within an environment of some conditional regard and the extent to which individuation subsequently occurs varies with the pressures and modes of local history. The present state of the Western world, compared with the Victorian period, values the type of openness that enhances self-actualization, autonomy, and authentic-ity. The Victorian period enforced social propriety, manners, and pretence to gain a social conformity that ensured a deep double stan-dard in the lives of many.

There is a choice between a more *natural* person and a socially *artificial* one. We cannot perhaps predict precisely the effects of these social outcomes in sociobiological terms but we can argue that to be most true to one's own 'nature' requires a democratic society tolerant of idiosync-racy and spontaneity. If that is what we wish for our children then we must also begin to understand the unconditional manner with which we shall have to regard them. With rates of social change as high as they are, adaptable young people are much needed for the ordered recon-struction of society. Unconditional regard in the rearing of young people is perhaps the most adaptive response we, in our time, can make. With more stable conditions in the global future this pleasing idea may, however, be perceived as less than socially adaptive. Our sense of the appropriate is bound by time and the manner of our suffering goes with it.

Summary
(1) The neotenous human infant requires an especially lengthened period of maternal care and infanticide is not uncommon in many human populations. The mother's investment is high and caring for an unfit infant (or a fit one under social circumstances that are unlikely to lead to success) may lead to a severe decrement in her biological fitness. Deferment of breeding under such conditions may well increase the mother's fitness.
(2) Once the decision to rear a child is made the mother must make a further decision about when to reduce or discontinue care in favour of rearing a further child. Her choice will commonly be contrary to the wants although not necessarily the needs of the child.

(3) During the weaning process, the child necessarily experiences maternal withdrawal. The infant's frustration may be met by the mother in various ways some helpful to the child and some not.

(4) The child's natural anger at the mother's withdrawal may be deeply suppressed, especially if the child has to comply with her emotional demands in order to attract her attention.

(5) Children are in fact skilled at equilibrating their emotional responses to experiences of parental withdrawal. Natural selection may well have enhanced this capacity to cope with rearing conditions.

(6) Both emotional suppression and traumatic events of parental rejection lead to repression of the memories related to them. This denial of experience leads to the development of motivations the origin of which remains unknown or 'unconscious' with respect to the child's self-awareness. The unconscious memory remains very active however as a determinant of both attitudes and behaviour. Repressed material, far from being lost, remains covertly active and the discrepancies between a person's actual behaviour and his failure to enact an ideal gradually become apparent to a degree depending on their salience in his ongoing life.

(7) Research suggests that because the child cannot reject the mother (since it needs her) it restricts its own behaviour so that its activities fit an arena acceptable to mother. Coping with mother produces that programme of responses which the child feels able to perform without risk of maternal rejection.

(8) Research by Ainsworth and Main reveals that children behave in ways that strongly reflect their mothers personalities. In particular babies who avoid their mothers after brief separations tend to have cold restrictive mothers while babies who approach under the same experimental circumstances have warmer more expressive mothers. Avoidant and non-avoidant infants are equally cuddly as neonates so their behaviour at 1 year of age is a matter of differential development. Different cultures seem to have different proportions of avoidant to non-avoidant infants and mothers to match, suggesting that there is an intergenerational transmission of personality characteristics which are both the product of and determine the cultural norms for child rearing.

(9) Other research suggests that avoidant infants may experience the world as essentially uncontrollable and hence become prey to a learned helplessness, lack of initiative, low autonomy, and a tendency to depression. However, an avoidant adult may also seek to control others in ways that resemble those of his or her mother. Such an individual in a position of social power is likely to be particularly intolerant of the expressive behaviour of others.

(10) Social interactions designed to maintain personal security are a major effect of limiting childhood experience. The mutual support of

self-protecting intimates may become directed to the maintenance of a collusion in each others 'games'. Families afflicted with collusionist parents are often particularly damaging to children through the 'double binds' they inflict. These 'games people play' can be made explicit in therapy and individuals gradually become aware of the impact of their own actions. This then allows opportunities for change.

(11) Most persons seek clarity, poise, and intimacy. There is a tendency to self-righting which facilitates the task of the therapist. The key obstruction is fear of psychological discomfort as the individual risks behaviour it has long dreaded to perform.

(12) While the profession of therapist has been cheapened by psychological adventurers exploiting the personal growth industry, a general consensus focuses around the work of Carl Rogers and Frederick Perks, the initiators of 'client-centred' and 'gestalt' therapy respectively. Both therapists emphasized the importance of 'unconditional regard', the accepting attitude of the therapist who in a sense plays the role of a good yet provocative parent rather than an inhibiting one. The experience of such a relationship is therapeutic for the client in that it facilitates his or her exploration of a wider world of interpersonal interaction.

(13) The chapter ends with an assertion that the self-righting properties of the person that are so clearly indicated in the experience of psychotherapy may be aspects of a will to autonomy ultimately designed to maintain inclusive fitness. The extent to which parents in given cultures restrict their offspring's behaviours through conditional regard may, however, also be related adaptively to the socio-cultural conditions of their societies. Stable conformist cultures will be fertile environments for stable conformist children, conditions of rapid change provide environments of opportunity for non-conformist adventurers born from parents who allowed them to do very largely as they wished.

11 Consciousness, flow, and the two sides of the mind

> Thought is getting out of touch . . . Before men had
> cultivated the Mind, they were not fools.
> D. H. Lawrence 1978

Objective and subjective aspects of attention

To say 'I am I' is not the same as to say 'I am me'. This distinction lies at the root of an important set of dichotomies that is apparent in recent psychology and has great importance in the understanding of the human person. James's original treatment demarcated the field of 'consciousness' as the ground of action, the 'I', from the character, identity, role, and other attributes of the 'me' that comprised the subject-matter of 'personality' study in the previous chapter.

In both phylogeny and ontogeny, awareness of the environment doubtless develops initially through the perception and cognition of external stimulation. The sensory systems are adapted to the environment as filters that prevent the organism from being confused by the mass of stimulation that is potentially available from the complex flux of information that is constantly present. The brain functions primordially to govern transactions with distant objects, to allow prediction based upon stimulation emanating from objects yet far away (Sherrington 1906). We may assume therefore, that primitive conscious states are dominated by the input from the senses and are in effect derived from the sense impressions themselves.

Animal experience is contingent upon the sampling of information carried out by special senses designed for the particular ecological requirements of the species. Out of the complexity and richness of the information available to its eye, the frog selects only four distinct classes of events. Cats and monkeys show similar selectivity, but in a more complex way. Humans, too, are adapted to receive information in ways that are characteristic of the organs functioning in the main sensory modalities, and our social agreement about our perceived world is based on shared limitations that have ensured the biological survival of our species. Our *Innenwelt* is specific to us just as the worlds of animals are specific to each of them (von Uexküll 1909, see above p. 4). We can only guess at the consciousness of other animals through a study of their sensory apparatus and their cognitive abilities (Griffin 1977).

The arguments of Chapters 7, 9, and the last part of Chapter 10 suggest that the self-process whereby we entertain and evaluate concepts about our own nature and position in society is an evolved characteristic of our species. Language as a representational symbolism, intellect to compute the elaborate stochastics of human relationships, and self-representation in order to position oneself within society are all consequences of the increasing complexity of nepotistic and reciprocating interactions in our species. In particular, the development of reciprocating interactions with their opportunities for cheating and the corresponding need to detect the cheater, led to the particularly sensitive apparatus of trust–distrust that functions in all forms of partnering. Intellect and self-representation are linked to an emotional system that balances biological egotism against the more refined forms of co-operation. Psychological pain is experienced as an important social message when self-evaluation on scales of personal esteem, shame, or the expectations of a significant other diverge away from what is expected. Much of human action consists of the equilibration of self-presentation in the world in the face of ambivalence in relationships and the pain involved in its experience. The whole apparatus is subject to a lengthy growth process through personal development; for the autonomy of the adult is not assured except through the education of the emotions experienced in transactions with others.

In this chapter we are concerned with the person's own consciousness of the operations of his mental apparatus. Conscious awareness is limited to that which is admitted by perception and attended to in the course of cognitive evaluation. This includes the awareness of emotional states that arise from associations between current feeling, events, recalled evaluations, and assessments of personal condition or status. We also saw in Chapter 10 how emotional states and personal attitudes are deeply influenced by repressed information which is not available to the conscious mind.

In human action, involvement in a task with the senses focused on the activities to hand provides us with a state of mind probably closest to the primordial functioning of consciousness with its total environmental focus (see Sherrington 1940). Here the human self is unaware of itself, no self-critical feedback loop is in operation, the subject is completely absorbed in the work. Similarly, in less active conditions, a person may be absorbed by observing a train passing along a line or a bird in the sky. While thought may be present, the attention is totally focused upon the external object.

This state of mind has been termed 'subjective self-awareness' and contrasted with an alternative condition, 'objective self-awareness' in which the subject is aware of its 'self' as a focus of attention. Here the subject is itself the object of attention. The individual normally attends to his conscious state, his behaviour, personal history, circumstances, body, or character in an evaluative manner in which these features are rated in relation to other conditions of them. Duval and Wicklund (1972) argue that these two states of awareness imply that conscious attention cannot be focused simultaneously on an aspect of the self and be absorbed with a feature of the environment. 'When a person's attention is directed towards a consideration of his personal virtues, it is impossible at that same instant to focus conscious attention toward driving nails into a board.'

The terms 'objective' and 'subjective' were chosen by Duval and Wicklund because they express the directional nature of conscious attention. Consciousness is almost synonymous with attention, for to exist at all it must have an object, a thing of which the individual is conscious. When attention is directed on to an individual's body or person he is the object of his own consciousness—and hence exists in a state of 'objective self-awareness'. With attention directed away from himself he is the subject or source of that attention—hence 'subjective self-awareness'. In this state self-awareness is limited to the sensations of being the source of observation and action which are experienced simultaneously with the mental emanation of the object observed.

A characteristic of objective self-awareness is that it operates primarily in a comparative mode. Self-evaluation is based on the existence of a set of standards by which each person regulates his self-esteem and sense of social well-being. Standards of correctness or quality of performance become 'self-demanding' so that deviations lead to self-correcting behaviour in cybernetic fashion. To have one's attention drawn to oneself is thus to initiate a momentary evaluation of one's position on some dimension of personal desirability originally based in societal requirement but psychologically and existentially rooted in the subjective imperatives of a super-ego. These automatic comparisons and corrections can occur along a multiplicity of dimensions locally determined in relation to the culture of personal adaptiveness that defines the individual's world of norms. Duval and Wicklund argue that a sustained state of objective self-awareness with its concommitant process of judgemental evaluation is an uncomfortable one.

Objective self-awareness will lead to . . . negative affect whenever the person is aware of a self-contradiction or a discrepancy between an ideal and his actual state. Even without a prior failure, or loss in self-esteem, we would argue that the objective state will be uncomfortable when endured for considerable time. As the individual examines himself on one dimension after another he will inevitably discover ways in which he is inadequate, and at such a point he will prefer to revert to the subjective state.

This dichotomy has been expressed in other ways. Rotters's (1966) distinction between externalists and internalists with respect to the experience of locus of control (p. 270) is similar. The externalist is like the habitually objectively self-conscious person who feels judged or controlled most of the time. By contrast a person with an internal locus of control is less likely to be judgemental. The self-critical condition is furthermore one in which self-examination leads to dissatisfaction, lack of confidence, sensations of unattractiveness, and inadequacy. The opposite state is, by contrast, marked by a purposeful focus on action with commitment and involvement. To be at one with a task is to be relatively unaware of oneself as a separate entity open to self-criticism and inevitable fallibility. In the distinction between an objective and a subjective condition of conscious attention we seem to be at the beginning of a major exploration, for the territory has so far been of little interest in conventional psychology.

The conditions which in an adult give rise to objective or subjective self-consciousness are nothing more than the stimuli that cause an individual to attend either to himself or the environment. Theoretically, the direction of attention is governed by situations in the environment or by attempted manipulations of the environment. It is when these conditions necessitate an awareness of the individual himself as an object in the world that objective self-consciousness is most likely to arise. And of course it will be in transactions with other persons that this can be most usually expected. Social intercourse will be marked by rather long and recurrent periods of objective self-consciousness. Intimate friends, whose mutual acceptance and compatibility are high, will be able to dispense with much objective self-consciousness and, when it occurs, it can be as rewarding as it may be an occasion for self-concern. Generally, the creation of friendship will allow persons to increase the proportion of time in which they can be subjectively aware and at ease with one another.

Duval and Wicklund assume that a person may be made objectively self-aware simply by knowing that another is attending to him seriously. Since such attention is likely to be evaluative, the recipient is likely to seek to determine on what dimensions the evaluation is proceeding and to make some estimate as to where he himself stands on these dimensions. It will be clear that the negative affect experienced in these situations will be a function of many variables concerned with identity structure, role performance, and above all the way in which a person maintains his or her self-esteem.

Duval and Wicklund have given us a theory of the developmental origins of objective self-consciousness. In the early discussion of similar problems by Mead (1934), 'taking the role of the other' was seen as being the key to self-knowledge. By establishing an empathic relationship with another it is possible to envisage how he sees oneself—and hence to construct a picture of oneself as seen by other people. A self-scrutiny is essentially therefore an introjected scrutiny by another.

This externalization of oneself in order to 'see' oneself may, however, be only a part of the process. Conscious attention may have *ab initio* the capacity to focus on the self-process as well as upon any external object. An individual is not necessarily *dependent* on the views of others but may be capable of constructing self-awareness out of the experiences that arise from his own initiatives towards others. We have seen in Chapter 10 that babies are far from being passively dependent creatures functioning purely by a cybernetic regulation of need satisfaction. From the beginning they occupy themselves with strategies that set up transactions with their mothers. It seems unlikely that the growing child is entirely dependent on its mother for its self-definition as Mead's argument would suggest.

An individual may possess a single innate consciousness with the property of directional attention. As the interaction with the mother proceeds, the concept of self as an agent gradually emerges and becomes a field for the focus of attention. Because of the immense importance for human beings of social relating, it follows that for a high proportion of their time they will give at least some attention to ongoing self-processes. To varying degrees, individuals will develop habitual attentiveness to themselves, sometimes to a neurotic degree which then tends to preclude relating through self-absorption in introspection. The 'I' and the 'me' are not two self-processes but are the result of differential focusing of attention either upon the environment or upon the agent of experience. We are not therefore discussing a dual nature, but rather two directions of attention by the same unitary consciousness. Behaviourally and experientially, however, an individual can categorize his awareness of this differential attentiveness very clearly into one or the other of two mental states.

Very young children are, of course, not objectively self-aware. The development of this ability comes slowly. Piaget has maintained that the young child, ignorant of his own ego, behaves with 'absolutism'. He has absolute belief in his own ideas, believes that everyone understands what he says, cannot recognize his self-contradictions, and thinks that everyone else has the same viewpoint as himself. This 'egocentric' self-processes of others that are different from his own are made manifest to him. He then perceives that each person's perceptual world is differentiate the causal agent self only as long as his implicit belief in the universitality of perception is not contradicted by events in the environment' (Duval and Wicklund 1972). This contradiction occurs when self-processes of others that are different from his own are made manifest to him. He then perceives that each person's perceptual world is bounded, particular, and not universal.

The discovery that there are perceptions, thought, and behaviours that do not accord with his own arises in the course of an individual's

transactions with another person. When another person simultaneously presents a point of view of an object that differs from his own
awareness of it, a contradiction becomes apparent to the child and he
becomes aware of his self as distinctive. Mere observation may, however, not be enough. It is when the contradiction relates to opposition
which has practical consequences—for example, preventing the child
from getting what he wants—that the insight will be forcefully confirmed and elaborated. Once this stage is reached, objective self-
consciousness becomes part of an individual's interactional experience.
As we have seen (p. 275) a similar process may have occurred in the
gradual emergence of consciousness of self in history.

Duval and Wicklund have used their theoretical orientation in a
number of empirical research studies. By manipulating individuals
into differing degrees of objective self-awareness, they were able to
show that the uncomfortable affect has a variety of motivational consequences. In particular, a discrepancy in opinion between an individual
and a group projects the person concerned into a highly objective
self-consciousness in which he focuses on his apparent error. According
to the extent to which he believes himself to be wrong, he then seeks to
alter his opinion. Empirical studies with small groups showed that, in
the absence of any way of ascertaining error or correctness, an individual who is objectively self-conscious will tend to conform to the
opinion of the dominant group. The need to equilibrate to group norms
is very strong in human beings and is surely based in the survival value
of group cohesion to individuals in ancient times. Without a clear
marker for a correct opinion, correctness is normally assigned to the
opinion held by the group. Experiments also show that minority groups
will often conform to majority opinions under these circumstances.

The whole process of objective self-awareness appears to be bedevil-
led by an anxiety anchored in the dissonance produced by a discrepancy between personal existence, opinion, belief, behaviour, or
appearance on the one hand and social norms on the other. Social
security for an individual is, it seems, anchored in a felt togetherness in
which the pain of social dissonance is reduced to a minimum. Sadly, as
the work on conformity shows (e.g. see Milgram 1974), this need for
self-confirmation through agreement with others can lead many
people, including even the tough-minded, into conformity with action
against scapegoats or other victims which is cruel and involves a
depersonalization of the other with a suspension of the considerate
responsiveness that would normally be present in an interaction. The
need to conform to a group norm may lead to a perception of members
of an out-group as unworthy of the respect that is usual in encounters
with other people.

Civilization contains numerous status hierarchies and opportunities for differential ranking in relation to skills, behaviour, affluence, and influence. The behavioural dimensions of dominance–submissiveness necessary engage objective self-consciousness as the prime mover in setting up comparisons. Social life is thus constantly saturated with the mutual suspicion and self-rating that this mode of being entails. Habituation to established social patterns in well-integrated groups reduces self-consciousness of this type, enabling a more open, less defended, stream of interaction to occur, but there is a degree of tension present in all but the most intimate social settings. While this may be stimulating and pleasurable to achievers, it can be depressing and productive of anxiety to those with poor self-confidence, the shy loners of society whose skills may lie in solitary occupations. The discomfort of objective self-awareness with its attendant anxieties about acceptance and rejection suggests that many would prefer the state of subjective self-consciousness and will tend to participate in activities that induce it whenever relaxation from social interaction is possible. Many dis-satisfied persons develop passionate activities that involve them with objects of the environment. Fixing the attention upon the external world achieves subjective self-consciousness, which removes the disso-nance of the objective state. For many the *processes* of these activities are far more important than any goal or end. Yet, as we shall see, such behaviour is by no means confined to misfits and masochists. The release from ego-concern that passionate involvement in a task creates is the basis for many a form of self-expression in which individuals claim a sense of personal fulfilment that is unattainable through the introspective discrimination of objective self-consciousness.

Enjoyment, conformity, and personal independence

Perhaps the most optimistic study consulted in the preparation of this book is the research by Mihaly Csikszentmihalyi (1975) on the psychological basis of enjoyment. Traditional behaviourist psychology conceives of human motivation typically in terms of a 'deficit model'. Behaviour is seen as no more than a set of innate and learned responses directed cybernetically to the satisfaction of certain needs. Such theories carry a flavour of despondency because social needs can rarely be fully met, and in sexual life, for example, the practitioner with inventive plans for improvement soon bumps his head on social disap-proval. Only in play does there seem to be an unalloyed enjoyment that is restricted neither by recurrent deficits nor by time.

Play is more or less goal-less, is carried out for the fun of it, is relatively unrestricted by fatigue, and is usually conducted with subjec-tive self-awareness. As Csikszentmihalyi remarks, 'If we can find out what makes play such a liberating and rewarding activity we can start applying this knowledge outside of games as well.' Yet the enjoyment that occurs in games and sport is not limited to these activities. There are, even in these alienating times, forms of work which practitioners find absorbingly fascinating. We can note here again the equation between subjective self-awareness, absorption in a skilled task, and a pleasurableness that fulfils in the same open manner that play does. These games and tasks all require absorption in action, the condition of subjective self-consciousness that precludes introspective worrying about oneself.

In a set of experiments Duval and Wicklund describe how subjects were placed in objective self-consciousness primarily by increasing environmental surveillance in an obvious manner, or alternatively in subjective self-consciousness by the provision of a task requiring focal attention. In general it appears that with more subjective self-awareness individuals attribute responsibility for error to others rather than themselves and to be generally less self-critical, defensive, and lacking in assertive confidence. With high involvement in a focal task, individuals may indeed also attribute the positive consequences of actions to events outside themselves. The effect is thus not restricted to negative judgements. To a degree the involved task performer is simply less concerned with the judging process in so far as it may affect his esteem on some dimension. The same appears true of involvement in games and work that resemble total play.

Certain sports that clearly provide their practitioners with rich enjoyment are not easy to understand with any dry deficit model of behaviour causation. Why rock climbers should climb or mountaineers struggle to the peaks of inhospitable and often dangerous mountains is a classic question. When asked, climbers will report that it is the activity in itself that is important, more so normally than the goal. Csikszentmihalyi studied chess-players, 'rock' dancers, and surgeons and found much the same principle at work: the activity was in itself fulfilling—*autotelic*. The rewards are intrinsic to the activity and are cited again and again in terms of creative discovery and exploration, testing of competence through praxis, matching skills with another, a rock face or a disease, and the mysterious joy of the focal involvement and total attention that is perhaps the most characteristic feature of all.

The 'holistic sensation that people feel when they act with total involvement' is called 'flow' and Csikszentmihalyi makes it the focus of his theoretical model of enjoyment. 'Perhaps the clearest sign of flow is the merging of action and awareness. The person in flow has no dualistic perspective: he is aware of his actions but not of the awareness itself.' After a brilliant documentation of this experience from interviews with many practitioners of total involvement, Csikszentmihalyi suggests two conditions that interfere with flow and which are liable to produce moments of highly disruptive objective self-consciousness with accompanying self-doubts. When a person—a surgeon, chess-player, or rock climber, say—believes that the action is too demanding on his capabilities the resulting anxiety precludes the possibility of 'flow'. Conversely, when skills are greater than opportunities for use, boredom arises, followed by an anxiety stemming perhaps from a need for a more demanding performance. Figure 11.1 shows this model of autotelic praxis.

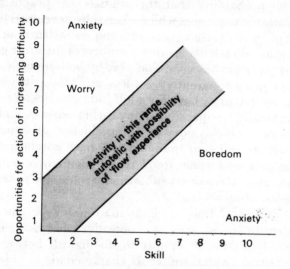

FIG. 11.1. Conditions for 'flow'. (After Csikszentmihalyi 1975.)

Autotelic activities then are modes of human action in which total involvement to the exclusion of introspective self-examination is the prime characteristic. Many of these activities are clearly tasks irrespective of whether they may be conventionally judged to be work (i.e. with economic or social gain) or play (i.e. without obvious economic or social gain). The activities are not necessarily solitary but, as with chess, basketball, or surgery, may be highly sociable or competitive. I myself remember states of flow in highly competitive rugby football matches at school, where for the duration of the game there was an almost trance-like state of suspension in which tolerance of exhaustion was a prime feature. It is probably also true of warfare, especially when a total physical exhaustion is involved, as for an infantry platoon in attack. Indeed, several soldiers who operated as special agents dropped to join resistance forces behind enemy lines have reported those days of extreme danger as the most fulfilling experiences of their lives. Clearly, such men, at the peak of physical fitness and military training, experienced the events as flow within the limits of their highly developed competence.

We should not leave the emphasis on playfulness in the flow experience without the realization that play in animal species other than our own remains a topic with problems not unlike those we are considering. Bekoff (1978), in his review of social play in animals, emphasizes that the biological function of play is still barely understood. Explanations in terms of exercise, reduction of excess energy, or maintaining arousal levels are all clearly weak. The strongest explanation for juvenile play focuses on the probability that the animals are practising innate activities in variable sequences which when fully developed become an essential part of an adult strategy. In addition, social learning about the relative strengths and talents of other members of the same generation is occurring. It is clear, however, that play by both juvenile and adult animals has the same apparently 'goal-less' and totally involving quality that autotelic activities have for adult humans. Bekoff emphasizes that play is normally co-operative in my earlier sense (Crook 1971) of being 'collaborative behaviours in the production of some common behavioural effect' and that many species have special signals that distinguish intentions to play from 'truly' competitive activities. In plax dominant animals may act subordinate roles; this never happens outside the play situation.

We can hardly argue that non-human animals experience the contrasting states of mind we call objective and subjective self-consciousness, but they do appear to distinguish between socially serious competition (which we see as characteristic of objective self-consciousness) and non-competitive social interaction and, furthermore, to mark the transition from one to the other in clear-cut fashion. If the sequences of play are practice for effective performance in the serious world of competition, we would expect collaborative play to occur mainly between relatives. In man, too, it may well be that skills generated in play generalize into use in social situations that are far from playful in their content. Total involvement is in either case a likely prerequisite for success in game or contest, for unrestricted focus on the task to hand is clearly the most effective means of integrating the input of information with skilful motor output in action.

If this is the case then one may well question the utility of objective self-consciousness with its accompanying tendency to introspective despondency. The answer must surely lie in the human need to formulate action ahead of the event, to create strategy and tactics prior to involvement in situations of great informational complexity. To achieve this a reflective withdrawal from ongoing events is needed: as, by analogy, when eyes are averted from gaze in the formulation of a conversational response. The objective self-conscious awareness may be momentary or prolonged or lie below the current of social interaction and monitoring performance. In all cases, however, the taking of one's own performance into account appears to be functionally projective. That is to say, it facilitates shifts in responding that appear to adapt the individual's behaviour more effectively to ongoing social transactions. However, conformity to conventionalized group norms is often neither a wise personal policy nor one of wider societal value. It is fundamentally antithetical to activities of social criticism upon which adaptive change cognisant of wide social issues can occur. Some balance between objective and subjective self-consciousness seems to be a requirement for integrating self-criticism and self-confidence into effective personal action.

Deep play and alienation

The capacity to enter flow differs from one individual to another, varying with abilities to relax from introspective anxiety dependent upon (objective) self-consciousness. The self-conscious person, in the colloquial sense of that term, cannot easily let go into the experience of an action. In his studies of 'rock' dancing ('rock and roll'), Csikszentmihalyi found that individuals differed in their abilities to experience the elements of flow described from interviews. As compared with relatively uninvolved dancers, those in flow were less easily distracted from the dance, perceived the passage of time as faster, felt at ease with their bodily movements as 'appropriate' to the dance, experienced direct physical sensation more, felt socially more in control, felt more in harmony with the setting of the occasion, and were less self-conscious in the sense of experiencing out-of-place sensations of embarrassment. Rock dancing is not a task; it is more a physical art-form in which self-expression in free movement is a criterion for full participation. In so far as dancers are observed by others, it is the grace, integration, and free release inherent in movement that is appreciated—and free release is of greater import than elegance. In general it seems likely that free flow in dance may carry over into other aspects of life; conversely, inhibited dancers are often inhibited in other areas of their lives. Learning to 'let go' into dance may well pay off in wider fields of living.

Jeremy Bentham described play in which the stakes are so high that it is from a utilitarian viewpoint irrational to engage in it at all as 'deep play'. Rock climbing is clearly a deep-play sport. Deep play in which the element of risk is great is peculiarly subject to disruption by anxiety or boredom. To achieve flow in this sport is thus particularly exhilarating and takes on 'out of this world' characteristics. Csikszentmihalyi's informants, who included some famous climbers, a number of local heroes, and ordinary enthusiasts, distinguished the deep flow experience on the rock from normal life along a number of dimensions that are highly revealing (Table 11.1). The main contrasts between flow and

TABLE 11.1
Deep-flow experience in rock climbing

Normative life	Rock-climbing experience
Informational noise: distraction and and confusion of attention	One-pointedness of mind
Nebulosity of limits, demands, motivations, decisions, feedbacks	Clarity and manageability of limits, demands, decisions, feedbacks
Severing of action and awareness	Merging of action and awareness
Hidden, unpredictable dangers; unmanageable fears	Obvious danger subject to evaluation and control
Anxiety, worry, confusion	Happiness, health, vision
Slavery to the clock: life lived in spurts	Time out of time: timelessness
Carrot-and-stick preoccupation with exotelic, extrinsic material and social reward; orientation toward ends	Process orientation; concern for autotelic, intrinsic rewards; conquest of the useless
Dualism of mind and body	Integration of mind and body
Lack of self-understanding; false self-consciousness; war between the selves	Understanding of the 'true self', self-integration
Miscommunication with others; masks, statuses, and roles in an inegalitarian order; false independence or misplaced dependency	Direct and immediate communication with others in an egalitarian order; true and welcomed dependency on others
Confusion about man's place in nature or the universe; isolation from the natural order; destruction of the earth	Sense of man's place in the universe; oneness with nature; congruence of psychological and environmental ecology
Superficiality of concerns; thinness of meaning in the flatland	Dimensions of depth 'up there' encounter with ultimate concerns

From Csikszentmihalyi 1975

normal life emerge as one-pointedness of mind, total involvement, timelessness, confident integration of mind and body, self-integration, egalitarianism with companions, oneness with nature, and contact with ultimate reality. So powerful can be the attraction of this experience that some climbers give up lucrative jobs in cities and seek out a simple life in the hills where some climbing can be done every day. Even the repetitive ascending of well-known faces never tires; the experience of an infinite variety of minor route changes, holds, weather conditions, personal moods seems to be an ever-absorbing novelty. In his book *Island*, a vision of a vulnerable Utopia, Aldous Huxley put rock-climbing as an educational imperative for everybody.

It is becoming clear that the language practitioners use to describe the deep-play experience approaches that used by mystics in their contacts with the 'divine'. Before we turn quite seriously to examine this similarity it is important that we look further at more 'superficial' flow experiences and the effects of deprivation from them. Csikszent-mihalyi set out to discover what experiences of flow people had in everyday life. A very wide variety of activities were classified as 'micro-flow' experiences that were felt to be without extensive rewards or particular goals yet in a quiet way fulfilling. While microflow is very different from deep play it has the same autotelic properties. In self-reports members of the experimental sample produced a range of 'unnecessary' behaviours classified under six heads: imaginative (i.e. daydreaming, talking to oneself, plants, or pets, humming, or singing), attentive (observing people or things, watching TV, hearing radio or records, reading), oral (smoking, chewing), kinaesthetic (walking, running, exercising, fiddling with objects), creative (artwork, playing music, sewing, letter-writing or other writing, doodling), and social (shopping, talking, joking, parties, dining out, sex). Over the range of subjects the highest percentage of microflow activities for an individual were: 82 per cent social, 61 per cent kinaesthetic, 27 per cent oral, 30 per cent attentive, and 32 per cent imaginative. A rating for the creative category was not obtainable. Of autotelic activities reported by the sample, 29 per cent were social, with sexual components probably underestimated, 25 per cent kinaesthetic, 20 per cent imaginative, 16 per cent attentive. Oral and creative activities account for only a little over 10 per cent of all activities. In general, people relax either with kinaesthetic activities or social ones, but rarely with both. Younger respondents were more kinaesthetic, relying on idiosyncratic private body movements to shape experience while older people (22 years +) were more social and less attentive. In general, all forms of microflow except the social tend to decrease with age. Sex differences were few in the sample; there was a tendency for women to be more involved in shopping, visiting galleries, etc., which is doubtless a cultural effect. In general, scores of alienation did not correlate with increased microflow; there is thus no suggestion that autotelic activity is used to compensate for an alienated experience of life. However, alienated people do tend to show oral activities and to talk to themselves. Adventure-seekers are also prone to find normal life meaningless. People whose autotelic activities are social are most rarely alienated, especially those who enjoy whiling away time in talk and joking. Thus, while the amount of microflow activity is unrelated to alienation, its type and patterning may well be so. The underlying personality traits that may be linked to these correlations remain to be studied.

Respondents asked to rate their current feelings on a checklist of adjective pairs (i.e. hostile–friendly, creative–dull, sad–happy, etc.) produced persistent patterns but these were strangely at variance with the results just quoted. Thus people who practise social microflow and are least alienated rate themselves consistently rather negatively, while those relying on kinaesthetic microflow choose more positive words to describe their mood. This fact, left unexplained in Csikszentmihalyi's work, may depend upon the higher degree of objective self-consciousness present in sociable than in unsociable microflow activities. Kinaesthetic flow may occur in the more alienated persons but because it is focused in body movement independent of others gives rise to a more positively expressed experience. Kinaestheticists call themselves happy, satisfied, free, and in control while socialites tend to describe their mood as sad, resentful, constrained, and not in control—comparisons certainly associated with subjective and objective self-consciousness respectively, irrespective of independent measures of alienation. A further finding supports these correlations, for kinaestheticists are more open and less stereotyped in problem-solving tasks than are the socialites.

We must remember that social microflow is especially represented in older members of the sample where the proportion of kinaesthetic activities is less. Sadly, therefore, it looks as if, with increasing age, people may become less alienated from others but, with increasing intellectual rigidity, more dependence on the company of others, and less delight in physical sensation, they become sadder rather than wiser and are understandably therefore more alienated from wider ranges of self-enjoyment.

Csikszentmihalyi completed his microflow study by asking 20 subjects to do without their autotelic activities (as reported by them) for a period of 48 hours. In general, this apparently mild self-deprivation had quite striking effects in which individuals variously described themselves as tenser, more irritable, listless, defensive, less decisive, machine-like, unfriendly, depressed, and lacking in vitality and concentration. Some subjects even thought they were going to have a 'nervous breakdown'. These effects, common also in numerous minor psychopathologies, suggest that moments of idling are not without restorative significance in daily life. The few subjects who enjoyed the experience (4 out of 20) seem to have been those for whom instrumental activities are especially important; prohibition of non-instrumental acts was thus for them a benefit rather than a deprivation.

The findings of these studies need replication and further development, yet there are certain lines of emphasis that are not only novel but of great importance for the understanding of conscious states such as alienation and enjoyment. First, the capacity and opportunity to idle at least for a while every day allows the psychological space within which the individual can release himself from the pressures of satisfying physiological needs or meeting social requirements. Idling allows the person to 'flow' in the same manner as an 'idling' motor-car engine simply purrs contentedly away. Idling or microflow seems to comprise mainly subjective self-consciousness and is associated with feelings of well-being and relaxation. Its after-effect may well be an increased confidence and ability to perform tasks with social 'relevance'. This effect seems to be reduced in the more sociable forms of idling and I presume that this is due to more frequent occasions of objective self-consciousness in social settings.

Participation in activities of deep play, whether these be in forms of sport or acutely involving work such as surgery or warfare, tends to become a way of life, not so much because of the extrinsic rewards which may be present (prestige to the rock-climber, fame and money to the surgeon, national acclaim to the soldier), but because of an intrinsic satisfaction in the activity itself. Deep play allows deep flow, but only when the levels of anxiety and boredom have been minimized by the balanced relating of challenge and competence. The challenge focuses the attention and the unity of awareness and action produces feelings of profound fulfilment that are almost addictive (as illustrated by the surgeon who after a few days of holiday abroad proffered his services to a local hospital). When these feelings are related to a rationale, a way of life with heart-felt meaning for the individual concerned has been achieved.

Clearly it is socially desirable to try to maximize the opportunities whereby individuals can create a meaningful life for themselves. Csikszentmihalyi concludes:

In this society [the USA], where the opportunity to satisfy pleasure and to obtain material comforts is unprecedented, the statistics on crime, mental disease, alcoholism, venereal disease, gambling, dissatisfaction without work, drug abuse and general discontent keep steadily worsening. The rates of these indices of alienation are increasing more sharply in the affluent suburbs. It is not the bottling up of instinctual needs that is responsible for this trend, nor the lack of external rewards. Its cause appears to be the dearth of experiences that prove that one is competent in a system that is geared for efficient transformation of physical energy. The lack of intrinsic rewards is like an undiscovered virus we carry in our bodies, it maims slowly but surely.

That was written in 1975, in 1978 to this list of decadence we can add baby-porn and the sexual exploitation of children in California (to the extent of an illicit importation of young village boys from Mexico), and

the affluent middle-class girl terrorist—the brilliantly heartless mur-
deress without pity or future of contemporary West Germany.

Biomodal consciousness and the brain

It is perhaps no accident but a consequence of focused attention that
the experiences of climbers in the flow of deep play so transcend their
normal consciousness that they quite commonly make statements more
typical of post-meditational states. All deep-flow experiences have the
sense of a unity of awareness and action as the pivot of fulfilment. The
total certainty of this self-experience, this non-duality, is like a mysticism shorn of sentimentality and metaphysical shrouding. Do we have
here in fact something like the bare bones of those experiences that in
complex elaboration by institutionalized settings are usually considered to be religious? Certainly the 'here-and-now' non-duality of
experience that is the effortless 'play' of the Zen practitioner appears
identical to the involvement in action that we have been discussing.
Once, in a conversation with a Zen Master in a Kyoto monastery, I
discussed the relation between Zen and therapy. 'Zen,' he said almost
sharply, 'is *total* therapy.' It may be that there is psychological substance to this claim. To find out we need to probe more deeply into the
nature of consciousness itself.

The division of consciousness into two aspects is in fact a very ancient
theme. Classical writers, the myths of primitive peoples, and modern
psychologists of varying persuasions have all attempted to dichotomize
mental experience—so much so indeed that one wonders whether a
tendency to dichotomize is not itself an inherent mental process.
Recently this dualism has become closely associated with the
neurophysiological study of the two hemispheres of the brain and has
thus been given an anchoring in functional biology; this may be of
profound significance to the understanding of human nature.

Among earlier psychologists, Pavlov emphasizes that the 'first signalling system' concerned with acquisition of information was distinct
from a second signalling system primarily concerned with logical operations. Freud, too, whose ideas are otherwise rarely in accord with
those of Pavlov, distinguished between a 'primary process thinking'
and a secondary process, again mainly associated with logical thought.
More recently Bruner has considered the 'elegant rationality of science'
to be distinct psychologically and possibly biologically from the
'metaphoric non-rationality of art'.

Arthur Deikman (1971), who had already made experimental investigations on the consciousness of meditating subjects (1963, 1966a, b),
has argued that a number of contrary aspects of consciousness could
be conveniently explained if human consciousness were actually

'bimodal', that is to say operated on the information presented to it in two functionally distinct modes. He drew upon studies of the effects of hallucinogens, meditation, psychotic mystical states, autogenic training, and biofeedback as well as certain researches in perception to argue that mind may operate in either an 'action mode' or a 'receptive mode'.

The action mode is a state organized to manipulate the environment. The striate muscle system and the sympathetic nervous system are the dominant physiological agencies. The EEG shows beta-waves and base-line muscle tension is increased. 'The . . . psychological manifestations . . . are focal attention, object based logic, heightened boundary perception and the dominance of formal characteristics over the sensory; shapes and meanings have a preference over colours and textures. The action mode is a state of striving, oriented towards achieving personal goals . . . obtaining social rewards . . . symbolic and sensual pleasures . . . avoidance of . . . pain.'

Clearly the action mode is designed for interaction with the physical and social environment in sequences that occur in time and can be predictive and experimental. By contrast, the receptive mode is devoted to the intake and processing of environmental information rather than with the instrumental or logical manipulation of it.

'The sensory perceptual system is the dominant agency rather than the muscle system and para-sympathetic functions tend to be most prominent. The EEG tends towards alpha waves and base-line muscle tension is decreased.'

This mode also features diffuse rather than focal attention, lessened perception of boundaries and a preoccupation with the sensory rather than the formal. It appears characteristic of infants and is gradually submerged in development by an overwhelming education in striving for achievements through performance in the active mode.

Diekman's insightful contrast relates directly to the properties now ascribed to the distinctive functioning of the two hemispheres. As far back as 1844 the British surgeon A. L. Wigan observed surprising autopsies of formerly sick but quite consciously rational patients in whom one hemisphere was totally destroyed. He concluded that since one hemisphere appeared to be as good as two, each cerebrum must be more or less equipotent and the normal mind therefore a dual entity. Others subsequently became fascinated with the properties of the left, so-called 'dominant', hemisphere, the seat of reason, logic, and speech. This led to a neglect of the right hemisphere, which was varyingly treated as a sort of shadow, a mere computer of relatively little interest. Debates over whether the mind was single or dual led to opposite interpretations, sometimes passionately held for extra-scientific reasons. (For example, see Zangwill's article of 1974 contrasting the views of McDougal (unitarian) and Sherrington (dualist) early in the century and Eccles (unitarian) and Sperry (dualist) more recently.) These debates are not yet entirely settled, although the functional contrasts of the hemispheres are now clearly established by the famous split-brain experiments of Sperry (see, e.g. Levy 1974).

In parallel with Diekman, but with full reference to hemisphere function, Bogen (1969) has argued that while the left hemisphere is characteristically the seat of the 'propositional' mind, the right is the home of 'appositional' thought. Table 11.2 lists the properties of propositional and appositional mental functions as located in the two hemispheres. It will be seen that they match precisely Diekman's active and receptive modes of consciousness.

TABLE 11.2
Propositional and appositional properties and functions of the two hemispheres of the human brain

Left hemisphere	Right hemisphere
Temporal organization and synthesis	Spatial organization and synthesis
Conceptual, logical, 'digital' analysis	Visual, auditory gestalt composition
Perception of detail, part rather than whole	Perception of whole rather than elements
	Image creation and management
Linguistic and descriptive information management	Sensory data collection
Verbal construction	Musical appreciation
Speech performance	Visual thought, fantasy, dream
Symbolic thought	Appositional, receptive, continuum of here and now
Propositional, action-oriented, planning, manipulative	Poetic, contemplative
Prosodic, deliberative	No phonological analyser
No gestalt synthesizer	

Based on Bogen 1969; Levy 1974; Zangwill 1974; Dimond 1972; Ornstein 1972, 1973.

The relation between the two hemispheres is complex and incompletely explored. The splitting of the corpus callosum connecting them, as in operations designed to improve conditions of severe epilepsy, produces a pair of co-consciousnesses with contrasting qualities that can be experimentally examined by presenting stimuli to one and not the other. This work shows that the information is processed in distinctive ways. Even so, information is often subtly and indirectly conveyed between the hemispheres.

When one 'split-brain' patient was shown a female face registered in the right hemisphere but had a male face provided for the left he reported, using language originating in the left hemisphere, that he saw a male; after a momentary pause he added that it was none the less a very effeminate one. Similarly, when a series of one or two alternatives are presented solely to the right hemisphere, the left, called upon to report, can only make a guess with a 50 per cent probability of getting it right. A wrong answer, 'overheard' by the right hemisphere, elicits signs of internal disagreement, bodily discomfort, and movement and the reply may be corrected later.

If such events can occur in totally split-brain patients, one must conclude that in normal persons some form of collaboration must exist between the two functionally distinct minds, perhaps through some superordinate agency of integration and control. Gazzaniga (1974) has, indeed, pointed out that a wide variety of cerebral processes are involved in cognitive behaviour, especially in language production, and that these are located at a number of distinct sites in both hemispheres. He argues that the function of cerebral dominance in the left hemisphere has less to do with language function in itself but very much to do with decision-processing, bringing order and integration to diverse cognitive processes and forwarding commands to final cognitive and motor paths: 'The term cerebral dominance would (then) refer to the central control system that institutes order in a chaotic cognitive space.'

Up to the age of 2 years the child's hemispheres seem to process information equally and to have equal linguistic ability. After that, however, it seems likely that anatomical differences, including different neural circuitry, combined with a concomitant onset of right-handedness, lead to a prime location of language in the left cerebral hemisphere. From this it may well follow that the integrative mechanisms become largely located there also. This idea is supported by the more appositional quality of the child's early thought with its poor appreciation of time and its Piagetian 'absolutism'.

The rediscovery of the 'other side of the brain' led to a great emphasis on appositional experiences, skills, and values (Ornstein 1972, 1973). Modern Western civilization clearly fails to educate children in skills and abilities making a full use of the right hemisphere; our main educational preoccupation is with the numerate and literate left. The new emphasis on an integrative 'centre' or function relating the activities of the hemispheres suggests that recent pleas for more exclusively appositional education may not be entirely appropriate (see

Blakemore 1977). In searching for an equipoise of mind, both hemi-spheres require development and it is in some as yet poorly understood balance of these mental aspects that greater understanding may arise.

Before leaving this topic we should examine the evolutionary ques-tion. Why two minds? What may be the survival value of a distinctively contrasting set of functions for the two lobes? We really have little to go on here. Levy suggests that as lateralization has not been recorded in the great apes or in very young children, it seems likely that the original mental condition consisted in a functional equality of the two hemi-spheres. Furthermore the distribution of lateralization varies within the human population. Right-dominant (left-handed) persons appear to have little lateralization, while less than two-thirds of left-dominant people have full lateralization. What then are the advantages?

It seems likely that lateralization increases cognitive efficiency by a division of labour and a localization of functions in discrete regions of the brain. The greater the functional symmetry of the brain, therefore, the greater a deficit in efficiency there would appear to be. It could be the case, however, that symmetry involves a bilateral development of propositional rather than appositional functioning, because of the cru-cial importance of language, and that a sacrifice of normal right hemi-sphere function is not critical. Alternatively, it could be the case that symmetry entails a bimodal distribution, some persons having mostly propositional minds (academic mathematicians, say) and others appositional ones (artists).

Some research indicates that sub-maximally lateralized brains tend to be more propositional than otherwise; in any case, cognitive abilities as measured in conventional tests are known to vary widely between people and populations. Levy in fact suggests that the more symmetri-cal brains tend to be propositional specialists while those with greater lateralization have wider general ability. It could be that a need for planning specialists in early human populations, designing a hunt for example, established a basis for a balanced polymorphism between propositional specialists and people with wider-ranging abilities with-out whom the excessively propositionally minded could hardly survive. These speculations are in accord with contemporary evolutionary theory; but such matters remain firmly in the realm of mystery.

Levels of mental operation

The research on consciousness discussed in this chapter emphasizes a bimodal functioning of awareness involving a wide range of functions which appears to be anchored in the differential lateralization of the brain. We may guess that the primary localization of language in the left hemisphere predisposes this region to become a centre for those propositional functions concerned with naming, the differentiation of objects, abstract analysis, and calculation. We have seen, however, that lateralization of function varies in a population of individuals, implying that mental structuralization is largely a consequence of experience. The matter clearly remains poorly understood and an attractive field for further investigation.

The relation between objective self-consciousness, subjective self-consciousness, states of flow or constriction, and the propositional and appositional functions of cerebral activity do, however, have a degree of consistency that allows the construction of a simple model (Fig. 11.2). The analytical functions of the propositional mind must be the seat of the distinction between self and others and hence of self as agent open to evaluative comparison. These discriminative and introspective aspects of self-consciousness create the objective state that is found to be involved in all aspects of the operation of self-esteem. Self-esteem has a strong affective component which is basically fearful of unfavourable judgement, usually self-inflicted. Continued low levels of fear about possible negative evaluations result in anxiety that may reach neurotic proportions. In any case, a self-evaluative condition tends to be depressing, forcing the subject inward, limiting his self-expression through doubt, and inhibiting his emotional release in self-disclosure with friends. The defence of one's self-conception is accompanied by a feeling of closed solidity rather than the open roominess of feeling that accompanies fearless self-disclosure and trust (Jourard 1971). One

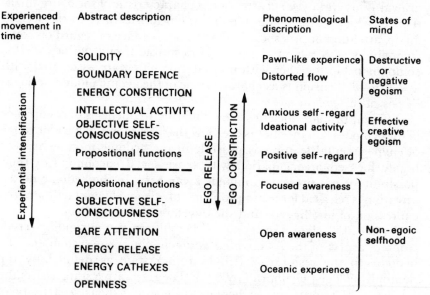

FIG. 11.2. A natural history of the basic conscious states.

feels like a pawn at the mercy of social pressures. Ego boundaries are tightly drawn and defended. Any movement in thought that involves objective self-consciousness tends towards contraction of ego boundaries, while activity that places attention in a task (subjective self-consciousness) releases experience from the constriction of ego boundaries. This release is attended by ease in self-expression and a freedom to be open to others. A total absorption in a task, a sport, or a physical activity leads to a loss of ego boundaries and an experience of unbounded flowing—sometimes called an 'oceanic' experience.

One way to achieve a degree of social equanimity between these polarities depends upon a capacity to risk trusting another with statements about one's feelings of pain or self-doubt. Self-disclosure in appropriate social circumstances leads to a release from ego constriction, energy flow, constructive self-expression, and new-found open confidence.

Michael Chance (1977b) has recently emphasized another bimodality of mental operation which can be distinguished from the propositional and appositional functions of the cerebral hemispheres. He argues that individual primates, human and otherwise, utilize their attention to the environment in two contrasting ways. In the first, attention is directed upon the social scene, and particularly to a centrally placed member of a group, usually a dominant animal, from which a distance is maintained in spite of its attractions. Interactions with this member may be carefully avoided or regulated by withdrawal. This *agonic mode* of attention is characteristic of social organizations in which status hierarchies are the prime feature. In the second mode, attention occurs socially in the maintenance of regard on some companion with whom closeness is desirable. Long periods of this companionship together with mutual interaction are associated with low arousal. Tension is as characteristic of the agonic mode as relaxation is of this *hedonic mode*.

Different primate societies show differing frequencies of occurrence of these modes. Chance holds the view that awareness of a wider range of environmental features is possible in the hedonic mode when the highly focused preoccupation with tense social encounters or their possibility is not present to impede awareness. In the hedonic mode, attention is released for use in problem-solving and hence facilitates the expression of intelligence and the development of intellect.

Chance also relates the agonic mode to the energy-expending (ergotrophic) aspect of the functioning autonomic nervous system and the hedonic to the restorative (trophotropic) state as defined by the neurophysiologist Geilhorn (1966–7). The restorative state assists the taking in of information, whereas the energy-expensive activity of agonism restricts it.

We have here again a possible link with the objective and subjective states of personal self-consciousness. The former anxious state of self-evaluation clearly connects with the agonic mode of attention. All studies are beginning to make clear the need for a better understanding of the relationship between patterns of social interaction (hierarchy, approach avoidance, distaste–empathy, trust–distrust, defence–disclosure) and related states of consciousness mediated by the autonomic and central nervous systems.

One possible way of relating them is shown in Table 11.3, where the outcomes of the four possible associations between the two cerebral modalities of consciousness and the two autonomic conditions of attention are shown. If the behavioural states could be induced by bringing

TABLE 11.3

Central and autonomic modalities in the control of mental attitude and resulting behaviour

Cerebral modalities of cognitive analysis	Autonomic component of mental attitude controlling attention	
	AGONIC	HEDONIC
PROPOSITIONAL	Social conflict	Companionship
	Disputation	Joy in exchanging information
	Objective self-consciousness	Subjective self-consciousness in constructive conversation
	Defence-aggression	
	Distrust	Collaborative problem-solving
		Conviviality
		Trust and disclosure
APPOSITIONAL	Withdrawal	Social awareness
	Arrogance	Mindfulness
	Closure	Zen contemplation
	Negative egoism	Apperception
	Defensive stasis	Self-expression
		Dance-like interaction
		Rituals of ecstasy and involvement with others and the world

about the appropriate underlying state of consciousness by an inner action it would be possible to gain control of social interactions through the use of that old attribute the 'will'. Changes in the conscious attitude affect behaviour, which inevitably then affects the course of a social interaction and the societal context that envelopes it. If we could gain control of the willed processes (including meditation and attitude change), the possibility of changing society from within rather than purely by external social engineering would become a real one. Indeed, it is this basic idea that underlies the Maharishi Mahesh's hopes for an enlightened world. On a wider front it is the prime focus of religious training in both Christianity and Buddhism.

Most of us oscillate between the poles of defensive social avoidance and confident self-expression. The way in which we perform is dependent upon the introjected 'games' we attempt to play and the relation between them and the social stage upon which we set them up. Equanimity can perhaps be found through discovering the way in which our states of closure or openness relate to the meanings we attribute to our acts and adjusting these in ways that balance propositional and appositional functioning to maintain an appropriate level of confidence.

With this thought we find ourselves in an area about which contemporary psychology has little more to say: strangely enough, however, it is an area that has been well worked over before in Asian cultures of distant epochs. The models of mind created by them have an almost uncanny resemblance to the ideas treated in this chapter but include a richness of detail and practical application unknown in the contemporary West. To these models and their origins we must therefore turn.

Summary

(1) The development of the brain seems to have been associated especially with the perception of objects at a distance to allow prediction based on stimulation from them. Primitive conscious states are probably dominated by the input from the senses and an animal's awareness is probably largely a representation of the world in which it lives and moves. This awareness is the result of a filtering of sensory stimulation by neural processes and has been evolved as appropriate to a species niche and way of life.

(2) In humans, active involvement in a task when the awareness is dominated by the job in hand represents the state of mind plausibly closest to primitive consciousness. In such a state of consciousness the subject is not aware of him or herself. The awareness is 'outward' based in sensory experience.

(3) Human beings have the capacity to turn their regard 'inward' and to become aware of themselves as an object for others and hence also as

an object to themselves. The state of consciousness when this activity is predominant is termed objective self-consciousness for the self is then the object of experience. The condition of outward regard has been termed subjective self-consciousness for then the subject is the source of the activity not its object (subjective self-consciousness).

(4) Experiments have shown that persons can be placed in either objective or subjective self-consciousness by providing situations in which the mental regard is focused either on self as object or outwardly in task performance. Long or intense periods of objective self-consciousness can result in despondency owing to an awareness of discrepancy between actual and ideal self-concepts acquired through social comparison and the need for self-esteem. There is a feeling of external control, of being manipulable, of a loss of self-confidence. By contrast, subjective self-consciousness results in a centering within a sense of self-worth without a focus on social comparisons and esteem.

(5) Human individuals have the capacity for a bimodal focus of attention, either in objective or subjective self-consciousness. This capacity develops with the child's sense of self as an object; personal stances in life determine the balance between the two modes. Different cultures or institutions also encourage a preponderance of one state or the other.

(6) Enjoyment in sport, games, and work is related to the occurrence of long periods of subjective self-consciousness which may be intellectual (chess) or physically based (dance, rock climbing) or both (surgery, martial arts). Subjective self-consciousness is a concommitant of play and is especially pronounced in 'deep play' when risk and competence are balanced at an appropriate level of personal challenge. Mountain climbing or hang gliding are cases where the experience of 'flow' in subjective self-consciousness may be especially enhanced. These are so-called autotelic or self-fulfilling activities. There are some close parallels with play in animals.

(7) Objective self-consciousness is related to planning and judgement. It is particularly important in assessment prior to decision-making. While uncomfortable and accompanied by anxiety which can become depressing, it is an essential activity in the designing of a meaningful and active life with relationships with others. Excessive preoccupation in objective self-consciousness can however become damaging and lead to neurosis. Contemporary Western culture is seen to be excessively located in enhanced objective self-consciousness allowing little chance for the deep relaxation that comes from 'flow' in autotelic activity.

(8) The distinction between objective and subjective self-consciousness can be related to other theories suggesting that the mind may function in two contrasting modes. In particular an analytical, rational, proposition-creating function has been contrasted with a non-analytical, apperceptive mode; they are associated with the func-

tions of the left and right hemispheres respectively. The importance of integrating these two modes of mental activity is emphasized.

(9) Conscious states show considerable variation depending on the degree of ego involvement which tends to constrict awareness through defence. High levels of attention without ego concern lead to experiences of openness, freedom, and unbounded energy and alertness. These distinctions parallel those within Eastern psychologies of mind.

12 Meditation

Meditation is not an escape from the world, but a means of looking deeper into it, unhampered by prejudices or by the familiarity of habit which blinds us to the wonders and the profound mysteries that surround us.

Lama Anagarika Govinda 1977

Types of meditation

If the attraction of deep play lies in the production of subjective self-conscious and a release from the concerns of habitual social life, may there not be a similar explanation for other ego-transcending activities, many of which amount to spiritual disciplines that are deeply embedded in some religious traditions? Many of these disciplines entail the focusing of awareness upon a single object, concept, or experience for long periods of time with the intention of reducing the flow of habitual thought and opening oneself to an alternative experience. In some traditions this experience is identified with the ultimate reality or the divine dimensions of the universe itself. In endeavouring to understand these disciplines it is important to separate a consideration of the psychological effects of such exercises (discussed in this chapter) from their role in relation to belief systems (Chapter 13).

The contemporary concern with meditation in the West is predominantly utilitarian and focuses on the medical benefits that deep relaxation may bring. Investigations of other personally and socially valuable benefits are also pursued, often with rather little experimental sophistication, by advocates of transcendental meditation, a commercially taught system derived from a basic Indian technique. So ancient a mind-changing technique as meditation must make use of some fundamental properties of the human psyche. What these may be is the subject of this chapter.

There is an enormous diversity of mental techniques to which the title meditation may be given. Their importance throughout history is manifest in the fact that they commonly form the kernel of the most significant religious practices of a particular culture. In such contexts meditation is concerned with bringing about a fundamental shift in the modality of an individual's being to establish the presence of a heightened capacity for equanimity and insights into life, death, self, and others. The achievement of this presence can transform individual lives, but it is generally recognized that the praxis needs persistence under guided instruction. While most learning involves the acquisition of habits or new conditioning, meditation is the very opposite, being a persistent effort to detect and release oneself from all compulsive habits and emotions. The unconditioned state is both the goal of the praxis and the praxis itself, for, with an increasing deconditioning of mental functioning, the consequences of inner freedom make their appearance quite naturally.

Naranjo (Naranjo and Ornstein 1971) presents a useful categorization of types of meditation under three headings. In the first approach, concentrative meditation upon a form or image, the individual attempts to enter into the power of the object functioning as a projection of his own experiences. The symbol represents that aspect of himself with which he seeks to identify. The second approach is expressive, permissive, orgiastic even, in which the hidden nature of oneself is allowed to emerge spontaneously. The third approach is a self-emptying through a relaxation into inner stillness and the cultivation of witnessing rather than action. All three approaches tend to overlap, and some complex systems, such as those of the Tibetan Lamas, make use of all of them.

Another way of distinguishing types is to contrast the concentrative inward focus upon a form or sound, as in Indian meditation, with the silently sitting moment-to-moment awareness of Zen. In the former an inward trance develops while in the latter the mind is allowed to open as a clear reflecting mirror.

It is important not to suppose that all meditations make use of the same mental mechanisms. While some factors are probably common, the different methods also emphasize mechanisms wcth subtly contrasting effects. It will be wise therefore to study contrasting methods individually and without too hasty generalization to 'meditation' as a whole (see further Goleman 1977).

Transcendental meditation and research on its effects

In recent years the most familiar system of meditation in the West has been the transcendental meditation (TM) of Maharishi Mahesh Yogi, who was himself trained by a traditional guru in an Indian concentrative meditation based upon Sankaracharya's eighth-century philosophy, itself much influenced by Buddhism. On his teacher's death the Maharishi obeyed his instruction to spread the knowledge of the technique throughout the world. The Maharishi, clearly an entrepreneurial genius as well as teacher, has established a commercially successful chain of international centres for instruction in TM, some of which, dignified by the name of University, have elaborate training programmes, propaganda campaigns, and research programmes. One suspects that research and transcendental evangelism easily became confused and that the former is often open to premature exploitation by the latter. Evaluation of this research reveals design errors among which, failures to take into account the 'demand' characteristics of the experiment are paramount. Meditators who have paid to learn a highly advertised technique are likely to respond positively to the experiments of researchers who, like themselves, are believers. Only recently has more sophisticated work begun which replicates and sometimes confirms the earlier rush of over-enthusiastic reports (West 1977).

The TM technique is imparted by accredited teachers and not by written description. This is done so as to keep the tradition pure, but it also adds a certain mystery to the proceedings which may attract new adherents. Initiations are the main source of finance. As West remarks, 'The whole process of learning TM subjects the individual to a variety of pressures. Expectation of benefit is fuelled and fanned throughout the stages of learning and complex double-bind explanations of differing effects deter the initiate from believing that TM practice could be harmful.' For example, good effects are attributed to TM, while possible bad ones are rationalized, for example, as being due to release of stress during so-called 'normalization' of the nervous system.

Basically the method comprises 20 minutes of relaxed sitting without breathing control, but with the mind lightly focused on a word or 'mantra' that is repeated mentally. The emphasis is on relaxation, an absence of forcing, lightness of touch, and enjoyment. It differs from some other systems in that powerful psychophysiological training in breath control is not employed and the duration of a session is, by meditational standards, short.

While the commercialism of the TM machine necessarily raises doubts about so skilfully packaged a product, it remains true that this is a technique of ancient respectability and that the Maharishi is a remarkable man. After his Guru's death, the Maharishi withdrew for three years for meditation in a Himalayan cave before launching himself into a lifetime of educational effort. His system is in fact quite straightforward, the only mystique being that surrounding the mantra, which is sometimes considered to be a 'power word' with quasi-magical properties. A simpler view would be that a repeated mantra provides a monotonous stimulation to the brain that tends to preclude thinking (i.e. objective self-consciousness) and allows relaxation (i.e. subjective self-consciousness) to follow. Naturally, a belief in special properties might increase the effectiveness of the mantra in some people. The mantra is kept secret in TM but a recent court case revealed that mantras are given according to age and that they usually consist of names of God or Sanskrit syllables of attractive sound. In other systems mantras are not secret, as in the Tibetan 'Om Mani Padme Hum'.

The basic effect of TM is deep relaxation. This alone has numerous effects in the relief of stress. The Maharishi claims however that a greater clarity of mind is achieved in that, with a reduction of noise and tension, the nature of thoughts and their meanings is more clearly understood (Russell 1976). In particular, a quiet mind observes the arising of thoughts, thereby allowing not only an appreciation of their subtle relationships but also of their dependence upon a ground state which is not itself thought. This ground state is perceived as a point of zero mental activity—a 'non-vibrating consciousness'. Claims that TM affects perception, creativity, and intelligence as a consequence of increased clarity have been made, but little research of a fully convincing nature has yet been carried beyond the assertions of an optimistic enthusiasm.

The ground of consciousness, the transcendental, is considered to be a fourth state of consciousness that is additional to waking, dreaming, and deep sleep. In this condition, *samadhi*, the duality of observer and observed is transcended and there is perfect stillness without boundaries and no self-awareness as an object: simply light, bliss, pure being (*sat-chit-ananda*). In this model of mind the state of *samadhi* is the 'true self' from which the duality of experience springs.

According to the Maharishi there is also a fifth stage of consciousness—cosmic consciousness—the knowgedge of which constitutes enlightenment. In TM the growth of this realization is said to be gradual. Repeated immersion in TM followed by normal activity constitutes a leavening path along which the later realizations come of themselves. Cosmic consciousness is an awareness of a continuity between one's ego-transcending self and the world as experienced 'out there'. It comes about through practice and insight into the meaning of the egoless state of mind. Maharishi himself talks of yet further stages, but we will not pursue him further here. Some account of them is provided on p. 369.

In an important doctoral thesis Michael West (1977, 1979) has paid particular attention to the research methodology employed in experiments on meditators. His findings, while dampening to the ardour of the more enthusiastic advocates, indicate the promise of meditation research. In a review of research he found many previous findings to be inadequately demonstrated. A list of claims and their relative credibility in terms of effective evidence is shown in Table 12.1.

In general, there is substantial evidence that physiological relaxation or 'de-arousal' occurs during meditation as measured by a number of important parameters. Evidence that repeated practice induces long-term changes is less secure. The role of de-arousal as an aid to psychotherapy is plausible in the treatment of some conditions but little adequate evaluation has been attempted. Surprisingly, in spite of much publicity, the actual evidence for meditation being important in the

TABLE 12.1
Effects claimed for the practice of transcendental meditation

Effect		Status
(i)	Increase in amplitude of alpha waves in EEG with decrease in frequency	A
(ii)	Presence of theta trains in meditation	A
(iii)	Decreased heart-rate	A
(iv)	Decrease in respiration rate	A
(v)	Increase in skin resistance	A
(vi)	Decrease in muscle tension	A
(vii)	Improved performance in tasks after meditation	C
(viii)	Improved learning ability	C
(ix)	Increased field independence in perception	B
(x)	Reduced anxiety	A
(xi)	Increased self-control	B
(xii)	Decreased neuroticism	B
(xiii)	Decreased drug abuse	C
(xiv)	Utility in psychotherapy	C

Status A, well established; B, moderately good evidence; C, uncertain. (Author's ratings after West 1977)

cure of drug abuse remains poor, largely because the reported improvements may be due to the adoption of new social roles by beginner meditators who were formerly abusers.

West undertook experiments to demonstrate changes in brain-wave activity and reactivity in meditators outside the action of meditation. He also attempted to compare relaxation during tasks performed after meditation and the same tasks performed after other types of relaxation. In general he was successful in both endeavours. Although listening quietly to music has some effects that are close to those of 20 minutes' TM, West concludes that 'stable differences between Meditators and non-Meditators have been shown'. He recognizes that the differences could still be due to chance contrasts between the experimental and control populations. Longitudinal studies should resolve these problems.

West also conducted a valuable questionnaire survey of a population of transcendental meditators in the Cardiff area. Eighty-three out of 315 contacts returned completed questionnaires on the regularity of practice, subjective experience in TM, and the effects of TM. West had the material analysed for relevant factors by a committee of psychologists. The clearest outcome was the reported increase in calm and relaxation. Subjective experiences suggested that the monotonous repetition of the mantra reduces arousal and slows thought and that in some cases relaxation persists in other activities so as to affect the life-style of persistent meditators. An Eysenck personality inventory was also completed by respondents to reveal that their neuroticism score was higher than the mean for the normal population and the extroversion score significantly less. There were no sex differences in these returns. A comparison between those still meditating with those who had given it up showed the former to have significantly lower scores for neuroticism and slightly but not significantly higher extroversion scores.

The analysis of responses shows a wide range of effects attributed to TM by meditators. These include reduction in blood-pressure, less migraine, more energy, better sleep, and improved depression. Greater confidence and appreciation of world and life concerns and less stress, together with improved capacity for empathy with others were also important. On the spiritual side, inner peace and awareness were often mentioned. The deep peace of *samadhi* seems to have been only infrequently experienced by these relatively casual meditators but when it occurred it was recognized as a goal 'achieved'.

Explanations of TM and other forms of deep relaxation

The major effects of TM on the average meditator are thus primarily effects of decreases in physiological arousal and arousability accompanied by decreases in subjective anxiety. It is by no means clear that TM actually offers more than other traditions of deep relaxation with a less exalted ancestry (see, for example, Smith 1976). In particular Autogenic Training appears to offer a very similar regimen without the mystification; it is quite commonly taught by doctors concerned with stress problems and psychosomatic conditions. Little research has, however, been carried out on Autogenic Training and its professional associations lack the attraction inherent in the mysteries of the East. In Autogenic Training practitioners are invited to sit in a prescribed relaxation posture and to repeat to themselves 'I am at peace'. After several sessions a further period of sitting while focusing the mind on 'Left arm heavy' is added in which the weight of the arm is experienced. Further periods with focused awareness on body processes occur in a developed training sequence: 'It breathes me'—a passive watching of the breath; 'Solar plexus warm'—a focused experience of warmth in the abdomen; and 'Forehead cool'. The sequence thus comprises focused attention over a period of 15–30 minutes on the experiencing of the body. The result is a profound relaxation with many attributed benefits closely parallel to those of TM. Further exercises involve focusing on mental colour and inner silence. Invented by a hospital doctor, J. H. Schultz, in the early years of the century, the system is perhaps most widely known in Germany (Rosa 1976).

Deep relaxation, whether in TM or in Autogenic Training, seems to be of especial utility to individuals rather high on scales for neuroticism. This apparent relation between a liking for de-arousal in meditation and certain personality features may be explained by reference to Claridge's theory of personality and arousal (Claridge 1967; see West 1977). Those attracted to meditation would be expected to have both higher arousal levels and stronger fluctuations in these levels than the normal population. Such individuals may well be subject to stress under arousal and seek to reduce the symptoms. In all probability the decreases in TM are primarily due to a partial sensory deprivation imposed by concentrated focus on a mantra coupled with the high level of attention inducing a light self-hypnosis. The resulting de-arousal compensates for high tonic arousal levels and the effect appears to generalize through learning to other life situations. This hypothesis is open to test in appropriately equipped medical laboratories.

Zen and enlightenment

The reduction of a meditative system to a relaxation technique explained by a medical model fails to account for all the claims that are made for the practice of meditation. Relaxation alone does not seem to provide a reason for the life-changing insights and profound philosophical ease expressed by the great mystics and their followers. Great contemporary teachers such as Krishnamurti or Bhagwan Shree Rajneesh are putting forward far more than a recommendation to relax. Meditation as practised by most modern Westerners (Table 12.2) probably amounts to little more than a relaxation of the stressed in a stressful society. Indeed, adepts in meditation do far more than sit for 20 minutes with their minds on a word. We must therefore ask what results from the practice of meditation in other ways. Few Westerners have attempted the three years' retreat from which the Maharishi started, and those who have gone deeply into Indian religions have

TABLE 12.2

Frequency of meditation reported by TM respondents in the Cardiff area (expressed as a percentage)

Two 20–min periods per day	13.4
One 20–min period per day	9.5
4–7 20–min periods per week	14.6
1–3 20–min periods per week	9.8
Less than once a week	9.8
Meditation currently abandoned	43

$n = 83$; after West (1977)
The maximum weekly duration of TM was thus 4 h 20 min and the minimum about 20 min.

profoundly interesting and far-reaching stories to tell (e.g. Ram Dass 1973, Sankarakshita 1978). What then might it mean to develop the 'cosmic consciousness' of which the Maharishi speaks? A more explicit understanding of this process may come from a consideration of recent research on Zen.

We have already noted that in Zen training there is an emphasis on an opening awareness to the world as it is in the here and now rather than a focus on the induction of trance in *samadhi*. Undoubtedly this emphasis stems from Taoism rather than Indian Buddhism and entered the teaching within China (see also p. 370). Taoism emphasizes the treading of a way in the present rather than working for a goal in the distant future.

In fact two rather contrasting aims are apparent in Zen training. Sekida (1975) makes a distinction between 'absolute *samadhi*', the trance achieved in deep meditation and 'positive *samadhi*' in which a quiet mind free of anxiety observes the world and its own presence in it without a withdrawal into trance. The world and bodily action are mirrored in awareness as in a still lake, but normal action in the world is not impeded.

In his examination of Zen psychology, Akishige (1977), head of the Zen Institute of Komazawa University in Tokyo, argues that Zen masters pay relatively little attention to the advanced trance states of consciousness that appear in Indian accounts of the mind. Rather the aim is to experience the stage of meditation in which an alert insightful attention is maintained. The various stages of concentrative meditation comprise successive abandonments of attachment; first to worldly thoughts and desires, secondly to more refined desire, thirdly to spiritual joy, and fourthly to bodily ease. In the fourth state, a freedom from self-concern and emotions comes into being. Insight into phenomena and the nature of the mind are then at their clearest and are undistorted by trance. Akishige regards the further stages (5–9) in the Indian lists as the induction of a 'non-structured, stupefied and homogenous ego . . . which lacks its own nature and quality.' In the fourth stage, by contrast, the structure of the ego remains active although transcended (p. 369).

To reach this fourth stage of meditation it is 'necessary to separate from and abandon all external and internal reference systems which centre on the possessive mind. Yet this abandonment does not bring about the destruction of consciousness through . . . sensual exclusion'. Such a destruction is highly detested in Zen Buddhism and is always rejected. The concept of separating from the reference systems that define identity while yet retaining an alert and active presence in the world is clearly shown in the numerous teaching stories of the great Zen masters and samurai. 'The ego is like a dragon which receiving water rises to heaven or the fierce but imperturbed tiger against the background of mountains, full of the power of life. Moreover, as expressed in the Zen phrase "to be a master of all places" the ego is free and unrestricted' (Akishige 1977).

In the Zen of the Soto school the training is primarily in silent sitting, eyes open facing a white wall. The mind is kept alert, fully aware, no mantra is used but there is sometimes a detailed concentration on a breathing praxis. Sekida describes this breath regulation as a means of maintaining a highly focused attention without interference from thoughts.

Attention or wakeful alertness is maintained neurophysiologically, Sekida states, by two oscillating cycles. In the first, signals pass from the wakefulness centre in the posterior hypothalamus into the anterior thalamus and thence through the cerebral cortex. The cortex in turn transmits impulses to the wakefulness centre, re-exciting it and initiating more stimulating impulses. This is largely a process involved in thinking and other cortical activities. The other cycle involves impulses from the wakefulness centre passing to the bulboreticular formation of the brain-stem to increase muscular tone throughout the body. Muscle tension in turn stimulates proprioceptors and other sensory systems resulting in feedback impulses that again stimulate the wakefulness centre. Sekida implies that control of the wakefulness centre by muscle tension alone and without the intervention of thought can be brought about by making a muscular alerting response, as if to danger. The whole body-mind is then vividly attentive, waiting in apperception, and thought is excluded. Voluntary control of thought-production thus becomes possible through producing muscle tension that gains command of the wakefulness centre.

Important groups of muscles in this praxis are those of the abdomen, which are vital to all powerful body movement, and those of the diaphragm, which control breathing. In deep belly breathing the diaphragm and the abdominal muscles act to a degree in opposition. In an alerting response, attention to a sudden sound for example, the breath is bated, held in suspension with the abdominal–diaphragm muscles in opposition. The tension creates a bodily preparedness for reflexive action in which analytical thought plays no role.

In *zazen* meditation this alertness is sought through a special breathing technique in which deep bated expiration is practised, thereby excluding thought and focusing attention on the abdomen, especially on the area called the *tanden* in Japanese, an inch or so below the navel. The method, which requires both attention to detail and the development of a personal style, leads to a progressive shutting down of disturbing emotional feelings as well as thought (see Sekida and several articles in Akishige 1977). With sustained practice the body image itself fades and an alert, bodily unbounded, thoughtless awareness arises.†

In Zen of the Rinzai school additional training is given. The meditator is asked to hold a paradoxical Zen question or *koan* in mind and to bring answers to it in confrontations with the master. Examples of such questions are 'What is the sound of one hand clapping?' or 'Who am I?' The meditation method and the breathing may be the same as in Soto Zen, the *koan* being, as it were, placed in the belly along with the breath. The mind, empty of analytical thought, comes to a realization of pure 'mirror-like consciousness' in which the world is reflected. Within this unstructured but alert consciousness the insights that resolve the paradox of the *koan* arise. As the saying goes: body and mind alike are dropped and the meaning of the *koan* becomes plain.

The Zen trainee is called upon to convert these wordless insights into demonstrations or statements that indicate his realization to the master. These actions are the means of communication between Zen adepts.

An instructive account of an encounter between an intellectual patron of painting and an enlightened Zen artist is given by Trevor Leggett (1978) in his book on the expression of Zen in the ways of being, martial arts, painting, the tea ceremony, etc. The artist, the seventh master of Jufukuji temple, was asked to portray the fragrance described in the line of poetry 'After walking through flowers, the horse's hoof is fragrant'. The artist drew a hoof with a butterfly fluttering round it. Then the line 'Spring breeze over the river bank' was set as a subject and the master presented a willow branch waving. The patron next asked the master to portray the heart in 'A finger direct to the human heart, see the nature to be Buddha'. The master picked up the brush and flicked a spot of ink onto the patron's face. The warrior was surprised and annoyed; so the master drew an angry face. Then the warrior asked him to paint the nature in the phrase, 'See the nature'. The artist broke the brush, saying, 'That's the nature.' But the patron failed to understand and the painter said, 'If you haven't got the seeing eye you cannot see it.' Puzzled, the patron said, 'Please take another brush and paint the picture of the nature.' To which the artist merely said, 'Show me your nature and I will paint it.' The patron had no more words.

These seeings into nature, demonstrations of *koan* solutions perceived in meditative insight, are so profoundly paradoxical because they are translations of 'no-mind' (mind unconstricted by thoughts but full of awareness) into the medium of communication by symbol. The message conveyed is always the same although presented in a myriad of

† Although awareness of breath is important in all Zen training systems not all use exercises in breath control as such. Like mantra repetition they are best thought of as thought-reducing practices at the start of a session.

ways. It is to the effect that the trainee has recognized that in essence he exists as a consciousness without thought, that intellectual constructs are mental fabrications, and that the basis of being is not limited by them.

Interpreting these experiences, we may argue that the cognitive insight consists in a sudden change in the balance of the propositional and appositional modalities of mind; the tyranny of the former is 'illusory', for propositional activity is relative to a social world rather than being real in itself. In going beyond this relativity the cage of the constructed self is opened often with an extraordinary release of bodily and mental energy with powerful psychosomatic effects. Both Sekida and Akishige have likened the experience to the realization that occurs when a paradoxical figure is suddenly seen in its alternative form.

Sadly, the inner freedom found in such events fades with the reimposition of habitual responding. The continuation of training is important and a deepening of the original insight occurs. The concern of the Zen master is to be in conformity with the *ri* or 'inner lines of the universal flow' (Leggett 1978) in every event and action; much as a great warrior overcomes an opponent by an intuitive insight into the balancing of his strength and skill in relation to the ongoing expression of those of his enemy. Living by Zen is to live extremely well, flowing in accordance with the multiple aspects of the ongoing moment.

And at this point we recall the flow of deep play experienced by the mountain-climber or surgeon (Chapter 11). Zen is a form of training in deep play of which life and death themselves are the essence. Through practice and insight the adept perceives the working of his own self-process and his attachment to the reference systems that define him. He is not a thing, a static identity, but a continuing awareness of a process of relating an inner and an outer world. Analytically conceived in the propositional mode this activity is dual. Appositionally perceived there is only one experiential continuum in space and time.

Zen training is arduous with an emphasis on intensive retreats (*sesshin*) in which practitioners may meditate in repeated sessions for up to 10 hours a day. Socially, the discipline and the silence emphasize conformity to a pattern in which the ego-exciting traits of individuality are de-emphasized and the continuum of selfhood increasingly experienced in a communal setting (Nakamura 1977).

The 'enlightenment' experience is not, however, restricted to those with experience of *zazen*. For many it has been a spontaneous and natural occurrence stumbled upon as if by accident. Even in training this is usual, for 'enlightenment' tends to appear under conditions of minimal intention and maximum attention which may arise at any time (p. 372).

When it happened to Douglas Harding (1965) it seemed to him that he no longer had a head. Instead, at the top of a headless trunk there was simply an experiencing space in an indivisible continuity with the world-space around him. He has spent much time devising perceptual means for evoking this experience for others. The provision of such 'mini-satoris' jerks the mind into a different perception that can lead to important changes in life. Harding's Zen philosophy (1974) has much in common with that of the ancient Chinese master Hui-Neng or Krishnamurti, both of whom advocate 'direct seeing' without an emphasis on long-term meditation and the pursuit of trance.

The relative importance of these forms of transpersonal experience need hardly be debated. There can, however, be no doubt that long-term training deepens an individual's understanding of experience, whether the focus be on deep trance or upon open awareness. Superficiality can occur in either, as when long periods in trance replace a more appropriate occupation in the world or gimmicky perceptual tricks lead someone to think he is 'enlightened'.

Other effects of meditation

One of the reasons why TM training is limited to 20 minutes a session is that longer periods of meditation without the control of attention induced by breathing exercises may allow repressed material normally held in the unconscious to appear in the conscious mind. In its less bounded, relaxed condition this experience can be frightening, for there seems to be some danger of the mind becoming flooded with unconscious imagery with which TM instructors are rarely competent to deal. Given guidance, however, such a dramatic 'recovery of the repressed' can be of great therapeutic value. Indeed, comparable processes form the root of R. D. Laing's (1960) attitude to the therapy of certain types of mental patient.

It is of interest that in the immensely rich repertoire of meditations practised over very long sessions by Tibetan Lamas the deliberate evocation of visually projected monstrous forms is a common feature for experienced monks working under the guidance of their teachers. These often horrifying projections, which may emerge as actual dancing figures before the eyes of the adept, seem in all probability to pick up unconscious forces and externalize them with great therapeutic effect. Little scientific work has yet been done with visualizations of this form but preliminary work by those interested in Assagioli's (1965) 'psychosynthesis' suggests their validity for the Western mind.

Another effect of prolonged meditation practice concerns psychosomatic phenomena of an exceedingly powerful kind which are not yet understood scientifically at all. Feelings of profound bliss arising as bodily sensations from the belly area between the navel and the sexual organs and travelling as energy flows through the body are experienced by many practised meditators. Such feeling states are often followed by experiences as if one were radiating energy outwards from the body or of a profound love for all beings and the universe itself. Again the mind can become totally silent as if in a void while the tumult of the world goes on around it.

The old Hindu tradition of raising the energy of *Kundalini*, symbolized as a snake coiled at the base of the spine, refers to even more powerful psychosomatic events that seem to arise when the structured control with which the thinking mind limits experience is relaxed. These events, experienced literally as 'mind-blowing' energy flows within the body, can however be destructive and produce debilitating sickness. Both Krishnamurti (see Lutyens 1975) and Pandit Gopi Krishna (1976) went through periods of intense physical agony as the *Kundalini* process began operating involuntarily within them. For others this physical concomitant of enlightenment proceeds with less danger to health, but for all aspirants a dabbling in the practices that evoke such experiences should never be attempted: an experienced teacher is required. And good teachers of tantra are rare indeed.

The relationship between identity, the enlightenment experience of identity release, and these powerful psychosomatic effects is not understood; except of course experientially by those few teachers who have taken this path to near its conclusion. Science has almost nothing to say here and the theoretical comprehension of these processes still lies in the future.

Conclusion

Meditational practices can provoke a number of psychological changes in individual lives. First, the powerful effects of deep relaxation and the discovery of a state transcending or different from normal consciousness begins a process which inevitably affects a person's attitude to himself and others. Secondly, meditation increases the possibility of sudden insights in which, while the world remains the same, the habitual functioning of the mind is suspended in a profound 'silence' and the cage of identity broken. These cognitive events result in a changed perception of a person's self-process and tend towards a new balancing of the propositional and appositional modes of being. Such balancing, as in a Zen master, means a fulfilled and flowing way of life in appropriate relation to circumstance. A final and little-explored benefit of meditation is that it may offer means to manipulate the unconscious mind in the direction of recovering and understanding repressed mental constructs. Meditation in the hands of a great teacher could, as I was told in Japan, indeed comprise a 'total therapy'.

Summary

(1) If the attraction of deep play lies in the production of subjective self-consciousness and a release from the anxieties of social life, something of the same effect may be operating in the practice of spiritual disciplines which are likewise based in activities often tending to diminish self-concern.

(2) There are numerous forms of meditation; the prime types being the concentrative, the abreactive, and a self-emptying attentiveness. Some systems make use of all of them. Probably different mechanisms are in play in the practice of contrasting techniques.

(3) The transcendental meditation system of Maharishi Mahesh Yogi is evaluated. Early research tainted by over-enthusiasm is giving way to more careful study. The 20-minute sessions of TM have their prime effect in relaxation allowing recovery from the stress of modern life. Anxiety is reduced. Other claims remain to be adequately substantiated.

(4) Other relaxation systems such as Autogenic Training appear to parallel TM in their effects. Dysthymic neurotics seem especially attracted to TM and to benefit from it through a relaxation compensating for high tonic arousal levels and which appears to generalize through learning to other life situations.

(5) Prolonged practice of meditation has effects that include the induction of states of consciousness that reduce anxious thinking and hence give release from self-monitoring through commentary. This freedom amounts to a cracking of the constricting hold that identity constructs maintain upon a person's experience of himself.

(6) Meditation can lead to trance states of profound relaxation called *Samadhi* which, in that they transcend thought, allow insight into the non-conceptualizing aspects of the self. Insight is further fostered in Zen by direct confrontation with a paradoxical question concerning a person's 'true nature' in the world. High awareness levels are maintained by certain breathing exercises so that attention remains focused on the question (*koan*) and trance does not develop. Insight then occurs with the ego and all other aspects of mind fully functional.

(7) These insights or 'enlightenment experiences' are realizations concerning a person's conceptual and emotional life. They arise through changes in conscious states that allow disidentification and hence a sense of release and consequent 'flow'. Fears of impermanence and of death are overcome as the relativity of identity within the wider experience of mind is apperceived.

(8) The occurrence of such an insight has been compared to the perceptual shift that occurs when an illusory figure flips from one appearance to another. The objective features of the mind-world relation remain unchanged but they are seen differently and with a fresh set of values.

(9) Interpretatively these experiences consist in a sudden change in the balance of values set upon the propositional and appositional aspects of mind. The tyranny of the proposition is broken by a comprehension of its relativity. The cage of the constricted self is thus opened often with an extraordinary release of bodily and mental energy.

(10) Very prolonged meditation practice has unusual effects on the psychosomatic balance of the nervous system. These effects remain almost unknown in biological psychology and are not understood.

(11) Meditation can lead to self-comprehension and a psychosomatic balance that allows fulfilment in a natural life of self-expression and creative work.

13 The quest for meaning: models of mind and ego-transcendence

> If you wish to know the road up the mountain, you must ask the man who goes back and forth on it.
>
> Zen saying, anonymous

> Zen practice is not clarifying conceptual distinctions but throwing away one's preconceived views and notions and the sacred texts and all the rest, and piercing through the layers of coverings over the spring of self behind them . . . To turn within means all the twenty-four hours and in every situation, to pierce one by one . . . deeper and deeper to a place that cannot be described . . . Whether you are going or staying or sitting or lying down, the whole world is your own self.
>
> Daikaku in Leggett 1978

Meaning and religion

Within contemporary civilization the practice of meditation is commonly for utilitarian benefits. The meaning of the activity lies in the achievement of some goal: relaxation, improved health, an altered state of consciousness, or greater self-understanding and tolerance of others. Yet this attitude towards meditation is simply one way in which an otherwise paradoxical activity is given meaning by a profoundly egoistic, opportunistic, and tension-ridden society. A deeper understanding of the historical roots of meditation reveals a rather different picture.

We have already seen that the various forms of advanced meditation technique developed at the very heart of religious systems. They provide the essential experience that validates 'theological' opinions providing an interpretation of the world and of life. At a time when communication between major cultures was limited it was not apparent that while meditation is much the same in all cultures the beliefs the practice supports vary greatly.

What then is a religion? We shall argue here that a religion is primarily a system of thought that gives meaning to the everyday lives and endeavours of its adherents. It is thus an interpretation of the world and of life; in fact a complex of interrelated interpretations, often at several levels: the practical, the ethical, the judgemental, the metaphysical. Such a system of meaning grows by consensus and is enhanced by charismatic authority; eventually it comes to represent the values of a community. When a community predominates over a wide area, its religion then becomes central to everyday civilization itself. The religion is like a mirror in which each individual can see himself as related to a system of meanings and values that gives his life significance in relation to the lives of others. An overarching set of principles emanating from a core of beliefs then rules the transactions—personal, commercial, legal, political—of a people.

A developed religion has an authority that is rooted not only in the apparent validity of the interpretative paradigm itself but also in the actions of specialists that give the interpretation an existential presence, maintain it in ritual, and present it to the people. At the heart of religion lies the magical act responsible for the manifestation of the 'good'.

Yet this is not all that the major world religions do for man. An inevitable consequence of the evolutionary development of the self-process and the ability to analyse personal events within the continuum of time was the growing awareness of death, of the fact that life itself had an end. Death-awareness and self-awareness are essentially two sides of the same coin, for the discovery that the body dies implies the ending also of personal experience. The problem that has teased man has centred around the question whether this is really so. The dread of death is the dread of the termination of personal existence. It is clearly anchored in the attachment to the construct of self as an identity. Ever wriggling on this hook, mankind throughout history has sought to make away with the pain of this realization, to rationalize an explanation for death, and to argue for some kind of continuity for the living experiencing principle. Those whose ideological stance on this matter brings comfort and relief are likely to achieve eminence in a fearing society and, when their beliefs are associated with selfless ethics in personal life, such persons receive charisma. Such of course are the great priests. Both the doctrines of life after death and the simpler ideas of reincarnation bring some hope of a personal resurrection or renewed round of existence. The release from grief and the revival of hope in face of despair are both achieved by such comforting thoughts.

In his book *The social reality of religion* Berger (1969) pointed out that the social world arises from the externalization of human consciousness to construct a world of roles, rules, institutions, and beliefs. Society appears to be a fact just as does the organic world; yet it is actually more a product of patterned consciousness than it is some 'thing' in itself. Born into such a world, the individual internalizes the values and beliefs of the social environment so that the structures of the outer consciousness become the subjectivity of his growing person. Yet from time to time, and especially in the face of death, the fragility of this consciously created world becomes apparent. Then the realm of social convention faces its shadow, a world of comfortless non-humanity before which a person, socially structured as he is, cannot but feel afraid. Religion is concerned with the sacred quality of power which man finds present in nature. He attempts to coerce this power within his conventional world, to socialize the unsocializable. His structured notions of the 'cosmos', in which he traditionally takes central place, still face the dread of 'chaos'; nature is not so easily fitted in and the raw aloneness of the person before the void of death keeps breaking through.

The sacred cosmos, which transcends and includes man in its ordering of reality, thus provides man's ultimate shield against the terror of anomy. To be in a 'right' relationship with the sacred cosmos is to be protected against the nightmare threats of chaos. To fall out of such a right relationship is to be abandoned on the edge of the abyss of meaninglessness. (Berger 1969, p. 27).

The structure of religious belief, dogma, commonly comprises an exercise in theodicy; that is to say rationalization and ritual that attempt to maintain a safe interpretation of the sacred cosmos despite the intrusions of potentially faith-breaking experiences of suffering, evil, and death. To stay within the 'canopy' of belief is security; to venture forth or to be forced to do so as cultural change devalues a prevalent system of meaning, is an adventure fraught with unavoidable fear and anguish. Yet in most periods of history some individuals of great fortitude have sought more robust responses to the obvious facts of death and the unlikelihood of personal rebirth in any form. Such thinkers move towards a philosophy and a practical psychology of acceptance, which inevitably necessitates a profound personal exploration of the meaning of existence for oneself.

Monasticism and the priesthood

Readily available to all is the knowledge that life consists of birth, reproduction, and death; that health and wealth are hazardous and that even the most carefully conceived plans can be circumvented by arbitrary interventions of fate. While social action operates by rules and through roles moulded by the conventions of a socio-economic system, 'life' itself escapes convention and provides only uncertain criteria for meaning. Making sense of life often entails a cultural projection; man's place in nature is thus seen in the images of seasonal necessities, of agricultural gods, or the fanciful dictates of science fiction. Ultimate meaning escapes practical sense and the awareness of this creates a class of arbiters who seek to understand the whole and relate to it for the communal good.

Making sense of life and death and, for some, the subscription to a culturally prevalent explanation, is a vital activity; for upon it depends an individual's sense of personal worth and purpose and his acceptance of an ultimately unavoidable fate. While collective explanations of the ultimate are usually patterned upon those of the proximate necessities of life, it is the former that provide the superordinate meanings that apply to all persons and relate humanity and the cosmos in human consciousness.

It is today not easy to imagine the primitive mental world from which systems of meaning that crystalized into the 'great' religions came. Early man was surrounded by inexplicable forces all more powerful than himself and as capable of his destruction as of the provision of some good. The world he experienced was one in which the enigmatic character of things was barely distinguished from the powerful forces within the psyche itself. The 'objective' and the 'subjective' were not distinguishable: experience was a flux of forces with contentment balanced against fear and unkind fate. To stave off fear and fate became the task of the magician, the shaman who, himself often possessed of strong psychological attributes, could move with unusual confidence in a world of elemental forces.

One of the chief ways of coming to grips with things is through naming them. Name and form are indeed the two first principles of the earliest religious writings of the Indian subcontinent (Govinda 1961). To name a form gives power. Forms are the embodiments of names; power through the name gives power over form. The utterance of a name with the mind appropriately concentrated upon its object was found to affect the extent to which the object had power over experience. In this way power could be transferred from the object to the subject and confident action could be once more restored. The great scriptures of the Vedas consist largely of incantations of this sort, chants expressive of an elementary relationship to a deeply experienced world, a fresh world not yet caged in intricate intellectual analyses that distance the subject from the object of his attention.

These chants or incantations 'were as free from moral or religious considerations as the prescriptions of a physician . . . because religion had not yet become an independent value, had not yet separated itself from life in its fullness—just as the individual had not yet separated itself from nature. A child will satisfy his desires with a natural and innocent egotism—innocent, because not yet being conscious of ego . . . if the self has not yet become conscious of itself there cannot be any concept of morality. The individuality of man had not yet been discovered and for that reason there could not be any idea to preserve it' (Govinda 1961). The idea of self as we know it today was not present in either Rigvedic or Homeric times and the 'hymns' of those periods reveal a different functional consciousness from that of later civilized worlds (Jaynes 1976). The chanting of names or 'ultimate propositions' as Rappaport calls them (see p. 274) formed no doubt a means for inducing shifts in consciousness which later became the basis for developed meditation practices.

The idea of gods arose from human powers which were projected onto objects and later turned into abstracted representations or themes. As Govinda puts it, man was universalized and the world anthropomorphized. The rituals involving incantations were now aimed outward for power was placed in the abstract god.

It was not at that stage realized how far this abstraction actually remained within the mind; for in experience it was projected outward, perhaps into an image. There were many rituals designed to bring the power of the project back into the person. Wearing the mask of the God, a man became the god; and initiation rites, as at Eleusis, gave access to the powers of the projected agent. To manage these rituals a class of specialists emerged, shamans, priests, and other intermediaries between 'God' and man.

One of the most striking features of the major world religions is their common association with both priesthoods and with monasticism. I shall argue that this is no accident nor a cultural parallelism but a phenomenon associated with other aspects of the socio-ecological adaptation of the major agrarian societies. Dickeman (1979, see above p. 213) argues that in an agrarian society where wealth accumulates in the hands of the powerful there is a trend towards the development of polygyny at the top of society and a consequential upward movement of women through the social strata (hypergyny). The consequences of this movement, together with the fact that only a few males inherit their fathers' wealth, perhaps through primogeniture, means that many men necessarily move to lower perches in the social hierarchy than those occupied by fathers and favoured brothers. Among the poorer classes this fallout of 'surplus' males may lead them into high-risk strategies including crime, banditry, soldiering, or perhaps merely *bragadoccio*. One may suppose that among the moderately educated a similar movement leads to careers in the army or as colonists of many kinds. An avenue of especial interest here is monastic life.

From the sociobiological viewpoint the life-strategies appropriate to a monk are of considerable interest. Let us suppose that our monk is sworn to celibacy and, at least as far as coition with women is concerned, he maintains his vows with diligence. According to Hamiltonian theory he has thereby sacrificed all possibility of a direct reproductive contribution to his inclusive fitness. There remain two paths by which he can cover this loss; social influence leading to nepotism and reciprocating altruism in which the return of his investment accrues not to himself but to relatives. One strategy therefore is for him to climb the ecclesiastical hierarchy in such a way as to benefit relatives through his social influence. This kind of action is not however characteristic of a monkhood in general although cases of it undoubtedly occur. In an uncorrupt monkhood something more subtle appears to be in play.

In joining a monastic order Christians and Buddhists alike renounce the ways of the world. Fame and gain are abandoned and the traditional wisdom of the order in question is cultivated. This wisdom focuses on the practice of selflessness. The task of overcoming 'sin' or 'illusion' is not an easy one; ritualistic regimentation, long hours of prayer or meditation, the deliberate patterning of life according to the values of the priesthood and actively practised compassion towards fellow monks, laymen, and even animals are modes of behaviour which assist the central task.

There is an implicit logic to all this whatever the surface rationalization may be. The co-operative compassion of the monks creates an environment in which some individuals thrive, reaching levels of insight and acquiring reputations of a goodness, benevolence and charity that are available to all equally. Such monks or priests gain charisma and sometimes immense social influence. Their presence assists the spread of the peaceful values of the monkhood among the population at large. The effect is a general increase in ethical behaviour, in insight concerning self and in relationship to others, and in acts of disinterested kindness in thought and deed alike. This lessening of the characteristic avarice, aggression, exploitation, and sheer brutality of agrarian life cannot but be of assistance to all families engaged in rearing children within the sphere of influence of the celibate brotherhood. Through their communal saintliness the 'brothers' (note the use of this kin term for non-kin living altruistically together) produce co-operatively a potential increase in the mean inclusive fitnesses of all associated with them. The fact that their influence extends to their non-kin as well as their personal kin is no objection here, since non-kin by increasing the frequency of reciprocally altruistic acts also benefit direct relatives in consequence. In agrarian societies, where competition and the acquisition of wealth by the powerful leads to many forms of legal abuse and where economic instability is as much due to lack of societal cohesion as it is to ecological variance, the influence of celibate 'brothers', 'fathers', 'sisters', 'teachers', or 'gurus' may be considerable.

In past times the power of priests and monks was very great both in Europe and in several civilizations of the East. It was often associated with ruling gerontocracies that emphasized nepotistic value systems and operated social strategies appropriate to a demographic pattern in which the carrying capacity of the land was often reached (i.e. K circumstances). The monkhood often tended to a strongly conservative political stance but one which could be beneficial to a society in that it assisted in the maintenance of economic stability (James, E. O. 1961).

The paradox of communal compassion is that it readily yields authoritarian value systems that under economic or external pressures respond with a coercion of the population in the interests of conformity. Minorities such as the saintly Cathars of southern France were ruthlessly suppressed by the Catholic inquisition not because their morality was in question but because they were heretics whose beliefs threatened or appeared to threaten the credibility of the ruling ecclesiastical authority (Ladurie 1977). In such cases benevolence switches into a malignant mode. The rules of monastic life are commonly controlled by 'priests' who have the power of contact with the divine authority in whatever guise he may appear. Priests may use this power either with an avarice in no way different from that of worldly potentates or they may adopt a strategy of total altruism with its egalitarian effect. The choice between these policies is between maximizing personal success and nepotism on the one hand or optimizing fitness on the other through the maximization of communal fitnesses. This latter policy, known to its adherents as 'charity', cannot in this perspective be separated from its plausible outcome in terms of sociobiological theory.

The history of religion is witness to periods when the misuse of political power by ecclesiastical authorities has been grossly exploitative of others. Yet there is a marked tendency for such 'evil' to be condemned and rectified through rigorous reform, tending once more to an emphasis on egalitarianism and compassion. It is as if the strategy of generalized charity is recognized as a valid alternative to coercion and avarice and that it is often more advantageous to an individual (socially and sociobiologically) to optimize rather than to maximize his personal and familial power. There is a parallel here between republicanism and monarchism.

Success as a professional celibate is far from easily attained. It entails a struggle with the flesh which perhaps only rarely ends with total victory for the spirit. It may, however, lead to a deep understanding of the self-processes and hence to a transcending of egoism in its grosser sensual forms. Under the wiser disciplines acceptance of the body rather than its denial, and equilibration of lust and tenderness rather than their suppression, can be a fortunate outcome. The struggle with the self leads to wisdom and compassion that is heartfelt rather than a product of theoretical knowledge. To this alone is due the respect and veneration that a people may accord their priests and religious teachers. Indeed, such respect depends upon the extent to which religious leaders literally incorporate the values which they profess. In following a policy of optimization adherents and leaders alike have to demonstrate renunciation.

While all priesthoods probably took their origins from the magician they later developed systems of mind and body training that yielded personal power over the self. Today many contemporary priesthoods have turned to secularized value systems in a search for popularity and credibility. The switch to rationalism cannot generate the charisma that accrues only to those whose inner practices give strength to the heart rather than to the thinking mind. Meditational practices that form the root of monastic life cultivate a balance between the propositional and appositional aspects of mental activity, predominantly in the hedonic mode (p. 332). It is in these practices and the willed actions in the world that fulfil them that so-called 'spiritual' strength arise. In the modern West the extensive secularization of religion has largely destroyed the relation between individual spirituality and the systems of belief to which it used to belong.

Individualism and the quest for meaning

The projection of gods, or, as in Judaism, of a God as the focus of religious security is sooner or later linked with a doubt.

> Who knows the secret? Who proclaims it here?
> Whence, whence this manifold creation sprang?
> He from whom all this great creation came,
> Whether his will created or was mute,
> The most High Seer that is in highest heaven,
> He knows it—or perchance even He knows not.
> (*Rigveda* X, 129. Translated by Max Muller.)

Even the postulate of an ultimate God is not immune from such questionings, which throw doubt upon even the most profound of rituals. Eventually the problem returns to its source and man becomes aware of his capacity for projection and its function in protecting experience. This realization is itself a source for renewed quest. Now, however, the quest is in terms of a humanism based on the awareness that man alone is the source of his experience and that his relationship with the world is the heart of the problem. Historically this realization is associated with the appearance of explicit analyses of the subject–object dichotomy in personal life in the major urban civilizations of the old world (Jaynes 1976).

The great world civilizations developed religious systems with varying degrees of humanistic recognition. Often there is an outward theism, a canopy for the masses, and a secret esoteric tradition (e.g. the Caballah in Judaism, Alchemy within Christendom, Sufism in

Mohammedanism) in which the focus is less on the outer projection and more on the inward task of understanding the self. Today, living as most of us do in multi-cultural societies, where people 'have' a particular religion or none at all, it is often difficult to realize how monolithic and all-pervasive the great religions once were. They were virtually identical with the great cultures of the past, a total source of reference for ultimate meanings for countless inhabitants, embracing orthodoxies defining whole cultures, and to differ from them was heresy, punishable perhaps by death.

Berger (1969) has traced the slow downfall of religion in the West to themes detectable in the historicism and rationalism of Judaic religion which sprang into the forefront of Christian thought at the time of the Reformation. Rather than a human life which in microcosm re-enacted the great macrocosmic cycles of projected naturalistic deities, Jewish and Christian thinkers insisted on an actual historical link between a single god and the affairs of men. When this link was weakened by philosophical humanism and the rise of science the whole structure became unstable. As a result secularization of religious institutions proceeded apace. The contemporary Christian denominations and other religious sects present varying belief systems, the credibility of which is always in question. The 'churches' are forced to compete like business organizations for adherents. The relativity of belief systems renders the fabric of the whole endeavour in doubt. An emphasis on pastoral care, social welfare, personal and marital counselling, and on 'therapy' emerges as the 'product' that a belief system can provide its adherents. Religion ceases to be a matter of vast collective belief; it is rather a matter of individual opinion and aesthetics. This 'pluralism' of modern religion necessarily focuses on individual choice in a market place of spiritual goods. If heaven is unbelievable, some 'togetherness' at least helps to stave off the chill clutch of an ultimate meaninglessness in life.

As they now exist the major religions may be seen as 'theological, ethical and ritual deposits left behind when the civilizations of which they were part lost their distinctive political and economic features' (Ling 1973). This is of course true of the modern West and even more so of such remaining religious life as is permitted in the Communist world, where however, current movements of dissidence suggest that the materialism of the Communist believer may eventually be included among the theologies in question. Even in their countries of origin, Islam in the Middle East for example, the fate of traditional religious culture in the face of extraordinary contemporary changes suggests an increasing fragmentation against which the religious character of the events in Iran can be read as a reactionary backlash against Western-style values. As Ling puts it, the traditional religions' 'viability is thus limited; they will last as long as theistic belief can be maintained in a modern industrial society. This may of course be longer than the unbeliever expects, especially among politically, socially or culturally deprived or depressed classes of society for whom traditional theistic belief can be a major source of satisfaction and comfort.'

Two routes to the solution of the world's problems are especially emphasized today; one, the rectification of social 'injustice', is the path of Marx; the other, an idea that personal enlightenment leads to social solutions, is provided, for example, by the transcendental meditation organization of Maharishi Mahesh. Marxism does not stop at sociopolitical analysis but extends into a materialistic utopianism that is sadly lacking in sociopsychological sophistication. By contrast, the altered states of consciousness achieved in advanced meditational practice do not of themselves alter the facts of societal injustice and conflict. Marx or Maharishi, public or private perfectionisms; neither can yield an answer, for the psychological naïveté of the former is matched only by the sociological simplicity of the latter.

Contemporary systems of meaning are shifting strongly in the direction of what I call a 'transpersonal humanism'; that is to say a value-system based firmly in the realization that experience stems from within man and cannot be attributed to supernatural intervention, a value-system that none the less questions the values of the assertive egotism at the root of modern life and seeks to move to a deeper understanding of the personal- or self-process and its relation to the perceived world. To an ethogenist this trend is most significant, for not only are shifts in social values and behaviour involved but the very models of mind used in explanations for praxis are of an advanced order and are attended by activities that attempt to make the intellectual component existentially realizable. This line of thought connects easily with that informed humanism that focuses upon the ecological dilemma that faces us all. Only by directly confronting the maximizing policies of collective egoism that lie at the root of excessive industrial exploitation and pollution can optimizing 'soft energy' schemes for conviviality of any kind be realized (Schümacher 1977; Laing 1979; Lovins 1979; Illich 1979).

A major component in this trend arose during the American experience of the civil rights movement, the trauma of Vietnam, and the interest in an 'alternative' to the capitalistic, commercial, and militarily based contemporary Western civilization. It was epitomized particularly in the hippy movement. It is no accident that the impetus came largely from the immigrant state of California where traditional cultural values are perhaps most fragmented and a need for new roots is most pronounced. In this context a quest for an experientially based existentialism involved a popularization of Western psychological

knowledge of individual and group processes in the encounter movement with its myriad of group events designed to aid personal growth.
Yet neither psychoanalytically based explanations of experience nor
Western existentialism (essentially intellectual and lacking a praxis)
have sufficed to provide the roots for the meaningful life that so many
seek. Instead, following the example of Aldous Huxley, Alan Watts,
and the founders of Esalen, attention has turned to the psychological
systems that underlie Indian religion. Here, lacking a repressive mono-
theistic orthodoxy, religion has retained a diversity of forms, all
emphasizing the role of psychological praxis, of salvation through
personal quest and effort rather than by grace, and the relativity of
personal paths to personal characteristics.

Given the contemporary sophistication of science and the emphasis
upon the behavioural sciences in higher education, it is clear that in a
personal quest for meaning no naïve religious, metaphysical, or ethical
system is likely to gain adherents among educated people today. The
fact that Buddhism is at present said to be the fastest-growing religion
in Britain suggests that here at least is a system of world and life
interpretation that is sufficiently sophisticated to appeal to contemporary young people who must comprise one of the most educated
generations ever to have lived on Earth. This present-day example of
man as a maker of meaning merits scrutiny here for it illustrates
particularly clearly how a system of meaning can function in moulding
and sustaining individual life, and its potential for social influence.

The merits of Buddhism in the contemporary West seem to lie in the
following prime characteristics:

(1) It lacks both metaphysical and ethical dogmatism, and the
stance of its most prominent figures is not authoritarian.

(2) It provides a profound and subtle analysis of the human
dilemma which never trails off into empty philosophical speculation or a purely intellectual analysis, but both starts and ends in
a close examination of human experience.

(3) This analysis is anchored in what I term a 'subjective empiricism'; an 'experimental' study of experience under the closely
controlled circumstances of the everyday life of a community
and in precisely structured psychophysical disciplines. This
tradition stems, indeed, from the Buddha himself, who set out to
discover in personal experiment what the limits of human
understanding of the self might be.

(4) Buddhism invites those concerned with problems of life to follow
a phenomenological pathway which, in its various forms,
remains recognizably that of its originator. The exhaustive
nature of this path becomes apparent only to a practitioner, and
a merely intellectual questioner is given short shrift.

(5) Although contemporary Buddhism is as much afflicted with pluralism as is Christianity—Zen masters, Tibetan lamas, Thai monks, and Indian gurus jostle for space in the advertising sections of Buddhist journals—there is an underlying unity which is no mere matter of doctrinal belief. This unity focuses on the notion of individual search. 'Go work out your salvation with diligence' is a message for individual persons. A path is provided that can yield psychological results which enable the individual to meet 'chaos" on its own ground without fear. The task is to tread the way. Faith in a doctrine is of little importance. An inner atheoretical knowledge of self is acquired by transmission from a teacher or by personal discovery.

(6) The Buddha was directly concerned as much with social issues as he was with individual self-salvation. This fact is little understood but, as Ling (1973) makes clear, the creation of the *Sangha*, or community of practitioners, was intended to lead to the formation of a state governed by rational principles derived from personal and social understanding. Indeed, such a state did in fact emerge for important periods in the histories of India, Ceylon, Burma, Thailand, Tibet, and Japan, and China was at times much influenced by a combination of Taoism and Buddhism.

The sociological context of the origin of Buddhism provides an insight into its contemporary advancement. The Buddha lived at a time when the kingdoms of the Ganges plain were crystallizing out of the failure of small 'democratic' republics of tribal groups. The power vested in kingship allowed at best more efficient government but, at worst, extreme abuse of power and vivid demonstrations of the effects of personal avarice. Kingship, moreover, stressed the ultimate in individual 'achievement' in a society rooted in socio-economically pivotal cities where a new division of labour created an awareness of individuality that was not present in smaller-scale, rural societies derived from simple subsistence economies. The key to these changes lies in the shift from a semi-nomadic cattle-raising mode of life to intensive rice cultivation that allowed a sharp increase in human population. Settlements increased in size so that small villages on key routes or rivers emerged as nascent cities. The urban population had an influence over the countryside through the control of exchange, and various industries were already organized into guilds by the Buddha's time. Trade and exchange, i.e. a monetary economy, provide opportunities for specialization in ways of living that emphasize individual talent and increase the range of opportunities available. Individualism, the cult of personal difference, complementarity, and advancement, is a concomitant of urbanization. But individualism raises problems of a new kind (Ling 1973).

The village or settlement entails a simplicity of relationships based upon kin and the certainties of a life whose essential features are pre-ordained by matters of family position and birth order. The city provides acquaintances rather than kin and interchange rather than friendship. While an individual is freed to a degree from the conformity of intimate groups he loses the sense of social integration, the mutually supportive morale, and the conventional spontaneity of small-scale living. Acquaintanceship is more functional than personal and these functions relate to fame and gain rather than to mutual understanding. The role becomes all and the person is diminished.

The Jataka stories and other sources show clearly that the Buddha was not only himself the son of a leading citizen in a small, fading republic but that his life and work were focused purely in the cities of his time. His ministry found appeal because of the needs of urban people.

The transition that many people were then experiencing from the familiar small scale society of the old tribal republics to the strange large scale and consequentially more impersonal, bleaker life of the new monarchical state, was accompanied by a psychological *malaise*, a heightened sense of dissatisfaction with life as it had to be lived. It was this *malaise* which the Buddha was to take as the starting point of his analysis of the human condition (Ling 1973).

This description does not read unfamiliarly among city-dwellers of today, among whom the *malaise* goes by the ill-defined term 'alienation'; that sense of existential loneliness, a not-belonging which arises from the functional egotism of our times, from reductionist interpretations of life, and from an environment of concrete symbolizing an arid loneliness of mental encapsulation; physical walls like Piranesi's prisons, that gain their effect, from the economics of our commercialized psychic space.

The Buddha's personally achieved response was a doctrine of liberation coupled with an experientially testable model of mind. In its focus on the renunciation of egoism in all its forms and through his personal influence on the rulers of his time the Buddha's solution amounted also to a social policy that remains open to test today.

The Buddhist model of mind in the *Abidhamma*

The previous chapters dealt with a number of themes concerning the nature of consciousness. The Buddhist model of mind provides an embracing set of concepts concerning consciousness that are more inclusive than any model based solely upon modern psychological inquiry.

This defect in contemporary thought arises mainly because of the reductionist tenets of so much of modern psychology. Indeed, without a renewed concept of man as an active agent with powers (p. 267) there has been little hope of a sustained modelling of mind that can treat human experience with any fullness.

What sort of 'meaning' then does a Buddhistic approach provide? The Buddha's system sprang naturally from the story of his life. There seems no reason for doubting the validity of the essential elements of this story. Raised in an influential household he was at first a spoilt child given every luxury and from whom the difficulties of life were hidden. The discovery of the facts of sickness, old age, and death came as a personal shock. The sight of a wandering Sadhu on a quest for 'truth' opened the young man's mind to the possibility of a path or way of life. Finally, unable to resist his questioning as to the meaning of life and death, he bade his sleeping wife and son goodbye and left to become a wandering mendicant. After a period of intense asceticism that provided training for his body and mind, the young Siddhatha, having nearly killed himself with extremes, came to the conviction of their futility. He treated himself kindly, fed well and sat beneath a tree resolved to complete his quest. In profound meditation the inner barriers finally collapsed and he experienced 'enlightenment'. By this is meant that the boundaries of his ego-structured mind dissolved in an inner act of disidentification. He found himself in an unbounded, timeless, non-naming, primordial, and all-inclusive state of awareness which he recognized as the ground of experiencing within which all cognitive structures of named form are created and back to which they can dissolve. In the days that followed he not only systematized his understanding through logical comprehension but, after a period of doubt, decided that this was no mere private event but a solution that he could and should convey to others of his time.

The Four Noble Truths of his first discourse were:

(1) The fact of suffering: all human beings experience a lack of ease, an anxiety if not actual pain in the very fact of being conscious, alive, and self-aware. Self-awareness entails death-awareness also.

(2) This suffering (*dukkha*) is due to a clinging or attachment to phenomena, which being naturally impermanent, cannot give the satisfaction of security. Above all, attachment to one's own individuality (ego) is the prime source of suffering, for this too is necessarily impermanent, undergoes change, and dies. Indeed, upon analysis it is seen to be no entity at all, but a process. The illusion that one is an entity to be preserved is the prime source of psychological pain.

(3) There is a possibility of relief from suffering which stems from a profound inner realization concerning the nature of the self-process.

(4) The path or way to such a realization entails attention to right views, intentions, speech, action, livelihood, effort, mindfulness,

and concentration. The word 'right' implies that the feature in question should be expressive of a stance in life that is primarily directed at comprehending and transcending personal egoism and which involves constant watchfulness for its fulfilment. Effort, mindfulness, and concentration are basically the means whereby right livelihood is maintained.

The essential message is that while personal growth must involve self-definition and a role in life (livelihood) too great an emphasis on individuation produces a defensive ego-consciousness that becomes closed to change through fear concerning its own maintenance. This closure is a sign of ignorance (*avijja*) which only a profound emotional education can dispel.

The Buddha's initial insight was developed by generations of scholars who lived within the order of monks he created. This order, the Sangha, was by no means parasitical on society. In exchange for alms, robes, books, and simple shelter the monks provided education, spiritual advice, insight, and support for those who remained householders. It was a system of mutual exchange. Buddhism was, however, to remain primarily monastic and it was this that led, on the one hand, to the depth of psychological scholarship and, on the other, to a sociological frailty. When the monasteries were destroyed by Islam, the roots of the praxis thus failed to survive in the populace at large. The result was a return in India to the complexities of a village-based and polytheistic Hinduism which, in its subsequent philosophical development by Shankara, owed much to the earlier insights of the Buddhists.

Buddhist scholarship entailed an analysis of the fruits of experience and especially of the effects of meditation. The analysis is described in the *Abidhamma* (also spelt *Abhidharma* in some books), a voluminous body of literature only recently subjected to study by adequately equipped western scholars (Govinda 1961; Guenther 1976). The model of mind in this literature underwent a variety of transformations throughout a long history but the prime ideas in early Buddhist thought were already comprehensive.

It is essential to realize that the *Abidhamma* analysis addresses itself to the nature of experience. It treats a process, and the terms in the argument refer to functions that interrelate so closely in the system that they cannot properly be examined as elements mechanistically separable from one another. Experience is determined by attitude (*citta*)†

---

† This and the following terms, as in Fig. 13.1 are given in the Pali of the earliest Buddhist canon as described by Govinda (1961). In later Buddhism developments of this system occurred in the closely related Sanskrit language. For an account of Buddhist history in India see Thomas (1933).

which in the average person is a product of conditionings that are the results of previous actions (*Kamma*, e.g. Karma). The conditioning of the average person comprises a structured striving in relation to acquired wants (superimposed upon basic biological needs) and an anxiety about both the achievements and the existence, status, or significance of the person himself. In short, greed, anger, and illusion are the drives that maintain the attitude of a conditioned mind (*citta*) and produce the whole panorama of experiences which, as a result of actions entailed by them, yield a yet further set of similar events. The karmic process is cyclic and self-maintaining. Ignorance (*avijja*) of the cause of the cycle maintains the striving, desiring, or wanting associated with expectations of permanence and security. The full cycle is represented in Fig. 13.1. Ignorance and precipitated karmic consequences from the past (*saṅkhāras*) produce a consciousness (*viññāna*) involving the naming of particulars (*nām-rūpa* in the world of forms, *rūpadhātu*) and the patterned cravings for ego-satisfaction (*tanhā*). If these cravings are temporarily satisfied the result is attachment to the object (*upādāna*). Failure to achieve satisfaction leads to longing in disappointment (*lobha*) or aversion to the apparent obstacles (*dosa*). The patterns of attachment result in what we may call character-formation of identity, the 'becoming a person' (*bhava*), while sustained disappointment and aversion ends in disintegration (death—*jarāmarana*). Character-formation initiates through *jāti*—the principle of 'rebirth'—further karmically conditioned actions under illusion (*avijja*), and the cycle, in the form of successive spirals in time, recurs.

The analysis of perception is detailed. *Nāma-rūpa* includes body awareness involving the activation of the senses (*salāyatana*). This results in sensory experience (*phassa*), which includes the recall of earlier images and emotional feelings (*vedanā*) in relation to particular objects.

The growth of identity (*bhava*) through emotional attachment to ideas (*upādāna*) implies a clinging to the perceived; yet since life is in flux this involves an inevitable contradiction and disappointment. It is important to realize that ignorance of the nature of the whole conceptual and emotional cycle is not seen as causal to the cycle in any simple sense nor as some cosmogenic principle, but rather as the *attitudinal condition* that assembles the whole iterating cycle of consciousness in this mode. The whole system of the conditional arising of the co-related functions is known as the dependent origination (*paṭiccasamuppāda*) of mind.

The cycle of dependent origination begins to be broken through a change in attitude that arises once the possible effects of following the Eightfold path have been glimpsed either intellectually or in deeper experience. The eight steps in the path do not really form a sequence:

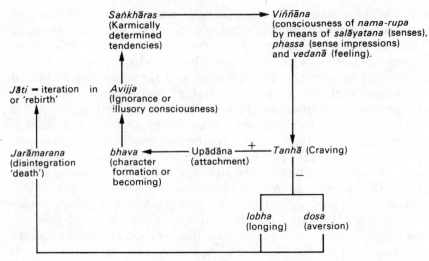

FIG. 13.1. The cycle of dependent origination in the Pali *Abidhamma*. (After Govinda 1961.)

they operate at differing levels. Right views and intentions arise from intellectual appreciation and create a favourable attitude of aspiration for right speech, action, and livelihood which involve ethically determined activity in daily life. These are sustained by right effort, mindfulness, and concentration (the last two being essentially components of the meditative praxis in everyday life) which yield a heightened awareness of being that tends towards a harmony of mind and equanimity. The Eightfold path components are seen as opposed to the functions descriptive of the cycle of dependent origination. Thus

Right views oppose illusion
Right intentions oppose karmic tendencies
Right speech/thought opposes false comprehension of name and form.
Right livelihood opposes uncontrolled emotional expression (*vedanā, tanhā, upādāna*)
Right effort ⎫   ⎧ illusory craving (*tanhā*) and its
Right mindfulness ⎬ oppose ⎨ consequent effects in becoming
Right concentration ⎭   ⎩ (*bhava*).

So far as mental work on the path is concerned, there are five factors which belong to the development of a contemplative mind. The first two, *vitakka* (thinking) and *vicāra* (sustained contemplative analysis), are initial steps applied to the existential problem of life, identity, and death. Sustained focus on this problem in meditation can provoke an experience of *pīti* (rapture or bliss) and *sukha* (quiet happiness) as a degree of comprehension and acceptance of the nature of mind emerges. In addition, one-pointedness of attention (*ekaggatā*) arises in the deliberate practice of *jhāna* (concentrative meditation). *Jhāna* in the *Abidhamma* has five levels in which the subject lets go successively of the several functions of mental activity. Sustained focus on the issue at hand leads first to a release or relaxation from thinking. This is the first *bhūmi* or level. In the second stage *vicāra* goes; in the third *pīti*; in the fourth *sukha*; and at the advanced fifth stage only absorbed attention, one-pointedness, remains, producing a neutral equanimity or the 'peace in voidness' (*upekkhā* of pure concentration. At this point the meditator attains the 'realm of no-form' which, being ineffable, is not analysable in words.

These *bhumis* are described in Buddhaghosa's *Visuddhimaga* of the fifth century AD: a summary in fact of the whole *Abidhamma* canon. They are virtually identical with the meditative stages described from a derived tradition by the Maharishi Mahesh. Concentrative meditation which gives rise to them has the property of suppressing everyday mental activity, which resumes its habitual actions without difficulty outside a sitting session. Clear insight into the meaning of these actions is acquired, however, only through a further traditional form of meditation which, instead of using concentration, applies watchfulness or mindfulness of every thought as it arises. After recognition the thought is simply allowed to fall away. Mindfulness or insight meditation (*Vipassana*) is of equal importance with concentration in the *Abidhamma* teachings and it is a key element in Zazen. It leads to a clear comprehension of the nature of the mind's action as a process and the realization that the ego is not a finite 'thing' but more like a bubble on a stream. The practice of bare attending to thought activity tends in itself to induce a level of concentration just short of the first *bhumi*. At this level the mental panorama is fully available for inspection but not flowing so powerfully as to engulf awareness in its stream. Up until about the fourth stage *Vipassana* can function (p. 344) but beyond this mental phenomena are too suppressed to allow mindful witnessing. At refined levels of awareness the paths of insight and concentration tend to flow together. It is however awareness or insight that secures the final conceptual release and not the level of concentration that may be attained. In fact in both the Theravadin and the Zen practice, the higher levels of *jhana* are thought of as concentration 'games'. The main emphasis is on the attainment of insight into the processes of self rather than on levels of deep trance (see discussion in Goleman 1977). The sequence of progressive release from those very attributes that in the cycle of dependent origination produce egoism may also be seen as stages of capacity in a personal development ranging from the beginner or stream-enterer (*sotāpanna*) through the once-returner and non-returner to the arahant or realized being (*arahā*). In brief, release from attachment to the concept of self purely as an identity also releases one from the fear of death. Change, including mortality is accepted as the nature of the real.

The arahant ideal in one school of Buddhism (Theravada) implies a final withdrawal from the world as the fires of becoming finally burn out. Yet this concept is quite at odds with the actual behaviour of the Buddha, who at this point chose to become a teacher. In later schools of Buddhism (e.g., the Mahayana) this choice indeed becomes a vow, the Bodhisattva vow, in which the process of self-enlightenment entails a decision to work for others until all have reached the goal. This means in practice that in his livelihood and in his politics the Buddhist acts in such a way as to counteract the effects of greed, anger, and illusion in public life and to encourage a fair distribution of resources, opportunities, and means of personal education. The coincidence of spiritual development and a life of practical affairs is idealized in the important *Vimalakurti Sutra* (Luk 1972), which presents the life story and teaching of such a man.

Developments in Mahayana psychology

The basic model of mind revealed in the *Abidhamma* literature gradually changed as Buddhism entered the rich phase of philosophical and psychological expansion that produced the Mahayana schools (the 'Great Vehicle') and the huge monastic universities at Nalanda and other sites in northern India. These were the foremost educational establishments of their day, giving rise to the patterns of thought that came to influence in many ways the religious life of Tibet, China, and Japan.

A prime change in the model of mind basic to Mahayana probably depended on an increasing emphasis on the winning of sudden enlightenment while following a natural way in this life rather than on a gruelling advance over many incarnations of increasingly spiritual existence. This emphasis is pronounced in the Dhyana School that led to the emergence of Ch'an and Zen (both words being the Chinese and Japanese versions of Dhyana respectively) and in the Tantric practices that became so influential in Tibet. As we have seen Zen utilizes breathing yoga and often focuses on the 'enlightenment experience' rather than on the development of extended meditation in Samadhi. Tantric Buddhism likewise makes use of a great range of breathing exercises, bodily yogas, psychosexual visualizations, and other practices that operate with modes of attention as well as trance. These practices favour the occurrence of sudden insights into the self-process.

In the ancient *Lion's roar of Queen Shrimala* (Wayman and Wayman 1974) it is argued that only a direct experiential knowledge of the Fourth Noble Truth of the Buddha, the cessation of suffering, is the true 'refuge' of the Buddhist. Everything else is preliminary. One who wishes to understand himself needs to discover experientially that he is no other than the 'suchness' (*tathata*) of existence and that the experience of suchness is nothing other than a particular way of 'seeing'. Suffering ceases when the contents of mind are apperceived without evaluation or discrimination. In simply observing the patterns of experience emotional attachment plays no role. Because there are no attachments the mind is experienced as free, empty, void (*sunyata*), a condition which is thus a real refuge in a troubled world.

The voluminous bulk of the *Lankavatara Sutra* (Suzuki 1930, 1932; see also Dumoulin 1959; Govinda 1971; Crook 1977*b*) includes an explicit account of mental functioning and enlightenment. The cycle (represented in Fig. 13.2) of dependent origination forms the basis for the model, but especial attention is paid to the new concept of the 'storehouse consciousness' (*ālayavijñāna*) in which all the accumulated traces of experience lie passively within an unconscious, likened to a sea that may be activated by a wind on its surface producing waves. Stimulation activates this storehouse of memories which are discriminated one from another by the analytical activity of thought (*manovijñana*). Thought both structures the process of sensation and generates the logically interwoven pattern of the contents of the storehouse. Essential to thought is attention (*manas*) which focuses awareness upon the cognitive elements with which thought operates. A basic distinction made by thought is the division between the subject and the object of thought. Thinking for the most part operates dualistically.

In insight meditation bare attention (*Vipassana*) to an object focuses awareness, without necessarily incurring analytical thinking. This separation of bare awareness and thought is not easy to achieve. When it happens and thought largely disappears, the object of awareness is no longer distinguished from the subject who is aware. Indian Buddhists had discovered that when they attended to each thought with clear awareness they could find no self because they completely *became* their experience without awareness of a separate experiencer. The subject of experience is thereby freed from a patterned way of viewing the external world which arises through time with the construction of the reference systems of his thought.

Attention (*Vipassana, Zazen*) to the roots of the conscious process itself allows a person to experience his own natural being or 'suchness' in its primordial non-constructed state. The whole process of looking inward meditatively is thus called 'seeing into one's own nature'. In the *Awakening of faith* (Hakeda 1967) it is argued that one may experience the contents of the store either as many or as one. The meditator comes to realize that he can either view suchness discriminatively and with ego-attachment or experience it as one field containing duality. To

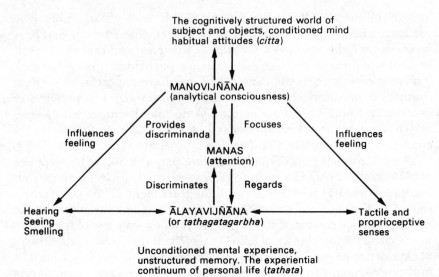

Fig. 13.2. The model of mind in the *Lankavatara Sutra* (Suzuki 1930, 1932). The ongoing continuum of sensory experience is both registered and stored in the *ālayavijñāna* or 'storehouse consciousness', also known as *tathagatagarbha* or 'womb of suchness'. This concept refers to the continuum of experience (sensory impressions and interior recall) basic to consciousness but as yet unanalysed by an intellectual function. *Manas*, a factor translated as attention, regards or inspects the experiential continuum and discriminates between its contents. These discriminanda become the material for analytical consciousness (thought), the *manovijñāna*, which thereby constructs the cognitive world of subject-object relations. I have assumed that this world feeds back to influence sensory experience. In Buddhist meditation the activity of *manovijñāna* is lessened by concentrated focusing of *manas* (attention) on the flow of experience itself. This breaks the control of the conditioned mind over experience and allows the relation between self and world to be experienced in its 'suchness' (*tathata*). This model in many ways resembles modern ideas on attention structure and the filtering of experience (Broadbent 1958) resulting from Western psychological science over a thousand years later.

discriminate or to see without discrimination are both ways of viewing the mind: hence the numerous paradoxical assertions in Zen to the effect that one's obviously unenlightened mind is already the mind of Buddha and questions to seekers such as 'what is your original face before you are born?

We remarked in the previous chapter that modern Zen students (Sekida 1975; Akishige 1978) have compared the 'enlightenment' experience (*kensho* or *satori*) to that of a person perceiving an ambiguous object or picture in which the figure–ground relationship flips over periodically to reveal a contrary reality. Both aspects of the figure are present at any one time but only one of them is perceived. The paradoxical questions (*koans*) of Zen training closely resemble ambiguous figures and yield their meaning only after the conditioning to read them in narrowly bounded ways has been overcome. The trainee has to make an existential jump from one mode of cognition, the discriminatory, to another, non-duality. There is no way by which a discriminatory mind can find out how to do this. All a person can do is to attend vigorously to the processes of his own mental activity.

When the changeabout occurs the alteration lies not in the contents of mind but in the relationship between the mind-discriminated ego and the world-as-experienced. Once this shift has been fully experienced an individual's vision of himself in the world is altered. His prospects for action arise from a base other than that of a frightened defensive ego. This ego is now an organ of a more totally integrated and awakened self. I should like to illustrate this concept of an insightful 'flip' by a quotation from a different yet relevant context. In his book *The cult of the fact* Liam Hudson (1972) discusses the way in which authoritative academic training can focus and restrict a student's view of the world. He refers, by way of an example, to a personal experience in which his 'common sense' as an instructed and received interpretation of perceptual experience was suddenly challenged by a new insight.

Walking in London one day, soon after completing my Ph.D.—to be pedantic, in Welbeck Street, on the left hand pavement as you walk south—it occurred to me that the figures coming towards me were not walking objects, but fields or foci of perception. Just as they were elements in my perceptual field, so was I in theirs. Ontologically, we were all of the same status; we were all the same kind of thing. Welbeck Street was full, suddenly, not of clusters of flesh and bone in motion, but of sensation. A belated discovery to be sure; but it arrived at the time with the force of revelation.

This event led Hudson to his first reading of the works of Ronald Laing. To be noted is the fact that the experience followed a period of hard mental work, that 'it occurred' as if by some agency independently of the experiencer's intentions, that the discovery was in some sense banal, belated, obvious, yet arriving with the force of revelation and accompanied by a vivid immediacy that forced Hudson in description to place the incident with a seemingly pedantic precision in Welbeck Street on a given occasion. The episode provoked in Hudson a powerful tendency to revise his view of psychology in an increasingly humanistic perspective.

In Zen the 'flip-over' from worldliness to 'enlightenment' occurs easily once a trainee has discovered how to abandon intention. It then becomes possible to arrange the circumstances in which enlightenment experiences come about. The event is predictable, however, only if the intention to experience it is utterly abandoned. Any *intention* is an act of ego, whereas heightened *attention* need not be so. Many such experiences arise therefore unexpectedly, far from the monastery, in the train going home, walking down Welbeck Street, whenever and wherever the handle of the bucket breaks.

The great Zen patriarch Bodhidharma taught that the root of experience lay beyond the realm of the rational. He refused to allow anyone to indulge in intellectual discussion of it. He said he had brought to China:

> A special transmission outside the Scriptures,
> No dependence upon words and letters,
> Direct pointing to the soul of Man,
> Seeing into one's own nature.

It is therefore not surprising that Zen literature and philosophy are paralysingly paradoxical, and deliberately so. Even so it was Bodhidharma himself who, sensing that his death was near, handed to his chief disciple, so the legend goes, the great tomes of the *Lankavatara Sutra*. Intellectual examination of the topic is thus not precluded. Scholarship can continue. But scholarship is no path to enlightenment, only a description in pale colours of what it may comprise.

Towards a Western Zen: from theory into practice

The East, deeply troubled by the need to acquire proficiency in Western technology, is in danger of losing its traditional wisdom as the anxieties now conspicuous in the West spread there too. Japan today is a clear example. It seems quite likely that the West must discover the truths buried in the ancient Eastern practices in its own way and thus perhaps, one day, return even the East to itself.

Western understanding of consciousness (Chapter 11) and Eastern models of mind and praxis can now be related together in a broader comprehension of some of the more mysterious functions of mind. We must tread warily and with humility here, for abstract theory is so often distanced from the intuitive knowledge known only by 'masters' which is transmitted by personal contact and wordless mutual understanding.

The benefits of meditation and similar practices can be far more than a cure for incipient stomach ulcers and recurrent anxiety. We have seen enough to realize that a serious malaise of the Western world takes its root in the problems of an identity structure alienated by intellectualizing abstraction from its experiential base. This is to go further than the relatively simple distinction between a self-concerned and a task-oriented consciousness (p. 312). The tight, conceptually ruled control of self-processes based in the need for the psychological security of the ego lies at the root of the matter. Its effects are not only personal, for our politicians and governors suffer the same malaise; which is thereby transferred into the very fabric of our material culture and into our suspicion of groups of people unlike our own.

The rediscovery of 'flow' in deep play is a prime function of sport; and, as we have seen, 'flow' plays a crucial role in professional self-fulfilment. Meditation offers an opportunity for deep play involving not only the concepts but also the most profound feelings we have about life and death. The aloneness of the meditator, if he can stick it, ensures the ultimate confrontation with himself. The successful outcome of this confrontation is a profound deepening of individual selfhood so that 'flow' becomes central to all activity, both public and private. The centre of gravity has shifted from one's head to one's heart. Socially, altruism rather than egoism predominates and natural assertiveness takes the place of defensive aggression. Alienation is no more.

Fine words these—but the practical application of such ideas requires the provision of learning circumstances within which men and women can test for themselves the basically Buddhist notions of human health that seem so needed. In the West today there are numerous centres providing instruction in Eastern 'ways'. Many of these are excellent and do good work. This is especially true of those that stick closely to the simplicities of a basic psychological practice and teach the elements of meditation, be it *vipassana*, *zazen*, Tibetan, or the tantric bioenergetics of Bhagwan Shree Rajneesh. Such practices can be closely linked with Western psychotherapies of the more dynamic modern kind; neo-Reichian bioenergetics and gestalt therapy in particular. Other centres are probably more harmful than helpful. Where there is indoctrination into a view of life by means of evangelism that persuades by pressure we find the gullible trapped and the intelligent converted into exploitative persuaders. The charlatans and their converts abound.

In general the traditions of Sufism, Zen, or the Tibetan lamas cannot *in themselves* help Westerners who are bound into a cultural world that is totally unlike those which these traditions developed. The immense psychological insights of these ancient philosophies and practices need to be approached simply. It is not the frills of Lamaism—the millions of mantras, deities, buddhas, and meditational devices—that are important, but the heart of meditation in the hour of sitting together. Teachers like Lama Chögyam Trungpa (1969, 1973) are well aware of this and are devising means of instruction that are adjusted to Western difficulties and culture.

My personal concern has been to develop a Western Zen retreat suited to urban Europeans. In this 5-day event Buddhist terminology is reduced to a minimum and is replaced by common-sense psychological concepts in everyday English speech. The idea is to provide a powerful group structure that stops the habitual preoccupations of the anxious and alienated mind by dropping it sharply into meditative (subjective self-) consciousness. This is then followed by work on a *koan* using a

communication exercise devised by Charles Berner in the late 1960s
from his studies of Kapleau's (1967) accounts of the interviews given by
Zen masters on the one hand and the practice of reciprocal co-
counselling on the other.

The retreat is constructed from several components:
(1) The overall format of a Soto Zen retreat (*sesshin*)
(2) Zazen (Zen meditation)
(3) Communication exercises using a *koan*
(4) Bioenergetic and breathing exercises

The reason for collating these differing types of experience is to allow
for individual variation in response. Those who find Zazen difficult
may find the communication exercises helpful and vice versa. The
outcome of a retreat can, however, be equally effective by simply using
Zazen in a Soto Zen *sesshin* or a group process using the communication
exercises alone. Putting them together increases the power of the event
and its range in reaching a variety of persons all with differing needs.
Each component is now described in turn.

Soto Zen sesshin

In the Soto Zen sect of Japan a retreat consists of a highly disciplined
daily regime over a period of a week or more. Activities include manual
work, zazen sessions, meals, and some rituals. Silence and a strict
adherence to rules of politeness, tidyness, and consideration for others
are enforced. Progress is checked by frequent interviews with the
master. In the Western Zen Retreat this format forms the basic structure of the event which begins with simple ritual and a recital of a
contract to work together. The first two days consist in learning the
regime, instruction in Zazen, manual work, or walks and Zazen practice. Interviews are given on the evening of the first day. Subsequently
other features are introduced but the pattern of daily life and periodic
Zazen is retained.

Zazen

Zazen in Soto Zen consists in silently sitting facing a wall. Breathing
exercises, as we have seen, form an essential part of this practice and a
deep relaxation into light meditational trance in which a high degree of
unfocused alertness to the environment is maintained, is gradually
acquired. With practice, sessions of meditation become easier for participants and the focus on exercises reduced.

Communication exercises

In the Rinzai school of Zen the meditator contemplates a paradoxical
question or *Koan* the resolution of which constitutes *satori*. Charles
Berner's exercise has individuals sitting in pairs asking each other a

Koan. One person asks and the other answers for five minutes, then positions are reversed. After 40 minutes everyone takes a fresh partner and the process continues. Each group session lasts about an hour and several sessions are run each day starting early in the morning.

The traditional *Koans* such as 'What is the sound of one hand clapping?' are derived from Buddhist philosophy. In Berner's system there are four core questions which are usually worked with in a series: 'Who am I?', 'What am I?', 'What is life?', and 'What is another?' In the Western Zen retreat additional *koans* related to each of these are also used. The first one is always 'Who am I?'

In the communications exercise the questioner is required to attend alertly to all responses given by his companions but no discussion is allowed. The respondent is thus forced into a free association and a progressive outpouring of themes related to the *Koan*.

At intervals the practitioners visit the facilitator of the process and undergo a question session with him. When a *Koan* is felt to be resolved, the resolution must be presented to the facilitator for a test of authenticity.

'Answering' a *Koan* is not necessarily in itself more than a glimpse of *satori*; but it may predispose a person for a deeper non-verbal experience which accompanies or follows it, often hours or days later.

Bioenergetics
Struggling with a fundamental *Koan* and the problems involved in presenting oneself to another arouse deep feelings and resistance to expression. Self-disclosure (Jourard 1971), in itself highly therapeutic, is experienced as risky, especially when strong feelings are involved. Reichian bioenergetic exercises assist the expression of blocked emotions and thereby accelerate the occurrence of disclosures that are an essential element of progression in the communication exercise. The exercises used in the Western Zen retreat resemble neo-Reichian bioenergetics. They are based on exercises derived from traditional tantra by Bhagvan Shree Rajneesh, a contemporary Indian teacher. They consist mainly in various forms of vigorous breathing coupled with active body movement to music. Some of them are derived from the chanting meditations of Tibetan lamas.

The retreat is so programmed that an individual experiences progressive realizations of successive aspects of his own identity. Introjected identity components are released through self-disclosure often involving a great deal of emotional expression. The structure of the process makes it safe for this to happen and the authority of the facilitator is firmly maintained to ensure an essential group security. Individuals often experience relief from inhibitions and tensions, renewed confi-

dence and vitality, and sometimes a major shift in their attitude with
respect to their existence in the world.

Western approaches to Buddhism emphasize an active mode.
Berner's system and its pressure to solve the question appear especially
purposive. Yet it is only when the new Western methods are placed
within an attitudinal framework of non-pursuit that they can be said to
have made contact with the spirit of traditional Zen.

I am aware of a danger in these Western approaches that so easily
collude with the average Westerner's need for demonstrable personal
success. The intensity of Japanese Zen retreats and their Western
derivatives may produce powerful insights which in profound paradox
may yield only a subtler egoism on the rebound into normal life. It is for
this reason that the Gelugpa tradition of Tibetan Buddhism emphasizes the priority of generating compassion before wisdom. In the
Mahayana attitude, without a total dedication to the release of all
sentient beings from suffering an understanding of Buddhism is not
attained. This attitude of mind requires that all 'merit' which accrues
through any personal practice be deliberately dedicated to the task of
personal enlightenment undertaken solely in the service of others. Only
this dedication can assist the laying aside of an egoism which may
become only more deeply entrenched by spectacular insights and
meditational 'highs'. The basic training of the Gelugpa order, to which
the Dalai Lama belongs, thus emphasizes a graduated path (the *Lam
Rim*) in which the meditator reflects again and again on the suffering of
others and the sources of personal strength that can relieve them. The
whole business of 'achieving' insight is set somewhat to one side as a
potentially misleading cul-de-sac. Insights arise naturally as one walks
this path. This message is an important one for Westerners, who so
often desire to reach the end before the beginning, to acquire the powers
of meditation without hard work or the sense of responsivity to others,
and to succumb to the temptations of 'spiritual materialism' on the
strength of a single retreat.

In the *Lam Rim*, the first step is to spend months seeking to recognize
the nature of 'ignorance'. *Avijja*, ignorance, is the failure to perceive
that the whole of suffering is due to cherishing the self. What then is
emptiness? It is an emptiness of the self-cherishing process. The path of
'thought transformation' means the repeated recognition that every act
of self-concern is itself the enemy to be annihilated. Thought transformation also arises with repeated reflection on the idea that beneath a
surface egoism all human beings are essentially bearers of love and
affection; that all are as capable of compassion as one hopes oneself to
be. These reflections pave the way for an altered attitude to other
people that is the heart of the path; concentration and insight into the
self-process are means to this end and in no way ends in themselves.

Indeed the practice of taking on the sufferings of others is one of the highest activities upon which the Gelugpa teachers place great emphasis (Rabten and Dhargyey 1977).

Thich Nhat Hanh (1974), a Vietnamese Soto Zen Buddhist, clearly understands the need to abandon all ideas of achieving a personal goal when he lists the five Soto principles (my italics):

(1) It is *sufficient* to sit in meditation without a subject of meditation
(2) Sitting and awakening are not *two* things
(3) There is no need to *wait* for awakening
(4) There is no awakening to *obtain*
(5) Mind and body become *one*

Modern practices need to anchor themselves in a training that breaks the attitude of pursuit, that fosters acceptance, and encourages surrender. True meditation leads to mindfulness and gratitude. Gratitude is the amazed awareness of the universe, for is it not surprising that anything has ever happened at all? Or has it?

In stories the Zen master often concludes a dialogue by 'returning to his room'. Lu Kuan Yu (1974) interprets this as the master's return to substance after his function in teaching. The movement between substance and function comprises the life of the master: for him the movement is not between an awakened and some other state for his life has become consistent and balanced. After interaction he returns by a natural necessity to the suchness of his own being. Untroubled, yet fully concerned, the master goes his way.

It is said that at a recent conference in Japan various proposals were being put forward enthusiastically for the spreading of Zen around the world. The oldest and most revered master said nothing. On being hustled to the microphone to express his opinion he maintained silence for a long while. Finally he said, 'I don't suppose this will do much harm'—and sat down. Such impressive sanity is rarely comprehended. It does not preclude vigorous action in the world but it maintains a reflective base which most of us so readily lose.

It is important not to deny the fact that Christianity, in spite of the mess the churches seem to make of it, also has a profound existential and meditative tradition. Indeed, many of the desert fathers, the Hesychasts, Eckhardt, and the unknown English author of the *Cloud of unknowing* (Wolters 1961) clearly match the Zen and Tibetan masters in their comprehension of the depths of mind. The *Cloud* prescribes a meditative practice in which the meditator conceives himself as sitting on a mountain-top. Mist swirls before and below him. He searches for God gazing into the cloud of unknowing before him. Every concept he has of God arises one after the other, and each in turn is dropped into the cloud of forgetting that lies below him. This disidentification from all concepts of God, a profoundly apophatic process doubtless more easily understood in Athos than in Rome, clearly resembles the disidentification process involved in wrestling with 'Who am I?'. In fact the *Cloud of unknowing* makes an excellent basis for a Christian Zen retreat. Participants could work with 'Tell me what the Cross *is*?'—a theme that undoubtedly preoccupies Western Christians who are not as yet attracted by Asian thought but desperately need an experiential praxis with which to anchor their faith in a living life.

Conclusion

I have used this chapter to illustrate that in the ethogeny of persons a search for meaning is pre-eminent. This search has given rise to elaborate models of mind that attempt to explore the processes of ego-transcendence. I could, given sufficient scholarship, have treated Christianity, alchemy, or Sufism in following this theme but Buddhism seems especially important because its contemporary popularity is based on 'needs of our time' that are not dissimilar from those with which its founder worked. The explicit nature of its existential philosophy, psychological models, and training systems are an aid in exposition and an encouragement to praxis.

Yet however important self-understanding may be, its expression can be realized only in society itself. Buddhism was from the beginning involved in state-craft and, although this is rarely true today, there is no reason why improved self-understanding should not be beneficial in politics. Much meaning-making is arbitrary, bound by fantasy and egotism. Buddhism has the strength to invite a test of itself by providing training and experience within which theory may be confirmed.

In the next chapter we need to analyse not so much the ways by which personal equanimity may be discovered as the effects of 'identity' as a process operating within society. We can then attempt some concluding interpretations.

Summary
(1) While meditation is used in the modern West primarily for its utilitarian value in stress reduction, the origin of meditation systems lies at the core of the major world religions.
(2) Religions are systems of thought that give meaning to everyday lives; they are world and life interpretations maintained by the personal charisma of priests, the power of ritual, and by their relevance to cultural conditions.
(3) Religions are primarily concerned with the insecurities of life and death. The naming of terrors was one of the earliest ways by which the mind could gain control over fear. The use of names in chant and ritual

gave power to the one who chanted. Later this power was projected into images or gods that became objects of worship. Yet in time this gave rise to doubt and Man became aware of his capacity for projection and its function in protecting experience.

(4) This humanistic recognition gave rise to systems of self-exploration that lie, often esoterically, at the heart of major religions. At the present time these religions are little more than the relics of former systems of belief that have largely collapsed with the disappearance of the socio-economic structures that gave rise to them.

(5) Contemporary systems of meaning are shifting in the direction of a transpersonal humanism: a value system based on the realization that experience cannot be attributed to supernatural intervention but which rejects the acquisitive egotism at the root of the consumer society. A deeper understanding of fulfilment in life is sought.

(6) It is in this context that the ancient systems of meditative self rediscovery have been found of great value. Those of India, especially in Buddhism, have proven especially relevant and attractive to the educated and sophisticated youth of today.

(7) The origin of the Buddhist ethical and meditative system lay in the developing urban centres of northern India where rice cultivation had given rise to a socio-economic structure leading to city forma-tion. Buddha's message was in large measure in response to the urban alienation of his time. It is this that gives it especial significance now.

(8) Buddhist scholars developed extremely sophisticated models of mind. While personal growth must involve self-definition, ego-formation, and a role in life, too great an emphasis on individuation produces a defensive ego-consciousness that becomes closed to change through fear regarding its impermanence. This is 'ignorance' which can only be dispelled by an emotional re-education in which meditation plays a key role.

(9) The nature of the psychological trap in which the individual finds himself is described as the cycle of dependent origination, fully ana-lysed in the Abidhamma cannon. The trap is sprung by opposing greed, anger, and illusion in all their various aspects by activities that undo their power and reduce their occurrence. The result is mindful equanimity.

(10) Later schools of buddhism (e.g., the Mahayana) emphasized sudden awakening and their explanatory models of mind reflect this shift in emphasis. Meditative methods that almost shock the mind into self-recognition are stressed. Since thought is itself the prime cause of the mental dualism that limits self-understanding many of these teach-ings are profoundly anti-speculative and rely on paradoxical injunc-tions to provide the self with non-conceptualized realizations.

(11) Western Zen is gradually taking its own form. To ensure that a true grounding in the ancient values has been attained emphasis on non-pursuit, non-achievement, acceptance, and surrender is essential. The commercialization of the consuming ego is so deeply entrenched in the West that it needs a vigorous challenge from totally opposed values.

14 The dialectics of change

History by itself does
nothing, dear friends,
It does absolutely nothing.
                    Padilla

I began this book by expressing a deep dissatisfaction with the contemporary relations between ethology and psychology. This discontent stemmed from the failure of ethologists interested in human evolution to do more than compare animal and human features in the light of their evolutionary continuity. Few evolutionists have addressed themselves to the unique features of *Homo sapiens* although authors as different in their origins as Sir Julian Huxley and Teilhard de Chardin have stressed the view that man exists on a distinct psychosocial level of evolutionary emergence. The nature of that emergence has been little examined in spite of the wealth of non-human primate research initiated originally with the idealistic assumption that this very question would be addressed in primatology. Sociobiological theory, while extending Charles Darwin's principle of natural selection to complex social organization, remains essentially reductionistic and has so far failed to treat the existential realities of the human person.

In our attempt to specify the distinctive psychobiological attributes of the species *Homo* and the historical process of his emergence, we have followed two main lines of thought: the sequence of societal evolution and the nature of the transition from organism to person. These lines are interdependent and cannot be separated from one another. Throughout we have been concerned on the one hand with whole-animal biology in relation to social evolution and, on the other, with whole-person psychology in relation to cultural evolution.

In this chapter I attempt to draw together in an overview the main themes in a definition of humanity and to discuss some aspects of the contemporary human dilemma. I then try to locate these ideas in relation to the contemporary *Zeitgeist* in the behavioural sciences with especial reference to the marked shifts in paradigm that have influenced our view of man in the last few years and continue to show a persistent direction of change.

The biological function and progressive development of the human person

The debate concerning the unit of natural selection is of profound importance in the philosophical understanding of the biological func-

tion of the organism and, by implication, of the human person. Dawkins's (1976) focus on the particulate gene as the selected entity has
clarified an often rather confused understanding of the meaning of
function in biology. Numerous and complex problems still surround
the definition of the gene and the conditions under which it can be
treated as uniquely responsible for traits selected at the level of the
phenotype (Alexander and Borgia 1978). Even so, one may argue that
in so far as the genes determine the traits of organisms, which then
undergo differential selection so that some genes enhance their presence in a gene pool over others in successive generations, the organism
is 'nothing but' the genes' strategy to maximize their inclusive fitnesses.
This argument is a powerful case of functional reductionism; the organism is not perceived as an entity in itself but only as the instrumental
expression of evolutionary strategies of gene combinations. Likewise, in
this perspective, the human organism has no other significance than
that of expressing its properties in such a way that its genes are passed
on into successive generations.

This totally materialistic basis for life rests ultimately on an interre-
lation between the replication of certain complex chemicals, their
modifiability through an inherent instability expressed in mutation,
and their differential survival through reproductive success in an environment. Organismic life depends very much on context. Organisms
require energy from the environment for growth, maintenance, and
reproduction and need to maintain steady states in relation to fluctuations in their ecological setting. There is thus a continuous and transgenerational exchange between organisms and environment that
determines the structure and strategic properties of the living creature.

Our discussion of human cognition began with the concept that the
cognitive functions of the brain were essentially means of relating the
motivational system governing the mechanisms of metabolism and
reproduction to short-term fluctuations in the environment. Learning
is the prime example and became the means whereby innate
behaviours are adjusted to wider, more variable situations. Cognitive
dissonance theories establish that the way in which an inner representation of the world emerges is through the progressive assimilation of
novel experiences. This representation of knowledge assimilated earlier
allows behavioural adjustments to occur quickly through the recall and
use of past events.

The most distinctive emergence of cognitive capacity at the human
level concerns the development of an effective representation of objects
and events in the symbols of language; a sequence associated with the
recognition of the functioning self as an object in a world of interactive
objects; of the self as the subject for social transactions.

In several chapters we endeavoured to trace the complex and still poorly understood autocatalytic process whereby this most significant of human characteristics developed. We argued that a number of structural features of a terrestrial ape responded to climatic changes necessitating dietary shifts by enhancing the use of hands and tools and by bipedalism in the development of scavenging and hunting. Man, as a secondary carnivore, needed to parallel the co-operative hunting skills of the pack-hunting carnivores in order to exploit effectively the new protein resources open to him. The ecological shift in turn elicited societal and social changes that were linked. In particular, the dispersion of a population into small gathering units with needs for collaborative hunting seems to have precipitated bond-formation out of the more promiscuous sexual style that is characteristic of an ape such as the chimpanzee. The formation of the bonded family created problems of intergenerational sexual succession that are closely parallel to those observed in harem-forming baboons such as the gelada. In addition the use of tools and artefacts gradually introduced problems of material inheritance.

The responses to these challenges rest upon three foundations: first, emotional equilibration that allows a contractual structuring of interpersonal transactions and reciprocality; secondly, a motivational system able to compute and express an appropriate balance between the trust and distrust that are inherent in reciprocal partnering, and thirdly, the time- and space-binding properties of language, which makes it possible to rehearse the past to admit innovations of use in predictive planning for the future. In ecological (economic) exploitation, and especially in intra- and inter-group relations, these capacities are of prime importance. They became the vehicles whereby the nepotistic and reciprocal altruisms of animals were transferred into conscious awareness.

Man is above all the information-using organism who, as a result of self-reference, has become aware of his own personal role in the social process in which he participates. It is this self-awareness of unique being that leads him to attribute to his self-bounding experiencing the importance of an ultimate entity. The survival, social prestige and power, reproduction and transmission of possessions by inheritance of a person become the criterion processes whereby the good and successful or bad and unsuccessful life is judged and upon which egoistic value systems are based. From the biological point of view all this, however, is no more than the process whereby a genetic system is strategically engaged in the maximization of inclusive fitness at a high level of phenotypical complexity.

Human biostrategies are detectable in the behavioural universals of the species. The study of humanity in this light suggests that *Homo sapiens* may be characterized behaviourally and socially as follows:

(1) Sexual dimorphism and bonded polygyny entail differing reproductive strategies in men and women. In particular sexual
competitiveness and risk of cuckoldry for the human male has
produced culturally mediated behaviours that emphasize male
control of women. This is expressed in numerous aspects of
marital systems that are found repeatedly in many cultures. It
has led to a variety of kinship systems regulating marital
exchange, descent, and lineage through which familial nepotism
and personal prestige are expressed within economic systems.

(2) Reciprocation between groups turns into mutual competition,
exploitation, and conflict with increasing distance and decreasing genealogical relatedness. Communities of interrelated
families tend (a) to increase their welfare through co-operative
ecological exploitation and (b) to defend themselves against
enemies. In both cases a major enhancement of reciprocation is
required to facilitate partnership and teamwork.

(3) Since reciprocating behaviour is open to exploitation by cheating, natural selection appears to have produced an emotional
system whereby personal expression is regulated by trust or
distrust according to an elaborate monitoring of the state of play
in partnering. The evolution of this process also entailed an
intuitional ability to represent one's own motivational condition
to oneself in order to distinguish between one's own feelings and
one's responses to another person. The self-process is the
evolved outcome of this process; and its possessor, through
social education, comes to act with autonomy in effecting his
biostrategies in interaction with others. The importance of the
individual as the unit of selection at the level of the phenotype is
thus emphasized by the evolution of processes that encourage
the effective action of autonomous persons in a social world.

(4) The self-process also eventually led to objective self-
consciousness. This enables an individual to assess his standing
on scales of social comparison with others, and leads to positive
or negative experiences of self-esteem. Man's inherent existential anxiety seems to be rooted in this focus on the monitoring of
identity constructs in social comparison. Our argument demon-
strates that this subtle and continuous process of evaluation is
based in the ancient strategies of reciprocal altruism.

The prime consequence of language is the transformation of information from one generation to the next so that successful techniques for
ecological exploitation can be utilized by the young and successive
innovations can be accumulated progressively through the years. Cultural innovation was a new form of socio-ecological adaptation based
on the ability to transmit information between generations.

Kinship systems vary with ecology, and whereas hunter–gatherers remain largely egalitarian the emergence of agriculture allowed economic power to accumulate more in certain descent lines than in others. The basis for an economic 'contradiction' or have–have not tension was thus created quite early in human societies and has remained present through the emergence of archaic civilizations and into contemporary modern states.

We argued too in Chapter 7 that ethical rules governing relations between individuals and groups did not develop in an historically arbitrary manner but reflected closely the nature of the economic and political structure. Economic demography, like ecological demography, is influenced by the relation between numbers and the turnover of resources. Under economic conditions analogous to those described as r conditions of ecology one can predict individualistic, entrepreneurial, exploitative ethics; under K conditions ethics emphasizing altruism are more likely to have evolved. Indeed, this latter principle is likely to underline the history of the religious systems that legitimated the major civilizations of the medieval period. Of course there have been enormous surface fluctuations that tend to obscure the underlying principles.

The human person was doubtless fully constituted by the time the later hominids were gathering and hunting on the African plains. This is not to say, however, that men and women viewed themselves then in anything like the way we do now. It is clear from tribal studies and from the writings of the early Greek or Indian civilizations that people have conceived themselves differently in successive historical periods, and that the structure of their identity attribution has varied and shown development within history from a more diffuse to a highly individuated condition.

In terms of capacities or powers the human organism has the following personal attributes:

(1) Self-recognition and a bimodality of consciousness showing trends towards differing degrees of objective and subjective self-awareness;

(2) A structural division of the psyche into a more and a less conscious part based on the inhibitive effect of motivational balancing during the long period of childhood. The child inhibits angry responses to powerful parental figures, and a habit of inhibition is commonly produced. The human being has the capacity to withstand such inner pressures, which appear to be an inevitable aspect of the ambivalent mother–child association. Repression of feelings creates an 'unconscious' reservoir of emotional associations that colour in highly disguised ways the relationships that young people form with elders and peers. The

capacity to repress some aspects of motivational expression rather than others accounts for the diversity of human 'personality'.

(3) Human persons conceptualize themselves in relation to other people they know. Their identity concepts may be positively or negatively evaluated. A need to maintain self-esteem is often an important motivating force in a person's social relations with others and may determine his maintenance or achievement of positions in society.

(4) Values taken over from society and impulses involving unconscious motivation can be most misleading guides for personal conduct. The growing person of necessity attempts to balance reality against fantasy. This balancing function Freud located in the 'ego'. A strong ego has established a workable relationship between the 'unconscious' and those conscious but not always clearly comprehended constructions of his own identity. The 'ego' enables individuals to relate together with a degree of stability and integrity. A weak ego functions poorly in these respects. The achievement of personal autonomy through a realistic appraisal of oneself and others is an important criterion of adult life.

While these 'powers' are of great antiquity, it is again important to emphasize that the way in which they have operated at different stages in human history is relative to the nature of the society and the child-rearing practices of the time.

It seems clear that the achievement of a balanced adulthood for either man or woman is not a foregone conclusion. The development of the adult person may be moulded to an extraordinary degree by circumstances of birth, by economic and social conditions, and by the influence of other personalities, quite apart from initial contrasts in natural endowment. The social and reproductive success of a human being perhaps depends far more on fortune in social life than it does on genetics.

Since this is the case, the predictive capacity of the genetic constitution with respect to the success of reproductive strategies would appear to be more in doubt in man than in other less flexible creatures. It is important to emphasize here that so far as man is concerned it is the *capacity* to behave rather than *behaviour* itself that has been stressed by natural selection. This important point for the study of man perhaps needs further elucidation.

Biological factors that are ultimately of genetic origin may pattern human interactions within a limited number of dimensions, of which dominance–submissiveness and openness–closedness to another (i.e. approach–withdrawal, love–hate, warmth–coldness, etc.) are likely to be pre-eminent and to be modulated in various ways by gender differences in endocrinology and conditioning.

The consequences of these patterns of interaction are structured relationships arranged in the hierarchical tiers that eventually become the subject-matter of the anthropologist and sociologist. Yet, as one ascends these tiers, for example from family to village structure to community life to government, the information that programmes the structure at each level and maintains the process operates with further interacting dimensions to produce ordered relations that are quite independent of those of the lower level, although still constructed from elements that are important there. This can only mean that biosocial evolution has created superordinate societal structures that encompass the individual as an environment to which (as to an ecology, indeed) he contributes and of which he is a part. These societal structures undergo processes of historical change that are contingent upon shifts in both economic and sociopolitical dimensions, but the unit of which they are made, the human person, remains relatively invariant. While the behaviour of persons adapts and changes, the structure of the person is the product of the biological evolution of personal powers.

This concept carries the further implication that natural selection may have adapted the attributes to the human person to his society and may still be taking place in the same way that organisms adapt to their environments. The human animal is adapted primarily to a culture that was itself originally an expression of the adaptation of *Homo sapiens* to environmentally labile parts of the world's surface. Material and social culture is the life-support system for the human organism, be it at Timbuktu, in Novosibirsk, or on the Moon, and this culture has been in existence long enough to have had some feedback effects on the organism that created it. Cultural economy is the buffer between the human organism and its unpredictable ecology.

The human person thus exists within a set of organizational tiers, each constructed from the materials of that below it, but each to a large degree independent from the others as processes. These tiers relate together much as does a box of self-enclosing Russian dolls. A vital question then concerns the interfaces between these tiers. Even the way in which our sciences are partitioned into biology, psychology, and sociology suggests that while we can carry out effective analyses at each process level, we encounter severe conceptual difficulties at the interfaces. These problems are possibly not a matter of historical chance but represent real discontinuities in structural organization that are more difficult to handle analytically than are process operations that have become defined at distinctly identified levels.

The emergence of civilizations with elaborated infrastructures entails especially difficult problems of understanding. In such organizations individuals no longer occupy single roles according to relatively simple rules of kinship and reciprocality. There are many interwoven roles for each individual and these occur in different organizational tiers. Ours is not the only civilization to have become aware of the severe problems of alienation that multiple roles impose on the human person. Ours is, however, perhaps the only civilization in which the speed of change in both role occupancy and in the structure of society itself has been so challengingly fast. This problem particularly concerns the interfaces between levels of personal identification in contrasting realms of life. To this then we shall now pay some attention.

Social identity: the interface of societal and personal processes

A set of identity constructs that each person entertains concerns his perceived membership of social groups or factions. Here we are not speaking so much of small face-to-face groups of long or short establishment but rather of groups the cohesion of which depends upon an idea. Such groups include train-spotters clubs, weekend sailors, bird-watchers, the Winchester Townswomen's Guild, the National Front, Welsh Wales, Great Britain, Israel, the United States. Each of these collective entities is of value to its members more from the idea it constitutes for them than from any other aspect, its geographical reality say. The part of one's self that subscribes, say, to an old girls' club or the Campaign for Homosexual Equality and is disturbed by the phrase 'Little England' is called one's 'social identity'. It plays a major role in each person's orientations and motivations in civilized society. It underlies Emerson's (1960) assertion that 'The simplest statement that can be made about a nation is that it is a body of people who feel that they are a nation'. While some contemporary nations seem more 'tribal' than others (Russia and Germany, for example), countries like Britain and Ethiopia, comprising many different ethnic or tribal factions that have become part of the national fabric over many years, clearly owe their unity to a guiding set of ideas that, not always without interior contradictions, make up the collective identity. The United States flag, with all the ceremonies that attend it, symbolizes the same kind of idea and evokes that aspect of social identity that pertains to US citizenship.

Members of a social group exist when they categorize themselves with a high degree of consensus in an applicable manner, and are likewise categorized in the same way by others who are not members. Such a consensus represents the psychological aspect of social reality that interacts with the political and economic events that determine intergroup relations and consequently, in large measure, inter-individual relations too.

In recent years Tajfel and his colleagues at Bristol University have elaborated a valuable descriptive analysis of the relations between social identity and historical events (Tajfel 1978). This analysis hinges upon the relationship between a set of closely linked concepts: social categorization, social identity, social comparison, and relative deprivation. The particular relations obtaining between these factors results in one of two outcomes: social mobility or social change.

In order to place themselves conceptually in a multiplex community individuals utilize their natural categorizing abilities to define their membership or non-membership of perceived groupings among their fellows. The process of categorization itself tends to sharpen perceived contrasts between categories, even to the extent that criteria for boundaries are often created when these are far from prominent or even relevant. Thus, for reasons that are historical and culturally received, a brown skin becomes a powerful boundary-marker while brown eyes do not. These judgements concerning arbitrary physical and social stimuli cease to be merely neutral when social categorization is intimately linked with a differentiation of values attributed to the categories concerned. Neutral characteristics come to mark social groups by virtue of the social values attributed to these groups by their members or by those who do not participate in them. Social categorization provides individuals with a system of orientation in the social world. The individual realizes himself in society to the extent that he recognizes his identity in socially defined and socially functional terms (Berger and Luckmann 1966).

One of the surprising findings of the research of Tajfel and his group concerns the minimal conditions necessary for inter-group discrimination. In one experiment a group of schoolboys was led to divide into two sections, each merely indicating a preference for one painter (as shown in colour slides) over another. The boys were later found to distribute small monetary awards among themselves in ways that reflected an in-group preference, even when this preference reduced the total sum available to the boys as a whole. It seems that quite small criteria are used to create distinctions between 'us' and 'them' and that these distinctions arise very easily and naturally in any group. Encounter group facilitators, for example, know the powerful inter-group effects they can create by dividing a group into two or more portions for as little as an hour, even when such a division is not created to arouse inter-group antagonism. When inter-group antagonism is deliberately aroused, as in the famous experiments of Sherif and Sherif (1973), the effects in the community concerned are deep and far-reaching.

While social psychologists may be uncomfortable with the suggestion, ethologists may well be tempted to see a possibly universal trait in this facility for in-group formation among human beings. It seems plausible that among the sociobiological rules that structure groups convened from a population of humans there could be one that brings about a close in-group loyalty, which in turn readily triggers out-group suspicion and antagonism. The functional value of such a tendency can be seen intuitively in the need for operational and emotional cohesion in small groups, especially hunting parties of young men, in the earliest days of hominid history.

In modern society this trait generalizes from actual face-to-face groups to notional groups; that is to say, to groups that exist for ideological reasons but rarely meet in their entirety as such (see Crook in press *b*). Such groups are better referred to as *factions* in society, which may or may not have some form of codified contractual membership as such. Welsh Welshmen may or may not enlist in some society to promote independence for Wales or the Welsh language, but all in some measure share powerful feelings of affectionate loyalty to 'Wales'.

Tajfel and his colleagues argue that the recognition of personal identity in socially defined terms (i.e. social identity) has a number of consequences that are of great importance in the structuring of events in modern society. Individuals may evaluate the group within which they categorize themselves either positively or negatively. If participation in a group or faction does not contribute positively to an individual's totality of identity constructs (Horrocks and Jackson 1972), he will tend to leave it and to seek membership of a different faction that will confer a more positively valued social identity.

All groups or factions interact in a modern society, but the extent to which an individual can move from one social identity to another varies according to a complex set of contextual relationships. Changing a social identity may be impossible for 'objective' reasons. For example, while a Welshman can acquire a better command of English than many Englishmen and hence be unrecognizable in an English cultural setting, the same is never possible for a man whose skin is black or whose eyes are shaped by a Mongolian fold. Changing a social identity may, however, be difficult for other, 'deeper' reasons. It may, for example, conflict with important values, including those involved in concepts of loyalty or honour. If changing his social status to improve his salary or his prestige conflicts with other values in this way, an individual is likely to rationalize his membership so as to justify remaining a member or, alternatively, to justify abandoning former fellows. It is also possible for him to accept a social identity, even if it is negatively evaluated, and to work to change the evaluation in which the faction is held by a wider public.

The decision to shift or not to shift a social identity is dependent upon a process of social comparison. The evaluation of oneself, *vis-à-vis* another, is paralleled by the evaluation of the group to which one subscribes in relation to other factions in society. 'A group becomes a group in the sense of being perceived as having common characteristics or *a common fate* mainly because other groups are present in the event' (Tajfel 1978; my italics). A common fate may be one of inferiority (and hence relative deprivation on an economic or some other scale of prestige and social opportunity) or one of superiority, again either in an economic sense or in terms of social opportunities. The vital point here is that it is the perception of a relative deprivation that is likely to start an individual on a course that either changes his social identity or engages him in social activity that changes the social situation of his group on the scale upon which it is seen to be deprived. The first course of action involves *social mobility* and the second *social change*.

Individuals become socially mobile when the barriers to movement between categorizable groups in a society are either absent or low. One may argue that the whole ethos of the Unites States of America hinges about the notion that a man who works hard will rise from a relatively deprived condition to one in which he has access to the goods of this world, perhaps to an unprecedented degree. Indeed, the history of the USA contains many remarkable examples; some heroic, some not. In principle, conditions that allow social mobility are those of 'freedom' in the sense that the capitalistic Western world uses the term. One of the effects of such freedom is that antagonisms between factions do not often reach an organized or violent level because those who experience dissatisfaction are able quite simply to change their social identity. Needless to say, there remain countless numbers of people in these societies who, for whatever reason, are unable to change the socio-economic circumstances of their lives and are thus stuck within their social identities while being 'deserted' by those climbers who move out into wider pastures and who could, by their very ability, do something for their fellows. It is indeed in recognition of this fact that (primarily through the efforts of trades unions) welfare states of varying degrees have come into being, so that gross inequalities of wealth and prestige no longer so easily arise.

Under circumstances where barriers to changes in social identity are high because mobility is denied (i.e., under conditions of racial prejudice or political oppression the perception of deprivation is increased together with a sense of in-group loyalty and the desire for social action leading to change. These are the conditions under which communities led by effective leaders agitate for change. In relatively open conditions of parliamentary democracy these agitations may bear fruit so that the sense of deprivation is diminished and the community rises in status within the population as a whole. A negative evaluation of the identity then changes its sign; black becomes beautiful.

Sometimes, however, the agitation may concern matters which the democracy by its nature cannot handle, a resolution being beyond the control of the government concerned. For example, the case of the South Moluccans in Holland seems unresolvable within the Netherlands, and the aspirations of the group need to be reformulated in the direction of fresh conceptions of their identity within Europe.

In extreme cases of social agitation revolutionary movements may be created as the only alternative to continuing oppression. Led by a charismatic leader, Martin Luther King for example, a movement may become an important crusade which enhances the principles of the rights of men and women, not only of the community in revolt, but throughout the world. Problematic cases arise when the revolutionary movement is that of a minority, or concerns the preservation of traditional freedoms by small peoples. Over such issues bodies such as the United Nations necessarily dispute and rarely come to conclusions that can appear just to all.

As Tajfel points out, 'relative deprivation' is essentially a failure in expectancies which can become a variable in social behaviour independently of a material or economic base. Expectancies are often contradictory in nature and operate at many levels in a social structure. The sense of relative deprivation is maintained so long as expectancies that are unfulfilled are supported by a sense of their legitimacy. A farm labourer may not expect to own a Rolls-Royce, for he recognizes certain realities of social stratification and ability as legitimate. He may expect, however, that his son will have the right to such social mobility that his talents and interests lead him to expect. Both son and father would sense the illegitimacy of a situation in which social mobility were prevented by reasons of skin colour or linguistic usage. In fact, it will be the sense of illegitimacy in such a situation that will generate social categorizations enhancing the boundedness of an individual's social identity.

In this context it is often the statements of politicians that, by revealing prejudice, enhance the social comparison, the sense of relative deprivation, and hence the distinctiveness of social identity of minority groups, irrespective of the truth or falsity of their actual socio-economic opportunities. Expectancies arise from comparisons, and comparisons arise from differentials that may be based on almost any distinguishable property or attribute of one group compared with another. The process of history largely consists in the mobilities and changes that are both the responses to social comparison and the factors that generate it.

The perceived illegitimacy of an intergroup relationship is thus socially and psychologically the accepted and acceptable lever for social action and change in intergroup behaviour. It is most often a shared perspective on the social world, actual or potential . . . it provides a basis for the . . . ideologising of arousal, discontent or frustration (and) the basis for their translation into . . . the achievement or the preservation of . . . psychological group distinctiveness. (Tajfel 1978.)

In the case of 'inferior' groups perceived illegitimacy legitimates the sense of deprivation and the urge to action; in groups already undergoing change it justifies the alterations in society that have begun; and in 'superior' groups it legitimates the defence of a *status quo* seen to be under threat.

A sense of grievance can arise from almost any disparity between either individuals or groups. It introduces a pressure into any system within which it arises, and socially it comprises the substance of 'contradictions' in society. The resolution of grievances is a matter for negotiation, and the context of these negotiations is at a higher structural level than the grievance itself. The rules for changing the rules comprise the ideologies that define the varying styles of government in the modern world.

Values: sociopolitical contradictions and the hope for a world community

Grievances between factions are settled within a governmental structure that is legitimated in modern states, not by organized religions, but by the social application of ethical values to which the population subscribes or, in totalitarian states, with which the people are forced to concur.

There is a substantial agreement about the 'rights' of man matched only by the equally substantial disagreement about the how and where of their implementation. These 'rights' have a history and since they provide the criteria whereby rules governing the relations between social factions are judged it is important to consider them here, if only briefly.

The ethical sense of human beings would appear to have its sociobiological roots in the nepotistic and reciprocal altruism of primate species. These traits are very old and form part of evolutionary stable strategies, doubtless with a genetic basis. At an early hominid level one can imagine human beings to have become gradually aware of the rules operating within their social systems and to have structured these in a loosely codified way in linguistic injunctions. The 'may' and 'may not', 'can' and 'cannot', 'ought' and 'ought not', 'should' and 'should not' aspects of the verb began to be expressed in interpersonal regulations of behaviour. At the same time the expansion of cultural over biological determinants of action meant that as grievances arose new codifications of propriety came into being.

It seems likely that the expansion of the ethical sense within the guidelines of the original biological prescription has been purely with respect to the inclusiveness of the target groups concerned rather than in gross changes in value or behaviour. We see here once more a stress in hominid evolution on the selection for a capacity or power to adumbrate social rules and social group definitions within very old and primitive guidelines rather than a selection for the details of behaviours themselves.

The increase in the complexity of social systems in the series from hunter–gatherers through tribal organizations to civilizations is correlated with an increase in the guarantees required to provide social security and satisfaction to individuals. This means both an increase in the specificity of detailed rules for grievance settlement and a generalization to principles that apply to all citizens irrespective of differentiation in ethnic, linguistic or caste terms. Vine (1977) argues that the increase in the target audience for principles of right (i.e. law) is the chief feature of the cultural evolution of moral thought. He points out that the value of life attributed to fellow human beings has increased down the ages. Thus cannibalism of out-group members, the human sacrifice of prisoners, killing in torture of captives, and slavery of the defeated have disappeared and infanticide and ill-treatment of children reduced. Even today, however, under conditions of prejudice, conflict, or social change members of out-groups may still be depersonalized or even dehumanized in the minds of their adversaries and then treated with humiliating psychological or physical brutality.

Kohlberg (1969) has argued that the development of moral thought in the child can be matched against stages of cultural evolution in ethical thinking. In both cases the direction of change is from an equating of life-worth with values of physical or social status towards a general principle of the universal sacredness of human life. With this trend go the specific rights to which each human being should ideally be entitled. Essentially these generalized rights are recognizably similar to those that commonly obtain between close kin. This can only mean that in civilized people there is a tendency to recognize any fellow human being as a member of the same family.

We also argued that in cultures under K conditions gerontocratic imposition of altruistic ethics is likely. We can now see how this can serve both the biological fertility and the social security of individuals in a state. This principle could become so universal as to apply to the global population as a whole. In that altruism would then be no longer a discriminating but a generalized rule of action, the distinction between nepotistic, reciprocal, and 'real' altruism would cease to have much significance in a culturally altruistic world community. Altruism here functions to preclude ungovernable discord and it is backed by powerful legal sanctions!

This view of a global law, embracing altruism as a key concept and structured for settling inter-group grievances according to principles of agreed fairness, is an obvious requirement of civilized life at the present time. The human community with its conspicuous overconsumption of the last hundred years faces a severe limitation in resources. The Earth as a whole is approaching its carrying capacity, which, on the exhaustion of fossil fuels, will in fact decrease. Not only do we need to utilize resources to discover how to tap extra-terrestrial energy but we need to envisage how life can be governed without excessive personal distress during a period of K circumstances on a global scale.

In particular, the gross differences in standards of living between the industrially developed and 'Third World' nations and the communication blockage between the advanced communist and Western democratic powers are such blatant contradictions in the face of universal human needs that further social change on a world-wide scale is inevitable.

Movement towards a global socio-economic interdependence between peoples on principles of equity under law is prevented by the narrowness of political conceptions engraved in the thinking of power-block governments. One aspect of this is the continuing conflict between the value system of a historical origin in the colonialist, expansionist 'frontier' spirit of Europe on the one hand and its reciprocal, the socialist struggle for the rights of working and colonized people, on the other.

Capitalism emphasizes the value of individualism, free enterprise through personal initiative, hard work, and free exploitation of seemingly endless resources. The result, at an extreme, is maximum competition between individuals and factions with an extreme inequity in the distribution of resources and standards of living. New York is the prime example. There is minimal development of an adequate taxation system to provide social welfare and the protection of the disadvantaged and minority groups. Since social mobility of the talented is encouraged and possible there remains an unskilled residue at the bottom of society who in personal defeat and moral despair take to drugs, drink, and arson to enliven their lives.

At the other extreme, in the totalitarian communist world, well-developed state-organized exploitation of resources distributes standards of living more equitably and prevents the taking of competitive initiatives that result in some persons making fortunes at the expense of others. However, an excessive governmental control over the aspirations of people produces a growing personal alienation from a mechanical system which severely limits individuals and allows the expression of certain grievances while suppressing others.

Both systems have their positive values and both their limitations. Each expends a fortune on arming itself to deter attack by the other. If such an attack developed the likely outcome would be the total destruction of world civilization. Upon this monumental inability to risk trust the future of the human race rests suspended. On an enormous scale we have here the working out of comparison, perceived legitimacy, and social change between vast collectivities of persons who in substantial degree share opposed and indoctrinated social identities. For such a dispute there is no court of appeal except a return to an examination of the nature of the human dilemma itself.

While Marx lacked psychological subtlety and the Maharishi lacks an understanding of socio-economics there is no reason why the polarities symbolized by these two names should not meet. While the world's economics are under treatment the capacity of individuals to withstand social pressure, changes in standards of livung, and alterations in value-judgements will be tested to a limit. The need to comprehend the nature of personal involvement in social movements based in social identity will be especially great.

The women's liberation movement has given us the idea of 'consciousness-raising'. It means becoming aware of social issues in a deeply involved and responsibly personal way in which an understanding of self is related to an understanding of others, both individually and collectively. Consciousness-raising is crucial to the problem of the individual man and woman in relation to the pressures of our time.

In particular the relativity of standards of living needs examination. People can be truly happy living under quite primitive conditions, under the rather poor conditions of Eastern Europe, or under the wealthy condition of Western Europe and the USA. Happiness is not necessarily correlated with standards of living. So long as basic human needs are satisfied and opportunities for creative work are possible, men and women can be happy. We do not need to provide every world citizen with the consumptive power of the middle-class north American white. Instead, by population control and a just distribution of resources, a balance between a satisfaction of needs and opportunities for a creative individual life could one day be met.

Happiness depends upon attitude. Where needs are met and opportunities for self-expression and creativity are available, happiness is precluded only by the operation of greed, pride, and illusion. Greed is the asking for more than one's fair share; pride is thinking oneself more important and deserving of more power than others; and illusion involves the failure to understand the relation between the self-process and the social process. It is no accident that these three aspects of egotism fill the central hub of the Tibetan Wheel of Life, that teaching document which, in iconic form, portrays the passage of the human mind from hell to an illusory heaven and back again. An understanding of these forces at a deep level is almost completely neglected in world education systems. A world education system that focuses upon the problematical and paradoxical nature of the human self as well as the socio-economic state of mankind is urgently needed.

In this book we have attempted to trace the evolutionary and cultural history of the human person in his or her close dependence upon the emergence of forms of society. In particular we have discussed the determinants of the human personality, consciousness, and sense of identity as the three elements that are basic to understanding the self-process that comprises each one of us. It is my belief that these subjects, together with active emotional education and experiential acquaintance with the effects of meditation, should form the roots of a reformed educational system to which the study of the exploitative sciences that power the world economy are then appended. If we learn the elements of world citizenship at school, the chances of producing leaders less tainted with their own cultural and political assumptions and more open to the possibilities of a mutual understanding between peoples will gradually be increased. It is not impossible: we have had great men. Perhaps if we took Dag Hammarskjöld (1964) as a first exemplar we would not be going far wrong.

Dialectics in the behavioural sciences

The great turnabout in biopsychology produced by the revolution in cognitive studies initiated by Chomsky and the linguists has a major bearing on the development of behaviour study. As yet not many academics have become aware of the shifting sands in which psychology now stands and the extent of the changes in basic paradigms that are under way yet far from completed.

In brief, the change is from a reductionist to a dialectical view of explanation in the behavioural sciences. In a reductionist view, terms that once referred to processes become easily reified into static principles and the old desire to model psychology in the fashion of classical physics remains. In a dialectical view, the terms used in explanation reflect a dynamic opposition of forces operating to create change through time, and these terms thereby become subject to change themselves. Truth in such a system is necessarily relative; the underlying principle is the flux of Heraclitus rather than the constructed world of Aristotle. In a less marked degree, the same change has been occurring with the application of systems analysis in biology and in ethology. Indeed, as the movement gathers strength, it becomes easier to topple the old barricades between the classically defined sciences and to work in the intermediate domains. This is because the patterning of thought and expectations regarding the types of explanation that one may use are becoming less bound by the metaphysical scholasticisms of the sciences of the first half of the century.

In particular, dissatisfaction with the predominance of the behaviourist approaches and conceptions of psychology which have ruled so much of American thought in the behaviour sciences since the First World War is today leading to wider consideration of the more conceptually elaborated and philosophically explicit theories already developed in Europe. In particular, structuralist, existentialist, and dialectical materialist approaches have deepened recent American thinking to an almost revolutionary degree (Riegel 1975). One of the effects of this shift is that psychology has now left the safe harbours of English empiricism (Locke, Hume) for the barely plumbed oceanic depths of Hegelian and post-Hegelian thought. Here indeed is a turn-about that must be quite disturbing to many working scientists: so much so that some further spelling out of its meaning is important here.

Science developed out of metaphysical thought which structured the world in metaphorical formulations and principles in which categories were applied abstractly and with an exclusion of their opposites. Modern empiricism often remains enslaved by uncritically fixed categories. In discussing concrete phenomena the finite and the particular are discussed rather than the process; the law rather than the context. 'Empiricism continues to refer the complex objects of experience to general categories of thought . . . involving the abstract principles of formal logic. The world is viewed as an aggregate of things juxtaposed to one another in space and succeeding one another in time' (Lawler 1975). In psychology the 'black box' construct invited the discovery of fixed laws relating stimulus and response under controlled conditions and produced easily reified constructs such as drive and specifications of behavioural determination intended to hold for all time and all species. The metaphysical consequence of this empiricism is clear enough (Hudson 1972). So too, in classical ethology, the hydraulic model of motivation led to reifications of 'instinct' under a plethora of fixed terms for what are actually process variables (Lehrmann 1953). Other reifications of process terms embedded in metaphysical empiricist theories are IQ and concepts of the racial fixity of human potential, supposedly on ethnic and biological grounds.

By contrast the post-Hegelians, who in particular included the important Marxist philosophers of the Frankfurt School, focused on the way in which a set of empiricist terms tended in time to generate their 'opposites'. Indeed, the case of learning theory within the Behaviourist tradition is itself a fine example of this principle, as the relations between the scholasticisms of B. F. Skinner, Clark Hull, and Edward Tolman so beautifully show. Engels himself argued that although analytical abstraction is a vital element in science it is, as it were, but a moment in a conceptual progression. The concepts that result from analytical categorization tend to become isolated from the phenomena they describe, seen as 'detached from the whole vast interconnection of things; and therefore not in their motion, but in their repose; not as essentially changing, but as fixed elements; not in their life, but in their death' (Engels 1966, p. 2).

Clearly in experimental science the empiricists' formulation of explanatory theory must freeze the phenomena in a 'momentariness' of explanation. And, indeed, science would not progress without the difficult acquisition of data and the construction of 'metaphysical' models. Yet the increasing use of systems-analytical methods is moving even the 'hardest' sciences in the direction we are discussing here.

The benefit of a dialectical approach lies in its wider comprehension of the relativity of 'fundamental' ideas in themselves and their relationship to the style of experimentation and patterns of thought of the time. Thus, although Piaget's stages of intellectual development in children are dynamically conceived, it has now been shown that they are relative to the cultural context in which a child grows. In particular the final stage, the concrete operational, is particularly characteristic of Western middle-class children and this can be interpreted as linked to their comprehension of a modern society's economic structure (see Buck-Morss 1975). There is thus a dilemma for educators in the developing countries, where children do not commonly exhibit this stage, as to whether to promote it or not. It relates to economic changes which, while they may link the 'emerging' country to the industrial world, do not in themselves imply any beneficial change in the well-being of individuals except in a materialistic sense. Since the values and the future of the current type of industrial society are in question, the answer to this problem is less obvious than might be thought.

Perhaps the most forward of dialectical psychologists, Klaus Riegel (1975) focuses on the value of analysing short-term dialectical exchanges in development; the mother–child system of transactions, the social–personal dialogue in character development, and longer-term developmental changes such as the interpersonal effects of different timings and directions in the careers of husbands and wives. The dialectical approach emphasizes continuing changes brought about by the contradictions between the interacting processes that are operating and it provides explication in terms of an analytical understanding of those contradictions, their nature, their outcome, and their transmutation into new situations in which other contradictions arise.

More generally Riegel argues for an analysis of the relations between levels of determination in temporal sequences of development. As we have seen, the interpretation of human behaviour requires an understanding of several interdependent levels of process, each one of which makes use of elements of other levels but within which the forces operating are distinct. Riegel considers the asynchronies that arise in developmental processes at the biological, personal, cultural, and environmental levels of determination and the crises or catastrophes that result from an asynchrony of development between 'programmes' on different levels. The study of the interactions between levels replaces research that relies for the most part only on one analytical level. The resolution of contradictions between levels produces a cessation of conflict that parallels the synthesis that arises from the meeting of thesis and antithesis. The resulting position is not, however, to be conceived as static, for new forces in conflict or in asynchrony will already be arising.

As a descriptive and philosophical orientation the dialectical approach is a powerful one. It does not displace empirical experimentation and analysis of particular processes and questions in science, but it provides such studies with a contextual structure that will tend to preclude the defence of scholasticistic positions beyond a period of reasonable time. It will accelerate the progression of ideas.

The types of temporal change discussed in this book, (1) biological evolution by natural selection, (2) sociobiological evolution of behaviour systems in non-human organisms, (3) the origin and evolution of self-reference and the emergence of the person, (4) the cultural progression in human history, and (5) socio-economic history, are all as open to this approach as are analyses of ontogeny in both animal and human behaviour. The transactional nature of historical change has been emphasized throughout this text: organism–environment, group-structure–ecology, economy–ecology, person–person, person–cultural grouping, identity–social-identity. Transactional analyses are of necessity dialectical in form, although at times in their development they may be institutionalized temporarily in a metaphysical position (classical ethology, behaviourism, social-learning theory). Such a position will, however, contain within itself conceptual contradictions that a closer analysis of terms, meanings, usages and metaphor will reveal. This book can be seen as a representative of this particular movement in the thought of our time.

It is therefore important to note that this way of thinking is itself a product of the predominant sociocultural–economic condition of our period. The rapid changes in industrial life, the 'future shock' that social change engenders, the multiplicity and short duration of many roles that people perform, all focus upon a dialectic of transactions in process and person alike.

It is perhaps no accident that dialectical thinking first came to the fore in practical as opposed to philosophical psychology in the early years of the Soviet Union. To a Western reader it feels strange to find important contemporary orientations being expressed vividly in the past writings of Engels, Lenin, and Mao as well as by leading psychologists in the Russia of the 1920s (Wozniak 1975). The historical context in the great class upheaval of that period is very evident. The present context in a crisis of over-population and diminishing energy resources is no less apparent.

Dialectics and equanimity in life

A number of features of contemporary Western life are profoundly disturbing to individuals. There is more to this than the conventional emphasis on the stress and hassle of modern city life, the pressures of office work, the status and salary competition in commerce, and the overarching threat of atomic destruction. To some extent all these problems have been with us before, although admittedly not to the same degree. The sophisticated court life, intrigue, and status-consciousness of ancient China led the poet Po Chü I to dream of the hills and a simple peasant life (Waley 1949). These have been aspects of civilization ever since cities with multiple roles and divisions of labour were invented. The very complexity of modern urban life makes comprehension difficult, and evasion, the failure to confront issues with commitment, easy. People want comfort and words are easily provided. Action is more problematical.

It is in the particular quality of contemporary alienation that the deepest roots of the malaise lie. The speed of change in the meanings individuals attribute to life itself has resulted in an almost total absence of those old legitimations of life and praxis that were the constants of traditional societies. Science has replaced religion with the scholastic metaphysics of an empiricism which, as in contemporary physics itself, leads to no certainty. The great unknown, like an abyss, yawns before the inquirer. The dark satanic mills of Newtonian science have melted into the void. Theology, too, retreating into parallel abstractions, or existentialist visions of despair in some way blessed in the experiencing, no longer provides the simple heart with the meaning of what lies before it. Birth, copulation, and death, no longer sanctified, become the stages of a mechanical life. The ultimate in abstraction is the concept of man as the genes' way to inclusive fitness. The metaphors in Dawkins's expression of theory remain unanalysed and, as it stands, the abstraction can provoke feelings of utter personal insignificance in which the enjoyment of human libido can become distanced from its fruition.

A common response to such alienation is the development of an attitude, all too common today, in which the ruling emptiness of meaning is hidden behind a false hedonism, a gross consumption of the riches of this earth, and a gentle submergence into an old age of tranquilized passivity. The ego, paralysed before a realization of nonentity and insignificance, reinforces itself in a pretence of comfort and a 'good life'.

Faced by the challenge of his own insignificance an individual experiences deep existential anxiety. For a time in the late 1960s and early 1970s the pressures of American life (Vietnam, civil rights, the questioned morality of a commercial military complex, Maslow, Marcuse, and all that) generated a grass-roots concern with identity and personal values. In those almost incredible years in California men and women took enormous risks in the service of knowing, in the search for personal realization. Today that courage has gone; the anxiety is once again too big to face, the new techniques are back in the hands of the professionals. The growth 'industry' has institutionalized itself. 'Doctor save me!' is the cry. But the doctors travel in the same boat and the young journey to desert lands to seek the gurus of a decaying world.

Only through crisis can an individual apprehend change and the resistance to change. Seeking stability and security, men and women resisting change come to inhibit their own growth. Vivian Clayton (1975) asks 'Where are the wise men?' Erikson's theory of human development argued that in the last stage of life the individual faces the emergence or submergence of the final ego strengths that build integrity and individuation: love, care, and wisdom. The choices are between intimacy or isolation, generativity or stagnation, and integrity or despair. It remains unclear to Clayton whether this is an idealistic conceit: whether contemporary individuals ever face the last crises of individuation or are even prepared to do so.

Clayton points out that we live in an era that (in the USA at least) cannot provide the elderly person with a feeling of either continuity or value. Tradition, which used to allow a sense of a lifetime's wholeness, is no more. Not only are the old segregated, isolated even, without communication with the young, but life-styles and attitudes change so rapidly between generations that the very roots of their stance in life is eroded by history before they die. An old person may be fit and well but the world he lives in is no longer a world he knows or really understands. The rising generation cannot receive whatever wisdom the old may have, and, in a new world, the old have no relevant wisdom to give. Yet both old and young need one another, for the young need a received vision from those who have gone before. Their world is as empty as that of the elderly.

Erikson himself argued that an inability to face crises produces either a foreclosure in which the crisis is denied or a moratorium consisting in a persistent but low-profile identity problem that remains unresolved. The failure to meet crises in youth or early middle years often fossilizes into one or other of these false solutions, which then run on till death. In Erikson's view the life-cycle is then never completed. People die, 'uncommitted, unresolved and frustrated, never having arrived at the stage where they could fully integrate and utilize their accumulated years of experience and knowledge' (Clayton 1975).

Where then are the wise men? That they are rare in our culture seems assured. Yet those of us who travel the world have seen them, known them. They do exist; in the poor villages of India or Africa or tilling the bare subsistence pastures of some mountain-locked Himalayan valley. This is no idealism of the alienated Westerner. Acquaintance makes it clear that given stability of culture and a continuity, not necessarily a fixture, of tradition the wise, both men and women, appear. The life-cycle can be terminated in the way that Erikson proposes. It is not surprising then that the young turn for their gurus to these cheerful old gentlemen in far-away lands. The result is problematic, for the wholesale importation of alien values into a Western setting is apt to lead to a later disillusionment; but the sense of need and its temporary resolution is clear. Sadly, the equally clear exploitation of these needs by subtle charlatans is obvious.

Michael Chandler (1975) pushes this viewpoint further. He points out that modern Western education trains the propositional mind in metaphysical empiricism and social relativism at an age when the young lean to an adolescent conformity in values. This must almost inevitably produce alienation by its very stress on the use of operational thought. The discovery of the particularity of minds, that each person views the world from individualized and idiosyncratic perspectives between which there is no means of judging, a world in which everyone 'does his own thing', is one of isolated individualism. While this understanding is an important aspect of personal growth, its negative side in a world without tradition is a complete uncertainty regarding personal value. The 'vertigo of relativity' (Berger and Luckmann 1966) produces a sense of estrangement and loneliness that is often solved only by forms of conformity that may be simply regressive.

Rogerian psychology may have a significant role to play here; especially as it continues to make a wider impact outside the clinical setting. By clearly identifying the conditions of worth that rule individuals' lives and through subjecting them anew to the organismic valuing process the Rogerian approach restructures attitudes to create a sense of independence in a self-valuing person for whom the primitive fears of the overwhelming 'other' are largely relegated to the past (see p. 301). The independent man or woman can negotiate with others in the creation of social form. There is then the discovery that one need not remain a conformist if one can accept the risk of a changing commitment.

Riegel has argued for a further stage of cognitive development in addition to those enumerated by Piaget. This is a stage when the ability to appreciate dialectical operations in the process of crisis, conflict, and change arises. The mature contemplation of change involves more than the propositional mind; it means coming to terms with deep feelings of loss and relationship, with personal experience in the harsh now of living, discovering the meaning to be given to the experienced fact of change. It could well be argued that Riegel's proposal would be met through the provision of careful training in the experiential understanding of the Buddhist dialectic that underlies Zen (Akishige 1977), for this indeed is a philosophy for the self-actualizing person that a Rogerian education may achieve. Indeed a deliberate education to achieve this advanced level of cognitive operation is rapidly becoming a matter of priority in the industrial world of today. The grass-roots concern with Eastern thought is a clear indication of such a need.

There is however no special reason for supposing that the present hectic pace of social and economic change will continue indefinitely. While the prophets of doom may be right, it seems more likely that we shall muddle through to a new level of socio-economic organization, this time on a global scale. The physicist–philosopher John Platt (1966) argues that eventually a society of stabilized socio-ecological homoeostasis will probably develop and spread throughout the planets of our solar system. Fast travel, instantaneous communications, artificial environments facilitating the exploitation of differing planets, a steady standard of living, and a controlled demography in what will eventually become a K-dominated society will all become accepted norms. Platt points out that stable conditions and advanced medical techniques will produce a population of youthful elders with only a small proportion of children and young persons. Education will be especially valued and will doubtless include psychological education for social stability and creativity as an important component.

We have already suggested that under demographic conditions ruled by the carrying capacity of the environment, with an emphasis on altruistic self-understanding based on organismic valuing, a sense of personal worth arising from individuation, and a commitment to social creativity within the necessary socio-economic structure we can begin to envisage hopes for a better world. Neither the acceptance of continuous or accelerating stress in life nor doom-laden expectations of catastrophe necessarily fit our historical circumstance. We are merely experiencing, Platt remarks, the shock wave of dramatic cultural change contingent on the expansive exploitation of fossil fuels. It cannot go on for ever. A new stability must in the end emerge and we need to plan possible adaptations to it. Future shock may have only another hundred years to run.

We return finally to those wider reaches of mind that lack training in modern democracies, but which, even so, are within the grasp of almost every man. The contemporary intuition that feeds the growth of an interest in the practical psychology of Buddhism in its many forms is based in the sense that a training of the mind in appositional experience, in the balancing of formal operationalism in thought with gestalt-like apperceptions of an aesthetic value in the paradox of life within death, can lead to an appreciation of being that is independent of roles, rules, rates of change, urban hell or rural tranquility, youth or age. Wisdom is not out of reach; it requires a recalibration of the ego. The subjective empiricism of the Indian monk has given us systems of mind-training that accept with a ruthless totality the concept of the relativity of the world, that all is change, that illusion is the structure of the valuing ego, that an appreciation of life within the silence of death that surrounds it leads to wisdom. To insist further becomes pointless. The old training systems need adjustment to the coming world but their heart is firm and that is where wisdom lies.

Krishnamurti (1976, p. 139) says of this subject:

The brain is restless, an astonishingly sensitive instrument. It is always receiving impressions, interpreting them, storing them away; it is never still, waking or sleeping. Its concern is survival and security, the inherited animal responses; on the basis of these, its cunning devices are built, within and without; its gods, its virtues, its moralities are its defences; its ambitions, desires, compulsions and conformities are the urges of survival and security. Being highly sensitive, the brain with its machinery of thought, begins the cultivation of time, the yesterdays, the todays and the many tomorrows; this gives it an opportunity of postponement and fulfilment; the postponement, the ideal and the fulfilment are the continuity of itself. But in this there is always sorrow; from this there is the flight into belief, dogma, action and multiple forms of entertainment, including religious rituals. But there is always death and its fear; thought then seeks comfort and escape in rational and irrational beliefs, hopes, conclusions. Words and theories become amazingly important. . . . The brain and its thought functions at a very superficial level, however deeply thought may have hoped it has journeyed. The brain and its activities are a fragment of the whole totality of life; the fragment has become completely important to itself. . . . Thought can never formulate the whole of life. Only when the brain and its thought are completely still, not asleep or drugged by discipline, compulsion or hypnosis, then only is there the awareness of the whole.

Krishnamurti's book is a celebration of that awareness. Here are some passages in which he seeks to relate experiences of it.

Of a sudden it happened, coming back to the room; it was there with an embracing welcome, so unexpected . . . meditation was going on below the words and beauty of the night. It was going on at a great depth, flowing outwardly and inwardly; it was exploding and expanding. One was aware of it; it was happening, one wasn't experiencing it, it was taking place. There was no participation in it; thought could not share it for thought is such a futile and mechanical thing . . . It was happening at such an unknown depth for which there was no measurement. But there was great stillness. It was . . . not at all ordinary.

The complete stillness of the brain is an extraordinary thing; it is highly sensitive, vigorous, fully alive, aware of every outward movement but utterly still. It is as still as it is completely open, without any hindrance, without any secret wants and pursuits. It is even without a centre, without a border.

Walking down the crowded street, smelling and sordid, with the buses roaring by, the brain was aware of the things about it . . . but there was no centre from which the watching took place. It is always surprising, after it is over.

These deep experiences of the self do not preclude a concern with society nor vital action within it. Potentially they are available to all, of any age. Equanimity in action is a possibility for every man and woman. The way lies through the experiencing of contradiction, through paradox, through pain. Such is the deliberate path of the wise.

Summary
(1) This final chapter attempts to assemble in brief the definition of humanity implied by the preceding chapters of this book. It also endeavours to place this definition within the world of ideas (the *Zeitgeist*) that gives rise to it. Finally I offer some contemplations on the implications of this definition in relation to the contemporary human dilemma.
(2) The idea that the organism and hence the person is no more than the gene's way of enhancing its inclusive fitness has a dual affect. On the one hand it clarifies greatly ideas about the function of an individual in the living world. On the other hand it raises profound doubt in relation to personal self-evaluation.
(3) Evolutionary emergence led to the development of human cognitive abilities allowing an effective representation of objects and events in the symbols of language. This included the recognition of the functioning self in a world of interacting objects. The evolution of such processes is briefly surveyed.
(4) The main structural features of the person comprise capacities or powers. These attributes are

(a) Self-recognition and a bimodality of consciousness into objective and subjective forms of self-awareness.
(b) A division of the psyche into a more and a less conscious part. The 'unconscious' is the consequence of the inhibitive effects of motivational equilibration during childhood socialization. Repression of feelings and motivational expression varies enormously and produces the diversity of human 'personalities'.
(c) Individuals interact in a kind of sociodrama designed to ensure that they live and have their being only within those social settings with which they can cope.
(d) Persons have identity constructs or beliefs about themselves. Much of an individuals activity is directed to maintaining a high self-esteem through comparison with others.
(e) The growing person has the task of balancing fantasy and reality. The achievement of a mature psychological adulthood is not necessarily assured. The achievement of a functional personal autonomy through realistic appraisal of self and others is a criterion of developed adult life.

(5) The extent to which human behaviour results from the interaction of causal dimensions that are inherited is still debated. There are a number of reasons for supposing that dimensions of dominance–submissiveness and openness–closedness in relation to others determine the patterning of human relationships.

(6) Interactions both create and occur within superordinate societal structures, the village, the community, the state. The information that programmes these structural tiers is at each level independent from that below it yet constructed from elements important there.

(7) Biosocial evolution has thus created super-structural organization as an environment within which the individual person lives. The human animal is adapted primarily to culture which was originally an expression of the biological adaptation of *Homo sapiens* to environmental lability. Cultural economy is the buffer between the human organisms and its unpredictable ecology.

(8) The way in which the several tiers of the superstructure interface poses severe analytical problems. In particular the way in which a person's view of himself relates to the values he sets on the social groupings with which he identifies and which may exist on more than one of the tiers of the super-structure is of crucial importance in processes of historical change.

(9) Categorization of one's resemblances to others in common interests or grievances leads to a sense of communality called one's social identity. A negative evaluation of one's social identity can lead a person to change his work and affiliations until he reaches a social position in which he is content. This is social mobility. Societal conditions may

preclude mobility however whereupon social identity may be strengthened, a sense of deprivation and a common course with other deprived people developed and action taken to bring about social change. Much of the action of history is constructed from social mobility and social change. The values that are generated in these processes provide the prime determinants of personal ethics.

(10) Grievances between factions are settled at a higher tier in the superstructure. While the 'rights' of majorities are easily respected those of minorities and dissidents generate debate and conflict in which 'justice' for all is rarely assured. While the evolution of ethics has included a broadening of the target population for altruism such values can still collapse under conditions of prejudice and conflict when a dehumanization of the opponent permits cruelty and brutal humiliation. The generalization of human rights to wider target populations continues to develop slowly. Essentially such rights are recognizably similar to those that obtain between close kin. Thus among civilized people there is a tendency to recognize any fellow human as a member of the same family.

(11) The need for a global generalization of rights is never more apparent than now when K conditions arising through the overexploitation of the planets resources will enforce severe constraint upon human activity. This can lead either to chaos and mutual destruction or to a new, altruistic world order from which the next great civilization, based on new energy processes, can develop. The needs of our time are very obvious but the means to overcoming suspicion between nations, prejudice between races and exploitation through economic imperialism by both capitalist and communist super-powers are little developed. The institutions (United Nations) are in place but the will, the capacity, and the training are all weak or even absent. A fundamental revision of education systems on a global scale is essential.

(12) This book emphasizes transactional approaches to social evolution and personal development. This places it firmly within a modern movement in the behavioural sciences which emphasizes dialectical analyses rather than old fashioned empiricism. The benefit of a dialectical approach lies in its wider comprehension of the relativity of 'fundamental' ideas and their relationship to the style of experimentation and patterns of thought of the time.

(13) We live in a period characterized by unemployment, alienation, despair and apathy. The speed of change in the meanings individuals attribute to life often leads to situations where the young and the old virtually inhabit different worlds of thought. Such wisdom as the old may have is not relevant to the young although they indeed need a received vision of value from the preceding generation. A pessimistic

but passionate US writer, where these conditions are most developed, doubts the possibility that individuals today can reach the self-fulfilment in old age that Eric Erikson believes to be a natural consequence of a full life—a fulfilment that needs to be demonstrated to the young.

(14) If the wise of the world only remain in the traditional cultures it is not surprising that the young seek their gurus often in strange places. The Western models are simply not enough. Yet these far-away cultures too are threatened as the flux of modern times continues to roll. The 'vertigo of relativity' engendered by the alienation of our times often produces a sense of estrangement and loneliness only solved by forms of conformity that are often simply regressive.

(15) In such a dilemma we need to return to the source. Klaus Riegel has argued for a further stage of development additional to those of Piaget. He envisions a stage in which an ability to appreciate the dialectical nature of the process of crisis, conflict and change arises. This means coming to terms with deep feelings of insecurity, loss and relationship in uncertainty. Such a dialectic in a formal sense already exists and underlies the praxis of Zen training. If human beings on a wide scale are to attain the cognitive level Riegel proposes then an emotional education is needed to supplement the isolating cognitive training that is all most modern schools can provide.

(16) Wisdom is not out of reach. It requires a recalibration of the ego. The mental equipment is there but unused. Like chimpanzees, who do not know how intelligent they are, we are only dimly beginning to perceive the possibilities of which our minds, operating in society, are capable. There is an almost desperate need to focus on this theme educationally for it is as important to our future as the resolution of our crisis in material things.

References

Abbeglen, J. J. (1976). On socialisation in hamadryas baboons. Ph.D. thesis University of Zurich.

Ainsworth, M. D. S. (1969). Object relations, dependency and attachment: a theoretical review of infant–mother relationship. *Child Dev.* **40**, 969–1025.

—— and Wittig, B. A. (1969). Attachment and exploration behaviour of one-year-olds in a strange situation. In *Determinants of infant behaviour* Vol. 4 (Ed. B. M. Foss). Methuen, London.

Akishige, Y. (1977). The principles of psychology of Zen. In *Psychological studies on Zen* (Ed. Y. Akishige). Zen Institute of Komazawa University, Tokyo.

Albee, E. (1962). *Who's afraid of Virginia Woolf?* Atheneum, New York.

Aldrich-Blake, F. P. G., Bunn, T. K., Dunbar, R. I. M., and Headley, P. M. (1971). Observations on baboons, *Papio anubis*, in an arid region of Ethiopia. *Folia Primatol.* **15**, 1–35.

Alexander, R. D. (1971). The search for an evolutionary philosophy of man. *Proc. R. Soc. Victoria* **84**, 99–120.

—— (1974). The evolution of social behaviour. *Ann. Rev. Ecol. Syst.* **5**, 325–83.

—— 1975). The search for a general theory of behaviour. *Behav. Sci.* **20** (2), 77–100.

—— (1977). Natural selection and the analysis of human sociability. In *The changing scenes in natural sciences, 1776–1976.* Academy of Natural Sciences Special Publication No. 12, pp. 283–337. Philadelphia, Pa.

—— (1978). Natural selection and societal laws. In *Morals, science and society*, Vol. 3 (Ed. T. Engelhardt and D. Callahan). Hastings Center, New York.

—— and Borgia, G. (1978). Group selection, altruism and the levels of organization of life. *Ann. Rev. Ecol. Syst.* **9**, 449–74.

Andrew, R. J. (1963). The origin and evolution of the calls and facial expressions of the primates. *Behaviour* **20**, 1–109.

Ardrey, R. (1966). *The territorial imperative.* Atheneum, London.

Argyle, M. and Kendon, A. (1976). The experimental analysis of social performance. In *Advances in experimental social psychology* Vol. III (Ed. L. Berkowitz). Academic Press, New York.

Assagioli, R. (1965) *Psychosynthesis: a manual of principles and techniques.* Hobbs, Dorman & Co., New York.

Aziz, B. N. (1978). *Tibetan frontier families: reflections of three generations from D'ing-ri.* Vikas, New Delhi.

Barasch, D. P. (1977). *Sociobiology and behaviour.* Elsevier, Amsterdam.

Barkov, J. H. (1975). Prestige and culture: a biosocial interpretation. *Curr. Anthropol.* **16**, 553–72.

—— (1977). Attention structure and the evolution of human psychological characteristics. In *The structure of social attention* (Ed. M. R. A. Chance and R. Larsen). Wiley, London.

—— (1978a). Culture and sociobiology. *Am. Anthropol.* **80**, 5–20.

—— (1978b). Social norms, the self and sociobiology: building on the ideas of A. I. Hallowell. *Curr. Anthropol.* **19**, 99–102.

—— (1978c). Conformity to Ethos and reproductive success in two Hausa communities. *Ethos* **5**, 409–25.

Bateson, G., Jackson, D. D., Haley, G., and Weakland, J. (1956). Toward a theory of schizophrenia. *Behav. Sci.* **1**, 251–69.

Bateson, P. P. G. (1976). Rules and reciprocity in behavioural development. In *Growing points in ethology* (Ed. P. P. G. Bateson and R. A. Hinde). Cambridge University Press.

Becker, W. C. and Krug, R. S. (1964). A complex model for social behaviour in children. *Child Dev.* **35**, 371–96.

Bekoff, M. (1978). Social play: structure, function, and the evolution of a cooperative social behaviour. In *Comparative and evolutionary aspects of behavioural development* (Ed. G. Burghardt and M. Bekoff). Garland, New York.

Berger, P. L. (1969). *The social reality of religion*. Faber and Faber, London.

—— and Luckmann T. (1966). *The social construction of reality*. Penguin, Harmondsworth.

Berne, E. (1966). *The games people play: the psychology of human relationships*. Deutsch, New York.

Bertram, B. C. R. (1976). Kin selection in lions and evolution. In *Growing points in ethology* (Ed. P. P. G. Bateson and R. A. Hinde). Cambridge University Press.

Birdwhistell, R. L. (1959). Contribution of linguistic–kinesic studies to the understanding of schizophrenia. In *Schizophrenia: an integrated approach* (Ed. A. Averbach). Ronald Press, New York.

Bischoff, N. (1975). Comparative ethology of incest avoidance. In *Biosocial anthropology* (Ed. R. Fox). Malaby Press, London.

Bitterman, M. E. (1965). The evolution of intelligence. *Scientific American* **229** (6), 24–37.

Blakemore, C. (1977). *Mechanics of the mind*. Cambridge University Press.

Block, J. (1971). *Lives through time*. Bancroft, Berkeley, Ca.

Blurton-Jones, N. and Sibley, R. M. (1978). Testing adaptiveness of culturally determined behaviour: do Bushmanwomen maximize their reproductive success by spacing births and foraging seldom? In *Human biology and adaptation* (Ed. V. Reynolds and N. Blurton-Jones). Symposium of the Society for the Study of Human Biology.

Bogen, J. E. (1969). The other side of the brain: an oppositional mind. *Bull. Los Angeles Neurol. Soc.* **34** (3), 135–62.

Borgatta, E. F. (1969). The structure of personality characteristics. *Behav. Sci.* **9**, 8–17.

Bowlby, J. (1953). *Child care and the growth of love*. Penguin, Harmondsworth.

—— (1969 and 1973). *Attachment and loss*. Vols. 1 and 2. Hogarth, London.

Broadbent, D. E. (1958). *Perception and communication*. Pergamon, London.

Brosset, A. (1978). Social organisation and nest building in the forest weaver birds of the genus *Malimbus* (Ploceinae). *Ibis* **120** (1), 27–37.

Brown, J. L. (1974). Alternate routes to sociality in Jays: with a theory for evolution of altruism and communal breeding. *Am. Zool.* **14** (1), 63–80.

Brown, R. (1965). *Social psychology*. Collier Macmillan, London.

Bruner, J. S. (1974). The organisation of early skilled action. In *The integration of a child into a social world* (Ed. M. P. Richards). Cambridge University Press.

Buck-Morss, S. (1975). Socio-economic bias in Piaget's theory and its implications for cross-culture studies. *Hum. Dev.* **18,** 35–49.

Buechner, H. K. (1961) Territorial behaviour in Uganda kob. *Science, NY* **133,** 689–99.

Cairns, R. (1972). Attachment and dependency: a psychobiological and social learning synthesis. In *Attachment and dependency* (Ed. J. L. Gewirtz). Wiley, New York.

—— (1976). The ontogeny and phylogeny of social integrations. In *Communicative behavior and evolution* (Ed. M. E. Haber and E. C. Simmel). Academic Press, New York.

Carr-Saunders, A. M. (1922). *The population problem: a study in human evolution.* Oxford University Press.

Carson, R. C. (1969). *Interaction concepts of personality.* Allen and Unwin, London.

Carter, L. F. (1954). Evaluating the performance of individuals as members of small groups. *Personnel Psychol.* **7,** 477–84.

Caspari, E. (1972). Sexual selection in human evolution. In *Sexual selection and the descent of man, 1871–1971* (Ed. B. Campbell). Aldine, Chicago.

Cassirer, E. (1944). *An essay on man.* Yale University Press, New Haven, Conn.

Cernik, H. and Thompson, H. H. (1966). Decision-making by teenagers in six problem areas: response to the problem of choice of mates. *Character Potential* **3,** 162–8.

Chagnon, N. A. (1968a). *Yanamamö: the fierce people.* Holt, Rinehardt, and Winston, New York.

—— (1968b). Yanamamö social organization and warfare. In *War: the anthropology of armed conflict and aggression* (Ed. M. Fried, M. Harris, and R. Murphy). Natural History Press, American Museum of Natural History, New York.

—— (1978). Kin selection theory and Yanamamö reproductive and social behaviour. Paper presented at the Symposium on Kin Selection and Kinship Theory. Maison des Sciences de l'Homme, Paris. October 1978. (In press *Social sciences information.*)

—— and Irons, W. (eds.) (1979). *Evolutionary biology and human social behaviour: an anthropological perspective.* Duxbury, North Scituate, Mass.

Chance, M. R. A. (1962a). An interpretation of some agonistic postures: the role of cut-off acts and postures. *Symp. Zool. Soc. Lond.* **8,** 71–89.

—— (1962b). Social behaviour and primate evolution. In *Culture and the evolution of man* (Ed. M. F. Ashley Montagu). Oxford University Press.

—— (1977a). Attention structure as the basis of primate rank orders. In *The Social structure of attention* (Ed. M. R. A. Chance and R. Larsen). Wiley, New York.

—— (1977b). The infrastructure of mentality. In *Ethological psychiatry: psychopathology in the context of evolutionary biology* (Ed. M. T. McGuire and E. Fairbanks). Grune and Stratton, New York.

—— and Jolly, C. J. (1970). *Social groups of monkeys, apes and men.* Dutton, New York.

—— and Mead, A. P. (1953). Social behaviour and primate evolution. In *Evolution.* Symposium of the Society for Experimental Biol. 7. Jonathan Cape, London.

Chandler, M. J. (1975). Relativism and the problem of epistemological loneliness. *Hum. Dev.* **18,** 171–80.

Charles-Dominique, P. and Martin, R. D. (1972). Behaviour and ecology of nocturnal prosimians. *Adv. Ethol.* **9.**

Charlesworth, W. R. (1979). Ethology: understanding the other half of intelligence. In *Human ethology: claims and limits of a new discipline* (Ed. M. von Cranach, K. Foppa, W. Lepennies, and D. Ploog). Cambridge University Press.

Cheney, D. (1977). The acquisition of rank and the development of reciprocal alliances among free-ranging baboons. *Behav. Ecol. Sociobiol.* **2,** 303–18.

—— (1978). Interactions of immature male and femal baboons with adult females. *Anim. Behav.* **26,** 389–408.

Childe, G. (1951). *Social evolution.* Watts, London.

Clare, A. (1976). *Psychiatry in dissent.* Tavistock, London.

Clark, G. and Piggott, S. (1965). *Prehistoric societies.* Hutchinson, London.

Clayton, V. (1975). Erikson's Theory of Human Development as it applies to the aged: wisdom as contradictive cognition. *Hum. Dev.* **18,** 119–28.

Cloak, F. (1975). Is a cultural ethology possible? *Hum. Ecol.* **3,** 161–82.

Clutton-Brock, T. (1974). Primate social organisation and ecology. *Nature, Lond.* **250,** 539–42.

—— and Harvey, P. (1976). Evolutionary rules and primate societies. In *Growing points in ethology* (Ed. P. P. G. Bateson and R. A. Hinde). Cambridge University Press.

—— —— (1977). Primate ecology and social organisation. *J. Zool., Lond.* **183,** 1–39.

Cooley, C. H. (1902). *Human nature and the social order.* Scribner, New York.

Coopersmith, S. (1967). *Antecedents of self-esteem.* Freeman, San Francisco.

Crook, J. H. (1964). The evolution of social organisation and visual communication in the weaver birds (Ploceinae). *Behaviour,* Supplement 10. Brill, Leiden.

—— (1965). The adaptive significance of avian social organisations. *Symp. Zool. Soc. Lond.* **14,** 181–218.

—— (1966). Gelada baboon herd structure and movement: a comparative report. *Symp. Zool. Soc. Lond.* **18,** 237–58.

—— (1970a). The socio-ecology of primates. In *Social behaviour in birds and mammals* (Ed. J. H. Crook). Academic Press, London.

—— (1970b). Social organisation and the environment: aspects of contemporary social ethology. *Anim. Behav.* **18,** 197–209.

—— (ed.) (1970c). *Social behaviour in birds and mammals.* Academic Press, London.

—— (1971). Sources of cooperation in animals and man. In *Man and beast: comparative social behaviour* (Ed. J. F. Eisenberg and W. S. Dillon). Smithsonian Institute, Washington, DC.

—— (1971). Sexual selection, dimorphism and social organisation in the primates. In *Sexual selection and the descent of man 1871–1971* (Ed. B. Campbell). Aldine, Chicago.

—— (1973). Darwinism and the sexual politics of primates. In *L'origine dell'uomo*. Accademia Nazionale dei Lincei, Rome.

—— (1974). *Towards an ethology of human relationships*. Unpublished lecture to the Ethology Summer School, University of Utah.

—— (1975). Primate social structure and dynamics — conspectus 1974. *Proc. Symp. 5th. Cong. Int. Primate. Soc.* 3–11. Japan Science Press, Tokyo.

—— (1977*a*). On the integration of gender strategies in mammalian social systems. In *Reproductive behaviour and evolution* (Ed. J. S. Rosenblatt and B. R. Komisaruk). Plenum, New York.

—— (1977*b*). Personal growth: East and West. *Consciousness and Culture* **1** (1), 59–84.

—— (In press *a*). Social change in Indian Tibet. *Soc. Sci Inform.*

—— (In press *b*). The evolutionary biology of social processes in man. In *Group cohesion: biological, psychological and sociological reflections* (Ed. H. Kellerman). Grune and Stratton, New York.

—— and Aldrich-Blake, F. P. G. (1968). Ecological and behavioural contrasts between sympatric ground dwelling primates in Ethopia. *Folia Primatol.* **8**, 192–227.

—— and Butterfield, P. (1970). Gender role in the social system of Quelea. In *Social behaviour in birds and mammals* (Ed. J. H. Crook). Academic Press, London.

—— and Gartlan, J. S. (1966). Evolution of primate societies. *Nature, Lond.* **210**, 1200–3.

—— and Goss-Custard, J. D. (1972). Social ethology. *Ann. Rev. Psychol.* **23**, 277–312.

——, Ellis, J. E. and Goss-Custard, J. D. (1976). Mammalian social systems: structure and function. *Anim. Behav.* **24**, 261–74.

Csikszentmihalyi, M. (1975). *Beyond boredom and anxiety: the experience of play in work and games*. Jossey-Bass, San Francisco.

Daly, M. and Wilson, M. (1978). *Sex, evolution and behaviour*. Duxbury Press, North Scituate, Mass.

Darwin, C. (1858). *On the origin of species*. Murray, London.

—— (1871). *The descent of man and selection in relation to sex*. Appleton, New York.

Dawkins, R. (1976). *The selfish gene*. Oxford University Press.

—— (1978). Replicator selection and the extended phenotype. *Z. Tierpsychol.* **47**, 61–76.

Deag, J. (1977). The adaptive significance of baboon and macaque social behaviour. In *Population control by social behaviour* (Ed. F. J. Ebling and D. M. Stoddart). Institute of Biology, London.

Deikman, A. J. (1963). Experimental meditation. *J. Nerv. Ment. Dis.* **136**, 329–43.

—— (1966*a*). Implications of experimentally induced contemplative meditation. *J. Nerv. Ment. Dis.* **142**, 101–16.

—— (1966*b*). Deautomatization and the mystic experience. *Psychiatry* **29**, 324–38.

—— (1971). Bimodal Consciousness. *Arch. Gen. Psychiat.* **45**, 481–9.

418   References

DeVore, I. (ed.) (1965). *Primate behaviour: field studies of monkeys and apes.* Holt, New York.

—— (1971). The evolution of human society. In *Man and beast: comparative social behaviour.* Smithsonian Institute Annual III, Washington, DC.

Dickeman, M. (1979). The ecology of mating systems in hypergynous dowry societies. *Soc. Sci. Inf.* **18**, 163–95.

Dimond, S. (1972). *The double brain.* Livingstone, London.

Dobzhansky, T. (1967). *The biology of ultimate concern.* New American Library, New York.

—— T. and Ashley Montagu, M. F. (1947). Natural selection and the mental capacities of mankind. *Science, NY* **105**, 587–90.

Downhower, J. F. and Armitage, K. B. (1971). The yellow-bellied marmot and the evolution of polygamy. *Am. Nat.* **105**, 355–70.

Dumoulin, H. (1959). *A history of Zen Buddhism.* Faber and Faber, London.

Dunbar, R. I. M. (1977). Feeding ecology of gelada baboons: a preliminary report. In *Primate ecology* (Ed. J. H. Clutton-Brock). Academic Press, London.

—— and Dunbar, P. (1975). Social dynamics of gelada baboons. *Contributions to primatology* 6. Karger, Basle.

Durham, W. H. (1978). The coevolution of human biology and culture. In *Human behaviour and adaptation* (Ed. V. Reynolds and N. Blunton-Jones). Taylor and Frances, London.

Duval, S. and Wicklund, R. A. (1972). *A theory of objective self-awareness.* Academic Press, New York.

Eibl-Eibesfeldt, J. (1970). *Ethology: the biology of behaviour.* Holt, Rinehart, and Winston, New York.

Eiseley, L. C. (1956). Fossil man and human evolution. In *Current anthropology,* 61–78. Wenner-Gren Foundation, New York.

Eisenberg, J. F. (1966). The social organisation of mammals. *Handb. Zool.* **8** (10/7). Leiferung 39: 92pp.

—— Muckenhirn, N. A., and Rudran, R. (1972). The relation between ecology and social structure in primates. *Science, NY* **176**, 863–74.

Ekman, P. (1973). Cross cultural studies of facial expression. In *Darwin and facial expression* (Ed. P. Ekman). Academic Press, New York.

Elliot, P. F. (1975). Longevity and the evolution of polygamy. *Am. Nat.* **109**, 281–7.

Emde, R., Gaensbauer, T., and Homas, R. J. (1976). *Emotional expression in infancy: a biobehavioural study.* International Universities Press, New York.

Emerson, R. (1960). *From empire to nation.* Harvard University Press, Cambridge, Mass.

Engels, F. (1966). *Anti-Dühring.* International Publishers, New York.

Erikson, E. (1950). *Childhood and society.* Pelican, Harmondsworth.

—— (1959). Growth and crises of the healthy personality. *Psychol. Issues* **I** (1) 59.

—— (1968). *Identity, youth and crisis.* Faber and Faber, London.

Estes, R. D. (1966). Behaviour and life history of the wildebeeste (*Connochaetes taurinus* Burchell). *Nature, Lond.* **212**, 999–1000.

Etkin, W. (1954). Social behaviour and the evolution of man's mental faculties. *Am. Nat.* **88,** 129–42.

Etter, M. A. (1978). Sahlins and sociobiology. *Am. Ethnol.* **5,** 160–9.

Festinger, L. (1954). A theory of social comparison processes. *Hum. Relations* **7,** 117–40.

Fisher, J. (1958). Evolution and bird sociality. In *Evolution as a process.* (Ed. J. S. Huxley, A. C. Hardy, and E. B. Ford). Allen and Unwin, London.

Fisher, R. (1930). *The genetical theory of natural selection.* Clarendon Press, Oxford.

Foppa, K. (1979). Language acquisition — a human ethological problem? In *Human ethology: claims and limits of a new discipline* (Ed. M. von Cranach, K. Foppa, W. Lepennies, and D. Ploog). Cambridge University Press.

Forde, C. D. (1934). *Habitat, economy and society.* Methuen, London.

Fox, R. (1967). In the beginning: aspects of hominid behavioural evolution. *Man* **2,** 415–33.

—— (1971). The cultural animal. In *Man and beast: comparative social behaviour* (Ed. J. F. Eisenberg and W. Dillon). Smithsonian Annual 3, Washington, DC.

—— (1972). Alliance and constraint: sexual selection in the evolution of human kinship systems. In *Sexual selection and the descent of man 1871–1971* (Ed. Bernard Campbell). Aldine, Chicago.

Fried, M., Harris, M., and Murphy, R. (1968). *War: the anthropology of armed conflict and oppression.* American Museum of Natural History, Natural History Press, Garden City, NY.

Fromm, E. (1978). *To have or to be.* Cape, London.

Gallup, G. C. (1970). Chimpanzees: self recognition. *Science NY* **167,** 86–7.

Gavron, H. (1966). *The captive wife: conflicts of housebound mothers.* Pelican, Harmondsworth.

Gazzaniga, M. S. (1974). Cerebral dominance viewed as a decision system. In *Hemispheric function and the human brain* (Ed. S. J. Dimond and J. G. Beaumont). Elek, London.

Geilhorn, E. (1966–7). The tuning of the nervous system. In *Perspect. Biol. Med.* **10,** 559–91.

Geschwind, N. (1970). The organization of language and the brain. *Science, NY.* **170,** 940–4.

Godelier, M. (1979). Territory and property in primitive society. In *Human ethology: claims and limits of a new discipline* (Ed. M. von Cranach, K. Foppa, W. Lepennies, and D. Ploog) Cambridge University Press.

Goleman, D. (1977). *The varieties of the meditative experience.* Rider, London.

Goldstein, M. C. (1971). Stratification, polyandry and family structure in central Tibet. *Southwest. J. Anthropol.* **27,** 64–74.

—— (1976). Fraternal polyandry and fertility in a high Himalayan valley in Nepal. *Hum. Ecol.* **4,** 223–33.

Goodall, J. van Lawick. (1971). *In the shadow of man.* Collins, London.

Goody, J. (1977). *The domestication of the savage mind.* Cambridge University Press.

Gould, S. J. (1977). *Ontogeny and phylogeny.* Belknap, Cambridge, Mass.

Govinda, Lama A. (1961). *The psychological attitude of early Buddhist philosophy.* Rider, London.

—— (1971). *Foundations of Tibetan mysticism.* Shambala, Berkeley, Ca.

Griffin, D. R. (1976). *The question of animal awareness.* Rockefeller University Press, New York.

Grossman, K. E. (1977). Frühe Entwicklung der Lernfähigkeit in der Sozialen Umwelt. In *Entwicklung der Lernfähigkeit in der Sozialen Umwelt* (Ed. K. E. Grossman). Kuder, Munich.

Guenther, H. V. (1976). *Philosophy and psychology in the* Abidhamma. Shambala, Berkeley, Ca.

Hakeda, Y. (1967). *The awakening of faith.* Columbia, New York.

Haley, J. (1959). An interactional description of schizophrenia. *Psychiatry* **22**, 321–32.

Hall, K. R. L. (1965). Behaviour and ecology of the wild patas monkey, *Erythrocebus patas*, in Uganda. *J. Zool., Lond.* **148**, 15–87.

Hallowell, A. I. (1950), Personality structure and the evolution of man. *Am. Anthropol.* **52**, 159–73.

—— (1956). The structural and functional dimensions of a human existence. *Q. Rev. Biol.* **31**, 88–101.

Halstead, W. C. (1956). *Brain and intelligence: a quantitative study of the frontal lobes.* Chicago University Press.

Hammarskjöld, D. (1964). *Markings.* Faber and Faber, London.

Hamilton, W. D. (1964). The genetical theory of social behaviour. I and II. *J. Theor. Biol.* **7**, 1–52.

—— (1971*a*). Geometry for the selfish herd. *J. Theor. Biol.* **31**, 295–311.

—— (1971*b*). Selection of selfish and altruistic behaviour in some extreme models. In *Man and beast: comparative social behaviour* (Ed. J. Eisenberg and W. Dillon). Smithsonian Annual 111, Washington, DC.

—— (1972). Altruism and related phenomena: mainly in social insects. *Ann. Rev. Ecol. Syst.* **3**, 193–232.

—— (1975). Innate aptitudes of man: an approach from evolutionary genetics. In *Biosocial anthropology* (Ed. R. Fox). Malaby, London.

Hamilton, W. J. and Watt, K. (1970). Refuging. *Ann. Rev. Ecol. Syst.* **1**, 263–86.

Harding, D. (1965). *On having no head: a contribution to Zen in the West.* Harper and Row, New York.

—— (1974). *The science of the first person.* Sholland Publications, Nacton.

Harlow, H. F. (1958), The evolution of learning. In *Behaviour and evolution* (Ed. A. Roe and G. G. Simpson). Yale University Press, New Haven, Conn.

—— and Harlow, M. K. (1965). The affectional systems. In *Behavior of nonhuman primates* (Ed. A. M. Schrier, H. F. Harlow, and F. Stollnitz). Academic Press, New York.

Harré, R. (1974). The conditions for a social psychology of childhood. In *The integration of the child into a social world* (Ed. M. P. Richards). Cambridge University Press.

—— and Secord, P. F. (1972). *The explanation of social behaviour.* Blackwell, Oxford.

Harris, M. (1968). *The rise of anthropological theory.* Crowell, New York.

—— (1974). *Cows, pigs, wars and witches: the riddles of culture.* Random House, New York.

Hewes, G. W. (1973). Primate communication and the gestural origin of language. *Curr. Anthropol.* **14,** 5–11.

Hinde, R. A. (1960). *Animal behaviour: a synthesis of ethology and comparative psychology.* McGraw-Hill, New York.

—— (1974). *Biological bases of human social behaviour.* McGraw-Hill, New York.

—— and Spencer-Booth, Y. (1969). The effect of social companions of mother infant relations in rhesus monkeys. In *Primate ethology* (Ed. D. Morris). Weidenfeld and Nicolson, London.

—— and Stevenson-Hinde, J. (eds.) (1973). *Constraints on learning: limitations and predisposition.* Academic Press, New York.

Hobhouse, L. T. (1901). *Mind in evolution.* Macmillan, London.

Hogan-Warburg, A. J. (1966). Social behaviour of the Ruff *Philomachus pugnax* (L). *Ardea* **54,** 109–229.

Homans, G. C. (1961). *Social behaviour: its elementary form.* Harcourt Brace, New York.

Homans, P. (1974). Carl Rogers' Psychology and the theory of Mass Society. In *Innovations in Client-Centred Therapy* (Ed. D. A. Wexler, and L. N. Rice). Wiley, New York.

Hoof, J. A. R. A. M. van (1969). The facial displays of the Catarrhine monkeys and Apes. In *Primate Ethology* (Ed. D. Morris). Weidenfeld and Nicolson, London.

Horrocks, J. E. and D. W. Jackson. (1972). *Self and Role: a theory of self-process and role behaviour.* Houghton Mifflin, Boston.

Hrdy, S. B. (1974). Male–male competition and infanticide among the langurs of Abu, Rajasthan. *Folia Primatol.* **22,** 19–58.

Hudson, L. (1972). *The cult of the fact.* Jonathan Cape, London.

Humphrey, N. K. (1975). The social function of intellect. In *Growing points in ethology* (Ed. P. P. G. Bateson and R. A. Hinde). Cambridge University Press.

Huxley, J. S. (1942). *Evolution: the modern synthesis.* Allen and Unwin, London.

Illich, I. (1979). Vernacular values. *Resurgence* **72,** 28–30.

Irons, W. (1978). Is Yomut social behaviour adaptive? Paper delivered at the Conference on Kinship and Kin selection, Maison des Sciences de l'Homme, Paris, October 1978.

James, E. O. (1961). *The nature and function of priesthood.* Barnes and Noble, New York.

James, W. (1890). *The principles of psychology.* Dover, New York. [Reprint of 1950.]

Jarman, P. J. (1974). The social organisation of antelope in relation to their ecology. *Behaviour* **58,** 215–67.

Jaynes, J. (1976). *The origin of consciousness in the breakdown of the bicameral mind.* Houghton Mifflin, New York.

Jenni, D. A. (1974). Evolution of polyandry in birds. *Am. Zool.* **14,** 129–44.

Jolly, A. (1966). Lemur social behaviour and primate intelligence. *Science, NY* **153,** 501–6.

Jolly, C. J. (1970). The seed-eaters: a new model of hominid differentiation based on a baboon analogy. *Man* **5**(1): 5–26.

—— (1972). The classification and natural history of *Theropithecus (Simopithecus)*. In Baboons of the African Plio-Pleistocene. *Bull. Brit. Mus. (Nat. Hist.) Geol.* **22**, 123.

Jourard, S. M. (1971). *Self-disclosure. An experimental analysis of the transparent self.* Wiley Interscience, New York.

Kant, I. (1784). Beantwortung der Frage: Was ist Aufklarung. In *Werke.* **4**, 167–76.

Kaeserman, M. L. (1977). Cited in Foppa (1979).

Kapleau, P. (1967). *The three pillars of Zen.* Beacon, New York.

Katz, S. H., Hediger, M. L., and Valleroy, L. A. (1974). Traditional maize processing techniques in the New World. *Science, NY* **184**, 765–73.

Kawai, M. (ed.) (1978). *Ecological and sociological studies of gelada baboons.* Karger, Basel.

Keesing, R. M. (1975). *Kin groups and social structure.* Holt, Rinehart, and Winston, New York.

Keith, Sir A. (1948). *A new theory of human evolution.* Watts, London.

Kelly, G. A. (1955). *The psychology of personal constructs.* Norton, New York.

Kendon, A. and Ferber, A. (1973). A description of some human greetings. In *Comparative ecology and behaviour of primates* (Ed. R. P. Michael and J. H. Crook). Academic Press, London.

Koestler, A. (1967). *The ghost in the machine.* Hutchinson, London.

Kohlberg, L. (1969). Stage and sequence: the cognitive-developmental approach to socialisation. In *Handbook of socialization theory and research* (Ed. D. A. Goslin). Rand McNally, Chicago.

Kortlandt, A. (1972). *New perspectives on ape and human evolution.* Stichtung Psychobiologie, Amsterdam.

Krader, L. (1968). *Formation of the state.* Prentice Hall, Englewood Cliffs, NJ.

Krishna, Pandit Gopi (1976). *Kundalini: path to higher consciousness.* Orient, New Delhi.

Krishnamurti, J. (1976). *Krishnamurti's Notebook.* Gollancz, London.

Krocber, A. L. (1952). The superorganic. In *The nature of culture* (Ed. A. L. Krocber). University of Chicago Press.

Kruschinsky, L. V. (1965). Solution of elementary logical problems by animals on the basis of extrapolation. *Prog. Brain Res.* **17**, 280–308.

Kummer, H. (1975). Rules of dyad and group formation among captive gelada baboons (*Theropithecus gelada*). In *Proc. Symp. 5th Cong. Int. Primat. Soc. Japan.* Science Press, Tokyo.

—— (1968). *Social organization of hamadryas baboons.* University of Chicago Press.

—— Gotz, W., and Angst, W. (1974). Triadic differentiation: an inhibitory process protecting pair bonds in baboons. *Behaviour* **49**, 62–87.

Lack, D. (1954). *The natural regulation of animal numbers.* Oxford University Press.

—— (1968). *Ecological adaptations for breeding in birds.* Methuen, London.

Ladurie, E. Le Roy (1977). *Montaillou, village occitan de 1294–1324.* Gallimard, Paris.

Laing, R. (1960). *The divided self.* Tavistock, London.
—— (1979). Ecology of mind. *Resurgence* **72,** 12–16.
Larsen, R. R. (1977). Charisma: a reinterpretation. In *The social structure of attention* (Ed. M. R. A. Chance and R. Larsen). Wiley, New York.
Lawler, J. (1975). Dialectical philosophy and developmental psychology: Hegel and Piaget on contradiction. *Hum. Dev.* **18,** 1–17.
Lawrence, D. H. (1978). Apocalypse. *The Guardian,* Monday, 23 October and Wednesday, 25 October 1978, London.
Lazlo, E. (1969). *System, structure and experience: towards a scientific theory of mind.* Gordon and Breach, London.
Leakey, R. R. and Lewin, R. (1977). *Origins.* Macdonald and Jane, London.
Leary, T. (1957). *Interpersonal diagnosis of personality.* Ronald Press, New York.
Lederer, W. J. and Jackson, D. D. (1968). *The mirages of marriage.* Norton, New York.
Lee, R. B. and DeVore, I. (eds.) (1968). *Man the hunter.* Aldine-Atherton, Chicago.
Leggett, T. (1978). *Zen and the ways.* Routledge and Kegan Paul, London.
Lehrmann, D. (1953). A critique of Konrad Lorenz's theory of instinctive behaviour. *Q. Rev. Biol.* **28,** 337–63.
Levy, J. (1974). Psychobiological implications of bilateral asymmetry. In *Hemispheric function and the human brain* (Ed. S. J. Dimond and J. G. Beaumont). Elek, London.
Lévi-Strauss, C. (1949). *Les stuctures élémentaires de la parenté.* Presses Universitaires de France, Paris.
—— (1962). *La pensée sauvage.* Paris.
—— (1969). *The elementary structures of kinship.* Beacon, Boston, Mass.
LeVine, R. (1973). *Culture, behaviour and personality.* Aldine, Chicago.
Levita, D. J. de (1965). *The concept of identity.* Mouton, Paris.
Lewis, M. and Brooks, J. (1977). Self-knowledge and emotional development. In *The development of affect* (Ed. M. Lewis and Rosenblum). Plenum, New York.
Lewis, M. and Brooks, J. (1979). The search for the origins of self: implications for social behaviour and interaction. *Proceedings of the symposium on the ecology of care and education of children under three,* February 1977, W. Berlin. (In press.)
Lewontin, R. C. (1970). The units of selection. *Ann. Rev. Ecol. Syst.* **1,** 1–17.
Liberman, A. M. (1979). An ethological approach to language through the study of speech perception. In *Human ethology: claims and limits of a new discipline* (Ed. M. von Cranach, K. Foppa, W. Lepennies, and D. Ploog). Cambridge University Press.
Lieberman, M. A., Yalom, I. D., and Miles, M. B. (1973). *Encounter groups: first facts.* Basic Books, New York.
Ling, T. (1973). *The Buddha.* Penguin Books, Harmondsworth.
Lloyd Morgan, C. (1909). Mental factors in evolution. In *Darwin and modern science* (Ed. A. C. Seward). Cambridge University Press.
Loevinger, J. (1966). The meaning and measurement of ego development. *Am. Psychol.* **21,** 195–206.

Lovins, A. (1979). Safe energy. *Resurgence* **72**, 17–27.

Lorenz, K. (1950). The comparative method in studying innate behaviour patterns. *Symp. Soc. Exp. Biol.* **4**, 221–68.

—— (1963). *Das sogenannte Böse.* Borotha-Schoeler, Vienna.

—— (1970). *Studies in animal and human behaviour.* Methuen, London.

Luk, C. (1972). *The Vimalakirti Nirdesa Sutra.* Shambala, Berkeley, Ca.

Lu Kuan Yu (1974). *The transmission of mind outside the teaching.* Rider, London.

Lutyens, M. (1975). *Krishnamurti: the years of awakening.* Avon, New York.

McGuire, M. T. and Fairbanks, L. A. (1977). *Ethological psychiatry: psychopathology in the context of evolutionary biology.* Stratton, New York.

MacKinnon, J. (1974). The behaviour and ecology of wild orang-utans (*Pongo pygmaeus*). *Anim. Behav.* **22**, 3–74.

MacMurray, J. (1957). *The self as agent.* Faber and Faber, London.

—— (1961). *Persons in relation.* Faber and Faber, London.

McNeill, D. (1979). Language origins. In *Human ethology: claims and limits of a new discipline* (Ed. M. von Cranach, K. Foppa, W. Lepennies, and D. Ploog). Cambridge University Press.

Main, M. (1978). Analysis of a peculiar form of reunion behaviour seen in some day-care children: its history and sequelae in children who are home-reared. In *Social development in day-care* (Ed. R. Webb). Johns Hopkins University Press, Baltimore, Md.

—— (1980). Avoidance in the service of proximity: the biological origins of detachment and defensive processes. In *Behavioural development: the Bielefeld interdisciplinary project* (Ed. K. Immelmann, G. W. Barlow, M. Main, and L. Petrinovitch). Cambridge University Press.

Maitland-Bradfield, R. (1973). *A natural history of associations: a study in the meaning of community.* Duckworth, London.

Marler, P. (1976). Social organisation, communication and graded signals: the chimpanzee and the gorilla. In *Growing points in ethology* (Ed. P. P. G. Bateson and R. A. Hinde). Cambridge University Press.

—— (1979). Development of auditory perception in relation to vocal behaviour. In *Human ethology: claims and limits of a new discipline* (Ed. M. von Cranach, K. Foppa, W. Lepennies, and D. Ploog). Cambridge University Press.

Masland, R. L. (1972). Some neurological processes underlying language. In *Perspectives on human evolution* (Ed. S. L. Washburn and P. C. Dolhinow). Holt, Rinehart, and Winston, New York.

Maslow, A. H. (1962). *Toward a psychology of being.* Van Nostrand, Princeton, NJ.

—— (1964). *Religions, values and peak experiences.* Ohio State University Press, Columbus.

Mason, W. A. and Berkson, G. (1975). Effects of maternal mobility on the development of rocking and other behaviours in rhesus monkeys: A study with artificial mothers. *Dev. Psychobiol.* **8**, 197–211.

—— (1976). Windows on the mind. *Science, NY* **194**, 930–1.

—— (1979). Maternal attributes and primate cognitive development. In *Human ethology: claims and limits of a new discipline* (Ed. M. von Cranach, K. Foppa, W. Lepennies, and D. Ploog). Cambridge University Press.

Mauss, M. (1950). *Sociologie et Anthropologie*. Paris. Republished in 1969.
May, R. M. (1967). *Psychology and the human dilemma*. Van Nostrand, Princeton, NJ.
—— (1978). Human reproduction reconsidered. *Nature, Lond.* **272**, 491–5.
Maynard Smith, J. (1966). *The theory of evolution*. Penguin, Harmondsworth.
—— (1969). Group selection and kin selection. *Nature, Lond.* **201**, 1145–7.
—— (1976). Evolution and the theory of games. *Scientific American* **64** (1), 41–5.
Mead, G. H. (1934). *Mind, self and society*. University of Chicago Press.
Menzel, E. W. (1973). Chimpanzee spatial memory organization. *Science, NY* **182**, 943–5.
Milgram, S. (1974). *Obedience to authority*. Tavistock, London.
Montagu, M. F. A. (1957). *On being human*. Abelard-Schuman, London.
—— (1960). Time, morphology and neoteny in the evolution of man. In *An introduction to physical anthropology* (Ed. M. F. A. Montagu). Thomas, Springfield, Ill.
—— (1961). The meaning of neonatal and infant immaturity in man. *J. Am. Med. Ass.* **178**, 156–7.
—— (Ed.) (1962a). *Culture and the evolution of man*. Oxford University Press.
—— (1962b). *Prenatal influences*. Thomas, Springfield, Ill.
Morris, D. (1967). *The naked ape: a zoologist's study of the human animal*. McGraw Hill, New York.
Morton, D. Exchange and the development of human society. Unpublished MS in possession of Robin Dunbar, King's College, Cambridge.
Moscovici, S. (1972). *La societé contre nature*. Union generale d'editions, Paris.
Murdock, G. P. (1956). How culture changes. In *Man culture and society* (Ed. H. L. Shapiro). Oxford University Press.
—— (1957). World ethnographic sample. *Am. Anthropol.* **59**, 664–87.
—— (1967). *Ethnographic atlas*. University of Pittsburgh Press, Pa.
Murphy, R. F. (1960). *Headhunter's heritage*. University of California Press, Berkeley.
Nagel, U. (1973). A comparison of anubis baboons, hamadryas baboons and their hybrids at a species border in Ethiopia. *Folia Primatol.* **19**, 104–65.
Nakamura, S. (1977). A psychological study of life in a Zen monastery. In *Psychological studies on Zen* (Ed. Y. Akishige). Komazawa University, Tokyo.
Naranjo, C. and Ornstein, R. E. (1971). *On the psychology of meditation*. Viking Press, New York.
Nelson, J. B. (1970). The relationship between behaviour and ecology in the Sulidae with reference to other sea birds. *Oceanogr. Mar. Biol. Ann. Rev.* **8**, 501–74.
—— (1978). *The Sulidae: Gannets and Boobies*. Oxford University Press.
Newman, R. W. (1970). Why man is such a sweaty and thirsty naked animal: a speculative review. *Hum. Biol.* **42**(1), 12–27.
Ornstein, R. E. (1972). *The psychology of consciousness*. Freeman, San Francisco.
—— (ed.) (1973). *The nature of human consciousness*. Freeman, San Francisco.
Packer, C. (1977). Reciprocal altruism in *Papio anubis*. *Nature, Lond.* **265**, 441–3.

—— (1979). Inter-troop transfer and inbreeding avoidance in *Papio anubis*. *Anim. Behav.* **27**, 1–36.

Papousek, H. and Papousek, M. (1979). Early ontogeny of human social interaction: its biological roots and social dimensions. In *Human ethology: claims and limits of a new discipline* (Ed. M. von Cranach, K. Foppa, W. Lepennies, and D. Ploog). Cambridge University Press.

Parke, R. D. (1977). Parent–infant interaction, progress, paradigms and problems. In *Observing behaviour*. Vol. 1: *Theory and applications in mental retardation* (Ed. G. P. Sackett). University Park Press. Baltimore, Md.

—— (1978). Perspectives on father–infant interaction. In *Handbook of infancy* (Ed. J. D. Osofsky). Wiley, New York.

Parsons, T. (1966). *Societies: evolutionary and comparative perspectives*. Prentice Hall, New York.

Patterson, F. (1978). Conversations with a gorilla. *Nat. Geog.* **154**(14), 438–65.

Pearson, P. H. (1974). Conceptualizing and measuring openness to experience in the context of psychotherapy. In *Innovations in client-centered therapy* (Ed. D. A. Wexler and L. N. Rice). Wiley, New York.

Phares, E. J. (1976). *Locus of control in personality*. General Learning Press, New Jersey.

Piaget, J. (1971). *Biology and knowledge: an essay on the relations between organic regulations and cognitive processes.* Edinburgh University Press.

Pitelka, F. A., Holmes, R. T., and Maclean, S. F. jr. (1974). Ecology and evolution of social organization in Arctic sandpipers. *Am. Zool.* **14**, 185–204.

Platt, J. R. (1966). *The step to man*. Wiley, New York.

Popper, K. R. and Eccles, J. C. (1978). *The self and its brain: an argument for interactionism*. Springer, London.

Premack, D. (1976). *Intelligence in apes and man*. Erlbaum, New Jersey.

Prince Peter of Greece and Denmark (1963). *A study of polyandry*. Mouton, The Hague.

Radcliffe-Brown, A. E. (1952). *Structure and function in primitive society*. Free Press, Glencoe.

Rabten, Geshe, and Dhargyey, Geshe N. (1977). *Advice from a spiritual friend*. Nepal Mahayana Gompa Centre, Katmandu.

Rajneesh, Bhagwan Shree (1975). *Tantra: the supreme understanding*. Rajneesh Foundation, Poona.

Ram Dass (1973). Transcript of a lecture at the Maryland psychiatric Research Center. *J. Transpersonal Psychol.* **2**, 171–9.

Rappaport, R. A. (1968). *Pigs for the ancestors*. Yale University Press, New Haven, Conn.

—— (1971). Ritual, sanctity and cybernetics. *Am. Anthrop.* **73**, 59–76.

—— (1978). Adaptation and the structure of ritual. In *Human behaviour and adaptation* (Ed. V. Reynolds and N. Blurton-Jones). Taylor and Francis, London.

Rasa, O. (1977). The ethology and sociology of the dwarf mongoose (*Helogale undulata rufula*) *Z. Tierpsychol.* **43**, 337–406.

Reich, W. (1945). *The sexual revolution*. Farrar, Straus, and Giroux, New York.

—— (1949). *Character analysis*. Farrar, Straus, and Giroux, New York.

—— (1970). *The function of the orgasm.* Panther, London.

Rensch, B. (1950). *Evolution above the species level.* Columbia, New York.

Reynolds, V. and Reynolds, F. (1965). Chimpanzees of the Budongo forest. In *Primate behaviour* (Ed. I. DeVore). Holt, Rinehart, and Winston, New York.

Reynolds, V. (1976). *The biology of human action.* Freeman, San Francisco.

Richard, A. (1977). The feeding behaviour of *Propithecus verreauxi*. In *Primate ecology* (Ed. T. Clutton-Brock). Academic Press, London.

Riegel, K. F. (1975). Toward a dialectical theory of development. *Hum. Dev.* **18**, 50–64.

Riesman, D. (1954). *The lonely crowd.* Doubleday, New York.

Robertson, J. and Bowlby, J. (1952). Responses of young children to separation from their mothers. *Courr. Cent. Int. Enf.* **2**, 131–42.

Robinson, B. W. (1972). Anatomical and physiological contrasts between human and other primate vocalizations. In *Perspectives on human evolution* Vol. 2 (Ed. S. L. Washburn and P. C. Dolhinow). Holt, Rinehart, and Winston, New York.

Romanes, G. J. (1884). *Mental evolution in animals.* Kegan, Paul, Trench, & Co., London.

Rosa, K. R. (1976). *Autogenic training.* Gollancz, London.

Rotter, J. B. (1954). *Social learning and chemical psychology.* Prentice Hall, New Jersey.

—— Chance, I., and Phares, E. J. (Eds.) 1972. *Applications of a social learning theory of personality.* Holt, Rinehart, and Winston, New York.

Rowell, T. E. (1972). *The social behaviour of monkeys.* Penguin Books, Harmondsworth.

Russell, P. (1976). *The TM technique: an introduction to transcendental meditation and the teachings of Maharishi Mahesh Yogi.* Routledge and Kegan Paul, London.

Ryle, G. (1949). *The concept of mind.* Hutchinson, London.

Sahlins, M. D. (1965). On the sociology of primitive exchange. In *The relevance of models for social anthropology* (Ed. M. Banton). Tavistock, London.

—— (1968). *Tribesmen.* Prentice Hall, Englewood Cliffs, NJ.

—— (1977). *The use and abuse of biology: an anthropological critique of sociobiology.* Tavistock, London.

Sameroff, A. J. (1975). Early influences on development: fact or fancy? *Merrill-Palmer Q.* **21**(4), 267–94.

Sankarakshita (1976). *The thousand petalled lotus.* Heinemann, London.

Sayre, K. M. (1976). *Cybernetics and the philosophy of mind.* Routledge and Kegan Paul, London.

Schachter, A. and Singer, J. E. (1962). Cognitive, social and physiological determinants of emotional state. *Psychol. Rev.* **69**, 379–99.

Schaeffer, E. S. Q. (1959). A circumflex model for maternal behaviour. *J. Abn. Soc. Psychiat.* **59**, 226–35.

Schaeffer, H. R. and Callender, M. A. (1959). Psychological effects of hospitalisation in Infancy. *Pediatrics* **24**, 528–39.

Schaller, G. B. (1963). *The mountain gorilla: ecology and behaviour.* University of Chicago Press.

428   References

Schaller, G. (1972). *The Serengeti lion: a study of predator–prey relations.* University of Chicago Press.

Schumacher, E. F. (1977). *A guide for the perplexed.* Abacus, London.

Sekida, K. (1975). *Zen training: methods and philosophy.* Weatherhill, New York.

Selander, R. K. (1972). Sexual selection and dimorphism in birds. In *Sexual selection and the descent of man, 1871–1971* (Ed. B. Campbell). Aldine, Chicago.

Seligman, M. E. P. (1975). *Helplessness: on depression, development and death.* Freeman, San Francisco.

Service, E. R. (1962). *Primitive social organization: an evolutionary perspective.* Random House, New York.

Seyfarth, R. M. (1976). Social relations among adult female baboons. *Anim. Behav.* **24**, 917–38.

Shapiro, H. L. (ed.) (1960). *Man, culture, and society.* Oxford University Press, New York.

Shefer, J. (1971). Mate selection among second generation kibbutz adolescents and adults: incest avoidance and negative imprinting. *Arch. Sexual Behav.* **1**, 293–307.

Sherif, M. and Sherif, C. W. (1953). *Groups in harmony and tension.* Harper, New York.

Sherrington, C. (1906). *The integration action of the nervous system.* Scribner, New York.

—— (1940). *Man and his nature.* Cambridge University Press.

Short, R. V. (1976). The evolution of human reproduction. *Proc. R. Soc. Lond. B.* **195**, 3–24.

Shotter, J. (1974). On the development of personal powers. In *The integration of a child into a social world* (Ed. M. P. Richards). Cambridge University Press.

Sibley, R. and MacFarland, D. (1974). A state–space approach to motivation. In *Motivational control systems analysis* (Ed. D. Macfarland). Academic Press, London.

Simpson, G. S. (1944). *Tempo and mode in evolution.* Columbia, New York.

Skinner, B. F. (1971). *Beyond freedom and dignity.* Knoph, New York.

Smith, J. (1976). The psychotherapeutic effects of transcendental meditation with controls for expectations of relief and daily sitting. *J. Cons. Clin. Psychol.* **44**, 630–7.

Snell, B. (1960). *The discovery of the mind: the Greek origins of European thought.* Harper, New York.

Sokolov, E. N. (1960). Neuronal models and the orienting reflex. In *The central nervous system and behaviour* (Ed. M. A. B. Brazier). Macy, New York.

Spinetta, J. J. and Rigler, D. (1972). The child-abusing parent: a psychological review. *Psychol. Bull.* **77**, 296–304.

Stein, R. A. (1962). *Tibetan civilisation.* Faber, London.

Stenhouse, D. (1974). *The evolution of intelligence: a general theory and its implication.* Allen and Unwin, London.

Steward, J. (1955). *Theory of culture change.* University of Illinois Press, Urbana.

Storr, A. (1972). *The dynamics of creation.* Secker and Warburg, London.

Struhsaker, T. T. (1969). Correlates of ecology and social organisation among African Cercopithicines. *Folia Primatol.* **11**, 80–118.

Studdent-Kennedy, M. G. (1976). Speech perception. In *Contemporary issues in experimental phonetics* (Ed. N. I. Lass). Academic Press, New York.

—— (1977). Universals in phonetic structure and their role in linguistic communication. In *Recognition of complex acoustic signals* (Ed. T. H. Bullock). Dahlem, Berlin.

Sullivan, H. S. (1955). *The interpersonal theory of psychiatry.* Tavistock, London.

Suzuki, D. T. (1930). *Studies in the Lankavatara Sutra.* Routledge and Kegan Paul, London.

—— (1932). *The Lankavatara Sutra.* Routledge and Kegan Paul, London.

—— (1953). *Essays in Zen Buddhism* (3rd series). Rider, London.

Swenson, C. H. (1973). *Introduction to interpersonal relations.* Scott, Foresman, and Co., Brighton.

Szalay, F. (1975). Hunting–scavenging protohominids: a model for hominid origins. *Man* **10**, 420–9.

Tajfel, H. (ed.) (1978). *Differentiation between social groups.* European Monographs in Social Psychology, 14. Academic Press, London.

Teleki, G. (1973). *The predatory behaviour of wild chimpanzees.* Bucknell University Press, Lewisburg, Pa.

Thibaut, J. W. and Kelley, H. H. (1959). *The social psychology of groups.* Wiley, New York.

Thich Nhat Hanh (1974). *Zen keys.* Anchor Press, New York.

Thomas, E. J. (1933). *The history of Buddhist thought.* Routledge and Kegan Paul, London.

Thompson, W. A., Vertinsky, I., and Krebs, J. R. (1974). The survival value of flocking in birds: a simulation model. *J. Anim. Ecol.* **43** (3), 785–808.

Thorpe, W. H. (1956). *Learning and instinct in animals.* Methuen, London.

—— (1962). *Biology and the nature of man.* Oxford University Press.

Tiger, L. (1969). *Men in groups.* Nelson, London.

—— and Fox, R. (1966). The zoological perspective in social science. *Man* **1**, 75–81.

Tinbergen, N. (1951). *The study of instinct.* Clarendon Press, Oxford.

—— (1972). Functional ethology and the human sciences. *Proc. R. Soc. B.* **182**, 385–410.

Tirykian, E. A. (1968). The existential self and the person. In *The self in social interaction.* Vol. 1 (Ed. C. Gordon and K. J. Gergen). Wiley, New York.

Tobias, P. (1967). *Olduvai Gorge,* Vol. 2. Cambridge University Press.

Trivers, R. L. (1971). The evolution of reciprocal altruism. *Q. Rev. Biol.* **46**, 35–57.

—— (1972). Parental investment and sexual selection. In *Sexual selection and the descent of man, 1871–1971* (Ed. B. Campbell). Aldine, Chicago.

—— (1974). Parent–offspring conflict. *Am. Zool.* **14** (1), 249–64.

Trungpa, Chögyam (1969). *Meditation in action.* Stuart and Watkins, London.

—— (1973). *Cutting through spiritual materialism.* Shambala, Berkeley Ca.

Uexküll, J. von. (1909). *Umwelt and Innewelt der Tiere.* Berlin.

Vayda, A. (1968). Hypotheses about functions of war. In *War: the anthropology of armed conflict and aggression* (Ed. M. Fried, M. Harris, and R. Murphy). Natural History Press, New York.

—— and McCay, B. J. (1978). New directions in ecology and ecological anthropology. In *Human behaviour and adaptation* (Ed. V. Reynolds and N. Blurton-Jones). Taylor and Francis, London.

Vine, I. (1970). The faceal-visual channel. In *Social behaviour in birds and mammals* (Ed. J. H. Crook). Academic Press, London.

—— (1971). The risk of visual detection and pursuit by a predator and the selective advantage of flocking behaviour. *J. Theor. Biol.* **30**, 405–22.

—— (1977). Some parallels between moral development and moral evolution. Circulated typescript.

Vries, M. de (1979). The problem of infanticide: a reinterpretation of the post-partum attachment period. In *Behavioural development: the Bielefeld interdisciplinary project* (Ed. K. Immelmann, G. W. Barlow, M. Main, and L. Petrinovitch). Cambridge University Press.

Waddington, C. H. (1957). *The Strategy of the genes.* Allen and Unwin, London.

Waley, A. (1949). *The life and times of Po Chü AD 772–846.* Allen and Unwin, London.

Ward, P. and Zahavi, A. (1973). The importance of certain assemblages of birds as 'information centres' for food finding. *Ibis.* **115**, 517–34.

Washburn, S. L. and Lancaster, C. S. (1968). The evolution of hunting. In *Perspectives on human evolution* (Ed. S. L. Washburn and P. C. J. Washburn). Holt, Rinehart, and Winston, New York.

Watson, J. S. (1971). Cognitive-perceptual development in infancy: setting for the seventies. *Merrill-Palmer. Q. J. Behav. Dev.* **17**, 139–52.

—— and Ramey, C. T. (1972). Reactions to response-contingent stimulation in early infancy. *Merrill-Palmer Q. J. Behav. Dev.* **18**, 219–77.

—— (1972). Smiling, cooing and 'the game'. *Merrill-Palmer Q. J. Behav. Dev.* **18**, 323–39.

—— (1977). Depression and the perception of control in early childhood. In *Depression in childhood diagnosis: treatment and conceptual models* (Ed. J. G. Schulter Brandt and A. Raskin). Raven, New York.

Wayman, A. and Wayman, H. (1974). *The lion's roar of Queen Shrimala.* Columbia, New York.

Watzlawick, P., Beavin, J. H., and Jackson, D. D. (1967). *Pragmatics of human communication: a study of interactional patterns, pathologies and paradoxes.* Norton, New York.

Werner, E. E., Bierman, J. M., and French, F. E. (1971). *The children of Kanai.* University of Hawaii Press, Honolulu.

Werner, H. (1948). *Comparative psychology of mental development.* Follett, Chicago.

West, M. (1977). Psychophysiological and psychological correlates of meditation. Ph. D. thesis, University of Wales, Institute of Technology.

—— (1979). Physiological effects of meditation: a longitudinal study. *Br. J. Soc. Clin. Psych.* **18**, 219–26.

Westermarck, E. (1891). *The history of human marriage.* Macmillan, New York.

White, N. F. (ed.) (1974). *Ethology and psychiatry.* University of Toronto Press.

Wickler, W. (1967). Socio-sexual signals and their intra-specific imitation among primates. In *Primate ethology* (Ed. D. Morris). Weidenfeld and Nicolson, London.

Williams, G. C. (1966). *Adaptation and natural selection*. Princeton University Press, NJ.

Wilson, E. O. (1975). *Sociobiology: the new synthesis*. Belknap, Harvard, Mass.

Wittfogel, K. A. (1957). *Oriental despotism*. Yale University Press, New Haven, Conn.

Wolf, A. P. (1970) Childhood association and sexual attraction: a further test of the Westermarck hypothesis. *Am. Anthropol.* **72**, 503–15.

Wolters, C. (1961). *The cloud of unknowing*. (trans.) Penguin, Harmondsworth.

Wozniak, R. H. (1975). A dialectical paradigm for psychology research: implications drawn from the history of psychology in the Soviet Union. *Hum. Dev.* **18**, 18–34.

Wrangham, R. W. (1975). D.Phil. thesis, University of Cambridge.

—— (1976). Research Report to SRC London.

—— (1977). Feeding behaviour of chimpanzees in Gombe National Park, Tanzania. In *Primate ecology* (Ed. J. Clutton-Brock). Academic Press, London.

Wright, R. (1972). Imitative learning of a flaked stone technology in the case of an orang-utan. *Mankind* **8**(4), 296–306.

Wynne-Edwards, U. C. (1962). *Animal dispersion in relation to social behaviour*. Oliver and Boyd, Edinburgh.

Zangwill, O. L. (1974). Consciousness and the cerebral hemispheres. In *Hemispheric function and the human brain* (Ed. S. J. Dimond and J. G. Beaumont). Elek, London.

Zuckerman, S. (1932). *The social life of monkeys and apes*. Harcourt Brace, New York.

Author Index

Figures in bold type refer to pages where full references appear

Subject Index

polyandry   105, 157, 216–18
polybrachygyny   53
polygyny   48, 53, 54–5, 157, 165, 213–214
population control   207–9, 210–11
population dynamics   18, 39
population genetics   2, 3, 94, 152
predation
    mother–child bonding and   105–6
    protection from   46, 48, 51, 52, 63–4, 85–7
    sexual   85–7, 114–15
pride   260, 265, 293, 398
primates   60
    adaptive radiations   61–3, 65, 151
    apes   65–73; see also apes
    baboons see baboons
    insectivores, evolution from   61, 63
    social organizations   51, 56–8
    socio-ecological factors in   61–5
propagation   41
property, concept of   134, 146
propositional mind   328–30, 331, 405
Prosimians   61
protection see under predation
psychobiology
    of the person   232–42, 296
    of reciprocation   176–8
psychotherapy   298–306
    client-centred   304
    evolutionary cognitive ethology in   306–8
    gestalt   305
    TM and   348
    transactional analysis   294–5

r, intrinsic rate of natural increase   45, 185, 222
Ramapithecus   67, 103
ranking, social   159–60
rearing strategies   49–50, 52, 82, 93
    dwarf mongoose   56
    human   104, 145
    lion prides   57
    marmosets   57
receptors, distance   22
reciprocation   3, 43, 176–8, 244, 386; see also altruism; exchange
reciprocity   173–5, 185
    balanced   174
    generalized   174
    negative   175

reflex
    arc   22
    conditioned   16, 23
    neuronal integration of   21–3
reinforcement concept   233
religions   223–4, 352
    Buddhism see Buddhism
    functions of   353–5
    of great civilizations and collapse   186, 224, 359–60
    monasticism, priesthoods   356–9
    objects of worship   356
reproductive strategies   51, 52–6
    of apes   68, 69
    of humans   156–8
    of weaver birds   46, 48, 49
resources, limitations   38–9, 44
responsibility, interior   269
ritual   273–4
r–K continuum   48–9, 58
role   265, 267–9, 273
role-figmentation   266
role-playing   266
role-taking   266
ruffs   54

Samadhi   340, 342, 344
satisfaction, psychological   153, 174, 182, 212
scavenging mode   102, 111, 129
schizoid personality   284
schizophrenia   296, 297
selection
    kin   43, 55, 57, 94
    natural   8, 19, 27, 45
        humans and   150–1, 152, 388–9
        r, K conditions   45–6
        theory of   37, 38–9, 94
        unit of   39–40, 383–4
    sexual   40–1, 61, 64, 94
    social   41–3
    see also altruism
self see self-process
self-actualization   300–1, 302, 305, 406
self-awareness   2, 155, 253, 267, 353, 365, 385
    agonic, hedonic attention   332–4
    bimodal mind and   326–30, 331, 387
    development of   315–16
    egocentric   315
    history of   273–6
    objective   312–17, 320–1, 331–2, 386